The ANTIQUE COLLECTOR'S ◄ GUIDE ►

The ANTIQUE COLLECTOR'S ◄ GUIDE ►

DAVID BENEDICTUS

M

**To the generous and cheerful race of antique stall holders —
may their profit margins be vast
and their slow days few and far between.**

Drawings by Chris Partridge

Copyright © David Benedictus 1980
Drawings Copyright © Macmillan London Ltd 1980
All rights reserved. No part of this publication may be
reproduced or transmitted, in any form or by any means,
without permission.

First published by Macmillan London Limited
London and Basingstoke
First published in 1981 by
PAPERMAC,
a division of Macmillan Publishers Limited
London and Basingstoke

Associated companies in Auckland, Dallas,
Delhi, Dublin, Hong Kong, Johannesburg,
Lagos, Manzini, Melbourne, Nairobi,
New York, Singapore, Tokyo, Washington
and Zaria

Filmset by Filmtype Services Limited, Scarborough
Printed in Great Britain by
Redwood Burn Limited, Trowbridge
and bound by Pegasus Bookbinding, Melksham

British Library Cataloguing in Publication Data
Benedictus, David
    The antique collector's guide.
    1. Antiques
    I. Title
    745.1   NK1125

ISBN 0-333-24242-4
ISBN 0-333-31923-0 (Papermac)

Contents

Introduction

I should have been a surgeon. Complicated as it is, the human body is seldom more than six feet high by two feet wide by one foot thick, and the scope for the doctor's expertise is accordingly limited. The poor antiques expert has no such limitations. To be an expert he needs to have immersed himself in all civilisations, all cultures, all religions, all disciplines. How can one hope fully to appreciate a piece of jade without a working knowledge of Chinese philosophy? Or a Tompion clock without knowing what makes it tick? Or a Bugatti without driving one?

I make no claim to being such an expert. But in this book I have tried to pass on such expertise as has come my way in the hope that it may help the reader to understand a little more about a treasured possession, to avoid a disastrous purchase, or to illuminate a dusty corner of the fine arts repository. Accordingly after each major, and many of the minor entries you will find details of a book or books (readily available in most cases) in which you may learn more about that subject, and of museums and galleries in which examples of the item may be seen and perhaps even touched. For there is no substitute for looking and touching. The differences between hard- and soft-paste porcelain, between jade and soapstone, between elm and oak, between a genuine Stradivarius and a nineteenth-century imitation, these are things which are clumsy to describe but thrilling to discover for oneself. To learn all there is to learn about someone (or all that *can* be learnt) one needs to live with them for a lifetime. Similarly with antiques. And if it is not possible to live with them, one should at least handle them, break them (you learn a great deal from fragments), repair them, even buy and sell them.

In an antiques dictionary which lies before me as I write, there is a definition of a chamber-pot as follows: 'A round, metal or china pot with rim and handle for night-time use, when lavatories were distant or non-existent.' I don't find such a definition particularly helpful and have excluded from this book such basic information, which most of us learnt at our mother's knee — so to speak. I have also avoided giving prices, since they are so volatile and dependent upon outside forces, so little representative of the inherent quality of materials and craftsmanship. Who would have believed that a Ravenscroft decanter would sell for less than a nineteenth-century paperweight, a handsome antique silver tray for less than its modern equivalent, the finest products of the finest porcelain factories of the eighteenth century for less than a twentieth-century china bird? Price guides in all major areas of collecting are now produced annually and may be consulted in public libraries; their up-to-date valuations are, of course, extremely useful for those who wish to ensure that they are not being dunned.

I have also included a glossary of names, concentrating particularly on those which crop up most frequently in saleroom catalogues and magazine articles; also a chronological chart which should help to set antiques in their historical context. If your brain overheats, as mine does, when faced with dates, this chart may provide a shady oasis in which to cool yourself, and take your ease — and your dates.

You will also find that I have included a few subjects which some of my learned colleagues might not consider particularly 'antique'. In the traditional definition of that term (a hundred years old according to the British Antique Dealers Association) they would be right, but when so many art nouveau and art deco pieces fetch such substantial prices in the salerooms, when a suit worn by Elton John at a pop concert is on view at the Victoria and Albert Museum, and when people are prepared to pay more for an old car than a new house, we must obviously take notice.

Finally an apology to those whose research has provided the fruit which I have plucked to make this salad of a book. Just as a patient under the knife is grateful that the surgeon does not rely entirely upon original research and uses the benefits of anaesthetics, so I have tried for your continuing good health to take what was useful, and discard what was not, from the scholarship of others.

My thanks are due to Jan King and Henrietta Browne-Wilkinson for their help in researching the book, and to Henrietta for typing so much of this book so cheerfully.

DAVID BENEDICTUS

acanthus   There must be something profoundly satisfying about the leaf of the acanthus tree, for we find it used as a motif in Greek and Roman sculpture and in a great deal of European design. There are several varieties of this herbaceous plant, but the most commonly found are *Acanthus mollis* and *Acanthus spinosus*, one, as you might expect, soft and rounded in contour, the other spiny.

In Britain, the acanthus design is often found on the scrolls of classical Regency furniture — the ends of chair arms and the feet of tables sprout acanthus leaves most pleasantly — and as a frieze on silver and plate.

accordion   The introduction into Europe of the Chinese mouth-organ led to the suggestion that there might be other applications of the free reed principle. In 1829 Frederick Buschmann devised an accordion with bellows operating on a push-me-pull-you basis; its popularity led to many other models with fanciful names such as Flutina, Aoline, and Melophone.

act of parliament clock   In 1727 William Pitt imposed a levy of 10s per annum on all clocks, 5s on gold watches, and 2s 6d on cheaper watches. However, he soon recognised the error of his ways and repealed the act the following year.

The popular explanation for the name act of parliament clock is that large dialled clocks were hung up in public places, such as inns, post-houses (which were required by law to display a clock), and large kitchens for the benefit of those who could not afford to pay 2s 6d. The name is now generally applied to any English clock with a large unglazed dial and a short trunk enclosing the weights and pendulums. Such clocks are robust and keep excellent time; the old-fashioned railway clocks were probably made in imitation of them, and are very nice too.

Act of parliament clock

Adam (style)   Robert Adam, born at Kirkcaldy on 3 July 1728, was the son of Scotland's leading architect. When he was twenty, on the death of his father and in association with his brother John, he took over his father's business. In 1754 he embarked on a Grand Tour, but remained in Rome for three years, sketching and researching. Then, after studying the excavations at Pompeii and Herculaneum, he travelled to Dalmatia.

These formative years in Europe proved of inestimable value. When he returned to Britain he began designing his own buildings and furniture in what is now known as the neo-classical style. Not all his work was classically informed — he worked in both the rococo and Gothic revival styles — but the best of it was. So powerfully did he enforce his predilection for classical columns and porticos, for urns and swags, honeysuckle, rams' heads and paterae, that after a while any object with a classical flavour was attributed to him. He did not invent neo-classicism, but he gave to it what Wedgwood gave to ceramics, respectability, and so became a powerful influence upon such men as Thomas Sheraton.

He experimented with filigree carving, and employed a number of talented assistants to help paint his furniture, including Angelica Kauffmann. A great deal of Victorian and Edwardian furniture is described as 'Adam-style', meaning that it has vaguely classical attributes. But few craftsmen shared Adam's excellent sense of proportion and few could hope to emulate his tactful attention to detail. He made it his business to take responsibility for everything in a room, from wall coverings and furniture to fire irons, door-plates and handles; everything had its allotted place in the room. A Titan among minnows.

Books: *The Furniture of Robert Adam* by Eileen Harris (Tiranti, 1963); *Decorative Work of Robert Adam* by Darril Stillman (Tiranti, 1966)

Collections: Sir John Soane's Museum, London; Kenwood House, London; Osterley Park, London (mainly created and wholly decorated by Adam); Kedleston Hall, Derby (an Adam house with Adam furniture); Harewood House, Leeds; Hopetoun House, South Queensferry (started by Adam senior and completed by his sons)

air-twist glass   The air-twist stem glass was a development of the tear-stem glass, and was introduced in the first half of the eighteenth century. The glass was made in three separate sections (the stuck-shank method) by plaiting strips of opaque glass, sometimes coloured with enamel. By 1760 it had given place to twisted canes of glass, and to cut decoration.

Book: *Illustrated Guide to Eighteenth-Century English Drinking Glasses* by C. M. Bickerton (Barrie & Jenkins, 1972)

alabaster   It is important to distinguish between what was anciently known as alabaster, and what we now refer to as alabaster. The older type, oriental alabaster, is formed by water dripping through limestone: stalactites and stalagmites are pure alabaster. This substance, being indissoluble in water and ideal for weathering the elements, was frequently used for outdoor statuary. It is easy to work (a hardness of only 3 on the Mohs scale) and has patterns of concentric rings, much like the patterns in tree trunks. Many treasures worked in oriental alabaster were found in Tutankhamen's tomb.

Modern alabaster is a fine-grained form of gypsum, translucent and cloudy with impurities. It is soft and fragile, and takes a high polish gratefully. Alabaster was often used for church effigies, sometimes painted and gilded, until the Reformation put an end to such levity. A fine collection of alabaster retables is the Hildeburgh Bequest at the Victoria and Albert Museum, in London. Today alabaster is usually used for vases, lamps, and desk furniture.

Opaque glass with a matt finish, manufactured in France in the early nineteenth century, is known as alabaster glass.

Book: *English Medieval Alabasters*, a Victoria and Albert Museum publication (HMSO, 1976)

Albert   That Prince Albert of Saxe-Coburg-Gotha (1819–61) was not the rigidly virtuous, formally correct, and dull character many xenophobes have made him out to be, is clearly displayed in Daphne Bennett's excellent biography *King Without a Crown* (Heinemann, 1977). Apart from his political career, he was the instigator of the Great Exhibition of 1851 at the Crystal Palace, he designed the settings for some of the Crown Jewels, and various other jewellery, medals and orders, and he was responsible for the great South Kensington museums and the Royal Albert Hall. Obviously a man of parts. This was recognised in 1845 by a group of Birmingham jewellers who presented the Consort with a watch-chain, seal and key. From this derives the name for the Albert.

The classical Albert was a gold watch-chain with a bar that fitted into the buttonhole of a waistcoat; the two ends of the chain were fed into the two pockets of the waistcoat nicely situated to receive them. The links of the chain were graduated, and the *tout ensemble* fitted well over the nursery slopes of a swelling corporation. There were also ladies' Alberts with bars and tassels in gold chain.

The wrist-watch saw the Alberts off, although recently, converted as ladies' necklaces, they have enjoyed a new vogue.

amber   A fossil resin derived from the sap of an extinct variety of pine. Amber jewellery from Asia Minor and Tibet was promoted all along the trade routes from Africa to China in the Middle Ages.

The colour varies from yellow to brown. Sicilian amber of a reddish hue became fashionable among the Victorians. During the arts and crafts movement strings of plain amber beads were thought to be quite the thing. Rough amber shapes, hung as pendants, are considered lucky, luckier still

4

if they contain a trapped fly. As Pope put it:

> *Pretty! in Amber to observe the forms*
> *Of hairs, or straws, or dirt, or grubs, or worms!*
> *The things we know are neither rich nor rare,*
> *But wonder how the devil they got there.*

Book: *Magic of Amber* by Rosa Hunger (N.A.G.Press, 1977)

amboyna wood   The amboyna tree (*Pterospernum indicum*) grows in the Amboyna and Ceram Islands in Indonesia. Its hard wood is a light reddish brown and has a beautiful mottled grain. It is ideal for veneers and inlays, and was eagerly seized upon by art deco furniture designers.

amen glasses   See *Jacobite glasses*.

American clock   Shelf and wall clocks were exported from America by the shipload from about 1842. In England they retailed at 7*s* 6*d* each and created very real competition for native products. They came in wooden cases, shaped like beehives and steeples, or sometimes simply rectangular. Below the dial they often featured coloured prints of American scenes or romantic landscapes. Early examples usually bore trade papers signed by individuals such as Seth Thomas, Chauncey Jerome, Eli Terry and the Willard family, later ones by companies (Ansona Clock Company, Newhaven Clock Company), indicating the prosperity which this trade enjoyed. These American clocks were sturdy time-keepers, horological model-T Fords.

amethysts   The most highly regarded of the quartz gemstones, the amethyst used to be worn as a protection against intoxication. It is graded as Siberian, Uruguay, and Bahia in decreasing order of desirability. The Siberian amethyst is blue-purple in daylight changing to red-purple under tungsten, and is the aristocrat of amethysts. At the end of the last century the market was flooded with poorer and less pure stones from Latin America. It is most unusual to find a Siberian amethyst larger than two inches in diameter. If you do, count yourself lucky.

andiron   See *firedog*.

apostle spoons   These charming spoons usually came in sets of thirteen. The Master spoon bore the figure of Christ with an orb and a cross, His right hand upraised in blessing. Each of the other spoons was topped with a figure of one of the Apostles, and bore the appropriate emblem, as follows:

St Peter: a key, two keys, or a fish
St Andrew: a saltire cross

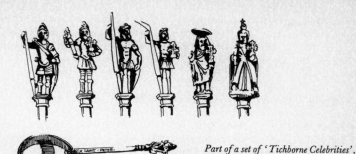

Part of a set of 'Tichborne Celebrities', by Christopher Wace, 1592

St James the Greater: a pilgrim's staff, scallop shell, or hat and wallet

St John: a cup, eagle or palm branch

St Philip: a cross, staff, knotted cross, or bread

St Bartholemew: a flaying knife (a reference to his martyrdom)

St Thomas: a spear, an arrow, a girdle, or a builder's rule

St Matthew: a wallet, a money-box, an axe or a T-square

St James the Less: a fuller's bat (a reference to his martyrdom)

St Jude (or Thaddeus): a carpenter's square, cross, club, boat or inverted cross

St Simon the Zealot: a saw, fish or oar

St Matthias: a halberd, axe or lance

The emblems are sometimes damaged or missing entirely. The Master spoon and the St Peter and St Andrew spoons are very rare. Sadly very few complete sets have survived, so those that have are much sought after: a complete set was sold at Christie's in 1903 for the record sum then of £4900.

The first reference to an Apostle spoon occurs in a York will, dated 1494: '*xiij cochilaria argenti cum Apostolis super eorum fines.*' The popularity of these spoons continued for two hundred years. In the late seventeenth-century examples the Apostles are dignified with haloes, and in some sets the figure of St Paul replaces one of the Apostles.

Collection: Holburne of Menstrie Museum, Bath

apothecary jars also known as **drug jars**   In the seventeenth century earthenware jars were found to be ideal for storing the roots, seeds, berries and herbal extracts which the apothecary needed to cure the plagues, agues and fluxes which must have played so tragically important a part in the lives of everyone. The jars would have been closed with a parchment membrane, or sealed with wax or chalk. In their finest form they married necessity with invention most agreeably.

There is some evidence that such storage vessels were used in Mesopotamia, Baghdad, Knossos and Rome. But collectors are not usually concerned with anything made earlier than the fourteenth century, when the albarello appeared. This was a cylindrical vessel with a flange at its open end, over which a parchment cover could be tied; it was imported into Italy from Persia and Syria.

In Tuscany — notably in Orvieto and Viterbo — decorated tin-glazed earthenware (maiolica) was painted in green and brown with simple abstract designs or animal representations. At the beginning of the fifteenth century more ambitious decorations were undertaken, sometimes portraits in relief, often against a background of cobalt blue. Since the arts and sciences were not regarded as mutually exclusive during the Renaissance it is no surprise that a simple chemist's pot became an object of some magnificence.

Jars were imported into Britain from Italy, Spain, and Holland in the fifteenth century, when the Italian maiolica and Flemish Delft became the faience of France and Germany, and the delftware of England. In the seventeenth century blue and white apothecary jars were made at the Lambeth potteries on the south bank of the Thames, and during this period naturalistic designs of birds, flowers, and, most frequently cherubs, were in vogue. In the eighteenth century jars were made in the Bristol and Liverpool potteries, but creamware increasingly replaced tin glaze, as Wedgwood conducted successful experiments into the production of an attractive, stable and hard-wearing ceramic.

One of the pleasures of collecting apothecary jars is the deciphering of the legends which they carry and the insight this provides into the ailments and treatments of the Middle Ages. *Simpliciae* were drugs of natural origins, or simples, while *Compositae* were compounds of more than one therapeutically active ingredient. Matters are complicated by the inclusion on occasion of the name of the physician who invented the formula and by the use of made-up or pidgin Latin. Thus: 'P:S: STAPH: AGR', a very straightforward inscription on an eighteenth-century Swedish jar, stands for *Pulvis Simplex Staphisagriae*, or simple powder of stavesacre.

A full glossary of the most important terms used on apothecary jars may be found in the excellent but expensive volume named below.

Book: *Apothecary Jars* by Rudolf Drey (Faber & Faber, 1978)
Collections: Pharmaceutical Society's Museum, London; Victoria and Albert Museum, London; Wallace Collection, London; City Museum, Birmingham; Polesden Lacy, Dorking; Ashmolean, Oxford

armada chests   Dating from the sixteenth century — and nothing to do with the Armada — these chests are heavy iron-bound coffers, usually of German, Dutch or Austrian origin, used for storing treasures. They have dummy keyholes in the front and are internally bolted.

armour The earliest surviving pieces of armour are the gold headpiece and the copper helmets excavated at Ur in Sumeria. They were probably worn with quilted capes or tunics and supported by a shield. The Greek soldiers wore cuirasses, back and front, embossed with rippling muscles; greaves below the knees; helmets, with high horsehair crests, covering the head, neck and sides of the face; and oval shields. All these pieces were moulded in bronze.

In the first century BC the Roman legionaries wore the *lorica segmentata*, consisting of tranverse iron hoops for the trunk, substantial shoulder pieces, helmets, and concave wooden shields. Officers might wear cuirasses in the Greek manner. At about this time mail was introduced for both horses and cavalrymen, whose faces would be covered by visors. In the Middle Ages solid plate armour was replaced by hauberks, shirts made of iron rings linked together, worn with conical helmets covering the skull and, giving extra protection, a nasal for the nose. Most of our information regarding early armour comes from the Bayeux Tapestry (*c.*1075), on which hauberks and nasal helmets are featured together with lozenge-shaped shields. Leg coverings in mail were normal and the sleeves of the hauberk were extended to cover the hands.

By the twelfth century cavalrymen were almost completely covered and the helmet was extended around the back of the head in what was known as the great helm, upon which a leather or parchment crest would identify the almost invisible wearer. Such crests and coats of arms were later featured on both the surcoat (a sleeveless gown covering the armour) and the shield.

In the thirteenth century 'tace' armour was introduced — small plated tiles sewn or riveted on to undergarments. With the plates, as these were known, came large back and breast pieces. By the mid-fourteenth century the soldiers' limbs would be almost entirely encased in plates, articulated at the joints and worn over mail. About this time the basnet appeared, a conical helmet fitted with a pointed visor and *aventail* (a sort of mail wimple) over the throat. Rectangular shields were also designed. By the end of the century a distinction was beginning to be made between battle armour and tournament armour.

By the fifteenth century armour had become as efficient a means of protecting the warrior as could be devised. Further changes were on the whole decorative, influenced by the Gothic mode. The Missaglia family in Milan and Lorenz Helmschmied in Augsburg were the finest representatives of northern Italy and Germany, where the best armour came from.

At the end of the sixteenth century armour of good quality was produced at Greenwich. By now a complete set would include, working from the top downwards: a helmet, whether basnet, or babuta (one piece extending over the cheeks), or sallet (Sou'-wester shaped with separate bevor or chin-piece), or armet (completely enclosing the face, but with hinged visor), or close-helmet (much like the armet); a cuirass, with a hoop skirt, attached to a padded undergarment with straps; and articulated plates covering all the limbs except the backs of the thighs. Tournament armour gave greater protection to the left side since one jousted right to left.

In the sixteenth century it became generally fashionable to have etched, engraved and/or gilded designs on the front of your armour. Damascening was employed more for show than for use, and by now the practical advantages of suits of armour had become questionable. The invention of the pistol *c*.1530, and the development of more sophisticated firearms, encouraged a greater weight of armour on the upper part of the body, compensated by as little as possible on the legs. By the outbreak of the Thirty Years War in 1618, musketeers, for instance, wore only a helmet and by the end of the seventeenth century armour was worn for ceremonial occasions but not in battle.

Book: *European Armour* by C. Blair (Batsford, 1972)
Collections: Tower of London; National Army Museum, London; Victoria and Albert Museum, London; Wellington Museum, London

Sixteenth-century German composite suit of armour

art deco   It was fast cars, it was the Hotsy Totsy Club, it was cocktail shakers and pink champagne. It was *Metropolis*, it was dancing the tango, and sniffing cocaine in one's Marcel wave to the wail of the saxophones, it was frantic and raucous and seemed like fun — at the time. It was a long weekend.

Art deco gets its name from L'Éxposition Internationale des Arts Décoratifs et Industries Modernes, which was held in Paris in 1925, ten years later than scheduled, the postponement being the fault of that horrid war, darling. Paris in 1925 brought together men and women involved in every kind of art and craft, people determined that the old order had gone for good and that cities and cinemas and jazz had come to stay.

Traditional standards of design had already been questioned by such innovators as Charles Rennie Mackintosh who offered his stark Gothic furniture to genteel Glaswegian tearooms; Walter Gropius, the father of the Bauhaus, who longed for a time when what was structural and what was decorative could no longer be distinguished (a principle perfected in the tubular steel chair, so very characteristic of the Bauhaus); and Rietveld, the Dutchman, who saw chairs as abstract structures.

Le Corbusier was dreaming of white cities, graceful and airy, and he and such visionaries as Frank Lloyd Wright, Max Reinhardt, Brecht and Cocteau, Modigliani, Brancusi and Man Ray, Juan Gris, Matisse, Mondrian and Leon Bakst, Picasso, Stravinsky, Milhaud, Erik Satie, Diaghilev, and many, many others, responded to the electricity in the atmosphere, the throb of the machines, the syncopation of the jazz, the flickering of the pictures on the cinema screen, by advocating and producing a new style, full of geometric patterns of zigzags and circles and curves. The prophet of the style was *The Studio* magazine, but the style scarcely needed prophets, so powerfully self-generating were these bold and seductive ideas.

The style pervaded every art form: the Ballet Russe, Donald Deskey's Radio City Music Hall, the choreography of Busby Berkeley, and Ruhlmann's furniture; Lalique's jewellery, Puiforcat's silver, and Brandt's interiors; Dunand's metal work, Erté's clothes and stage designs, Marinot's glass, Clarice Cliff's ceramics, Eileen Gray's screens, and the erotic figures of Preiss and Chiparus (now much faked).

Collecting art deco — the cocktail bar is a particularly rich seam to mine — was very much a minority interest until the late 1960s when the sale of a big French collection and an important exhibition in Minneapolis drew attention to what had become already, if you could be objective, an aesthetic revolution. And the aesthetics were all-important: if a piece was good enough, then the price was immaterial. This gave rise to the sale of a collection of furniture by Pierre Legrain for half a million pounds.

The reign of art deco was shattered by the rise of Nazism and the Second World War, after which utility furniture and clothes of a universal drabness took over. But plenty remains to remind us of that frenetic weekend when everything went a little crazy.

Books: *Spirit and Splendour of Art Deco* by A. Lesleutre (Paddington Press, 1974); *The Decorative Twenties* by M. Battersby (Studio Vista, 1976); *Art Deco of the 20s and 30s* by B. Hillier (Studio Vista, 1968); *The Decorative Thirties* by M. Battersby (Studio Vista, 1976)
Collection: Bethnal Green Museum, London

art glass An impressive phrase for a piece of glass designed for no
apparent purpose except to please the eye. Such aesthetic decadence crept
in about the time of the Great Exhibition of 1851, and the finest (or most
decadent) practitioners included such innovators as Lalique and Gallé in
France, and Tiffany, among others, in America.

Books: *European Art Glass* by Ray and Lee Grover (Tuttle, Tokyo, 1970); *Art Glass Nouveau*
by Ray and Lee Grover (Tuttle, Tokyo, 1975)

art nouveau To quote some well-known lines of A. P. Herbert:

> *As my poor father used to say*
> *In 1863,*
> *Once people start on all this Art*
> *Good-bye, moralitee!*
> *And what my father used to say*
> *Is good enough for me.*

The trouble with the unorthodox art nouveau movement was that there
was so much of it that it was not easy to ignore, and it flaunted its sexuality
on the street (with, for example, the wrought iron entrances to the Paris
Metro designed by H. Guinard). It is not easy to say just why it was erotic,
but to a stern Victorian all those fluid lines were horribly suggestive of a
woman's body, and one longed to get back to the good old British right
angle. Art nouveau had its origins in Britain. William Morris (1834–96)
and the arts and crafts movement, Arthur Mackmurdo (1851–1942) and
his century guild, Charles Ashbee (1863–1942) and his guild of handicraft,
Charles Ricketts (1866–1931) and the Vale Press, Charles Mackintosh
(1868–1928) and the Glasgow school, and Aubrey Beardsley (1872–98),
all prepared the ground for a European movement which, although it
lasted not much more than twenty years (*c.*1890–1910), shattered the old
ideas about style, fashion and design into such fragments that they could
never be reassembled. The new ones were promoted by the magazine *The
Studio* which was launched in 1893.

The name art nouveau comes from a shop, the Galeries de L'Art
Nouveau, opened in Paris by the German connoisseur, Samuel Bing
(1838–1905) in 1895. 'When English creations began to appear,' wrote
Bing three years later, 'a cry of delight sounded throughout Europe. Its
echo can still be heard in every country.' But the influence was not wholly
British. Japanese fashions in design, promoted and adopted by Christopher
Dresser (1834–1904), the botanist and designer, E. W. Goodwin
(1833–86), famous for his Anglo-Japanese furniture, and W. S. Gilbert,
librettist of *The Mikado*, among many others, had made a tremendous
impact. There were sympathetic groups of artists in Belgium, given
impetus by van de Velde (1863–1957) and Les Vingt (renamed La Libre
Esthétique in 1894). In France, Victor Horta (1861–1947) built a house,

Maison Tassel, of totally revolutionary design; in Austria Hoffman, Olbrich and Moser founded the Vienna Secession; and, in Germany, August Endell (1871–1928), Richard Riemerschmidt (1868–1957) and Peter Behrens (1868–1940) represented the Munich school. In America, Louis Comfort Tiffany (1848–1933) spread the gospel from the Tiffany studios, and in Czechoslovakia Alphonse Mucha (1860–1939) designed posters of Sarah Bernhardt which did much to popularise the new styles.

It is remarkable that so many men and women from so many different cultural backgrounds working in so many different disciplines should have agreed so on a matter of aesthetics. The Paris Universal Exhibition of 1900 was perhaps the crest of the new wave, while Brussels became the city, above all others, upon which it broke.

The characteristics of art nouveau were the use of shapes reminiscent of nature — rocks and waves and marine life, plants and flowers and insects — and the use of traditional materials in untraditional ways. Cabinet-makers used wood as if it was putty, glassmakers used glass as if it were jewellery, potters used china as if it were drapery, and very few were the craftsmen who did not work in more than one field of endeavour. Architecture, in contrast, disdained the art nouveau curve in favour of an abstract rectilinear style. The influence of the Glasgow school was particularly strong here, and it needed a genius like Antonio Gaudi (1852–1926), whose surreal buildings in Barcelona have to be seen to be believed, to extend the range of architecture. With a few exceptions Gaudi's vision has inspired no school of disciples. Perhaps it was *too* personal. But Gaudi apart, the art nouveau crusade shared by this versatile band of pilgrims made other such crusades not just possible but inevitable. Without art nouveau there would have been no Bauhaus, no art deco, no modern movement. Art nouveau was the least anxious to please. Three-quarters of a century later its influence is all-pervasive.

Books: *Art Nouveau* by R. Schmutzler (New English Library, 1970); *Art Nouveau* by G. Warren (Octopus, 1972); *Art Nouveau: Revolution in Interior Design* by R. Bossaglia, edited by M. Battersby (Orbis, 1973)

Collections: Bethnal Green Museum, London; William Morris Gallery, Walthamstow, Essex; Art Gallery and Museum, Brighton

ash Also called frene wood, the wood of the ash tree, *Fraxinus excelsior*, has a light brown, yellow or white grain. It is used where economy is considered more important than quality, for example for the framework of chairs (because it is strong though not heavy) and drawer linings. The spindles of Windsor chairs are frequently of ash.

ashtrays Ashtrays, or ash-pans as they were also originally called, became necessary during the early years of the nineteenth century when the fashion for cigar smoking caught on. Many porcelain ashtrays came from Germany around the beginning of this century, notably those featuring pigs performing various human actions. I bought one recently featuring a lady pig lying on her back, her frilly tu-tu spreading around her forming the edge of the ashtray. Cameras also feature frequently: another of my acquisitions shows a frog standing behind an old-fashioned plate camera taking a photograph of another frog, who is holding in front of his face the mask of a handsome prince. Many of these German porcelain ashtrays have life-like representations of pipes lying casually in them, and many of the duller examples are inscribed with 'A present from . . .'

There are many commemorative ashtrays, usually connected with royal occasions, that are already popular collectors' items. These are made in glass, metal, brass, and bakelite, as well as in china. Silver ashtrays tend to be plain and modest in design. The most beautiful examples are probably those produced by Gallé, Lalique, and Fabergé.

An ideal item for the small collector of limited means; examples are still cheap and much research remains to be done.

autographs   Autographs are much collected. Not solo signatures which are considered poor things, unless on presentation copies of first editions, or substantial cheques of course. What you should look for are what are known as A.L.S. (autograph letters signed). L.s are letters with only the signature handwritten. A. Docs are signed handwritten documents. Docs are documents with only the signature handwritten. And a T.L.S. is a signed typewritten letter.

The value of such things depends upon the amount of interesting information contained within them. A detailed letter from a Moderately Important Person is worth as much as a dull one from a Very Important Person. It also depends on the circumstances under which it was written. Recently an A.L.S., written by Nelson twelve days before Trafalgar, fetched £220, half what a bundle of letters from Dr Crippen fetched, but the same as nine miscellaneous A.L.S. from Einstein.

A certain archbishop of York had the right idea. To all begging letters he replied with the following autographed letter: 'Sir, I never give my autograph and never will.'

Books: *Four Hundred Years of British Autographs: A Collector's Guide* by Ray Rawlins (Dent, 1970); *Guinness Book of World Autographs* edited by Ray Rawlins (Guinness Superlatives, 1977)

automata   Automata – elaborate mechanical toys, operated by springs, clockwork and other such devices – were developed by the early clockmakers. However, the first important craftsman to turn his attention to automata was Jacques de Vaucanson. The Swiss Henri-Louis Jacquet-Droz (1752–91), talented son of a talented father, invented a singing bird music-box which had a clockwork mechanism and a small flute driven by miniature bellows to mimic the bird's cheeping. Vaucanson and Jacquet-Droz together produced a mechanical draughtsman who executed ornate baroque designs. James Cox, their contemporary in England, produced similar toys, and these gradually became more and more complex. Caterpillars crawled and acrobats somersaulted. Often such miniature marvels were made of gold, silver and gilded bronze, encrusted with precious gems, and the makers stamped their marks on their products when they felt particularly proud of them.

Throughout the nineteenth century the trade flourished with monkey orchestras, dancing dolls, shoe-cleaners, clocks with loudmouth trumpeters, and smoking monkeys which could inhale and exhale (Cartwright and Evans). There was little that the skill of these mechanical geniuses could not achieve. After about 1870 the German tin-plate industry swamped Europe and America with its 'penny toys'. Perhaps the wonders of the Industrial Revolution had turned adults' minds away from mere toys: when you could ride in a train or fly in a balloon, send a telegraph or experiment with electricity, the charms of automata began to fade.

Recently a number of reproduction singing-bird automata have come on to the market. These are of poor quality and should not be mistaken for the Victorian models they imitate.

Book: *Automata* by David Hopkins and Barbara Moss (Macmillan, 1976)

baby-walker The idea was ingenious in its simplicity: first catch your baby, then place it inside a circular structure of sturdy oak. The oak is hinged at one side and there is an opening which may be fastened with an iron latch on the outside. From the structure depend four legs with castors underneath, which curve outwards as they reach the ground. The baby, who is presumed to be just ready to start walking, may then push his walker around the room knocking aside any unfriendly objects with the legs. Occasionally, a tray may be attached to the ring for toys. Examples may be seen in the Snows Hill Museum, Broadway, and at Shakespeare's birthplace, Stratford. Most baby-walkers were made by country craftsmen.

Collection: Snows Hill Museum, Broadway

baluster A small circular column or pillar, with a bump in the middle or at the base. In sixteenth- and seventeenth-century tables, baluster legs were common (and in later Victorian reproductions of them). Turned balusters were an attractive feature of eighteenth- and nineteenth-century Windsor chairs. Longcase clock-hoods were decorated with balusters, bobbins and rings. A baluster-stem glass or a baluster glass or goblet is one in which the stem of the glass has a bump in it. Curiously the word banister is a corruption of the word baluster; next time you climb the stairs, have a look and you will see why.

bamboo The Prince of Wales (later to be crowned George IV) began building the Brighton Pavilion in 1802. In order to make the Chinese interiors seem more, well . . . Chinese, he bought Chinese furniture from Canton, later ordering imitation bamboo pieces to be made out of beechwood by Elward, Marsh and Tatham of London. Indeed most authentic Chinese bamboo furniture may be ascribed to the first thirty years of the nineteenth century. Look carefully for tight lattice-work, wooden pegs holding the joints in place, and bandings and stretchers which pass *outside* the legs and splats of tables and chairs.

Towards the end of the nineteenth century and the beginning of the twentieth, there were many manufacturers supplying the demand which the Prince had initiated. Although there was no such animal as Japanese bamboo furniture, the fashion for *japonaiserie* in the 1860s led to great quantities of lacquer, matting, and bamboo poles being imported; these were then made up into tables and chairs, whatnots and canterburies, wash-stands, cake-stands and stools.

A vast quantity of bamboo furniture was made, and plenty has survived. But it is not always in very good condition and repairs are arduous and expensive.

banknotes Once upon a time banks issued paper notes payable on demand and redeemable in gold. Even today the Chief Cashier announces on a modest £1 note, 'I promise to pay the Bearer on demand the sum of one pound'. Until 1826 there were no restrictions on the number or value of notes which banks could issue, but thereafter the law proscribed the issuing of notes under £5 in value. When joint stock banks were first permitted only those beyond a radius of 65 miles from the centre of London could issue notes. In 1854 a monopoly was created in favour of the Bank of England, other banks only being allowed to issue notes redeemable for the amounts they had actually in circulation at the time of the act.

For the collector the guiding rule is that the greater the stability of the country at the time the note is issued, the more value that note is likely to have. Face values are not related to current values. A five hundred million drachma note can be bought for peanuts. On the other hand banknotes made out of strips of shirt cloth and distributed by a British general in the Boer War (Uffington Border Scouts notes, redeemable by the Paymaster General) are among the most desirable of collected notes. Other banknotes have been made out of materials such as porcelain, leather, silk, and wood. Some modern notes, imperfectly printed, have a substantial value.

To clean banknotes, use soap and cold water, nothing more.

Book: *A Collector's Guide to Paper Money* by Yasha Beresiner (André Deutsch, 1977)

barbed wire A sort of barbed wire was invented in France, but its serious history began with the patenting of a wire fencing by Henry M.

Rose, an American, in 1873. His idea was improved upon by Joseph Glidden and Isaac Ellwood. Homesteaders used barbed wire to protect their smallholdings from cattle. There are now more than four hundred types of barbed wire, avidly sought by some 150,000 American collectors. They don't collect whole rolls, but only 18-inch lengths, which sell for a few dollars a 'stick'. The magazine for collectors, published in Texas, is called *The Barbarian*, and collectable makes of wire enjoy such names as Stover Clip, Meriweather's Snake, and Reynold's Hanging Knot.

Book: *The Wire That Fenced the West* by Henry D. and Frances T. McCallum (University of Oklahoma Press, 1965)

barley-sugar twist   A spiral-turning used on the cogs and underframes of furniture, and also on clock-hoods.

barometers   Early barometers had cases made by clockmakers including that genius Daniel Quare, and it is easy to date barometers if you are already familiar with the changing styles of clockcases.
Two distinct models evolved from the 1690s, when barometers were first made for the domestic market: the 'stick' and the 'wheel'. The stick barometer had a calibrated scale mounted against a column of mercury contained in glass. The wheel barometer had a circular dial with a needle operated by a float or a small reservoir of mercury. Sticks are generally more accurate and more expensive, being the design chosen by the finest craftsmen.

Mahogany bow front stick barometer

Mahogany wheel barometer

A barometer may be dated by its style, by the wood of which it is made — walnut (1690–1740), mahogany and, more unusually, satinwood (1740–1840), rosewood (1840–60), oak and again walnut (from 1860) — and by its engraving. Roman capitals and lower-case italics, or joined copper plate suggest the eighteenth century, while Gothic lettering indicates the first quarter of the nineteenth. Roman sans serif capitals returned towards the end of the nineteenth century. Generally, the more complete the details on the scale the later the barometer. The scales themselves were made of brass (preferred) and ivory.

The banjo-shaped wheel barometer was introduced by Italian craftsmen towards the end of the eighteenth century, the onion shape by about 1850. Robert Fitzroy (later Admiral Fitzroy), who devised a detailed wording for his barometer, was a British meteorologist who sailed on the *Beagle* with Charles Darwin. The Fitzroy barometer was mounted in a glazed, rectangular oak case. The aneroid barometer, popular from about 1850, measured the pressure variation on an evacuated chamber: as its name suggests it was liquid free. Aneroids are frequently found combined in a banjo case with thermometers and/or clocks.

In order to avoid air entering the mercury tube of your barometer, handle the instrument carefully and carry it at an angle of some 45 degrees.

Books: *Antique Barometers* by Edwin Banfield (Wayland Publications, 1977); *English Barometers 1680–1860* by Nicholas Goodison (Antique Collectors Club, 1977)
Collection: Hampton Court, Greater London (especially Tompion)

Bartolozzi prints   Francesco Bartolozzi (1727–1815) was engraver to George III for nearly forty years, a long time to work for so volatile an employer. A Florentine by birth, he was something of a journeyman, using Demortenu's red chalk style and stipple engraving to reproduce the works of the old masters – Cipriani, Angelica Kauffman, and others. Many prints which auctioneers and others claim are the work of Francesco came from his atelier but were the work of his students.

basalt or **basalte**   A highly vitrified black stoneware, developed by Josiah Wedgwood (and copied by others), in which he was able to fashion versions of the ancient antiquities brought back from Egypt by Sir William Hamilton. 'The Black is sterling and will last for ever,' Wedgwood claimed, and so far his claim seems to have been justified. Vases, teapots, urns and jugs were the most usual pieces to be found in basalt, and they were often decorated with friezes of classical scenes.

Collections: Lady Lever Art Gallery, Port Sunlight; Wedgwood Museum, Stoke-on-Trent

Battersea enamel   The enamelling factory at York House in Battersea was set up by Sir Stephen Janssen in 1753. Sadly by 1756 it had ceased production, and the stock was put up for sale. This included 'snuff-boxes of all sizes, of a great variety of patterns; of square and oval pictures of the Royal Family, history and other pleasing subjects, very proper subjects for the cabinets of the curious; bottle-tickets, with chains, for all sorts of liquors, and of different subjects; watch-cases, toothpick cases . . . crosses, and other curiosities, mostly mounted in metal, double gilt.'

The most celebrated copper-plate engraver employed at the works was Simon-François Ravenet (1706–74), who also engraved Plates IV and V of 'Marriage à la mode' for Hogarth. Most of the designs used at York House were from originals by Boucher (1703–70), transfer-printed on to white enamel, and then delicately overpainted.

Since the Battersea factory was open for no more than six years at the most, it is no wonder that genuine examples, the characteristic colours of which are bright blue, deep crimson and reddish brown, are extremely rare; nor that ignorant or unscrupulous dealers try to pass off as Battersea the inferior (but still very charming) products of the enamelling factories at Bilston especially, Wednesbury, Bickley and so on. These later Staffordshire pieces frequently carry legends on the lids, such as 'A Trifle from Harrogate' or 'Let us share, Joy & Care'.

Sir Stephen Janssen may sleep easy in his grave. He lost all his money, but he left the world a few trinkets of limited usefulness, perhaps, but of very great beauty. How many of us could claim as much?

Book: *English Enamel Boxes: from the 18th to the 20th Centuries* by Susan Benjamin (Orbis, 1978)
Collections: Blickling Hall, Norwich (candlesticks); Usher Gallery, Lincoln (Bilston); Nelson Museum, Monmouth; Bantock House Museum and Bilston Art Gallery, Wolverhampton (Bilston)

Baxter prints   George Baxter (1804–67) was the most brilliant of the mid-Victorian colour printers whose aim was to achieve a more popular application of the art of colour-printing. To this end he devised a new process, using a key plate on copper from which a number of impressions were printed in black. The oil colours were then applied from wood blocks to the prints taken from the copper. Up to twenty-four blocks might be needed to apply the colours to a single print. A Baxter print has none of the garishness of the later chromolithographs, but is vividly and excitingly coloured. The prints may be identified by one or other of the following legends printed on the picture or embossed on the mount: 'Printed in oil colours by Geo. Baxter, Patentee', or 'Printed by G. Baxter, the Inventor and Patentee of Oil Colour Painting'. It may be dated from this list of his London addresses: 1830–35, 29 King Square; 1835–43, 3 Charterhouse Square; 1843–51, 11 Northampton Square; and 1851–60, 11 & 12 Northampton Square.

Baxter's two most celebrated prints are probably 'The Coronation of Queen Victoria 1838' and 'The Opening of Queen Victoria's First Parliament'. He was also responsible for a handful of bird prints which in most cases appeared as little vignettes on the title pages of works by Robert Mudie. Baxter's later productions, Sunday School cards and pocket-sized prints (needle-box prints), are less remarkable and therefore cheaper.

When his patent expired, Abraham Le Blond was the most renowned licensee of the process. Le Blond's characteristic prints were small oval pictures of rustic courtship and the like. When he tried to reprint his master's work the results were not entirely successful.

With the high prices that early Baxter prints command it is no surprise to find a few forgeries around. A forgery may have its surface covered with a fine criss-cross pattern; on the other hand it may not. Be warned!

Book: *George Baxter and the Baxter Prints* by Max E. Mitzman (David & Charles, 1978)
Collections: National Museum of Wales, Cardiff; Museum and Art Gallery, Reading; City
       Museum and Art Gallery, Worcester

beadwork   Beads have been with us a long time: there are records of glass beads being manufactured in Egypt from about the third millennium BC. In Britain by the sixteenth century beads were being sewn to clothes and wall-hangings. But it was not until the years of Victoria's reign that beadwork, especially associated with needlework, was considered worthy of the attentions of any amateur who cared to take up the hobby. Beads were imported from Germany and Murano in Italy, and throughout the nineteenth century their design became more elaborate and varied. They could be made of glass, pearl, coral, wood, metal, cut steel, jet, gold, silver, and, eventually, plastic.

The beads would either be stitched over an entire area, as with cushions or firescreens, or incorporated into a design, as with Berlin woolwork pictures. Footstools were especially popular. Much beadwork was imported from the Red Indians of North America whose early works were usually in four colours, representing the natural colours of earth, air, water, and fire; these designs depicted flowers and animals.

Beadwork of any age is seldom found in perfect condition unless it has been kept behind glass. Repairs should be done with period beads; the Royal School of Needlework in London will undertake such work for you.

beechwood   The wood of the beech tree, *Fagus sylvaticus*, is semi-hard and light in colour. When growing it is often very majestic, but when cut up for furniture it is rather humble and self-effacing. In the fifteenth and sixteenth centuries it was used for coffermakers chairs, copied from French models. During the mid-nineteenth century when the furniture maker's art was becoming mechanised, it was sometimes stained and veneered to masquerade as mahogany.

Beilby glassware   William Beilby (1740–1819) and his sister Mary (1749–97) worked in Newcastle-upon-Tyne as glass enamellers at the glassworks of Dagnia-Williams. Initially they concentrated on putting heraldic devices (frequently fictitious) on wine glasses, goblets, and decanters. Before Beilby's father, a goldsmith and silversmith, died in 1765, William signed his pieces 'Beilby Jnr' or 'W. Beilby Jnr'. After 1774 William added rococo scenes to his repertoire. Some pieces are signed with the surname alone, so that one cannot distinguish between William and Mary. Another son, Ralph (1743–1817), was also an engraver.

Book: *The Ingenious Beilbys* by J. Rush (Barrie & Jenkins, 1973)

Beilby white enamelled goblet, c. 1770

Belleek Many fine things have come out of Ireland, my favourites being Bernard Shaw, Arkle, and Belleek porcelain. This is not the place to enthuse about the first two, but Belleek demands attention, with its brilliant white glaze, its elegantly modelled marine styles, and its flower-baskets, so delicately structured one wouldn't trust a puff of wind not to shatter them.

Parian ware, a form of china aping marble and ideal for small pieces of statuary, was developed around the middle of the nineteenth century, possibly at the Copeland factory. Its qualities were recognised by those in charge of the Royal Worcester factory, whose display of Parian ware caused much admiration at the Great Exhibition. Among others to be impressed was an Irish landowner, John Caldwell Bloomfield of County Fermanagh. In the grounds of his Castle Caldwell estate he discovered deposits of felspar (potassium aluminium silicate), the essential ingredient in Parian manufacture. He called in and sought the advice of Robert William Armstrong, an expert from Worcester. Surveys were favourable and within two years 'Irish statuary porcelain' was on the market.

Armstrong's taste and skill were backed by money from a Dublin businessman named McBirney. The factory they set up in the village of Belleek (where it is still in production) was known as D. McBirney and

Company. Production was varied and included such improbable necessities as porcelain insulators for telegraph poles. But there were three areas in which Belleek was outstanding.

The first was statuary. Classical figures were modelled by such skilled craftsmen as William Gallimore, and symbolic titles, like 'The Prisoner of Love' (a despondent lady posing amidst dead flowers and soulful doves) and 'Erin Awakening from her Slumbers', ensured that Victorian intellectuals were catered for. Then there were the marine pieces. A bismuth-based glaze, developed in France and applied to Cornish clay mixed with Belleek felspar, produced an iridescent glaze with a brilliant sheen strongly reminiscent of mother-of-pearl. Along the Donegal beaches were numerous sea-urchins, and these inspired shapes and styles for a great variety of Belleek pieces. Other marine designs followed, incorporating seahorses, flying fish, and shells of all kinds. The lustrous glaze was contrasted with pastel shades of coral-pink, green or gold. Queen Victoria commissioned a table service of a sea-urchin design for the Empress of Germany, and the Prince of Wales ordered an even more imposing one.

The third category was basketware. Baskets intricately modelled by hand from woven strips of porcelain were decorated with roses, thistles, and shamrocks in natural colours. When fired these baskets were reduced to three-quarters their original size, emphasising their delicacy.

Most Belleek porcelain is marked with an Irish wolfhound, a harp, and a tower, with the word Belleek in a cartouche. This mark is transfer-printed on the base of the piece, with 'Ireland' added after 1891. Where the base was too small to accommodate the mark, the word Belleek with or without the 'Co.' was regarded as sufficient. A few unmarked pieces were produced, and with these the only satisfactory test is the quality of the craftsmanship. Both Armstrong and McBirney died in 1884, and standards declined after that date, although later pieces are still attractive and of good quality.

Several American firms copied Belleek designs, notably the Ott and Brewer factory and the Willets Manufacturing Company. They sometimes even went so far as to mark their pieces with the name Belleek. Although Belleek porcelain is sometimes rather elaborate (winged monsters tend to feature more than perhaps they should) the best from the Belleek factory equals anything else from the nineteenth century.

bentwood It was a great day in High Wycombe when the bodgers and bottomers discovered that heat and steam could be enlisted to produce the harmonious and sensuous curve required for the Windsor chair. The wood would be steamed until it was pliable, bent, and clamped into position. In this way bows, spur stretchers and back-rails were fashioned, and, in this way, was bentwood furniture born. The technique was developed and extended by the Viennese Michael Thonet (1796–1871), who realised that beechwood bent in this way had interesting commercial possibilities. By

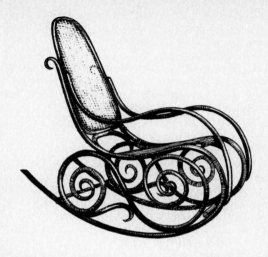

Thonet bentwood rocking chair, c. 1860

the 1850s he had established a London distribution centre from where his chairs, tables, hatstands and other pieces were sold in great quantity, the chairs being particularly popular. For restaurant chairs Thonet pioneered the use of plywood, usually pierced by a pattern of small holes, to replace the caning in the back panels.

Applied to the rocking chair, bentwood happily married the function of the chair to its design. Rockers were gracefully extended into arms and back in a single serpentine curve. One could rock oneself asleep in aesthetic security. However the makers of Boston rockers responded vigorously to the bentwood threat, and bentwood rockers were never very popular in America. In 1854 Heal's eagerly seized on the new furniture which could 'all be packed on the back of a Horse or Mule'.

The bentwood technique remained — and remains — as relevant in the twentieth century. In Finland Hugo Aalto (born 1898) applied it successfully to birchwood, and the Hungarian Marcel Breuer (born 1902) was much taken with it. (Breuer was the man who, inspired by the handlebars of a bicycle, designed the first tubular steel chair.)

Berlin porcelain   A generic term used to describe the output of three establishments: that of William Wegely in Friedrichstrasse (*c.*1751–61), that of Gotzkowski in Leipzigstrasse (1761–63), and that of Frederick the Great, who took over Gotzkowski's factory in 1763 and ran it as the Königliche Porzellan Manufaktur — the Royal Porcelain Factory.

Among the characteristic products of Berlin porcelain were lithophanes, in translucent biscuit panels with *intaglio* moulded decorations, from the

1820s to 1850, imitation maiolica, and later in the century elaborate glaze effects influenced by oriental shapes and colours. The Royal Factory employed painters and a modeller (F. E. Meyer) from Meissen. The marks to look for are: 'W' for Wegely (1751–61); 'G' for Gotzkowski (1761–6); a sceptre for pieces dating from the late eighteenth century; an orb with a cross and the initials 'K.P.M.' from about 1830; a printed sceptre from 1870; and, for modern pieces, a stamp in blue with an eagle in the centre and the initials F.R. with a lettering surround.

Collections: Museum and Art Gallery, Birmingham; Public Museum and Art Gallery, Hastings

Berlin woolwork   The idea originated in Germany at the beginning of the nineteenth century. You purchased a kit, consisting of paper patterns, squares of canvas, samples of wool, and, of course, instructions. You filled in the canvas squares with the wool, sewed the squares together, and added a border. The result was a completed picture which to your country cousins might appear an original work of art. The subjects most frequently tackled were old master paintings, Biblical scenes, and flower designs.

The kits were imported from Germany in great quantities by a Mrs Wilks who showed considerable acuity, for the craze caught on not only in Britain and France but also in America, where the kits were known as Zephyrs. The tapestry patterns were manufactured in the German town of Gotha, but the wool was dyed in Berlin, hence the name. Although the designs were unsophisticated and the colours coarse, many examples were considered well worth framing and glazing. Others were used for chair backs, firescreens, and cushion-covers, and coloured silks and beads were occasionally incorporated. A few examples were signed and dated, but the majority — perhaps wisely — were not.

Collection: Lauriston Castle, Edinburgh

Woolwork picture,
c. *1860*

Biedermeier   A particularly ugly style of furniture named after an imaginary Philistine character, Gottlieb Biedermeier, who appeared in the pages of a magazine, *Fliegende Blatter*. It was a cheapskate version of French

Empire style with much metal mounting, and black horsehair upholstery. Swans, griffins, and dolphins enriched (?) the chairs and sofas, and the excesses of the rococo style were adopted with enthusiasm. People are once again paying good money for Biedermeier furniture, which only goes to show that there's nowt so queer as folk!

Billies and Charlies   William Smith and Charles Eaton were illiterate mudlarks who lived during the second quarter of the nineteenth century. Since the London docks were then in the process of construction there was plenty of mud in which to lark, and plenty of antiquarians prepared to pay for any interesting artifacts which might be uncovered on the banks of the Thames. One day Billy and Charlie discovered a fifteenth-century medal and sold it to the British Museum for what seemed to them a generous price. Obviously mudlarking had greater charms than they had supposed, but, failing to turn up any more treasures, they decided to manufacture their own.

Using a small furnace and cock metal — a cheap lead alloy — they cast a quantity of items, such as goblets, badges, weapons and seals. By adding some indecipherable lettering, vaguely symbolic figures, and a healthy patina of good estuary mud, they managed to fool the experts. So successful were Billy and Charlie that they took to the wholesale business, passing the pieces to more anonymous mudlarks for retail; they continued to do so until an undeniable confusion between Roman and Arabic numerals led to a dealer of some repute being accused of selling 'antiques', knowing them to be fakes. The resulting libel action in 1858, in which a number of eminent experts insisted that Billy's and Charlie's medieval effusions were indeed the real things, created such a stir that these fake pieces began to be collected in their own right and were found to have — despite their unorthodox pedigree — considerable merit; 'vigorous' and 'original' were the words used. Billy's and Charlie's business continued to flourish, and their pieces are now highly regarded. The most satisfying irony is that since less than a thousand genuine Billies and Charlies are thought to have been made, there must be a great many *fake* Billies and Charlies making fools out of the experts just as they always did.

birdcages   Until the end of the Elizabethan age almost all the birds found in captivity were indigenous British species. Goldfinches, linnets, and siskins did the singing, jackdaws, crows, and magpies the talking. Before the fashion for soft furnishings, it was perfectly feasible to let your bird roam around the house — Sir Thomas More's private apartments were aflutter with imported parrots. But birdcages came in with carpets, curtains, and cushions, and kindness flew out of the window.

Early birdcages followed the fashionable furniture styles of the period, frequently Gothic, but Elizabeth I had birdcages specially created of silver and silver gilt, inlaid with diamonds, pearls and other gems. During the Civil War and the Republic birds were left to their own devices. With the Restoration birds and birdcages became fashionable once more, and a stroll down Birdcage Walk would have exposed you to a great variety of cages. Most were rectangular, flat-roofed, and made of carved wood, with an interior of wire mesh above a leaded floor to facilitate cleaning. They would stand on a table or hang by the window.

Regency cages were better adapted to the birds' requirements: tall, oval cages allowed parrots to spread their wings, spacious cages encouraged birds to enjoy the company of others of the same species. The Chippendale influence dictated delicate mahogany fretwork with tiny brass mounts on drawers and doors, silver drinking troughs, and fine porcelain feeding bowls. Really these cages were bird *houses*, and everything the Prince Regent could do to the Brighton Pavilion was done to the cages of what must have been rather bewildered birds. Bamboo and cane, lacquer, whatever the cabinet-makers used for human furniture, the birds had to put up with. Victorian taste elaborated the birdcage to such an extent that the birds became almost unimportant.

Under the influence of the architecture of the Crystal Palace, where the Great Exhibition was held in 1851, brass and white wire replaced bamboo and lacquer, and birds could live in transparent elegance once more. But this was only a temporary respite. The decline into architectural madness continued. However, if I were a budgie, I'm not sure I wouldn't prefer some manic Victorian cage to an unsteady perch in a chromium box within permanent view of the television.

Book: *Bird-keeping and Birdcages: A History* by Sonia Roberts (David & Charles, 1972)

biscuit Unglazed porcelain. The virtue of biscuit is that it has to appear naked and unashamed before the world, whereas glazed and coloured porcelain figures can hide their imperfections under their decorations. Much very fine biscuit was produced at Sèvres and Dresden, but the figures and groups produced at Derby from 1795 onwards are as fine. The surface of these Derby pieces has a waxy softness and glossiness which is far more lifelike than the chalky white of most other biscuit ware. Rockingham, for instance, in other respects the equal of Derby, is very white; so is Copeland.

Collection: Knowle House, Sevenoaks

blackamoor The fashion for Negro servants originated in Venice, that city dedicated to excess, the unfortunates concerned being brought to Italy by ships trading in the Orient. Those Venetians who found the real thing too expensive or too troublesome had candlestands made in the shape of Moorish servants. The fashion regrettably spread to England where these *torchères* or *guéridons* were given the Regency or Victorian treatment, and were used latterly more for trailing plants and aspidistras than for candelabra. That arbiter of Victorian taste, Mrs Haweis (1848–98), wrote in *The Art of Decoration*: 'A candlestand, lamp or any other support ought to be a pretty and consistent object . . . Large Negro lads with glass eyes and arsenic-green draperies starred with gold are not so suitable in a great hall as a bronze Hercules or a really well modelled elephant.'

blue and white china If you exclude oriental china (see *Chinese porcelain*), what is usually understood by the useful phrase 'blue and white china' is transfer-printed china in underglaze blue. A pattern would be engraved on a copper plate, spread with a heat-resistant cobalt blue dye, transferred on to the china. The border would be applied separately in two or three pieces: sometimes you can see the join where, as with wallpaper, the pattern is a little unsynchronised. The paper would be floated off, and the pattern would be 'set' in an oven and then glazed. Early glazes are blue and faintly rippled; after about 1830 they tend to be colourless and smooth.

Blue and white china of this traditional kind has enjoyed prolonged popularity in Britain and America. Much early blue and white china is almost impossible to attribute: there was a great deal of pirating of patterns among potters, with itinerant hawkers selling their borders several times over. The practice was stamped out by the Copyright Act of 1841.

Caughley is usually credited with the introduction of willow pattern designs; and in about 1780 it produced a steely blue oriental-style willow pattern, with pagodas and willows, bridges and windfall apples. However, the classical willow pattern did not emerge until 1830, when it may have been introduced by Spode. This pattern, with its romantic story (two lovers, being chased over a three-arched bridge by the girl's father, are transmogrified into birds) and its geometrical border of small flowers and scrolls, quickly established itself as the most popular design ever. Second in popularity was the Wild Rose pattern, two pairs of men in boats on a canal with a bridge, a cottage, a church, and a big house, within a border of wild roses. Other popular designs included the Hundred Antiques, the Lady of the Lake, and the Grazing Rabbits. Such patterns were used for the vast Victorian dinner services which vast Victorian households required. There were more artistic and more ambitious series in which the quality of the engraving is especially fine. These include Ridgway's 'Views of Oxford and Cambridge', Spode's 'Indian Sporting Series', and others, including American scenes, especially popular with, as you might expect, Americans.

Book: *Blue and White Transferware 1780–1840* by A. W. Coysh (David & Charles, 1974)
Collections: Museum and Art Gallery, Doncaster; Christchurch Mansion, Ipswich; Harris Museum and Art Gallery, Preston

blunderbuss The blunderbuss is a romantic looking weapon with a romantic sounding name. It speaks to us down the ages of pirates and highwaymen, and we would do well to listen for it would be rash to antagonise that flaming muzzle, that sly bayonet.

Literally a blunderbuss, derived from the Flemish *donderbuss*, is a thunder-tube, and it reached Britain from Germany and the low countries towards the end of the seventeenth century. Its bell mouth was not, as has been popularly supposed, intended to spread the shot, but to facilitate loading when one was operating under difficulties, from a coach maybe, or the deck of a ship, or the back of a horse. The muzzle of a fowling-piece was never more than three-quarters of an inch wide: how much more inviting the gaping mouth of the blunderbuss! (And how appalling the prospect for the unfortunate man who happened to be staring into that mouth once it was fully loaded.)

Originally a naval weapon, the blunderbuss became the householder's friend in an age of violence. Others who liked to have one to hand included landlords of taverns, prison officers, coachmen, seamen, private armies and, of course, the services.

Another misconception about the blunderbuss is that you could load it with whatever you happened to have to hand; in fact you would have done so at your peril, for you would have risked exploding the barrel and possibly yourself with it. The normal charge for a blunderbuss (fowling-piece or pistol) would have been lead balls or common shot; 'swandrops', a type of large-shot, was most often used. The majority of blunderbusses had brass barrels and brass furniture, although combinations of brass and iron are sometimes found. Early designs incorporated the flintlock mechanism, but a few of the later weapons were converted to the percussion technique.

Early in the eighteenth century the musketoon was developed, a long-barrelled blunderbuss with a slightly smaller bore and slightly less flared muzzle, ideally suited to shooting from horseback. However, by the end of the century the musketoon was discarded in favour of the more traditional blunderbuss.

There was usually a spring-mounted bayonet running along the top of the barrel the full length of the muzzle. The styles of furniture and lock accorded closely with prevailing fashions, although they were rarely worked in silver, since the blunderbuss was always regarded very much as a working weapon rather than an ornament. For this reason the greatest gunsmiths generally ignored the blunderbuss, which was left to lesser craftsmen. In the eighteenth and nineteenth centuries blunderbusses made with many disparate elements would be used on board merchant ships, most particularly during the Napoleonic wars. Such weapons are now virtually impossible to distinguish from modern pieces, so be warned.

bobbins Since it sometimes took two hundred bobbins to make a piece of bobbin lace (or pillow lace or bone lace), it is not surprising that so many old and pretty examples have survived, and are still quite cheap. Knitting needles only have numbers but bobbins have names, and very appealing some of them are. 'Old maids' were rather plain, 'leopards' had spots, 'butterflies' had splayed wings, and 'cows-in-calf' were big bobbins with little bobbins inside. The oldest ones, dating from the mid-eighteenth century and known as 'dumps' and 'bobtails', were short and fat; but they dieted considerably as time went by. Many were decorated with coloured beads, so that the lacemaker could swiftly distinguish between them. They could be made of gold or silver, ivory or bone, brass or any of a number of close-grained woods.

Collections: Buckingham County Museum, Aylesbury; Museum and Art Gallery, Luton; Castle Museum, York

bog oak   This hard wood was darkened by being buried in peat. It is similar in appearance to jet, and was used in much the same way. In the sixteenth century it was used for inlay work; after the Great Exhibition of 1851 it became a fashionable material for mourning and souvenir jewellery. Copies of ancient Irish brooches, set with Irish pearls, were evidently traditional and therefore much admired by the pre-Raphaelites and the arts and crafts set.

bohemian glass   Early in the nineteenth century there was something of a reaction in Britain against so many years of good taste and restraint; and nowhere was this reaction felt so strongly as in the glassmaker's craft. Suddenly everyone wanted colour, and the glassworks of Bohemia (now part of Czechoslovakia) were the most advanced in the production of coloured glass. During the Biedermeier period (c.1815–48) the middle classes found themselves with money to spend, and the manufacturers, such as Buquoy, Egerman and Riedel, were only too willing to soak it up.

They pioneered yellow glass in the 1830s, and ruby glass (most successfully) in the 1840s. They produced flashed glass, which was engraved through one or more layers of colours, and overlaid glass, for which panels of white are laid over the glass with paintings within the panels and gilding around the paintings. Figurative designs were used, and one finds symbols of health and happiness, with views of the resorts where one is expected to recover one's health and happiness.

The best examples of these techniques, which spread rapidly to the rest of Europe and America, may be dated between 1830 and 1850. Much of the rest is embarrassingly nasty.

Collection: Victoria Art Gallery, Bath (Huth Collection)

bombé   Literally, *bombé* means 'swelling' or 'bulging'. The word vividly recalls the appearance of certain items of furniture, especially eighteenth-century serpentine-fronted commodes.

bonheurs du jour Literally 'happy hours of the day', *bonheurs du jour* turn out to be no more than elegant little writing tables for elegant little French ladies. They stand on four legs with small bureaux atop, in which are tiny drawers for correspondence, and cupboards for writing materials. These charming pieces are made from light wood, especially satinwood.

bookcases If you should find yourself in Cambridge, a visit to the Pepys Library in Magdalene College may make a welcome alternative to yet another quadrangle. In the Pepys Library you will find Samuel's glass-fronted bookcases, twelve of which he had made in 1666 by 'Sympson the Joiner', who started quite a fashion since these were the first glass-fronted bookcases to have been made. Prior to that, bookcases, where they existed, had been architectural features rather than domestic furniture, and they were generally to remain so for another hundred years or so. Open pediments allowing space for vases or busts gradually gave way to continuous galleries, as may be seen illustrated in Chippendale's *Director*.

Eighteenth-century bookcases were generally large and heavy, being used for sections of complete libraries in country mansions; they were made of walnut or mahogany. Combinations of bureaux and bookcases offered intriguing challenges to the master craftsmen. Mirror plates on cabinet doors gave way to clear glazing or to mahogany panels. The breakfront style was popular and broken pediments were introduced.

In the mid-eighteenth century bookcases were much affected by Gothic and rococo styling. Geometrical patterns in the glazed panels, with pointed arches, carved and fretted friezes, pagoda roofs hung with tiny bells, gilt mounts, there was very little that was not tried, and — such was the confidence and craftsmanship of the period — there was very little that did not work.

During the Regency period dwarf bookcases were introduced and the walls were left clear for paintings and prints. According to Ackermann's *Repository* of 1823 one only needed a small stand or a few shelves 'to contain all the the books that may be desired for a sitting room without reference to the library.' In 1808 a patent was taken out for an ingenious revolving bookcase which could contain a healthy number of books in a limited area.

The Victorian age contributed little other than weighty carving and a general gloominess to the bookcase, but mention should be made of William Burges (1827–81) and his remarkable painted examples. Burges, with Pugin (1812–52), was a Gothic revivalist, but the bookcase which he exhibited in the medieval court of the 1826 Exhibition was restrained, though castellated, and was painted by eleven leading artists. It may be seen in the Ashmolean, Oxford.

book collecting During the first forty-five years of printing, up to AD 1500, some 38,000 books were printed, a number curiously close to the number now printed in Britain *in a single year*. From this it may be seen that anyone who sets out to collect books will soon be as frustrated as those Wiltshire rustics who (according to Grose's *Dictionary of the Vulgar Tongue*), upon seeing the moon in a pond, tried to rake it out — the original 'moonrakers'. Specialisation is essential. From the vellum Gutenberg Bible at Eton College — probably the most valuable book in the world and worth well over a million pounds — to a first edition of *Just William*, from the 1493 Nuremberg Chronicle, which has 645 woodcuts and 1809 printed illustrations, to Mary Tourtel's Rupert books, the range is so vast that books cease to be an area of collecting and become the tangible symbols of the world's culture. Just as the pen is mightier than the sword, so are authors mightier than the most powerful tyrants. Who would know about Tamburlaine if Marlowe (and others) had not chosen to write about him? It's a consoling thought.

A book may be desirable for the beauty of its binding, printing, or illustrations, it may be intellectually seductive — the fourteen leather-bound volumes and supplement of James Murray's *New English Dictionary on Historical Principles founded mainly on the Materials collected by the Philological Society*, for instance — or its appeal may be emotional, as the Penguin Classics edition of Nathaniel West's *Miss Lonely Hearts* is to me. It is hard to conceive of a book which would make no appeal to *any* collector, just as it is hard to imagine a book whose author would not experience a *frisson*, when he takes the first edition into his hands, and fancies that he is holding a tiny chunk of civilisation between his ink-stained fingers. On, however, to more specific matters.

Binding. The earliest books were unbound and consisted of rolls stored in cylindrical containers. Medieval manuscripts were bound in sheepskin or deerskin, and occasionally in cowhide. This cowhide (more often known as calf) was the most common sixteenth-century binding, and was accompanied by gold tooling. (Queen Elizabeth, however, preferred embroidered bindings.) Until the end of the seventeenth century English bindings were copied from continental models and executed, as often as not, by craftsmen from abroad who had settled in England. Morocco bindings — tanned goatskins originally from Moroccan or North African goats — in brown and olive green (1600–50) or in red and blue (1650–1700) represent the best the century had to offer. The fine mosaic bindings of John Houlden and the decorative leather of Samuel Meame (not a binder himself, but a bookseller who commissioned bindings from others) are examples of this golden age. The reign of Charles II saw the introduction of 'cottage' binding, decorated with a gilt or painted gable at the top and bottom of the central panel, which may be said to be Britain's first national binding.

Interesting eighteenth-century developments included neo-classical designs by Robert Adam and 'Athenian' Stuart, and surprisingly restrained bindings in a similar style used by Horace Walpole at Strawberry Hill. Towards the end of the century the finest work was coming from Dublin and Edinburgh: James Scott's rococo bindings, for example, and Roger Payne's 'gold studded' backs — when he was sober enough to do them justice. Many German immigrants also took to bookbinding. The nineteenth century saw 'cathedral' bindings in the Gothic style, sometimes including a rose window. A sharp distinction was made between 'fine' and 'trade' bindings when machinery made cloth bindings a cheap and accessible alternative to leather. The private presses of the late nineteenth century brought a return of emphasis to the binding and printing of books, and examples from the Kelmscott Press, for instance, are very fine.

It is often true in bookbinding that the more obscure the work the more elaborate the binding which embraces it.

Collection: Museum of Bookbinding, Bath.

Book jackets. The first printed, detachable paper cover for a book was made for *The Keepsake* (Longman, 1832). Thereafter, from the 1850s, beautiful abstract designs, developing from the tradition of the great bookbinders of the past, were used on books bound in paper on boards. Detachable covers did not come into general use until the 1890s when they tended to repeat the designs on the bindings.

The distinctive yellow jackets of Gollancz, promoted by Stanley Morrison, showed the commercial possibilities of such consistency. Distinguished figurative jackets have extended the range significantly, with work by artists of the calibre of Barnett Freedman, Edward Bawden, Rex Whistler, John Piper, Duncan Grant, Feliks Topolski, Edward Ardizzone, and Ronald Searle.

Modern paperbacks depend increasingly on 'stills' from films and television but the raucous vulgarity of some of the jackets from the 1950s and 1960s (see Ed McBain's thrillers) quickly acquires a nostalgic charm with which the latest television spin-off cannot begin to compete.

Book-plates (ex libris). Anatole France had it right. He it was who admonished: 'Never lend books, for no one ever returns them; the only books I have in my library are books that other folk have lent me.' There are only two ways to avoid such a situation. One is to put inside your books a plate, or ex libris, with your name on it; the other is to manage without friends. Book-plates, though a minor and pleasantly economical branch of collecting (few cost more than a couple of pounds) are often charmingly decorated, the designs frequently punning on the author's name or occupation.

The first English example is reputedly one belonging to Sir Thomas Tresham (or Tresame), dated 1585. Pepys had several in his books, now in the Magdalene College Library, Cambridge. His were engraved by Robert White, after Kneller; other notable artists who specialised in this field include Bartolozzi and Bewick (for Southey).

The armorial style (*c.*1700–20), the Jacobean style (*c.*1710–60), the Chippendale style (*c.*1750–80), the Georgian style (*c.*1770–1820), and the art nouveau style (*c.*1870–1910) are all much as you might expect. In the twentieth century modern calligraphers, such as Eric Gill and Reynolds Stone, added their pennyworths. The first known collector was Miss Jenkins of Bath in the 1820s. She was ahead of her time, however, and it was not for another fifty years or so that the fashion became current. There is now a book-plate society, in London, which keeps a list of modern artists who will accept book-plate commissions.

Children's books. The more loved a child's book has been, the more likely it is to be torn, battered, scribbled on, and generally disfigured. This in part is why the collecting of much-loved children's books of the past has become so sadly out of reach of the shallow pockets of today's children.

Age is less important than names in this field. Beatrix Potter, Kate Greenaway, Walter Crane, Kay Neilson, Arthur Rackham, Edmund Dulac, Cecil Aldin. Charles and Heath Robinson, these are the nine bright stars in the firmament of children's books. Kay Neilson illustrated only five books (Hans Andersen and *Hansel and Gretel* among them), while Rackham, who was extremely prolific, is most celebrated for *Peter Pan*.

The yellow Rupert books, published by Sampson Low in the 1930s, are now great rarities. There were 46 volumes which sold for a shilling (later sixpence) each. Many of the most colourful comics, such as *Tiger Tim*, *Teddy Tail*, and *Mrs Hippo*, owed their popularity (and owe it still) to the crazily cheerful designs of H. S. Foxwell, while A. A. Milne's success must have been greatly due to Ernest Shepherd's sympathetic realisations of Pooh, Kanga, Eeyore, Tigger, and Christopher Robin himself.

Myself, I collect books by Angela Brazil, whose illustrations are less than aesthetic; and I love beyond reason the doom-ridden woodcuts which transform the *Curious Lobster* books into fateful pilgrimages.

Colour-plate books. Somewhat arbitrarily booksellers exclude from this category all natural-history books and include few books published after 1830. What remains is rich enough anyway, since no matter what techniques were used for printing the pictures, the colour was nearly always added by hand. The books thus produced were invariably expensive (up to 95 guineas a volume for some of Ackermann's publications), but there seems to have been a public for them.

Some of these books, in the late eighteenth and early nineteenth centuries, were topographical in subject, such as Paul Sandby's much sought-after *Views in South Wales* (*c.*1775), and they contained little if any text. Gilpin's works, though sometimes uncoloured, were highly rated by his contemporaries. One of the finest of all topographical books must be Ackermann's *Microcosm of London*, illustrated by Rowlandson and Pugin. This contained no fewer than 104,000 hand-coloured plates. Some microcosm! Other subjects dealt with in colour-plate books include architecture (Nash and Soane), instructive drawing books (Cox and Morland), pictorial collections, sociological studies (Cruikshank), and sporting books (Alken and Leech illustrating Surtees' Jorrocks books, William Daniell, and others).

First editions. All copies of a book as first printed and published are first editions, including repeated printings with minor textual alterations. A first edition only becomes a second edition when the format or text has been re-set or changed. Obviously there will be no printing history in a first edition, but the date of publication is often the only sure guide to the 'firstness' of a supposed first edition. Many are collected. The great Irish evangelists, Joyce, Synge, Yeats and Shaw, are always in demand. So are D. H. and T. E. Lawrence, Norman Douglas, T. F. Powys, Maugham, Kipling, Eliot, Wodehouse, and many others. The First Edition Club was founded in 1922 by A. J. A. Symons and Max Judge to promote book collecting. They need not have worried.

A first folio Shakespeare or a Kilmarnock Burns, these are treasures indeed. Editions of Dickens, collected as part-works and with original wrappers, are worth a great deal more than Dickens editions published as books. Where *Pickwick Papers* is concerned one really needs to call in an expert, as the water is so muddy. And, of course, one needs to avoid buying first editions of books which never deserved second editions.

Limited editions. Any book that includes a statement that the printing has been limited is a limited edition. Such books are usually numbered and may be signed by the author and/or illustrator. Some limited editions may be for private circulation only. The most interesting are from the private presses, of which there were several in the eighteenth century (such as Horace Walpole's). However, it was William Morris with his Kelmscott Press, founded in 1890, who set to work raising the standards of book production and typography. The Doves and Ashendene presses followed soon after, with the Gregynog (1930–40 in Wales), the Golden Cockerel (founded 1921), the Lion and Unicorn (founded 1953), and others.

Books: *Glossary of Book Collecting* by G. A. Glaister (Allen & Unwin, 1960); *Book Collecting: A Beginner's Guide* by Seumas Stewart (David & Charles, 1972; revised ed. 1979); *Book Collector's Fact Book* by Margaret Haller (Arco, 1976).

boss   The word has three meanings, two ancient and one modern. The modern meaning of the word derives from one of the others; who can say which?

In architecture a boss is a carved projection covering the junction of ribs or beams in a roof or ceiling. By extension, to a cabinet-maker a boss is a similar decorative device to conceal an intersection of mouldings. In early English architecture some roof bosses are worked into complex patterns of heraldic symbols, armorial bearings and beautiful or grotesque animals and birds.

In armour a boss is the stud in the middle of a shield. Sometimes this tapers to a spike, which could come in very useful in hand-to-hand combat.

boulle (confusingly also known as **buhl** or **boule**)   A style of marquetry named after André Charles Boulle (1642–1732), the ingenious architect, sculptor, cabinet-maker, engraver, and marqueteur. But he did not invent the technique, which was of Italian origin. Boulle's version was to use very thin layers of brass and tortoiseshell. The sheets of both materials were clamped together, and the designs cut out of the partnership in a sort of fretwork. The layers were then either combined as *première partie* (the tortoiseshell inlaid with the brass), or as *contre partie* (the brass inlaid with the tortoiseshell). Thus pairs of furniture or opposing panels might be matched by patient craftsmen. The brass might be engraved and the designs heightened with black pigment. Those parts of boulle furniture not inlaid in this way are usually veneered in ebony and bear ormolu mounts. Disciples of Boulle tended to get rather carried away, adding pewter, horn, mother-of-pearl, ivory, and improbable colouring. The effect can be stunning, dazzling, or alarming, and migraine-sufferers would be well advised to keep away.

Boulle's original work was seen to best effect at Fontainebleau, where a whole wall was covered with his inlaid designs, but unfortunately it delaminated. Boulle work is always liable to come unstuck. Motifs are based on classical antiquity, and Louis XIV insignia frequently pop up. Boulle was made in both France and England during the eighteenth and nineteenth centuries; it is sold for spectacular prices in the twentieth.

Collection: Wallace Collection, London

Bow   Edward Heylyn and Thomas Frye were granted a patent in 1744 to manufacture porcelain in Stratford, East London. Frye, an artist and engraver, was the first to introduce bone ash into porcelain. He stayed on as manager of the Bow factory (under the ownership of Wetherby and Crowther) until 1759. Alas, for human aspirations! In 1762 Frye and Wetherby both died, and in 1763 Crowther went bankrupt. The men who had been responsible for so much fragile beauty were themselves fragile. What happened to Heylyn we don't know, but plates survive, inscribed 'Robert Crowther, 1770', which indicates that he cheated his creditors as well as death for longer than his colleagues.

Some early Bow porcelain is marked 'New Canton', and characteristics of the factory, besides this Chinese influence, include partridge and quail designs, and powder-blue pieces with oriental patterns in underglaze blue. But the glory of Bow was the figures, many attributed to John Bacon, who became an R.A., and Tebo or Thibaud, later employed by Josiah Wedgwood. These figures, much heavier than those produced at other factories, include the Muses, Mars and Venus, Flora, Charity, Thomas

Waterman, the Marquis of Granby, General Wolfe, Quin in the character of Falstaff, Woodward as 'The Fine Gentleman' with Kitty Clive as his companion piece, harlequins, boys riding goats, dancers, flower-sellers, and men with bagpipes.

Bow figures are often notable for their lack of gilding. The early ones bear no factory mark. They are vividly coloured in blue, red, and pinky-violet and feature blobs of red on the cheeks, where Chelsea used a more sophisticated stipple effect. Another clue to a Bow original is the presence of three spur-marks in a triangle on the front edge of plates. A square hole at the back of figures and groups is also frequently found. Look in the Victoria and Albert Museum, London, for the Schreiber Collection, the Herbert Allen Collection, and the Broderip Gift.

Book: *Chelsea, Bow and Derby Porcelain Figures* by Frank Stoner (Ceramic Book Company, 1955)
Collections: Fenton House, London; Usher Gallery, Lincoln; The Museum, Lancaster; Central Museum and Art Gallery, Northampton; Victoria and Albert Museum, London

boxes Question: what have the following got in common? Bibles, jurymen, buttons, corpses, paints, cricketers, chocolates, theatre audiences, snuff, horses, and hats. Answer: they are all to be found in boxes. There have almost always been boxes. It seems that the securing of personal possessions in a box is a statement of some significance. These are *mine*, therefore I exist. Not for nothing did the emperors of the past have their possessions buried with them.

The Venetian had velvet-lined coffers, the dandy had gold boxes for his snuff and patches, and for *cachous* with which to sweeten his breath. Apothecaries had boxes into which all their impedimenta fitted snugly, ships' captains had camphorwood chests. Games-players had compendia of games, fathers of families Bible boxes, letter-writers writing slopes or *bonheurs du jour*, conjurers had boxes of tricks. Scottish watchmakers had little wooden boxes made from sycamore trees, housewives had knife-boxes made to display their cutlery which would later be kept in brass-bound canteens. All these boxes — and many, many others — are collected today.

Lacquer boxes from Japan were imitated by *papier-mâché* boxes from Birmingham, so successfully, as it turned out, that the copies became worth more than the originals. Tunbridgeware boxes, porcupine-quill boxes, porcelain boxes from Germany, and gold boxes from Russia, set with precious stones, Victorian boxes with sentimental designs in chromo-lithography on the lids, all have charm and value and require more space than I can give them here. I suggest you turn to . . .

Books: *Boxes* by Brian Cole (Collecting for Tomorrow Series, Pitman, 1976); *The Collector's Book of Boxes* by Marian Klamkin (David & Charles, 1972)
Collections: Art Gallery and Museum, Brighton (work boxes); Wallace Collection, London (small boxes)

boxwood Being hard and close-grained, this tight brown wood from the box tree (*Buxus sempervirens*) is ideal for marquetry inlay. It was also regarded as the best material for chisel-handles, and, indeed, for boxes, which take their name from boxwood.

bracket foot In furniture, and especially in case furniture, a bracket foot is one which projects along two sides of the base. It may be cut in the style of a wall bracket, and exhibit characteristics of furniture styles such as cabriole or ogee. Bracket feet usually feature from the early eighteenth to the mid-nineteenth centuries.

Bracket foot

brass Some of the confusions arising from the vague use of the words brass and bronze are discussed under the entry for bronze. But brass is a vague enough substance anyway. In Elizabethan England the nearest thing to modern brass was latten, but after *c.*1730 it was recognised that bronze was copper with tin, while brass was (and still is) copper with zinc.

Thimbles were made from brass by John Lofting of London from 1693, and soldiers' buttons were also struck from this alloy. From *c.*1760 an industry grew up in Birmingham where such bits and pieces as furniture mounts, door-plates, knockers and handles, picture frames, oil-lamps, and horse brasses were made. Fire-irons, ink-wells, and candlesticks were also popular, and the only brass items produced in Britain with any pretensions were the chandeliers made in Bristol for West Country churches.

Dutch metal (a substitute for gold leaf on picture frames), bell metal (used for bells and candlesticks), Britannia metal, a poor quality type of pewter, gun-metal (for gun barrels), prince's metal (invented by Prince Rupert of Bavaria), and pinchbeck, the poor man's gold, are all alloys similar to brass, which itself could be drawn into wire, rolled or hammered into sheets, cast, and stamped. Birmingham-made brass objects with an oriental flavour (usually trays) are intriguingly known as Benares ware.

Books: *The Book of Copper and Brass* by Geoffrey Wills (Hamlyn, 1968); *English Domestic Brass 1680–1810* by Rupert Gentle and Rachel Feild (Elek, 1975)

breakfront or **broken front** A description applied to bookcases, wardrobes, and so on, where the central section projects slightly in front of the side sections. Such pieces have always been popular, but not always quite as popular as auctioneers would have you believe.

Bristol glass The rich deep blue of Bristol glass (which was also produced in green and other colours) came from cobalt oxide imported from Silesia. This was mixed with powdered glass to produce 'smalt' and the smalt, when infused into molten flint glass, resulted in the popular Bristol blue. Glasses, jugs, decanters and scent bottles were either left plain or given a gilded border. Sometimes an inscription, also in gold, would be added.

Collections: Museum and Art Gallery, Bristol; Ashmolean Museum, Oxford

Britannia metal Devised in 1769 by John Vickers and known then as Vickers metal, Britannia metal is an alloy of 90 per cent tin, 8 per cent antimony, and 2 per cent copper or bismuth. Later it came to be known as French metal or hard pewter. From about 1830 it was frequently used as a cheap substitute for pewter. Objects made of Britannia metal were machine-stamped or cut from flat sheets; they were soldered rather than riveted, with handles cast separately and then fastened to the main body. Britannia metal has a silvery look, altogether less dignified than pewter. Since it tarnishes it is often electroplated, in which case it will be marked E.P.B.M. Other marks are designed to pass it off as pewter; they still frequently succeed.

broken pediment On the top of bookcases and cupboards you may often see an arched or triangle pediment with a gap where the apex of the arch or triangle ought to be. This gap was usually fitted with some kind of decorative urn, but it was also permissible to leave it empty. The broken pediment is also used as an architectural feature.

Broken pediment

bronze To say that bronze is an alloy of copper and tin is true in the limited sense that books are alloys of printing and paper. But bronze is not composed solely of these two metals: lead, for instance, is usually added to facilitate pouring.

For over 4000 years bronze has been used for a wide variety of practical purposes, from weapons to cooking utensils. In all areas substitutes have been found which are more efficient than bronze, less extravagant, lighter, more elegant, and so on, but bronze is still used for casting sculptures in much the same way as it has always been used. It expands as it solidifies, contracts as it cools, so that it may easily be removed from the mould. Sadly (from the artist's point of view) it can also be melted down and recast. Many fine sculptures have been turned into cannons and cannon balls and only occasionally is the process reversed: the statue of Achilles in Hyde Park, London, was cast from the melted down French cannons captured at Waterloo. It is not at all easy to distinguish between copper and bronze in old manuscripts (the Bronze Age was more properly a *Copper* Age) and recently brass and bronze have been much confused. When Shakespeare and his contemporaries refer to brass they usually mean bronze.

Traces of ancient bronze statues were found in Crete *c.*2100 BC, and, in Britain, bronze was already being cast at the time Stonehenge was being built *c.*1800 BC. The Colossus of Rhodes, 120 feet high and one of the Seven Wonders of the Ancient World, was probably cast in bronze. In classical Greece and Rome bronze-casting for statues was frequently undertaken, the bronze being decorated with gilding, especially in Rome. Bronze, which has much tensile strength, was considerably more liberating than marble, for the marble sculptor could not put too much stress on an outflung limb or a carelessly positioned leg. To the Romans bronze, and especially Corinthian bronze, was valued more highly than silver. Equestrian studies, portrait busts, many of emperors, and nude soldiers were the principal Roman subjects. Between the Roman Empire and the fifteenth century very few bronze sculptures were made. Some of the cannon, however, were magnificent, though they may not have been works of art: a cannon used at the Siege of Byzantium was 17 feet long and threw a stone ball weighing half a ton.

The Golden Age of bronze began in the fifteenth-century Florence of the Medicis. Magnificent bronze doors by Andrea Pisano for the Florentine Baptistry were cast by native Italian workmen, and so impressive were they that a competition was organised to find an even more stupendous pair of doors. Among the competitors were Jacopo della Quercia, Filippo Brunelleschi and Lorenzo Ghiberti, the winner. Besides these artists, Donatello, his assistant Michelozzo Michelozzi, and Andrea del Verocchio are the giants among a race of mighty men. Donatello's nude David, made *c.*1430 for the Medicis, was the first free-standing bronze statue since the Classical era and its almost hermaphroditic sensuality heralded the new aesthetic revolution. Equestrian statues became a test of sculptural horsemanship, because the weight of horse and rider had to be borne on such slender legs. Donatello had Gattemalata's horse rest one foreleg on a ball. Verocchio raised one foreleg of da Bergamo's horse into the air.

Leonardo da Vinci (1452–1519), Verocchio's pupil, raised both the forelegs of Sforza's horse, though his stucco model was never cast in bronze.

Smaller bronzes, after the Roman examples then being excavated, became fashionable towards the end of the fifteenth century. Some were even cast damaged and with missing limbs. Bertholdo da Giovanni, a pupil of Donatello, was tutor to Michelangelo (1474–1564), completing an important link in a miraculous chain. Michelangelo also worked in bronze, though sadly none of his pieces survive. The workshop of Andrea Briosco (born 1470 and known as Riccio, the Curly) from Padua produced many grotesques and a bronze candelabrum of astonishing complexity. Pietro Torregiano (1472–1528) worked on the tomb of Henry VII at Westminster.

Benvenuto Cellini (1500–71) was the archetypal Renaissance man ('the Genius of the Renaissance incarnate in a single person' — J. A. Symonds). In Rome he made coins and medals, in France (1540–45) he completed his gold, enamel and ivory salt-cellar for Francis I, and in Florence he worked for Cosimo I in marble and bronze, producing his bronze masterpiece, Perseus, in 1554. After Cellini many of the rules of the classical tradition were broken by the mannerist sculptors, among whom Gian da Bologna (1529–1608) is the most celebrated. His 'Rape of the Sabines' (1579–83) and 'Mercury' (1580) you will have seen in countless reproductions.

As the Italian Renaissance spread to the rest of Europe, the sculptors who worked in bronze became too numerous to mention here. In Austria Adrian de Vries (1546–1626), in Venice Jacopo Sansovino (1486–1570), in France Francesco Primaticcio (1504–70), in Germany Peter and Hermann Vischer, in England Pietro Torregiano (known by the English as Peter Torrysany) are just a few of the more notable.

The most significant figure in seventeenth-century sculpture, in both stone and bronze, is Giovanni Bernini (1598–1680), one of the originators of the baroque movement. He could encompass both the monumental (the Baldacchino and St Peter's Chair in St Peter's, Rome) and the intimate (St Theresa). But by the middle of the century Paris was taking the centre of the stage. The bronzes in the Parterre d'Eau at Versailles, cast by the Keller Brothers, were an impressive and substantial collection. Other important sculptors in seventeenth-century France include Antoine Coysevox (1640–1720), François Girardon (1628–1715), and Pierre Puget (1624–94).

In England Hubert Le Sueur, a Huguenot refugee, was commissioned to make the equestrian statue of Charles I which now stands at Charing Cross. He was paid £600, but was unable to complete the work before the King's execution. The statue was buried to save it from being scrapped and dug up again after the Restoration.

In the eighteenth century bronze statues and monuments were less in demand in France than 'gilt-bronze' (or ormolu) mounts for furniture, although these were highly elaborated, especially once the rococo style got under way. Small bronzes to stand atop console tables or *secrétaires* were fashionable, as were clock-cases, candelabra, ink-stands, paperweights, and so on. Many similar pieces were produced by Boulton and Fothergill at the Soho Manufactory in Birmingham, where brass foundries had been established since 1689.

A mistaken belief that white marble was the preferred material of the classical sculptors led to preference for this material over bronze during the classical revival. But in any case the great age of bronze was now over, and reductions and reproductions in spelter and other such dubious alloys of the great bronze pieces of the past were what the people wanted — or, more probably, what they could afford to pay for. Only the French *animalier* sculptors of the nineteenth century found bronze challenging and worth persevering with. Antoine-Louis Barye (1796–1875) was the founder of the group, which included Emmanuel Frémiet, Auguste-Nicolas Cain, Georges Gardet and Pierre-Jules Mêne. The best of these bronzes were cast by the *cire perdu* method, the rest by less distinguished sand-casting. Thereafter only Auguste Rodin (1840–1917), who was inspired by Michelangelo and Donatello for his nudes, and by Ghiberti for his magnificent but incomplete 'La Porte d'Enfer' (1880–1917), used bronze as though it were the most important thing in his life.

In London Landseer (1802–73) modelled the genial and somnolent lions which guard Nelson's column, Thomas Thorneycroft (1815–85) gave us Boadicea at Westminster Bridge, and George Watts (1817–1904) the Physical Energy Statue in Kensington Gardens.

Bronzes are particularly subject to faking and similar malpractices. Spelter is easily spotted, having neither weight nor quality, but accurate reproductions for multiple casting can be made by electrotyping. Many fakes are 'bronzed', not solid. As a general rule, one can say that bronzes darken with age: the lighter, therefore, the more modern.

Books: *A Concise History of Bronzes* by George Savage (Thames & Hudson, 1968); *Nineteenth Century Romantic Bronzes* by Jeremy Cooper (David & Charles, 1974)
Collection: Rapallo House Museum and Art Gallery, Llandudno

bun foot   A pad foot, in the shape of a rather squashed tomato, found on furniture from the second half of the seventeenth century. Sometimes bun feet are made of brass, and in mahogany they were often used for Victorian footstools.

Bun foot

bureau Any piece of furniture with a fall-front, which rests at an angle of 45° when closed and provides a writing surface when open. Behind this flap you may expect to find pigeon-holes and possibly a small central cupboard; below it drawers. A bureau bookcase has a bookcase, a bureau cabinet has a display cabinet, and a bureau dressing table has toilet glass above the writing slope. A bureau bedstead looks like a bureau but conceals a bed.

The bureau was introduced during the seventeenth century and many varieties were developed in France during the long and disastrous reign of Louis XV. The bureau *plat* was a straightforward writing table. The bureau *à cylindre* had a roll-top. The amazing Bureau du Roi Louis XV, designed by Oeben and Riesener, is to furniture what Versailles is to a Wimpy Bar. The bureau *à pente* had a lid which opened on a slant. The bureau *à dos d'âne* had an elegantly curving outline. The *bonheur du jour* had a small recessed superstructure.

Burmese glass An art glass, semi-opaque and with either a matt or a glossy finish. Some confusion exists between the British Burmese glass (known as Queen's Burmese glass) produced under licence by Thomas Webb & Son of Stourbridge from 1886, and the American Burmese glass, patented a year earlier by the Mount Washington Glassworks. What is certain is that no Burmese glass comes from Burma. The American glass is usually greenish-yellow shading to pink; the English is often decorated with a pattern of daisies known as the Queen's Burmese pattern (fairy-lights and night-lights are frequently found in this design).

buttons 'I pray you sir,' said Lear, 'undo this button.' And I am surprised he said it, because in ancient Britain buttons were not worn. Indeed buttons are not thought to have been worn on clothes before the reign of Edward III (1327–77). Three hundred years later, under Charles I, jewelled buttons were sewn to handkerchiefs, elegant certainly, but uncomfortable if you needed to blow your nose in a hurry. From 1860 buttons were used extensively on male costumes, and were made of wood, bone, metal or *passementerie*.

Button-making originated in the American colonies in 1706, and collecting buttons has been a popular hobby in America since the 1930s when a Mrs Gertrude Patterson expounded its charms in a radio talk. Cloth-covered buttons also originated in the U.S.A. In 1807, Sanders of Birmingham invented the metal button, made from two discs locked together by turning the rims. Other elaborate buttons were made by goldsmiths, silversmiths, potters (especially Wedgwood), copper beaters, and painters, who particularly favoured scenes *à la* Watteau and Boucher.

Collectors of military and naval buttons are particularly fanatical and, since the numbers of regiments were frequently stamped on the backs of the buttons (and tailors' names occasionally on the backs of civilian buttons), it is easy to trace the history of a set of buttons. Jennens and Company (established 1800) stamped their buttons with the Prince of Wales plumes, while Buttons Limited (now the Francis Sumner Engineering Company) used crossed swords.

After 1830 all regiments were required to use gold lace and gilt buttons, in place of silver, with the exception of regiments of militia. Other ranks had to make do with lead and pewter till 1855 and with brass thereafter. By 1914 it was estimated that four and a quarter million general service buttons were being made each week for other ranks.

Besides the above, hunt buttons (gilt, silver, vulcanite, or brass), police buttons (black and white metals, bone, horn, and composition), and livery buttons are also collected.

Books: *Buttons for the Collector* by Primrose Peacock (David & Charles, 1972); *Buttons: a Guide for Collectors* by Gwen Squire (Frederick Muller Ltd, 1972) — only military and service buttons; *The Collectors Encyclopedia of Buttons* by Sally C. Luscomb (Crown Publishers, 1976); *Buttons of the British Army* by Howard Ripley (Arms & Armour Press, new ed. 1979)

Collections: Gorey Castle Museum, St Helier, Jersey (regimental buttons); Local History Museum, Shaftesbury, Dorset

cabaret   A ceramic term derived from the French word for an inn or public-house. It is used to describe a small china service (usually porcelain) consisting of matching teapot, milk jug, sugar basin, one or two teacups and saucers, and a tray. Such services are also known as *déjeuner* and *tête-à-tête* services. Cabarets were popular in the late nineteenth and early twentieth centuries.

cabochon   There are a number of intriguing and colourful words in the English language which one gets few opportunities to use. Defenestrate is one. Caboched is another, and it means 'cut off just behind the ears'.

Cabochon derives from the same source as an old French word meaning 'the head' and it has two applications in antiques. It may be a convex gem that is cut and polished but not faceted, or a raised oval moulding surrounded by a rim on a piece of furniture, especially on the 'knee' of a cabriole leg.

cabriole leg   The cabriole leg is one of the seminal shapes in furniture design which originated in China over two thousand years ago. The word derives from a Latin word meaning 'to leap into the air', and the reference is probably to the hind leg of an animal, and especially a mountain goat. Cabriole legs, which curve outwards to a 'knee', then inwards to an 'ankle', are a common distinguishing feature on furniture from the late seventeenth to the late eighteenth century.

The cabriole leg looked sturdy on a chair, light and elegant on a table. Early cabriole legs were strengthened with stretchers, but these were found to be unnecessary. Usually only the front legs of chairs were cabriole legs, but, in especially luxurious examples, all four legs would be curved. There is some evidence that the cabriole leg was introduced into this country by Daniel Marot, a Huguenot, who entered the service of the Prince of Orange, later William III.

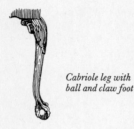

Cabriole leg with ball and claw foot

caddy spoon or **caddy ladle**   A short-handled spoon kept in the tea caddy, and made from silver, plate or wood. The caddy spoon was introduced in about 1770 in the agreeable shape of a scallop shell, so that it also became known as a caddy shell. Caddy spoons took other shapes, such as jockeys' caps or fish, and were mass-produced from Birmingham in the nineteenth century as cheap souvenirs.

cairngorm   A form of quartz, smoky brown in colour, found in the Cairngorm mountains of Scotland. Cairngorm stones, popular as souvenirs, were set, often in silver, in the form of shields or claymores and sold to the extravagant English.

cameo   Should you find yourself in Barlaston on a weekday, contact the Wedgwood factory and you will be able to arrange a tour. There you will see, among other treasures, a selection of the jasperware cameos which were used as medallions on fireplace surrounds, on chairs, workboxes, snuff boxes and, of course, as jewellery.

Cameos are small sculptures in low-relief made from precious or semi-precious stones. They were always ornamental, never functional. The Egyptians made them six thousand years ago, the Romans fashioned cameos from glass. From the fifteenth century cameos were carved from shells cut in such a way as to reveal the different layers of the shell. Helmet shells and conch shells were the most successfully used. Other materials from which cameos were cut include agate, onyx, opal, sardonyx, ivory, amethyst, emerald, garnet, and, latterly, plastic.

The golden age for cameo carving came between 1740 and 1850. Wedgwood employed celebrated artists like John Flaxman, William

Hackwood, and James Tassie to produce portrait cameos of kings and queens and politicians. The fashion for wearing cameos was given a new impetus when the Empress Josephine's fondness for the things was remarked. The Gothic revival led to cameos depicting subjects from medieval sculpture. The most elegant settings for cameos were gold and silver surrounded with pearls and other precious gemstones, although cut steel was quite the thing at the end of the eighteenth century.

What you should watch for is whether or not the cameo has been sculpted from a single piece of stone. Most modern reproduction cameos have the relief work carved separately and appliquéd on; they are also usually set in gilt. Ones made from plastic are particularly common, and particularly nasty. See also *Gallé, Émile*.

camphorwood The camphor laurel is a species of cinnamon tree which grows in places like Taiwan, Borneo, Kenya. Its appearance is similar to mahogany, and it is used principally for blanket and linen chests, since moths have no taste for it at all.

candlesticks The earliest and simplest British candlestick was an iron plate with a spike, or pricket, upon which the candle would be impaled. Sockets to hold the candle were introduced in the sixteenth century. Early examples of these have rarely survived. They are vulnerable to corrosion, and primitive socket-candlesticks often turn out to date only from the nineteenth century, and to have been made for the outhouses of farms. Slightly posher than iron were brass and pewter candlesticks. The brass trumpet-shaped candlestick with a straight stem, a wide drip-pan midway along it, and a flared base was the first distinctively English candlestick shape. Before 1670 these brass candlesticks were cast in solid moulds, but thereafter they were cast in vertical halves (the join may still be faintly visible) with levers and push-rods inside to eject the unwanted tallow.

Pewter is either cast or spun from thin sheets. The more desirable cast pewter 'rings' when flicked with a finger-nail. Britannia metal originated at the factory of James Vickers Limited in Britannia Place, Sheffield, and is a poor quality alloy with more tin than pewter should properly have. As to the various other alloys which answer to such names as paktong, bell-metal, gun-metal and latten, all I can say is that if you ask an auctioneer or dealer to explain to you the differences you can expect the sort of dusty answer which discourages further questions.

Silver candlesticks were introduced during the late Stuart period. These were dignified pieces on square or octagonal bases with baluster columns. The rococo style in silver was less extreme in Britain than it was in France, where it sometimes must have seemed as though the whole country had been afflicted with astigmatism, and was not long established before it gave way to the good sense of neo-classicism. A number of silversmiths specialised in candlesticks. James Gould and William Cafe, both from late Regency London, are typical examples. Whatever silver could do, base metals could simulate, and brass, Sheffield plate, and pewter candlesticks followed the prevailing styles obediently, Sheffield plate and pewter being sometimes stamped with unconvincing imitations of silver hallmarks.

Victorian brass candlesticks are the ones most frequently met with in more refined antique shops. Typical ones exhibit any number of knobs of different shapes and sizes along the stem. There are now so many reproduction candlesticks on the market that it is important to be on the look-out for signs of age. The genuine article should have plenty of weight (and not the sort of artificial weight which is created inside the base; look for the alteration in the centre of gravity), patina and richness of colour. A number of early metal candlesticks have improving messages stamped upon them, such as *Grace me governe*.

Candlesticks in glass followed the prevailing glass styles and may be roughly dated from the shapes of base, stem and rim. Waterford produced some heavily cut beauties. Porcelain candlesticks vary hugely from the elaborately painted and encrusted models from Sèvres, Meissen, and so on, to simple rose-patterned Victorian and Edwardian examples which featured, with ring-trees and little pots on china trays, as dressing table sets.

caneware   In the late eighteenth century caneware was produced independently by Josiah Wedgwood and by the Turners of Lane End, Staffordshire. Wedgwood's caneware was the colour of piecrust pastry, and was consequently used for pie-dishes. But he also produced charming teapots, tea dishes, and flower holders. Lane End caneware was less a realistic copy of bamboo canes and more a cane-coloured stoneware, upon which classical figures performed classical activities in delicate relief.

John Turner (not to be confused with the Turner of Caughley) produced bulb-pots, wine-coolers, jugs, dishes, ink-stands and tea services in his caneware. The factory operated from 1762 until it went bankrupt in 1806 (Turner died in 1786 or 1787, and was succeeded by his sons).

canterbury   Charles Manners-Sutton, the first Viscount Canterbury, Speaker of the House of Commons and elder son of the Archbishop of Canterbury (if I may be permitted to drop a name) is generally credited with the early nineteenth-century invention of the free-standing, four-legged book- and music-stand known as the canterbury.

Confusion may arise unless it is understood that a canterbury is also a stand with three transverse divisions for cutlery and a curved end for plates. This sort of canterbury dates from the late eighteenth century.

Canton   The capital of the Chinese province of Kwangtung, Canton has a seaport from which Chinese blue and white porcelain was exported in the eighteenth century. Hence Canton china is a general term for china exported from Canton, which china no more comes from Canton than Dover soles come from Dover. See also *Nankin*.

Book: *Oriental Blue and White* by Sir H. M. Garner (Faber & Faber, 1970)

carbine　A musket used by the cavalry, the carbine was shorter than its infantry equivalent because the cavalryman did not carry a bayonet.

car mascots　One sees car mascots only rarely nowadays. In the owners' and members' car parks at the smarter race meetings you can find them on the radiator caps of Jaguars and Jensens, but these are usually models of the car owners' most successful horses, and therefore of real interest only to the owners themselves.

Car mascots were introduced early this century and were usually made of some kind of cast metal. A few manufacturers supplied mascots with their cars; memorably this was so with Rolls Royce, whose 'Spirit of Ecstasy' was sculpted by Charles Sykes. Lincolns arrived with greyhound mascots, Duesenbergs with birds. Other mascots which had notable chic, but which were not tied to any make of car, include 'Speed' by Harriet Fishmuth (1928) and various designs by Lalique and Sabino. Caricatures and novelty animals, often in bronze and signed by John Hassall, have a crazy sort of distinction.

The Rolls Royce
'Spirit of Ecstasy'

carpets and rugs　One cannot and should not judge carpets and rugs from the Near and Far East by the standards one applies to Western antiques. The test of a good carpet can only be subjective. The glory of these beautiful things is that they each represent the personality of the weaver; one cannot successfully apply any other criterion. Variations in colour, irregularities in shape, are only to be expected. In Islam only Allah can make things perfect and regular. Which is as it should be. Furthermore tradition is a part — an important part — of Islamic culture. To understand the carpets, you must understand the culture. The only non-

Islamic culture to produce carpets of comparable value is the Chinese. The intricate repeating patterns are not representations of nature, nor do they tell a story, nor are they 'symbolic' in the Western sense. To say that a Senneh rug with a geranium border around a turtle design is concerned with geraniums and turtles is to miss the point. (Some Persian carpets do in fact display hunting scenes and gardens in a recognisable if ritualised form.)

The tradition is a continuing one. Despite the use of synthetic dyes which in turn require the use of synthetic ageing devices, carpets are still being made to traditional patterns (many of which have never been written down) and in traditional ways. Some of the finest Persian carpets have been woven as late as 1930.

It is perhaps worth pointing out that the distinction between carpets and rugs is just what you would expect: carpets cover all or most of the floor, rugs only a small section. (And one should add that carpets of fine quality were often regarded as *too good* for the floor — they deserved to hang on the wall.) Rugs were the speciality of the Asian nomads. A nomad with a carpet would find it difficult to go on being nomadic. Rugs, therefore, even more than carpets, provide a direct link with prehistory.

There are two main types of knots, the Turkish or Ghiordes knot, and the Persian or Senneh knot. The Turkish is the more secure, the Persian produces a tighter pile. However it is not so much the knot as the knotter that counts, and there may be over a million knots in a rug of moderate size. There is one kind of carpet without knots and without pile, and that is the Kilim, which is made entirely by weaving. Kilims were until recently quite inexpensive, and some, especially those of the Kurdish weavers, are of very fine quality.

Until some ninety years ago carpets were always dyed with natural dyes, provided by trees, flowers, berries, nut shells, and cochineal. Sour milk may be added to dyes in order to lighten the colour. In order to make it fast, a carpet will be hung over a stream and then dried in the sun. When the dye has been fixed unevenly the result is known as 'abrash'. This may add to the appeal of a carpet in the eyes of a connoisseur, to whom technical perfection means that a machine (and not Allah) has been at work. Synthetic dyes are increasingly convincing, but there is no doubt that the fading of colours with age and use gives added attraction to natural dyes.

There is no space here to detail the great wealth of variety that may be found in Eastern carpets and rugs, nor all the towns and tribes where and by whom they are made. But it may be useful to itemise the five main areas, at least, whence come these fascinating, magic carpets.

Persia. Probably most popular of all are Persian carpets and rugs. Carpets from Heriz and Georavan usually have a brick-red field with borders of dark blue and feature *herati*, that is rosettes within diamonds. Tabriz produced neat sophisticated patterns often with central medallions and geometric floral decorations. Kashan, where the *boteigh* design, shaped like a tear drop or gas flame, originated, and Isfahan, home of the 'vase' pattern, both produced carpets and rugs of the very finest quality.

Caucasus. Most Caucasian rugs resemble a mosaic, with abstract patterns of great antiquity based on animals and figures. Kuba rugs are long and narrow and depict geometrically anatomised dragons and phoenixes. Karabagh carpets from the Persian border are notable for the striking contrast between dark ground colours and bright patterns. Kazak rugs have a thick, glossy pile and a large, bold design which may contain two jagged 'eagles'. Dagestan carpets are rare and desirable. Their colours, combining brown, red and cream, are dignified and beautiful.

Turkey. Being Mohammedans the Turks were forbidden to treat human or animal representations in their work. Transylvanian (or Siebenbürger) carpets are frequently found in churches in the Balkans; they have an eight-sided central medallion with rosettes in the corners on a light ground. Bergama rugs are small, square and loosely woven. They can easily be mistaken for Kazaks (see above). Melas, near the Aegean Sea, produced prayer-rugs in pastel colours; these have a childlike charm by no means as simple as it appears, and are often an unusual greenish-yellow. Ghiordes rugs are bright and fresh and sometimes feature white cotton, indicating purity. Oushaks are short-piled and for centuries enjoyed complete supremacy in Turkey. In the nineteenth century Oushak supplied carpets to many fashionable hotels.

Central Asia. The Turkomans were nomadic and their rugs represented a dowry for their daughters, a covering for their camels, and the one

Afghan Ersari mat, c. *1850*

sustaining element in an existence made precarious by Mongol and Russian invaders, drought and famine. Turkoman rugs and carpets feature reflective repetitious designs, including the tribal emblem, or 'gul', an octagon, square or elongated diamond. The colours are restrained reds and browns. Bukharas is a generic name (carpets were sold, not made, in Bukhara) incorporating Tekes, Yomuds, and Beshirs. Afghan carpets, predominantly deep red and dark blue, became fashionable on the floor of nineteenth-century gentlemen's studies. They are sometimes woven with goat-hair in place of sheep's wool. Baluchi rugs are particularly wide with camel-coloured grounds.

China or East Turkestan. This area lies inside what is now the Chinese province of Sinkiang. It is hot desert, even less hospitable than Central Asia. Samarkand carpets (again, sold in Samarkand but made a few hundred miles to the East) and Kashgars are brightly coloured with bold uncluttered designs, but rather loosely spun with a poor density of knots.

Books: *Rugs and Carpets of the Orient* by Nathaniel Harris (Hamlyn, 1977); *The Book of Carpets* by Reinhard G. Hubal (Barrie & Jenkins, 1971); *Oriental Rugs and the Stories they Tell* by Arthur T. Gregorian (Frederick Warne, 1978)
Collection: Victoria and Albert Museum, London (Room 97)

carriage clock   You must discard from your mind the spurious notion that these small portable clocks were specially intended to be used in carriages. They were initially made *c.*1850 in France as cheap desk-clocks, the handle in the top and the leather case making it easy to take them from room to room, or from house to house. Many varieties were produced,

Carriage clock with chased gilt case

some extremely fine, with striking, repeating and alarm mechanisms. The movements were mass-produced in the provinces, but sent to Paris for assembly and finishing. Frequently the retailers' names would be printed on the dial. English and American carriage clocks are less complex than the French originals.

Collection: Wallace Collection, London

cartouche   (a) In architecture, a decorative scroll containing (usually) an inscription, such as 'Queen Elizabeth Slept Here'. (b) In metalwork, an oval tablet usually containing an inscription. (c) In cabinet-making, a surmount above a cornice or in the centre of a broken pediment. (d) The cartridge-shaped frame in which the hieroglyphic names of the Egyptian kings of the Second Dynasty onwards were enclosed.

cased glass or **cameo glass**   A technique in which two or more layers of different coloured glass are blown inside one another. The layers are fused together when reheated and decorations are carved, leaving the pattern in high relief. The result is known as cameo glass.

The Chinese used the technique for snuff bottles in the eighteenth and nineteenth centuries. It was also employed at the Bohemian glassworks and by many art nouveau glass artists.

The most famous example of cased glass is the Roman Portland Vase, whose history is long, varied and romantic. Josiah Wedgwood agreed not to bid for the vase at an auction in 1786 on condition that it was lent to him to reproduce in jasperware. (He later adopted it as a china mark.) It was cracked by the Duchess of Gordon, and smashed into more than two hundred fragments by William Lloyd in 1845. But you can't keep a good glass down, and it was subsequently restored.

Book: *Nineteenth Century Cameo Glass* by Geoffrey W. Beard (Ceramic Book Club, 1956)
Collection: Corporation Museum, Newport

castors or **casters**   Castors — small pivoted wheels attached to the underneath of furniture — were introduced in the late seventeenth century. Originally leather and wood, brass castors proved more practical in due course. The Victorians patented a wild array of castors.

Caughley   That there was a small earthenware factory at Caughley (pronounced Calf-ly) in Shropshire from 1751 we know, but we know little about what was produced there. In 1754 it was leased to Ambrose Gallimore, and he went into partnership with his son-in-law, Thomas Turner, who had worked at the Worcester factory. In 1772 Turner acquired the business, rebuilt the factory and set about the manufacture of soft-paste porcelain.

Turner's speciality was tableware made in imitation of the fashionable Chinese export porcelain, his trademark a violet-toned blue, a colour of unusual brilliance, his forms based upon those which he had known at Worcester. He had an outlet in London, a warehouse behind Lincolns Inn Fields which he called his 'Salopian China Warehouse'. Until quite recently Caughley china was more commonly known as Salopian, a trade name which frequently figures in the Caughley marks.

At Caughley much early willow pattern was produced, and a number of charming dolls' tea-services. Dishes in the form of six-pointed stars, painted in underglaze cobalt blue, are characteristic, and are known as 'salts'. Other output included 'shanked' or spiral-fluted tea ware of great elegance, and occasional sparrow-beak jugs painted with 'Long Elizas' — slightly sinister-looking ladies in kimonos and pyjama trousers. There has been much confusion in attributing Caughley tea ware of the 1780s and 1790s to the Flight period at Worcester and vice versa.

In 1799 John Rose took over the business, and in 1814 he transferred it to Coalport. Caughley had been in the porcelain business just twenty-seven years but Turner had been able to give it great distinction. Only recently has it been recognised as a factory to rank with the finest.

Collections: Christchurch Mansion, Ipswich; Art Gallery and Museum, Shrewsbury

cedar wood   An aromatic wood the smell of which is disheartening to small insects. Two main varieties were used by eighteenth-century cabinet-makers, the North American cedar (*Juniper virginiana*) and West Indian and Honduras cedar (*Cedrela mexicana*). Its quality was too poor for it to be much used, except on drawer-linings, boxes and chests.

celadon ware   This mysterious Chinese pottery with a felspathic glaze of pale watery green was first produced during the T'ang Dynasty (AD 619–906). During the Sung and Ming Dynasties more delicate varieties of celadon ware were produced with brownish blotches added to the green ground. Dark celadon of a brownish-green came from the northern provinces, while the more admired paler celadon came from the south. Kuan ware was a variety of celadon ware but displayed a number of coloured glazes, often with crackle, over a grey body.

Some celadon pieces were exported to the West, where they were much admired and much imitated. Sadly the admiration sometimes took the form of adding other features, such as ormolu mounts, to vases which need no embellishment. See also *Chinese porcelain*.

cellaret   Also known as a wine cooler, or a *garde du vin* (by Hepplewhite and others with grand ideas), this was a container for wine, usually lead-lined and sometimes with bottle divisions. When sideboards were introduced, the cellaret was incorporated in one, and sometimes both, ends.

chairs In the Middle Ages the chair was reserved for the master of the house or a distinguished guest, while the vulgar throng had to be content with settles, benches, and stools; hence the origin of the word 'chairman'. ('Lord North', said Dr Johnson, 'fills a chair.') It is curious that bishops and kings should be expected to hold court from a sitting position — Popes are hardly ever allowed to get into any other position — when it is well known that the brain is most active when its owner is on his feet.

Medieval chairs evolved from chests to which panelled sides and backs were added, but it was on benches and stools that the early English sat for their meals. The first chairs were of sturdy oak, walnut being introduced into Henry VIII's court by French and Italian craftsmen.

Throughout the eighteenth century chairs became more elegant under the influence of such men as Chippendale, Hepplewhite, Sheraton, and Adam. Chippendale reduced the heavy square legs to the attractive cabriole style, and curbed the excesses of the rococo movement. Hepplewhite removed the stretchers, pierced the backs and lightened the splats of the Chippendale chair. Adam brought the classical influence back from Italy, and added honeysuckle, rams' heads, swags (generally in ormolu) and urns. Sheraton encouraged ever lighter and more elegant designs with the use of satinwood and painted decorations. (Incidentally there is still some doubt as to whether Sheraton even had a workshop or produced any of the furniture which bears his name; but he did produce a highly influential *Drawing Book* of designs.) Sheraton's chair swelled visibly during the Regency (as it needed to, if it were to accommodate the ladies' bustles) and in Victorian England, whose Queen had a 46-inch waist, it became upholstered, overstuffed, button and balloon-backed, and at times rather ridiculous.

William Morris first put his furniture on public display at the International Exhibition in London (1862). His aim was to build a socialist Utopia in which the dignity of labour could be respected. 'The Firm' (Morris, Marshall, Faulkner and Company) produced two classes of furniture. One was state furniture, which attempted a perfection of the Gothic style — though not as elaborate a neo-Gothic as that of Pugin (1812–52). The other was cottage furniture, which was directed towards sturdy functionalism. A typical example of Morris's cottage style is the Sussex chair.

After Morris came the arts and crafts movement of the 1880s, which reinterpreted many of the traditional English forms such as the ladderback, brought back into vogue by Ernest Gimson. The Glasgow school, led by C. R. Mackintosh (1868–1928), produced some fine chairs in an art nouveau Gothic style. During the twentieth century perhaps the most significant influence on design came from Walter Gropius (1883–1969) and the Bauhaus. Their 'modular' furniture, which could be arranged in different combinations, included the tubular steel chair.

Chairs

*Sheraton mahogany
elbow chair*

*Adam carved mahogany
elbow chair*

*Chippendale mahogany
dining chair*

*Hepplewhite carved
mahogany dining chair*

Country furniture, with its Windsor chairs, is a continuing tradition, which has been little affected by changing fashions. Its standards have been tested by the centuries, and not found wanting.

Books: *English Chairs* by Ralph Edwards (HMSO, 1978); *Chairs in Colour* by Lanto Synge (Blandford Press, 1978); *The Englishman's Chair* by J. Gloag (Allen & Unwin, 1964)

chaise longue   Literally the chaise longue is a long seat, with a carved or upholstered back and sometimes arms or an arm. (The arms were shed during the nineteenth century.) Two types of chaises longues are illustrated by Sheraton in the third edition of his *Drawing Book* (1802). If the chaise was made in three parts, that is two chairs with a stool in the middle, it was known, spectacularly, as the *péché mortel*.

chamfer   A square edge that has been planed down, whether concave, moulded or recessed — a characteristic feature of Gothic reform furniture in the 1860s. Hence 'chamfering'.

champlevé   A process of enamelling on gold, bronze, and copper, by the addition of coloured glass pastes which fuse with the metals on heating. The areas of design are hollowed out declivities (champs) which are filled with enamelling to the level of the original surface.

In Western Europe from the twelfth century *champlevé* supplanted in popularity the similar process known as *cloisonné*. The three centres for *champlevé* enamels were the Rhine and Meuse valleys, where Godefroid de Clair and Nicolas of Verdun made their masterpieces; Limoges, notable for crucifixes, book-covers, candlesticks, caskets, and even horse-bits in *champlevé*; and Spain. The craft was revived in Victorian England and in 1860 Ruskin offered a prize for the best enamel work.

chasing   A technique of ornamenting metal (silver, copper, bronze, and so on), by punching and hammering it from the front (unlike *repoussé*, which is from the back) against a pitch-block.

châtelaines   Châtelaines are a gift to theatre directors with a vague historical sense and a taste for restrained symbolism. At the start of Act Two of Anton Chekhov's *Three Sisters*, it is not unknown for the dreadful Natalia Ivanovna to appear in her dressing gown *and wearing a châtelaine* to indicate her assumed role as head of the household. A châtelaine, literally mistress of the castle, is a clip with a hook from which hang keys, seals, watches, scissors and suchlike.

Originally an eighteenth-century fashion, it was revived in the 1870s and 1880s. Châtelaines could be made of silver, or base metals. The pre-Raphaelite versions came in enamelled gold set with precious stones, or gold pavé set with small diamonds. The list of items which hung from a

Châtelaine, c. 1735

nurse's châtelaine in 1899 is long: a pin-cushion, a vesta case, a caustic holder, two tongue-depressors, a director, a suture, forceps, a female catheter, an hour glass, two thermometer cases and one thermometer.

Collections: Anne of Cleves House, Lewes; Castle Museum, York

Chelsea The origins of the Chelsea factory, probably the oldest in Britain, are quite obscure, and some even argue that there were a pair of factories. The names of two men involved are consistently cited: Nicholas Sprimont and Charles Gouyn. Sprimont was a silversmith from Liège, and Gouyn a jeweller from St Cloud. It is possible that Gouyn was a refugee who brought with him the secret of soft-paste porcelain manufacture, possible also that he put up the capital for the factory which started operations in about 1743. Certainly Sprimont, as the first manager, made the works famous. Even without royal patronage, which most of the continental factories enjoyed, it built up a turnover of some £3500 per annum, with a staff of a hundred men and thirty apprentices.

There are four distinct periods of Chelsea manufacture, with four separate china marks to identify them.

1743 to 1750: incised triangle mark. Surviving pieces from this earliest period are rare, and can be found mostly in museums and fine private collections. They tend to be uncoloured, ungilded, with a satiny glaze, and to have been based in part on silver designs — Sprimont's speciality. Some of these early cups, saucers, plates, and dishes have brown borders. The influences are Chinese and German. The secretary to the Duke of Cumberland travelled to Dresden in 1749 and brought back a number of Meissen figures. Sprimont had moulds taken directly from these. Sprays of flowers and leaves, butterflies and insects may be found featured during the triangle period. It is probable that Gouyn severed his connection with the factory around 1750.

1750 to c.1753: raised anchor mark, sometimes outlined in red and placed on a raised oval medallion. The body now became thick, almost opaque. Designs were taken from George Edwards' recently published *Natural History of Uncommon Birds*, from Aesop's *Fables*, from the Italian *Commedia dell'Arte*, from a book describing the specimens in Sir Hans Sloane's botanical garden, and from Kakiemon patterns. Figures of Abelard and Héloïse were celebrated; a nun and a hurdy-gurdy player were also featured. Meissen was still an overriding influence.

c.1753 to 1758: red anchor mark, painted on and usually accompanied by a triangle of spur-marks. This was a period of great prosperity for the Chelsea factory. Large and exuberant tureens are found, in rococo style. A rabbit was made 'as big as life', according to the catalogue. The modellers worked on coiled eels, hens with chicks, bundles of asparagus. Small trifles also proliferated, including snuff-boxes, seals, scent bottles, *étuis*, and *bonbonnières*. Services after Vincennes and Sèvres patterns with birds, flowers, and insects were found, as were the famous nurse seated with a child — which had also been produced in the raised anchor period — and sets of figures depicting the senses, the seasons, ladies and gallants, and so on.

1759 to 1769: gold anchor mark. It is generally supposed that during this last and most fanciful period the factory came under the influence of the French sculptor Roubiliac. If so, he has a lot to answer for. This was a time of lushness and elaboration, of lavish gilding, rococo scrolls, *bocages*, bold ground colours, such as pea-green, turquoise blue, claret and ruby, and ornate vases — the porcelain equivalent of Chippendale furniture. 'The forms are neither new, beautiful or various', remarked Horace Walpole with all the confidence of a very rich man.

Such magnificence was more favoured by the Victorians than by us, and it is interesting that Lord Dudley paid 5000 guineas for two gold anchor vases in 1868, which vases were sold at Christie's in 1963 for £1500 the pair. Take note that neither the red nor the gold anchor marks are to be found on the bases of figures.

During the gold anchor period bone-ash had been added to the Chelsea paste, and this new formula saved losses during firing to such an extent that by 1763 Sprimont was a very rich man. He sold the business in 1769. Duesbury, the Derby proprietor, ran it until 1784 when it finally ceased trading.

Books: *Chelsea, Bow and Derby Porcelain Figures* by Frank Stoner (Ceramic Book Company, 1955); *Chelsea Porcelain: Red Anchor Wares* by F. Sevene Mackenna (F. Lewis, 1967); *Chelsea Porcelain: Triangle and Raised Anchor Ware* by F. Sevene Mackenna (F. Lewis, 1969)
Collection: Cecil Higgins Art Gallery, Bedford

chessmen The history of chess is as long as it is obscure. The word 'chess' is, literally, the game of kings, while 'checkmate' is the arabic *Shah-maat*, 'the King is dead'. It is of course a war game. Originally it was played by four players who each controlled a king, an elephant, a horse, a ship, and four soldiers. When the game reached Christendom the pieces were given a respectable social symbolism. Today most pieces are based on designs made for Harold Staunton, the British master, by Nathaniel Cook in 1835, but prior to that antique sets from France (ivory), from Germany (wood, ivory, amber, porcelain, silver, and cast iron), from Italy (ivory and glass), and from just about every country in the world, were used.

Chinese sets pit Chinamen against Mongols, some Russian sets pit communists against capitalists, and there are sets from Persia in which gold pieces inlaid and topped with silver play against silver pieces inlaid and topped with gold. The variety is enormous, and the opportunity to buy any true antique sets correspondingly rare.

Book: *Chessmen* by A. E. J. Mackett-Beeson (Weidenfeld & Nicolson, 1968); *Chessmen* by Frank Greygoose (David & Charles, 1979)

chestnut roaster A chestnut roaster is a circular or rectangular box with a hinged, perforated lid and a long handle; the roaster is usually made of brass, and the handle is either brass or turned wood. A few shovel-shaped types were also produced. The box is filled with chestnuts and placed in the embers of an open fire where the chestnuts roast, smelling most agreeably as they do so.

The experts are rather snooty about chestnut roasters, arguing that there is no evidence of their being produced much before the mid-nineteenth century, and that most of the ones found in antique shops have no right to be there. Nonetheless, what is an open fire on a winter's day without the smell of roasting chestnuts?

chiffonier The French *chiffonière* was a small case of drawers on legs. The Regency adaptation was an open cupboard for books, those books that were currently being studied (for most would stay in their library shelves), and it lived in the drawing room. Sometimes there would be a drawer or small cupboard beneath. In Victorian England the chiffonier moved to the dining room and became a poor man's sideboard, usually between three and four feet wide. In the 1830s and 1840s wire grille doors backed by pleated silk would lend dignity to the chiffonier, but later on bow-fronted shelves in front of mirror backs within ornate frames gave the article an importance it did not perhaps deserve.

china See under types of china (e.g., *soft-paste porcelain*), major potteries (e.g., *Chelsea*), types of ornamentation and glaze (e.g., *lustre*), and china articles (e.g., *teapots*).

Chiffonier

Chinese porcelain   There are three reasons why the Chinese achieved such sophistication in their ceramic products, at a time when in other parts of the world the best anyone could come up with was primitive earthenware pots. First, they had the resources, the clays and minerals necessary for a wide variety of glazes. Second, they had the skills to produce high temperatures in the furnaces. And third, they had an unbroken tradition for two millennia of a society in which the authorities, both secular and religious, regarded the arts as a necessity and not (as so often in the West) a mischievous and corrupting luxury. Some of the problems which the Chinese potters solved during the K'ang-Hsi period are problems which we, in the West, still find insurmountable. There are things we do better but making porcelain is not one of them.

   Until quite recently Chinese porcelain was referred to vaguely as Nankin or Canton, depending on the ports from which it was shipped West — for the valuable trade in ceramics was vital to the Chinese. But it is now regarded as helpful to think of it in terms of dynasties; I shall do so too.

Han Dynasty (206BC–AD220). Pottery of a rather primitive kind was buried when the owner of the pots was buried. Some of this earthenware, which is either grey or red, featured a lead glaze. Subjects include buildings, cooking implements, and figures, both human and animal. High-fired stoneware was reserved for domestic use and was grey-bodied and green-glazed.

The Six Dynasties Period (AD221–581). Green ware, a celadon type of stoneware, was first produced in Chekiang Province, and towards the end of the period large covered jars decorated with lotus petals appeared.

Sui Dynasty (AD581–617) and *T'ang Dynasty* (AD618–906). The first porcelain was created during this period, although it is unclear which kilns, even which provinces, have the best claim to its invention. The first pieces were shallow bowls with straight sides and a wide foot ring. The body was white with a slightly bluish tint, 'as though the piece had been dipped in skimmed milk', according to one expert. Some Greek influence was apparent, and much use was made of Buddhist symbolism. Figures of animals and birds survive, including a remarkable phoenix-head ewer from Chi-Chou, on view in the British Museum in London.

Sung and Nan Sung Dynasties (AD960–1279). During this great period in Chinese ceramics, stoneware and porcelain were made to the virtual exclusion of earthenware. Ting ware from the mountains in the province of Hopei consisted of bowls, plates, basins, and vases, white-bodied with glazes of various colours, chiefly ivory and dark brown. These glazes covered the base and the foot ring. The subjects carved, incised and moulded on the pieces included scrolls and sprays, lotuses, peonies and pomegranates, ducks, phoenixes, fish and dragons. Chun stoneware had a blue or green glaze over a dark-coloured body and was decorated with crimson or purple splotches. Besides the usual tableware we find flower-pots, bulb bowls, incense-burners, headrests, and, of course, vases. Ju stoneware, of which only some thirty pieces survive, is pale buff with a grey-blue glaze and a fine cràckle. The shapes are simple, the decoration is minimal, and the origins obscure.

Northern celadon stoneware has a grey body over which an olive-green or olive-brown glaze sits very happily. Vases, ewers, and lampstands may be found, as well as bowls and dishes. The decoration is carved, incised, or, most often, moulded, and features plants, animals and children. Early twelfth-century examples are the very best. They come from Shensi and western Honan. Tz'u-Chou stoneware made in northern China from the end of the tenth century varies enormously in body, glaze, decorative subjects and technique. In addition to the usual pieces, prunus vases (*mei-p'ing*) and headrests (*shên*), small figures and playthings are found.

Yuan Dynasty (1280–1367). After the fall of the Sung Dynasty, potters were given a freedom to improvise they had never before enjoyed. They concentrated on porcelain. Vessels became larger, colours brighter, and the kilns of the south, now the main centre of production, were run by syndicates rather than private sponsors. Overseas markets became impor-tant, and the revolutionary and hugely influential underglaze blue-painted porcelain of Jao-Chou was developed. This depended on the importation from the Persian Gulf of the cobalt blue dye. Almost all Chinese blue and white porcelain of this period was exported. The Chinese regarded it as vulgar. Lotus, peony and chrysanthemum, dragon, duck, pheasant, kylin, and bird, fish and insect, the repertory of decorative subjects makes familiar reading. More abstract border patterns were added and the designs were often formalised with bands and panels. The cobalt blue was often brilliant.

Besides this blue and white ware the Yuan Dynasty, short as it was, was also responsible for the heavy Shu-fu porcelain, possibly made for the use of the Mongol rulers. Shu and Fu are two characters who face each other across the inside of the bowls; they are thought to represent the Mongol equivalent of the privy council. There were also produced during this period monochrome vessels of red, blue or brown decorated internally with five-clawed dragons.

Ming Dynasty (1368–1644). Nankin was established as the first capital of the Ming Dynasty in 1368, and from this date the first reign marks of the Emperors were added to the china. By then porcelain was an important export about which the traders from Portugal (from 1516), and from Britain and Holland (from the early seventeenth century), were extremely enthusiastic. There were four main categories of Ming China. The first, blue and white ware, continued much as during the Yuan Dynasty but new subjects were featured: men and children, landscapes, and scenes from literature and drama. To please the Portuguese, coats of arms were sometimes added, and Latin tags — frequently misspelt. The second category was polychrome, and included Tou-ts'ai dove-tail colours; Wu-ts'ai, in which red, black and gilt outlines were added after glazing; and San-ts'ai, enamel glazes painted directly on to a biscuit body. Usually a warm yellow was combined with bright greens, blues, purples and blacks. During this period *famille verte* was introduced. Polychrome also included Fa-hua, which was like San-ts'ai but with the addition of strips of clay applied to the surface (like pastry) to create boxes within which the colours could be confined. Fa-hua pieces tend to be massive — wine jars and garden seats, for example — and are quite dazzling.

The third category was monochrome, a continuation of Yuan mono-chrome ware, but with a number of alternative colours. The celadon from Che-kiang was continued independently. The fourth was white ware. Early Ming white ware mostly takes the form of bowls, dishes, cups and ewers, some of which are enhanced by An-hua, or 'secret decorations', visible only when the piece is exposed to strong light. Later white ware was extended to include figures of the gods, notably Kuan-yin. This attractive porcelain is also known as *blanc-de-chine*.

After the death of the Emperor Wan-Li in 1619 a transitional period ensued before the Ch'ing Dynasty got under way. Many experiments were made, vases becoming taller and wider, decorations no longer being confined but spreading spontaneously over the whole surface of the piece. It was as though China were enjoying an art nouveau movement of its own nearly three hundred years before the countries of the West.

Ch'ing Dynasty—K'ang Hsi Period (1661–1722). The quality of body and glaze was then at its finest. *Famille verte* continued and *famille jaune*, *famille noire* and the glorious *famille rose* were introduced. *Flambé* or 'flashed' porcelain was also developed. The characteristic designs involving prunus, lotus, chrysanthemum, peony and rose were pressed into service and glazes imitating jade, marble and precious stones were expertly applied.

Ch'ing Dynasty—Yung-Chêng Period (1723–35) *and Ch'ien-Lung Period* (1736–95). By the middle of the eighteenth century the West, having discovered at the Meissen factory and elsewhere the secret of making 'hard-paste' or 'true' porcelain, had lost interest in Chinese products, while the Chinese market had become entirely dependent upon the West for its continuing prosperity. The result was export porcelain, especially large dinner services made for British and Dutch companies and exported by the Dutch East India Company. The products of the Ming Dynasty continued however, and a copper-red glaze was introduced to give the peach-bloom effect. Other opaque, coloured glazes produced satisfying monochrome vases, while white wares, both soft-paste and *blanc-de-chine*, were still produced. To the serious collector — and no collector is more serious than the collector of Chinese porcelain — nineteenth-century porcelain is of little interest.

Book: *Oriental Blue and White* by Sir H. M. Garner (Faber & Faber, 1970)
Collections: David Percival Foundation of Chinese Art, London; Gulbenkian Museum of Oriental Art and Archaeology, Durham; Melford Hall, Sudbury; Lady Lever Art Gallery, Port Sunlight; Lukis and Island Museum, Guernsey

Chippendale (style) Thomas Chippendale (1717–79), a charismatic Yorkshireman, was senior partner of Chippendale and Haig, the London firm of cabinet-makers. In 1756 he published the first edition of his influential work *The Gentleman and Cabinet-Maker's Director*, a catalogue of designs currently being crafted by the firm. A vast number of subscribers to Chippendale's *Director* were cabinet-makers themselves who bought the volume in order to steal — no, better perhaps to say *reproduce* — Chippendale's designs. Since other firms were as accomplished as Chippendale and Haig (Vile and Cobb boasted the royal warrant, while Gillow of Lancaster, Ince and Mayhew, and William Hallet could all turn out a handsome piece of furniture), few can now distinguish between what is genuine Chippendale and what is simply in the Chippendale style.

Chippendale's taste generally was to curb the excesses of rococo furniture, and to reduce the heavy curved cabriole limbs. But he was also eclectic. Since he worked to order on the decoration of his clients' rooms and each commission posed distinctive problems, he developed four styles under which most of his known pieces may be filed.

The classical style was already in fashion when Chippendale first came to London. The French style, which was loosely based on Louis XV, differed from it in the absence of finely chased and gilt metal fittings at the sides and corners of the pieces, the gilding of the woodwork and the beautiful tapestry coverings to the chairs. French Chippendale was chiefly used for mirrors, sofas, and chairs.

The Chinese style was the most consistent. Here the principal characteristics were open lattice-work in intriguing patterns, pagoda roofs with pendant bells, and the introduction of such motifs as mandarins, small buildings and Chinese birds into mirrors, and sconces. Finally there was the Gothic style, which attempted to combine elements of that ancient taste with Georgian delicacy and lightness of construction. Elements from some or all of these styles were sometimes used to produce pieces of genuine eccentricity, but the results are usually well proportioned and beautiful. Chippendale himself regarded the ribband-(or ribbon-)back chair to be his most successful innovation.

Evidently many of the designs in the *Director* were considered difficult to execute, for Chippendale introduced the third edition with these words:

> *Upon the whole I have given no design but what may be executed by the hands of a skilful workman, though some of the Profession have been diligent enough to represent them (especially those after the Gothick and Chinese manner) as so many specious Drawings impossible to be worked off by any Mechanic whatsoever. I will not scruple to attribute this to Malice, Ignorance, and Inability; and I am confident I can convince all Noblemen, Gentlemen, or others who will honour me with their commands, that every Design in the Book can be improved both as to Beauty and Enrichment in the Execution of it, by Their Most Obedient Servant Thomas Chippendale. St. Martins Lane Feb. 27, 1762.*

Book: *The Life and Work of Thomas Chippendale* by Christopher Gilbert (Studio Vista/Christie's, 1978)
Collections: Audley End House, Saffron Walden; Harewood House, Leeds; Braemore House, Fordingbridge; Littlecote House, Hungerford (Chinese Chippendale)

cigarette cards During the eighteenth century any self-respecting tradesman had a printed card giving details of the services offered by his company; very often he would also present his account on his card. Many cards survive, including a 'purveyor of asses' milk', a 'skeleton seller', a 'spadderdash and gaiter maker' and many 'chimbley sweeps'. The early Virginia cigarette manufacturers included 'stiffeners' in their packets to protect their product and after about 1870 the practice of printing these cards with attractive illustrations and informative texts became common. At this time most of the texts were concerned with the manufacture of cigarettes; but by the end of the nineteenth century the cards were being put to more imaginative use, as the commercial possibilities of running series of cards were recognised. The subjects reflect the interests of late Victorian smokers: buxom actresses and empire builders, for instance.

In the early years of this century there was an epic struggle between James Buchanan Duke, whose American Tobacco Company had taken over some 250 smaller firms and who paid over five million pounds for Ogden's of Liverpool, and the British manufacturers who huddled for protection under the umbrella of the Imperial Tobacco Company. The resulting conglomerate, the British American Tobacco Company, was vast, and the business of cigarette cards better organised thereafter.

Between 1920 and 1940 the craze was at its height and some 300 million cards were printed annually. Gold Flake, Black Cat, and Cadbury's were especially prolific, but among collectors the most desirable are those produced by the smaller companies, such as John Sinclair of Newcastle, Taddy of London, and W. Sandorides.

There was a pact after the last war that the issuing of cigarette cards be discontinued, but the pact was broken by Players with their Donicella series, and by Black Cat.

As with postage stamps, good condition is essential and cards pasted into albums are unwanted. The modern equivalents of the old tradecards are also collected, produced by such firms as Liebig's (whose 'chromes' come in as many as fourteen different colours), Kardomah, Lever Brothers, Rowntrees, Spratts and Typhoo.

Book: *Collecting Cigarette Cards* by Dorothy Bagnall (London Cigarette Company, 1972)
Collection: Harris Museum and Art Gallery, Preston

claw-and-ball foot Introduced during the reign of Queen Anne, the claw-and-ball foot was a suitable way of rounding off a cabriole leg on a chair, table or settee. It may have derived from a traditional Chinese symbol, a clawed dragon pursuing the pearl of wisdom, frequently found on Chinese porcelain and lacquer.

Cliff, Clarice A potter of the art deco period, Clarice Cliff (1899–1972) was born in Tunstall in the heart of the potteries. She studied at art school in Burslem and was then apprenticed to the firm of A. J. Wilkinson Ltd. Here she was encouraged to experiment with her craft and in the 1920s she

Clarice Cliff pottery

produced her Tibetan ware: large, brightly coloured jars. She also painted the pottery designs for such notable artists as Duncan Grant, Paul Nash, Frank Brangwyn, Laura Knight, Barbara Hepworth, and Graham Sutherland. Most of her output is eminently usable — tea services, vases, bowls, and so on — with an occasional decorative plaque.

In the early 1930s she held an exhibition at Harrods in association with the Foley Pottery. Her later work lacked the gaudy exhibitionism of some of her early designs, among which were 'Bizarre', 'Fantasque', 'Patina', 'Scarab Blue', and 'Biarritz'. Most of her pieces have a transfer-printed signature, while a few are marked Royal Staffordshire Pottery.

Book: *Clarice Cliff* by Peter Wentworth-Shields and Kay Johnson (L'Odéon, 1976)

clock   See individual types of clock (e.g., *longcase clock*).

cloisonné   A process of enamelling on gold, bronze, and copper by the addition of coloured glass pastes, which fuse with the metals on heating. The areas of design are confined by wires soldered to the surface. The finest examples of early *cloisonné* ware are the reliquary of the Holy Cross in the cathedral treasury at Limberg and the golden altar font in St Mark's, Venice.

Cloisonné was produced as early as the eighth century, and goldsmiths of the Middle Ages often used it as an alternative to decorating with precious gems. Much *cloisonné* was produced in China during the Yuan and Ming Dynasties and in Japan considerably later. The craft was revived in France with the fashion for things Japanese in the 1860s and 1870s, and it became generally popular with art nouveau designers.

Coalport   William Pugh, one of the proprietors of the Coalport pottery, went on a trip to London in the 1870s. There he found what he took to be a nice example of old Sèvres porcelain, which he purchased for £600 and took back to the Shropshire works. He showed it to the foreman, suggesting that they should study it in detail because it would help them to make their Sèvres reproductions more realistic. The foreman remarked — and one can imagine the look on his face — that they would have little trouble matching it because Pugh's piece of old Sèvres was in fact a piece of Coalport of a few years back.

The early history of the Coalport factory is more than a little confused, but, in brief, a John Rose, who had been apprenticed to Thomas Turner of the Caughley Salopian works, set up his business on the north bank of the Severn less than a mile from his old employer's works on the south bank. Having taken most of Caughley's business, Rose bought the Caughley works in 1798 and used them for the manufacture of his pieces which were then sent to Coalport for decoration (as they had previously been sent to Worcester). By 1815, when the seams of coal at Caughley had been worked out, the entire operation was removed across the river. Between 1820 and 1822, Rose bought up his two most formidable rivals at Swansea and at Nantgarw, employing both their proprietors, Messrs Billingsley and Walker. It is therefore not easy to distinguish early Coalport from Caughley, Worcester, Swansea or Nantgarw porcelain.

In 1820 Coalport won a Society of Arts award for the production of a leadless glaze, much less damaging to the lungs of the workforce than the usual glazes. At about the same time Coalport, which, as we have seen, had been imitating continental factories, turned to the rococo style with encrusted flowers and much lavish ornamentation. The works also introduced the Indian tree pattern, much imitated since by a host of other potters and *de rigueur* in pretentious Indian restaurants. Rose died in 1841 to be succeeded by his nephew.

Of the artists employed at Coalport the most notable was probably John Randall, a leading ornithologist. His studies of birds in their natural surroundings are much admired although, by a company rule, he was not allowed to sign his work. (The name of the London retailers, Daniell & Co., is frequently found however.) Another Coalport artist was Robert Abraham, who specialised in figure painting in the delicate French style, having studied on the continent, a rare qualification in those days.

The business was declared bankrupt in the late 1870s, but was bought up by Peter Bruff, an engineer turned porcelain manufacturer. Late nineteenth-century Coalport is extremely ornate. Tall, handled vases display well executed landscapes within jewelled surrounds. The table-ware, with flowers in panels, or lightly decorated on a pink or green ground, is more discreetly pretty. Parian ware was produced, as well as comports and centrepieces.

In 1924 the firm was bought by Cauldon Potteries and moved to Staffordshire. The best specimens of later Coalport are probably those pieces marked with a CBD monogram, standing for Coalbrookdale, with which Coalport was much associated.

Book: *Coalport and Coalbrookdale Porcelains* by Geoffrey Godden (Barrie & Jenkins, 1970)
Collection: Clive House Museum, Shrewsbury

coal scuttles In 1715 Lady Grissell Baillie spent 21s 6d on 'a coper scuttel'. She may not have known much about spelling, but she knew what she liked. Very few scuttles of this period have survived, and in the nineteenth century scuttles were replaced by the purdonium, the invention, I promise you, of a Mr Purdon. Two shapes dominated the short life of the coal scuttle: the helmet, which was always the more popular, and the shovel. Usually the scuttles were of copper with brass handles; but other examples in brass, bronze, and lacquered tin may be found. An ingenious device was shown at the Great Exhibition, whereby a small coal-scoop was kept full of coal released from the larger coal vase into which it slotted.

coasters When one had a long refectory dining table and an equally long evening's drinking ahead of one; when the women had been sent into the withdrawing room to get on with their needlework and their idle talk; when the faithful retainer had been dismissed because one could never *entirely* rely on his discretion; then one very real problem remained. How to get the drink from one end of the table to the other without the intolerable necessity of constantly rising to one's feet? The solution was the coaster, a small circular tray or stand on green baize, or on castors, which one could coast along the table, rather like the barmen in Western saloons sent Old Red Eye along the counter to Audie Murphy. Coasters came in silver or in Sheffield plate, and there were double-coasters which held two bottles.

coffee pots Coffee became a fashionable drink, together with tea and chocolate, in the late seventeenth century. At this time, the coffee pot was of tapering cylindrical form, with a conical cover and a long spout. It differed from the chocolate pot in that the latter had a hole in the lid allowing a rod to be inserted and the contents stirred. Many of the finest silversmiths made coffee pots which reflected the changing contemporary styles, and some of these silver pots were copied in ceramics, especially at the Chelsea works. By the end of the Regency period coffee services were made *en suite* with matching tea services, the styles being copied in Sheffield plate, lustreware, and pewter, and later on in electroplate. With the wider popularity of coffee drinking, earthenware and porcelain pots began to replace silver ones during the nineteenth century. Apart from other considerations, they were easier to clean.

coins A Mr Horace Burrows (well named) of Chelmsford was checking his change one day when he discovered a 1952 half crown, hitherto and since unrecorded. The coin was sold in America for £2000. Such stories as this may have encouraged people to hunt nervously through their pockets, but this is no longer a serious way to go about coin collecting. Indeed, since British currency went decimal, it is a pointless exercise. Also many of the rarer pennies found turned out to have been doctored.

Almost all coins struck in Britain before 1662 were made by hand; almost all coins struck in Britain after 1662 were made by machine. The earlier coins are known as the 'hammered series', the later as 'the milled series'. Coins are struck from dies, metal plates on which the design has been engraved. The die for the front of the coin ('heads') is known as the obverse, that for the back of the coin is known as the reverse ('tails'). For a hammered coin a series of pinches or 'irons' was made for the master die, and these irons slotted together like the pieces of a jigsaw puzzle to complete the design. Towards the end of the hammered period it became common for artists to engrave directly on to the master die with only the lettering added by irons; alternatively the whole coin might be a single die.

When the dies had been prepared a circle of metal or 'flan' would be cut or punched from a sheet and its weight would be tested: when coins were made from precious metals the weight and fineness of the metal used had to be exactly equivalent to the value of the coin. Of course, gold could not be used in a pure state, and a hardening alloy would be added: indeed most coins are composed of alloys. Then the 'flan' would be placed between the obverse and the reverse dies and hammer blows would imprint the design on the coins (which is why one speaks of coins being 'struck'). Hammered coins were usually imperfect in some detail. They were never quite circular, and a repetition of part of the pattern might appear if the coin had had to be 'double struck'.

Machine-made coins display none of these charming imperfections. With these a large plaster of Paris cast is made from the original designs, a mould is taken from the cast, the mould is plated with nickel and copper and then 'reduced' by the operation of an ingenious kind of pantograph. A large number of reductions, cut into a block of steel, can be taken from a single electrotype. The master punches which this technique produces are then used for a matrix which is 'incuse', or reversed, and from the matrix the coins themselves are struck. Modern coins are made from a cupro-nickel alloy, but early machine-made coins were made from ingots that had been rolled out or 'milled' by horsepower or a watermill.

When the coins leave the mint they are rarely in perfect or, as it is called by numismatists, 'uncirculated' condition. This matter of condition is of vital importance. In early coins variations in the spacing of the perimeter letters may be expected, and also in the positioning of the portrait (or 'device'). Such small variations are enough to give collectors thrillingly sleepless nights. More to the point, the detail on hammered coins is a great deal sharper than the equivalent detail on a machine-made coin. It is the difference between an original engraving and a reproduction — indeed, in a way, that's just what it is.

As regards condition, old coins (those produced before 1816) are graded as follows. The very best are known as F.D.C., which stands for 'Fleur de Coin'; these are in the best possible condition for their age, series and metal. Next comes E.F. (Extremely Fine), meaning a nice example showing only a little wear. Then there is V.F. (Very Fine), meaning average, F. (Fine) meaning battered, and Fair, which means horrible. In catalogues you may expect to find such subtleties as 'about very fine', 'extremely fine or better' — condition is, after all, subjective. With coins made post 1816 the term 'uncirculated' is used in place of F.D.C., and other descriptions are a little less stringent than with the older coins. The term 'proof' is used for coins specially struck for collectors. Some dealers also use symbols for rarity, from RRRR for a coin which is exceptionally rare to R for a coin which is just common or garden 'rare'. For modern coins the scale runs from R7 (only one or two examples known) to C3 (extremely common).

As to which coins to collect, the choice is wide. Pennies have a long and honourable history. They were the only coins in use for more than 600 years from AD725; they weighed either 19 or 25 grains, a grain being the weight of a grain of corn. They were minted in seventy different centres, from Dover to Durham, from Watchet to Wareham. Pure copper pennies were first circulated in 1797. Halfpennies, farthings, guineas, half guineas, crowns, sovereigns, and half sovereigns are also likely coins to collect. Or one can select a period, or a locality, or a subject.

Gold coins may be cleaned, but only with a weak acid, such as lemon juice, after which soap and water should be used. Soap and water is probably best for silver coins, though some recommend the use of ammonia on a cotton wool pad. Copper and bronze coins should not be cleaned.

Books: *Coin and Medal Collecting* by Howard Linecar (Pelham Books, 1971); *Collecting Coins* by P. Frank Purvey (Gifford, 1971)
Collection: British Museum, London

George I crown, half crown, shilling, and sixpence

comb-back A basic type of Windsor chair, the comb-back chair has a top rail rather like the back of a comb, and the vertical uprights remind one (resistibly, it must be said) of the teeth of a comb.

commemorabilia According to the Commemorative Collection Society, a commemorative is 'an item which has been produced commercially for sale which marks an event, occurrence or person contemporary with the time when it was produced.' Not, you will notice, anniversary pieces. Thus a Lyons Dundee Fruit Cake in a tin commemorating the Queen's coronation would be a commemorative item, so too would be a silk scarf woven with a likeness of the Derby winner of 1832, and a Stevengraph produced for the Great Exhibition, and a Jubilee mug. The range is vast. Silver salvers, crystal glasses, clay pipes, lapel badges, prints, Beatles T-shirts, almost anything. However, the majority of commemoratives are ceramic: beakers celebrating royal weddings and coronations; jugs honouring famous victories, the deaths of poets, the passing of acts of parliament, or the hanging of notorious criminals; plates bearing the features of Jenny Lind or Queen Caroline, Rudolf Valentino or Princess Anne.

The earliest commemoratives were issued to mark Charles II's exile and his restoration in 1660. Later the Staffordshire potteries found it profitable to produce souvenirs of everyone and everything to catch the public's interest. Obviously such events as the accession of young Victoria and her marriage to Albert were 'naturals'. Exhibitions, especially the Great Exhibition of 1851, produced flurries of souvenirs, many of which could be bought at the exhibitions themselves. Doulton and Spode specialised in classy commemoratives, Shelley and Foley less so. Wedgwood produced very little of this kind between 1830 and 1930, regarding such items as intrinsically vulgar. Some of them undoubtedly were. Take the instance of the chamber pot with General Sir Robert Napier and Theodore, the King of Abyssinia, transfer-printed on the side, and a frog crawling up towards the rim. As you will have gathered, in the matter of commemorabilia, *anything* goes. Large quantities of commemorative pieces were produced for Edward VIII, who was never crowned; a disaster for the manufacturers. More recently an enterprising firm, Panorama Studios of Buckfastleigh, issued a 'Watergate Jug' with pictures of Nixon and the conspirators on one side, and 'I can't tell a lie' on the other.

Book: *Commemorative Pottery 1700–1900* by J. and J. May (Heinemann, 1972)

commode   A highly decorated French chest of drawers dating from the eighteenth century. Commodes were graced with serpentine fronts, ormolu mounts, marquetry inlay, and all the other ingenious and elaborate ornamentation which that most stylised period could devise.

More often, the word is used for a portable 'convenience'. Rumour has it that one of our High Court judges (recently deceased) sat on one in court.

concertina   Sir Charles Wheatstone, Professor of Experimental Philosophy at King's College, London, and co-inventor of the telegraph, invented and patented the concertina in 1829. Not surprisingly, its pressnote system bears a striking resemblance to the morse keyboard.

The first concertina had twenty-four keys, but when Wheatstone joined forces with Louis Lachenal, a Swiss toolmaker, one with forty-eight keys and double-action was produced (double-action implies that the same note can be produced by pulling or pushing). Later, Lachenal started his own concertina business which was bought up by Boosey and Hawkes in 1934 — Lachenal's instruments have sometimes been defaced by the addition of other firms' labels. When Wheatstone's patent lapsed a number of other concertina makers set up in Islington: many of their instruments had beautifully decorated and fret-cut endplates.

The English concertina is purely a melody instrument. The Duet (known by the Salvation Army as the Triumph) is a solo instrument which can play both treble and bass. The Anglo (traditional for Morris dancing) has an action like a harmonica, one note for pushing, another for pulling; it also has the sophistication of a drone button.

Collection: Museum of Concertinas, Belper

console table A side table, supported either by brackets fixing it permanently to the wall, or with two or three legs at the front. The forerunner of the sideboard, the console table had its heyday in the late seventeenth century.

Copeland See *Spode*.

Copenhagen To say that the continuing existence of the Royal Copenhagen Porcelain Factory depended and depends upon a single commission may be overstating the case, but not by much. When Frederick VI, still the Crown Prince in 1790, ordered a dinner service from the firm which was owned by the Danish royal family, he may not have known just what the undertaking would involve. The Flora Danica service of over two thousand pieces — a hundred place settings — designed by Theodor Holmokjold and painted by the botanist, A. C. Bayer, was so successful that variations of it have continued to be produced for nearly two hundred years. It had been destined for Catherine the Great, who already owned vastly imposing services by Wedgwood (1774) and Sèvres (1778). But she died before she could take delivery, and the service remained in its own special room at Rosenberg Castle, in Copenhagen.

The early history of the Copenhagen factory is obscure. Production probably got under way about 1755 with soft-paste porcelain of very high quality in the much imitated Dresden style. The present factory was founded in 1772 by Franz Müller, a German chemist, who brought a largely German workforce with him. He adopted three blue wavy lines as the factory's mark, symbolising the three channels which separate Zealand and Funen from Jutland. In 1775 the factory received royal approval and, more practically, a fifty-year monopoly. During the years of the classical revival in Britain, Copenhagen was much influenced by Wedgwood. German and French influences also remained strong, so that the eighteenth-century output was little different from that of any other porcelain factory: there were table services, vases, figures and groups of figures, snuff boxes, *étuis*, and fluted blue and white domestic ware designed in the style of the celebrated Meissen onion pattern. Leaf and scroll handles to jugs and pots are characteristic, as are unusual curved finials on vases. Encrusted flowers are not uncommon in the styles made famous at Minton, Coalport, and Berlin.

Connections with the Danish royal family were severed in 1867, and the company was bought in 1882 by the Aluminia Faience Manufactory under

P. Schon. This led to a review of design standards, with interesting abstract patterns (in the 1890s), oriental-type glazes, and, in the early part of this century, bowls and vases with underglaze decoration in brown, yellow, blue, green, and purple.

Throughout this century such artists as Kyhn, Nielsen, and Salto have shown the rest of us a thing or two about porcelain design which, in the case of contemporary British manufacturers, who do little but repeat past successes, is not difficult.

> *What sealed my doom and made me a 'collector' for ever was the discovery of*
> *Royal Copenhagen pottery* (sic), *with the immensity of its range, from the*
> *almost sentimental little blue-grey figurines in which Christian Thomsen*
> *embodied the personalities of Hans Andersen stories to the heroic stoneware*
> *figures of Biblical characters by Jais Nielsen, having almost the magnificence*
> *of statuary.*
>
> from *In the Meantime* by Howard Spring

copper The word 'copper' derives from Cyprus, where large quantities of the metal were once found. It was known to medieval alchemists by the sign of the planet Venus and is the oldest working metal. Man mixed it with tin to make bronze, and with zinc to make brass, and from it he also produced such useful alloys as argentan, used for electroplating, Britannia metal, a cheap imitation of pewter, gun-metal, ormolu, pinchbeck, and speculum, which is used for mirrors. Copper is an excellent conductor of electricity, the best material for engraving plates for illustrations and maps, and ideal for kitchen utensils. In the form of horse brasses it has talismanic properties, and, when turned into coins, it is ideal for keeping at bay those evil spirits known as privation and bankruptcy.

In the eighteenth and nineteenth centuries most copper — more than half the output of the entire world — came from the Cornish mines, at which time it was the most popular metal for cooking-pots, kettles and warming pans. Such utensils had bases of double thickness and were internally lined with tin, as a protection against poisoning.

Copper ale and spirit measures came in sets of six, from five gallons down to a tablespoonful — the smallest size is now the most rarely found. Conical ale warmers were used to infuse ale and cider with spices. Copper jelly moulds (more desirable than glass or earthenware examples) were used for cakes, blancmanges and chocolates as well as for jellies. They sometimes have their owners' initials stamped on them. The range of antique items made from copper is extensive, and other collectables include chestnut roasters, doorstops, water jugs, tobacco tampers and boxes, trivets, scales, scientific instruments, hand-warmers, ecclesiastical items, and sconces.

There is more reproduction copper on the market than antique. Indeed most copper items of the eighteenth century or earlier have already found their way into museums. Genuine old copper often has a pleasantly battered look where it has been hammered into shape. The quality of the detail is finer than on modern examples, and careful examination usually reveals where the castings from modern moulds have been joined.

coral A marine gem, made up of calcium carbonate formed by the secretion of seawater by the coral polyp. As a material for jewellery coral became fashionable in 1845 after the marriage of the Prince of the Two Sicilies to the Duchesse d'Aumale. The groom presented his bride with some very pretty coral ornaments in a *corbeille*. For twenty years the fashion raged: in 1867 George Augustus Sala was moved to describe his contemporaries as going about 'bedizened with twisted sticks of seeming red sealing-wax.' This would have been natural coral but carved coral was more highly prized.

The dangers and difficulties of coral fishing may have been partly responsible for the myths attached to the gem. The Romans hung coral around their children's necks to ward off evil spirits, and in the Middle Ages it was used for amulets, rosaries, reliquaries, madonnas, and other such ecclesiastical bric-à-brac. Love brooches and christening rattles were frequently inlaid with coral. British babies wore coral branches around their necks to suck while teething. The most esteemed colours were dark red (mystically associated with blood) and pale pink.

Sicily, Naples, and Genoa were the centres for the coral carvers of the seventeenth and eighteenth centuries; more recently Japan has become celebrated for its carved coral. However, there was one English coral master, Robert Phillips (died 1881) of Cockspur Street, who received in 1870 a decoration from the King of Italy, acknowledging all that he had done for the Neapolitan coral trade.

Coral ranges in colour from the whitest of whites to the deepest of reds. Once, blue and yellow corals were also fished. Brown and black coral comes from coral bushes which have died. Mediterranean coral is thicker and heavier than Japanese coral, which has a profusion of branches. It is also more suitable for figure carving. Polished coral will display small pittings where the branches have been ground away, and such signs are a useful guarantee of authenticity. Another test is to pour sulphuric acid on a piece of coral, which, if genuine, will effervesce. But such a practice, if too freely indulged, will defeat its purpose by destroying the coral.

Collection: Public Art Gallery and Museum, St Helens, Lancashire

corkscrews The human race is at its most delightful when at its most eccentric, and I feel sure that the International Correspondence of Corkscrew Addicts, who write letters to each other beginning 'Dear Addict,' must be charming people.

There are certainly many varieties of corkscrew to collect, from Dutch silver corkscrews of the eighteenth century with mother-of-pearl embossed handles to the patent 'safety bar' model 'with counter clamp, spring-loaded neck handles, bladed worm and lever action'; from 'double-action' to 'rack and pinion' corkscrews; from folding and 'concertina' corkscrews to brass novelty models in the shape of a girl at a spinning wheel. As a general rule corkscrews are valued according to age, beauty, and mechanical ingenuity.

Silver rack and pinion corkscrew with bone handle and brush

coromandel A type of lacquer, named after the Indian Coromandel coast where East and West traded their furniture. Coromandel work features designs incised on to lacquered backgrounds, and filled with colours and gilding. Some massive screens were constructed out of coromandel, as well as chests and bureaux. The designs on some of the screens so puzzled British workmen, who cut them up to use for panelling, that they were often mounted upside down.

country furniture Until the second half of the last century Kensington, Blackheath, Islington, Hampstead, and Chelsea were still in the country. When T. H. Huxley was born in Ealing in 1825 it was 'as quiet a little country village as could be found within half-a-dozen miles of Hyde Park Corner'. 'Town' was the City of London with its East and West Ends. It stopped to the north a little way up the Tottenham Court Road and to the south somewhere near Elephant and Castle. But within those narrow confines all the classical names in English cabinet-making set up their workshops, and produced their *Directors* and *Drawing Books*. Their designs were copied and developed from the Orient, from France and Italy, from Austria, Germany and Holland, and were imposed on a receptive metropolitan public. It is worth remembering that Chippendale, Hepplewhite, Adam, and Sheraton all died within twenty-seven years of one another and that a revolution in furniture design (or four smaller upheavals) took place within the span of a single generation.

The provincial centres followed London's lead as soon as it was practicable, but in the country areas things move more slowly. The woods used — oak, beech, elm, ash, yew and various fruitwoods — were those most readily to hand. And if a customer got to hear that in London Chippendale was quite the thing, his local chairmaker would put together a handsome piece incorporating some of the features that suggested Chippendale to him (usually the chair-backs, the seat and legs remaining solid and sturdy). So arose Country Chippendale, which owes as much to that great innovator as Chippendale (himself a Yorkshireman) owed to those in China, France and elsewhere. (People in the big country houses had London houses as well, so they would be inclined to go to local craftsmen for furniture only for the servants' quarters and the cottages on the estates.)

Cupboards, dressers and presses, chests, stools and benches, tables, beds and wash-hand stands, longcase clocks and, above all, Windsor chairs are what comprise country furniture. Regional differences are important to the specialist, but not so important as the similarities: a confidence in the materials, a traditional way of working with traditional tools, and a clear idea of the uses to which the furniture would be put.

Book: *Country Furniture* by Jane Toller (David & Charles, 1973)

crackleware   A Chinese technique, imitated in nineteenth-century Europe, whereby a piece of porcelain was covered in tiny brownish crackles. The effect was produced as the porcelain itself was made more sensitive to heat and expansion than the glaze. The resulting crackles were then rubbed with black and red dyes for emphasis. Handles of crackleware vases were usually made in the form of kylin heads with movable rings inside the teeth; raised ornamentation of a bronze appearance was also added. European examples can be fairly hideous. It has been poetically suggested that genuine old crackleware was a symbol of the Chinese spring when the ice begins to crack.

cranberry glass   Originally this transparent pinkish-red glass was used at Stourbridge to make pharmaceutical jars more cheerful. In the 1880s most British glassworks began to turn out small items in cranberry glass (little bowls and vases with frilled rims, jugs and decanters enamelled with rather too sweet Mary Gregory children) as a cheap line. Cranberry glass is misleadingly and sometimes hopefully known as ruby glass, which was a German glass made with gold chloride, far richer in colour than the pale imitations of the Victorians.

creamware   In the early eighteenth century a new process of mixing white clay with powdered flint (silica) was introduced in the Staffordshire potteries. Enoch Booth of Tunstall was one of the early pioneers, and at the Leeds and Wedgwood potteries many refinements were undertaken. If the clay was fired at a high temperature a useful stoneware was produced, while a lower temperature produced a cream coloured earthenware which could be waterproofed by glazing. Lead glaze was used to give creamware its characteristic greeny-yellow gloss. The result was ideal in many ways:

you could pierce it, mould it, colour it with enamels, print transfers upon it, all with satisfying results.

Josiah Wedgwood developed it as Queen's ware, with great success; but William Hartley at Leeds produced the finest quality creamware. By the late eighteenth century it had replaced saltglaze as the most popular domestic earthenware in Britain and its popularity spread to the continent and North America. As time passed creamware became more and more etiolated, and was turned into cool, white pearlware by the addition of cobalt blue.

Book: *English Cream-Coloured Earthenware* by Donald Towner (Faber & Faber, 1957)
Collections: Temple Newsam House, near Leeds; Astley Hall, Chorley

crystal   A confusing term which may either be used specifically to mean rock-crystal, or vaguely for fine-quality, faceted table glass. Recent E.E.C. regulations state that no glass may be labelled crystal unless it contains at least 24 per cent (half-lead) or 30 per cent (full-lead).

damascene   A decorative technique, supposedly once practised in Damascus, which involves inlaying a piece of iron or steel with gold or silver wire. In the Near East the technique was principally used for swords and scabbards, and table tops. In Britain it was never much employed except for racing trophies.

Davenport (china)   The Davenport factory was founded in 1793 when it took over an established works at Longport in Burslem. It is true that the output of the factory is not of the finest quality, but it is durable, attractive and, more to the point, easier to come by than items from the more glamorous stables. Certainly Davenport china was highly considered at the time of William IV's accession to the throne, for the factory was commissioned to provide a coronation service. It also supplied a richly coloured service in the Sèvres manner to celebrate the union of Great Britain and Ireland. The stoneware was of good quality, rather similar to Mason's ironstone and the factory produced, as Mason's and Ridgway's also did, a great many octagonal jugs in the Imari style.

In the 1880s the factory specialised in tea services in the Japanese manner, trading on the success enjoyed by the Derby works with similar sets, but, since the company failed in 1887, it seems that somebody miscalculated. It was also a notable producer of strong earthenware for use on board ship, and included in its output porcelain plaques, some of which were decorated by independent artists working outside the factory.

Book: *Davenport Pottery and Porcelain 1794–1887* by T. A. Lockett (David & Charles, 1972)

davenport (furniture)   The davenport was supposedly named after a Captain Davenport R.N. who designed this compact and attractive piece of furniture. What is a davenport? It is a small writing desk with a sloping working surface, hinged to give access to stationery racks, pens and ink-holders within. Very often on the right hand side the davenport has a single deep drawer opened with a knob; several shallow drawers are to be found on the left hand side.

Early examples are high and square with a brass gallery rail on the top. Later one finds much elaborate carving added to the leg supports and elsewhere, with occasionally a secret drawer operated by a hidden spring. In some examples the upper section has been made to swivel. A simple form of davenport has done duty in schools for several centuries.

Victorian rosewood davenport

deal The wood of the fir or pine introduced from the Baltic in the seventeenth century. It is used by cabinet-makers for those parts which are not supposed to be visible, like drawer linings.

decanters The system that operated from the mid-seventeenth century was that wine was removed from the cask in a decanter bottle (or serving bottle) and brought to the table to be served. (A decanter bottle attributed to George Ravenscroft may be seen in the British Museum.) In the eighteenth century, when the binning of wine was introduced, wine would be decanted from the bottle into a decanter, leaving the dregs behind. In the very early years of decanters, say 1725–30, corks would be used and tied under the rim; the more sensible glass stopper was introduced from about 1730. Decanters were used for sherry, port, cordials, and ale as well as wine, and labels would identify what was in which.

1674 *serving bottle*	c. *1680* *serving jug*	c. *1730* *cruciform* *decanter*	c. *1750* *facet-cut* *decanter*
c. *1810* *straight-sided* *decanter*	*1810* *ship's decanter*	*1815* *hexagonal* *decanter*	*1850* *heavy green* *decanter*

There were many distinctive decanters. The bell decanter, logically, had a body shaped like a bell. The claret decanter (or claret jug) had a pear-shaped body, a long neck with a lip for pouring, and a curved handle. Many early versions (c.1800–50) were in silver and corked, later ones became ornate and fanciful. The Elgin jug was a claret decanter, engraved with part of the Elgin marbles in relief. A guest decanter was a small decanter placed on a house-guest's bedside table; it had no stopper. A magnum decanter held two quarts.

The piggy-dog decanter was a horizontal decanter shaped like a pig or a dog. You held the beast by the tail and poured through the snout — as with a cow-creamer. The shaft and globe decanter, made from 1725 of soda glass, had a globe body and a tall shaft neck. The spirit decanter was attractive: the contents of each of these decanters would be engraved or gilded on the bowl with sometimes the first letter repeated on the stopper. The stirrup decanter was carried at a hunt, and had a spike underneath which went through a hole in a tray, upon which tray matching stirrup cups were set. This decanter had a pouring lip and a handle. The toilet-water decanter was a small decanter or bottle for the dressing table, and would have held scents (usually eau de cologne) and medicaments. Whisky decanters are square, ideal for fitting into a tantalus, and often made from elaborately cut lead glass.

Should you have a decanter with unsightly wine stains inside, you can clean it with potato peelings and water; leave them there for a week or so, then wash with soda and fresh water and the stains will disappear.

It is also worth bearing in mind that stoppers can be cheaply ground down to fit decanters, and that those who sell old decanters may have done the same; check carefully! See also *ship's decanter*.

Book: *English Bottles and Decanters 1650–1900* by D. C. Davis (Letts, 1972)

Delft First of all a warning. When dealing with tin-glazed earthenware one can easily become confused, and a distinction must be made between Delft (with a capital D), Dutch tin-glazed earthenware; delftware (with a lower case d), English tin-glazed earthenware; maiolica, Italian tin-glazed earthenware; faience, French and German tin-glazed earthenware; and majolica, tin-glazed stoneware developed by Minton's and other factories in the nineteenth century.

Since Delft is often used as a generic title for all blue and white tin-glazed earthenware it is as well to be clear about its true meaning. In this volume delftware is discussed under *Lambeth*, while maiolica, faience and majolica are to be found under their respective headings.

Delft lies between The Hague and Rotterdam, a nice old village which produced apothecary jars and such like, in the Italian style, after the arrival in Antwerp in 1508 of Guido Andriesz, a potter from Casteldurante. But at the beginning of the seventeenth century Holland started importing large quantities of oriental porcelain (it was the only European power permitted to enter Japanese ports). Thereafter the Dutch slavishly imitated the Chinese hard-paste porcelain, reducing the weight, improving the figuration, and adding glaze to the underneath of the dishes. They became expert and some of the landscape plaques and polychromatic dishes (at the beginning of the eighteenth century reds and greens and pinks, blues and yellows and greens) were highly sophisticated.

Delft is always warmer to the touch and lighter in weight than the Chinese originals, but difficult to distinguish at a glance. No retouching was possible since the soft glaze dried very fast, and the Dutch artists had to work spontaneously and confidently to achieve their fine results. Their work was strictly controlled by the Guild of St Luc. Much early Delft was itself copied by Parisian forgers, and since the number of Delft marks is enormous, great care needs to be taken to tell the true from the false.

Book: *Delft Ceramics* by Caroline H. De Jong (Pall Mall Press, 1970)
Collection: Museum and Art Gallery, Reading

Derby Mysteriously and intriguingly there exists a letter written from Derby by the second Earl Cowper dated 1728, the postscript of which reads as follows: 'If 2 portmantoes should come to you I desire you to take them in — I have bespoke a set of China from the man who makes it here in

England.' Who was the 'man'? Where was 'here in England'? What was 'China'? We can only guess, but the most intelligent guess would seem to suggest that some sort of earthenware or stoneware — most unlikely to be porcelain — was being made in Derby as early as 1728. We do know that by 1756 a partnership had been set up between John Heath, a banker from Derby, Andrew Planché, an apprentice goldsmith, and William Duesbury, an enameller who had been employed at the Longton Hall Factory. Heath supplied the capital, Duesbury the energy and know-how.

Planché seems to have been excluded from the partnership (the deeds of which were never properly executed) since his name appears in no future records. But he produced white and coloured human and animal figures, slip-cast, with hollow interiors and a screw-hole (usually) in the base, some of which Duesbury painted in his London workshop. Among the animals is a 'hosterredg' (ostrich).

The factory based its early success on copying continental styles, and was called 'The Second Dresden' by Duesbury. These early Derby pieces (1756–70) were often incorrectly identified as Bow or Chelsea, but the presence of three unglazed patch marks on the base has helped to place them where they belong. Domestic pieces were painted with birds and butterflies copied precisely from nature. Figures were finely modelled because the paste which the potters were using — they experimented for a long time — was more pliable than that used at most other factories.

In 1770 Duesbury purchased the stock and plant of the Chelsea factory and for the next fifteen years (1770–84) he carried on production at both factories. This is the period known as Chelsea-Derby, and the output then, with models interchanged between the two factories, tended towards the neo-classical with subdued colours and such subjects as nymphs and shepherds, the four seasons, and children playing rather *too* sweetly with pet animals.

When the younger Duesbury took over a few months before his father's death in 1786, the most productive years of Derby output began. The firm now enjoyed considerable favour at court, was able to employ the best modellers and decorators, and specialised particularly in table services with handsomely painted landscapes. The figures produced at Derby in the 1780s were to form the originals for many of the nineteenth-century Staffordshire models, which in turn are so frequently reproduced even today.

The finest landscapes were painted by Zachariah Boreman, the more realistic flowers came from the brush of William Billingsley. Other notable artists included Brewer, Bancroft, Taylor, Robinson, Corden, Stanesby, Haslem, Cotton, Askew, and Pegg, a Quaker. All old English names and despite the Chinese, continental, and, in the nineteenth century, Japanese influences, there remains something powerfully English about the flavour of Derby pieces. The modellers of figures and groups included Spängler, a

Swiss who worked in the style of Adam's protégée, Angelica Kauffmann, Stephan, Coffee, Duvivier, Dear and John Bacon R.A.

In 1811 the factory was leased to Robert Bloor who had been Duesbury's clerk. There followed a gradual decline in standards, and the factory closed in 1848 or 1849 after the death of Bloor.

The history of the Derby works thereafter is confused. Locker and Company (including several former workmen at the factory), Stevenson, Sharp and Company, Stevenson and Hancock were just some of the firms to assume responsibility. The company traded as the Old Crown Derby China Works until 1935, and the Derby Crown Porcelain Company was established in 1876 by a former director of the Worcester factory. Japanese patterns were (and still are) popular, and much richly gilded and decorated tableware was produced — it found favour particularly in America, which was always keen on gold.

Books: *Ceramics of Derbyshire* by H. G. Bradley (published by the author at 14 Dorset Sq. NW1, 1978); *Derby Porcelain* by Franklin A. Barrett and Arthur L. Thorpe (Faber & Faber, 1971)
Collections: Museum and Art Gallery, Warwick (definitive); Royal Crown Derby Works Museum, Derby

Devon motto-ware This is usually found in teashops in the High Streets of old market towns. Cream pots, milk-jugs, ashtrays and teapots offer advice on table manners ('Go Easy With The Cream'), moral and philosophical tags, or legends identifying where the piece comes from. These are often in heavy — and sometimes *highly* suspicious — West Country dialect.

In fact this motto-ware comes from the Torquay area, from factories at Aller Vale, Long Park, and Watcombe. It all began after a nineteenth-century job creation scheme when the government of the time attempted to give a boost to cottage industries by running pottery classes — Mr J. Phillips presiding — at Aller Vale, Abbotskerswell, Kingskerswell, and Coffinswell. Around 1887 the motto-ware produced at Aller Vale became a commercial proposition and has been so ever since. The motto is brushed on in slip with a glaze over it or sometimes *sgraffito* may be used. At Watcombe, where the clay is said to be the finest in Britain, a pottery had been established since 1867 for a variety of products including fine ornamental terracotta. At the beginning of this century the two concerns merged to form the Royal Aller Vale and Watcombe Pottery Company. The Longpark Pottery was established in 1905 at Torre, where Isambard Kingdom Brunel's pumping station was.

There is a rich variety of patterns in Devon motto-ware. Aller Vale specialises in abstract designs based on natural history. Watcombe features rather primitive houses and cottages, while Longpark uses black cocks, kingfishers, sailing boats and thistles as some of their trademarks. More recent examples of this quaint pottery, which goes particularly well with cream teas, come from the Devonmoor Art Pottery, the Dartmouth Pottery, the Devonshire Potteries, the Babbacombe Pottery and the Carrigaline Pottery. As with Cornish serpentine rock, Devon motto-ware is sure to become highly collectable in the near future.

Collection: Royal Albert Memorial Museum, Exeter

*Devon motto-ware
coffee pot and loving cup*

dial clock   Only the best was good enough for the servants, and these simple, circular, mahogany-framed clocks were made to hang in the butler's pantry or the servants' dining-room. The very best examples of these handsome and trustworthy clocks had silver dials, punched out brass bezels, and spring-driven German movements. Similar clocks were placed in station waiting rooms, post offices, and anywhere else where time was of the essence. Drop-dial clocks had a case slightly extended underneath (like a sawn off longcase) to take in the pendulum.

diamonds   A pure crystallised carbon which rates 10 on the Mohs scale, diamond is the hardest substance known to man. It is chiefly found in South Africa, India, and Brazil, and is either colourless, or tinted yellow, pink, green, or blue. Of these colours the blue-white diamond is the one which is traditionally valued, and only one diamond in five hundred qualifies; however, 'fancies', or diamonds of a decided colour, are even rarer, and, if they are blue, red, pink or green, even more desirable. Yellows and browns are not sought after. The value of a diamond does not simply depend on colour, but also on clarity, size (of course), and cut. Diamonds were usually 'rose-cut', until Queen Victoria sensationally announced that she would have the rose-cut Koh-i-noor diamond 'brilliant-cut' to show it off to better advantage.

South African diamonds were first imported into Europe in the 1870s; the Boer War was not entirely unconnected with this trade. Electricity, introduced into the Savoy Theatre by D'Oyly Carte, gave brilliant stones the advantage over coloured stones, and the popularity of the diamond remained unchallenged until the Great War.

Book: *Diamonds* by Eric Bruton (N.A.G.Press, 1971)

dog grate   There was some anxiety in the eighteenth century that Britain was running short of timber. The population was increasing fast, and the ship-builders were taking all the available wood. Consequently the use of timber as a fuel had to be restricted by law. However, there was plenty of coal, and this would be brought south from Newcastle and elsewhere on sailing brigs which serviced little ports around the coast. Such coal was known as 'sea-coal'. Obviously firedogs were inadequate to contain coal fires (the coal would just fall through the holes on to the hearth), so they were gradually superseded by basket grates. Initially these were plain, constructed from wrought iron (two large firedogs joined together with a grid of iron bars), but within a hundred years polished, pierced and engraved steel facings were applied to the front of the basket, and these dog grates became objects of great significance in the overall design of a room. Blacksmiths gave way to steelworkers and brass founders, and grates reflected the changing furnishing styles. The very best examples, such as the one from the Old Rectory, Sutton Coldfield, were perfectly characteristic of Adam's style.

At the beginning of the nineteenth century grates became heavier and more florid, and, as chimney pieces became lower, increasingly disproportionate. With the reduction of the grand old fireplace to no more than a hole in the wall, the grate, and the fireback, would be completely enclosed. The surrounds then became supremely important, and they too reflected the tastes of the period, whether neo-gothic, Chinese, or Victorian rococo.

dolls   During the sixteenth and seventeenth centuries dolls were not the baby-dolls we are accustomed to today (which made their appearance *c.*1825), but were dressed like adults. They had wooden or wax heads, and bodies crudely carved from wood or suggested by stuffed rags. It is believed that *papier-mâché* dolls were made in sixteenth-century Germany, chiefly in Nuremberg, but these dolls' heads were moulded from a composition of paper, rye, and animal or vegetable glue — a mixture known as *brotteig* — loved by rats, so sadly few examples have survived.

It was during the early and mid-eighteenth century that the first dolls of real antique quality emerged. These are known as Queen Anne types; they have turned wooden torsos and gesso-covered heads and shoulders. They are primitive but full of character with oval eyes and tiny quizzical mouths. There are jointed limbs on the best examples, but linen and leather tubes stuffed with sawdust are cheaper. Protective import duties were levied against painted dolls from abroad and, although some unpainted German

Jumeau doll, c. *1880*

dolls made their way into Britain, most Queen Anne types were native British. Such dolls were often beautifully and fashionably dressed. A letter from a little girl in 1776 speaks of 'Miss Dolly's mode box just packed up containing a lady *à la mode* in accoutrements.' Dolls were sold door to door by pedlars throughout the eighteenth century. Dolls dressed as pedlars and carrying trays of goods were (and are) popular, the more varied and interesting the items in the tray the greater the popularity.

The Regency period was boom-time for doll makers, and a great many toyshops opened in London. The Old Argyle Rooms was extremely fashionable, and soon the Lowther Arcade in the Strand was to become the toyshop of Europe. Toy makers from Germany produced catalogues from which retailers could choose their lines. Regency *papier-mâché* dolls came with a wide variety of heads which could be attached to available bodies as required. They were often sold undressed and, as a consequence, considerable care was taken over the finish of the bodies. Hairstyles were moulded, unless a particularly complicated style was called for when a wig of human hair would be used.

Wax dolls originated from the effigy figures supplied *c.*1800 to grieving parents of dead children, of whom, alas, there were far too many — infant mortality being then so high. The ability to reproduce in wax precisely the texture and plasticity of human skin gave wax dolls a realism which some find as unnerving as a visit to Madame Tussaud's. The more formal and idealistic china-headed dolls usually prove the more popular. Poured-wax dolls were custom-made, sometimes even with the recipient's own hair, and the lengthy process involved resulted in high prices. For those who couldn't afford these, *papier-mâché* dolls dipped in wax with glued-on wigs (where the poured-wax dolls had hair inserted into the scalp) were a modest alternative.

There were a number of families of wax doll makers, two of whom particularly deserve a mention. Henry Pierotti (*b.*1809) and his family had shops in Argyle Street, Great Ormond Street and Oxford Street. Some of the dolls were modelled on his own children, and look rather Italian, although the hair, made of mohair, was fair or titian. Pierotti dolls have puce colouring and blue eyes. They turn their heads slightly to one side, and, since the same moulds were used for very many years, up until 1930 in some cases, they are not easy to date. (However, machine-made clothes, if original, date a doll after the 1870s.) The Pierottis made portrait dolls of 'The Royal Wax Babies', Queen Victoria's children.

The seven members of the Montanari family produced wax dolls for no more than fifty years during the mid-nineteenth century. Their dolls are plump with rolls of fat around the neck, dark hair and deep violet eyes. A display by Madame Montanari at the Great Exhibition of 1851 of all the ages from infancy to womanhood earned a rebuke from the jury — the dolls were thought too lifelike and, at prices from ten shillings to five guineas undressed, too expensive.

Other notable makers of wax dolls include Herbert Meech, doll maker to the Royal Family (a fruitful commission this, for the Queen had a collection of 132 dolls, now on exhibition at the London Museum), John Edwards, Charles Marsh, and, in the twentieth century, Lucy Peck.

China dolls of the nineteenth century in all their variations have generally survived better than wax dolls (although damage to a wax doll is regarded by collectors less seriously than damage to a china doll). The Germans had a monopoly of porcelain dolls' heads in the mid-nineteenth century. So attractive and so cheap were they that the French were reduced to buying German heads and attaching them to French bodies. German heads were full of character and most accomplished. They whistled, ogled, opened and shut their eyes, and were multi-racial. Simon and Halbig dolls, marked 'S & H' after 1875, wore national costumes, and could sometimes walk and talk.

The French fought back with their Jumeau dolls' heads, made by the Jumeau family between 1844 and 1898. These were made from bisque (unglazed biscuit) and had large, soulful glass eyes with bodies of kid on a wire armature, or jointed wood. The most sought after Jumeau doll is the one with a long face and a closed mouth. But not all dolls claimed by their owners to be Jumeaus in fact are; nor are Jumeaus the best of the bisque-headed dolls. Many believe the Bru doll to be the more remarkable.

In this century the most interesting bisque dolls have been the numbered series of 'babies' produced by the German firm of Kämmer and Reinhardt between 1909 and 1930. These developed the theories of Froebel and Montessori that dolls which were too perfect might be less helpful than more realistic 'character dolls'. One hundred and thirty-one of these were produced, but the last dozen or so are less interesting than the earlier ones, for which the slogan 'Realism combined with Beauty' was coined.

Books: *The Collector's History of Dolls* by C. Eileen King (Robert Hale, 1976); *Dolls* by Antonia Fraser (Octopus Books, 1973); *Dolls* by Marianne and Jurgen Cieslik (Studio Vista, 1979)

Collections: London Museum; Horniman Museum, Dulwich; Museum of Childhood, Bethnal Green, London; Pollock's Toy Museum, London; Penshurst Park, Sussex; Queen's Park Art Gallery, Manchester

dolls' houses The baby houses of the seventeenth century were not intended for children at all but were meticulous recreations in miniature of fashionable interiors. By the early eighteenth century solidly made simple structures, four feet high by three feet wide, with three or four rooms, were being made, chiefly in Germany. They were immensely popular with young girls who, for a few pence, were able to furnish them with all the accoutrements of a real house. (Some of the miniature furniture in rosewood by an anonymous craftsman is very fine.) From 1850 the houses were smaller and meaner proportioned, but the furnishings had become more and more elaborate, with miniature dinner services by Meissen, Spode, and other leading factories. Glass came from Bohemia, ivory furniture from China, and painted furniture from Bavaria. The kitchen equipment, and particularly the plaster food, is especially appetizing.

Books: *English Dolls' Houses* by Vivien Greene (Batsford, 1955; new ed. Bell & Hyman, 1979); *A History of Dolls' Houses* by Flora Gill Jacobs (Cassell, 1954)

Collections: London Museum (Queen Mary doll's house complete with dolls in costume having a picnic); Bethnal Green Museum, London; Queen's Park Art Gallery, Manchester

doorstop or **door-porter** The introduction *c.*1775 of automatic return hinges for doors necessitated the doorstop or door-porter, the earliest examples of which were moulded in earthenware with long handles. Others were manufactured in bronze, cast iron or brass — anything heavy enough to 'stop' a door, in fact — and the opportunity was taken to indulge in fanciful designs. By the 1840s flatbacks in cast iron and bronze were being turned out in large numbers by the Coalbrook Company, which also specialised in door-knockers. Thus we find an armoured knight under a Gothic canopy, Punch (based on Richard Doyle's famous drawing), Ally Sloper, David Lang, the Gretna Green Blacksmith, Jumbo, the zoo-celebrity of the 1860s, and many others.

The Kilner factory in Wakefield produced green bottle glass stops with flower bouquets in air bubbles, and the Nailsea glassworks was originating glass globes like fishing floats, known as 'dumps'. Terracotta, Derbyshire marble and carved wood were also used. There is much reproduction of doorstops, particularly of the skilful creations of the iron founders. The chances are your bell, your Judy, your highlander, your Duke of Wellington, will not be as old as you had supposed it to be.

Collection: Museum of Ironfounding, Coalbrookdale

Doulton   The firm of Doulton and Company has always been something of a contradiction: it was the largest producer of sanitary earthenware (and that means just what you think it means), and yet it was a pioneer in the field of art pottery. The firm was founded in Vauxhall in 1815, moving almost at once to Lambeth High Street; until 1860, it made its money in the tough masculine world of commercial and industrial stoneware, and yet it was among the first British firms to employ women on a significant scale, giving opportunities to such talented artists as Hannah and Florence Barlow, and Emily Edwards.

It was after the Great Exhibition of 1851, where its chimney pots created a modest sensation, that the firm set up, in association with the Lambeth School of Art, its art department, the output of which falls roughly into three categories, Doulton ware, Lambeth faience and impasto.

Doulton ware bears a design scratched by the artist in the soft surface of the clay. Design and ground colour are in harmonious shades, the whole is saltglazed, and given just one firing. Lambeth faience (introduced in 1873) has hand-painted designs on bands of white biscuit, the whole being given a dull glaze and several firings. Impasto (from the late 1870s) has coloured clays added to the surface, giving a design in slight relief with contrast between translucency and opacity heightening the effect. Doulton's designs are never printed, and are always signed with either the name or the monogram of the artist responsible.

In 1901 the factory received the royal warrant from Edward VII, and was thereafter authorised to call itself Royal Doulton. Production at Lambeth concluded in 1956.

Perhaps the most talented artist to practise at Doulton's was George Tinworth (1843–1913), who spent the last forty-seven years of his life at Lambeth and specialised in terracotta panels of religious subjects, including a reredos for York Minster, and series of animals behaving uncharacteristically (mice playing chess, frogs at the Epsom races and such like). Hannah Barlow (1851–1916) decorated her glazed stoneware with charming scenes of domestic animals in familiar landscapes. Her sister Florence (d. 1909) concentrated mainly on birds and flowers. Besides vases, tableware and tea services, Doulton produced some quite unusual pottery pieces, such as bells and menu-card holders.

Book: *The Doulton Lambeth Wares* by Desmond Eyles (Hutchinson, 1976)

dowel   A wooden peg, used in old oak furniture, where in later pieces one would have used a nail. Hence a dowel joint.

Dresden (Meissen) To those accustomed to eating and drinking off and out of ordinary pottery, the delicacy, translucency and whiteness of Chinese porcelain (imported into Europe during the sixteenth century by Portuguese traders) seemed almost magical. So revered was it that Augustus the Strong, King of Poland and Elector of Saxony, exchanged 600 of his soldiers for 117 pieces of Frederick William I of Prussia's Chinese porcelain. How was it made? Nobody could work it out. In Venice an opaque white glass was produced $c.1500$, and in Florence the Medicis pioneered a sort of porcelain towards the end of the sixteenth century. But the breakthrough in about 1708 is credited to E. W. von Tschirnhausen, a mathematician and physicist, and Johann Böttger, an apothecary's assistant and failed alchemist. The following year a factory was set up at Meissen, twelve miles from Dresden, the capital of Saxony. Böttger, whom some say found kaolin — the miracle ingredient for which he had been searching — in his hair powder, was put in charge of the factory but died nine years later, aged only 37.

The earliest Meissen ware was modest enough and limited mainly to tableware. But Böttger's successor, enameller Johann Gregorius Herold (or Höroldt), offered the public pieces with beautifully gilded lacy borders and medallions in the Chinese style. Wonderfully vivid colours were introduced: apple green, lilac, maroon and claret, and the unforgettable yellow which withstood firing best of all. By 1731 Johann Joachim Kändler became the master-modeller producing animals and birds, *Commedia dell' Arte* figures, wreaths, bouquets, chandeliers, and much else of superlative quality. Contemporary groups representing Countess Cosel, Count Brühl and Augustus II are among the very best examples. The same Count Heinrich von Brühl, a powerful minister of the crown, was entitled to all the porcelain he required for his own use free from the factory, and he did not stint himself. He was put in charge of the management of the works until his death in 1764.

The Seven Years War (1756–63) intervened, and many of the Meissen workmen removed to Berlin. The secrets of porcelain manufacture spread far and wide (Sèvres paid an industrial spy £6000 down and £3000 per annum for life for the formula), and Meissen never regained its pre-eminence, which was probably just as well.

But there were other talented artists involved at the factory. Michel Acier, a French sculptor, affected the rococo style for his pastoral figures, his 'Cries of Paris' and his fantastic and slightly sinister monkey bands. Concurrently the finest pictures from the royal collection were copied and white groups were modelled in the antique taste. The Marcolini period (1774–1814) under Count Marcolini's management had very rich decoration with a deep blue ground colour, and finely painted landscapes.

During the nineteenth century, in which the Meissen factory suffered a gradual decline, many parasite companies set up shop in Dresden, adding elaborate decorations in the grand old style to the less distinguished pieces from the parent factory. Such fragmentation, and a certain amount of sharp practice involving counterfeit marks and similar villainies, has meant that the collector should be particularly cautious before mortgaging his house to buy a fine piece of old Meissen.

Books: *Meissen China: An Illustrated History* by K. Berling (Dover Publications, 1973); *Meissen Porcelain* by Otto Walcha (Studio Vista, 1979)
Collections: Central Museum and Art Gallery, Northampton; The Museum, Lancaster

duelling pistol Duelling with pistols replaced duelling with swords in the second half of the eighteenth century. Everything about duelling pistols (also known as cased sets) was subserved to precision and reliability. Barrels were octagonal and true, butts chequered to give added grip, the trigger guards fitted with spurs, balls perfectly shaped, locks trustworthy, balance perfect.

Duelling pistols came in matched pairs, which were beautifully cased, with compartments for all the accessories. So precisely were they engineered that it would be blasphemous to use them for practice. But one had to practise, and for that purpose small-bore target pistols of the same balance and weight as the real thing would be provided. Etiquette required that the injured party offered choice of pistols to his adversary.

dumb waiter A revolving stand with two or three tiers around a central column, described by Sheraton (1803) as 'A useful piece of furniture, to serve in some respects the place of a waiter, whence it is so named.' Some dumb waiters had drawers, some corner-posts, most had a tripod base, and all had castors. In the United States a dumb waiter is a service lift.

Dumb waiter

earthenware   All objects made of clay and fired at temperatures of between 800 and 1200°C are earthenware. At these (comparatively) low temperatures the pieces do not vitrify but remain porous, and so require glazing. Any hotter than this, and the clay becomes stoneware. The whole matter of firing clay is highly delicate. Most primitive pottery was earthenware, and modern tiles, flowerpots, and cooking vessels are similarly made.

Collection: Penrhyn Castle, Bangor

ebony   A hard close-grained wood, heavier than water and almost black, from trees of the genus *Diospyros*. The best wood comes from southern India, Ceylon, and Mauritius. Too brittle to be used except in veneers, ebony became very fashionable in seventeenth-century France, so much so that cabinet-making became known as *ébénisterie*.

eggshell china   A term applied to very thin, white, glassy porcelain, much of which has been imported from Japan since the middle of the last century. Fujiyama is often represented, and decadent versions of older styles of Japanese decoration. The term has also been applied to porcelain produced in America, in imitation of, and sometimes fashioned by workmen from, the Irish Belleek factory of County Fermanagh.

electroplate   Sheffield plate was introduced in the middle of the eighteenth century, because it was cheaper than silver. It was killed a century later because electroplate was cheaper still.

   Electroplate is silver electrolytically deposited on base metal. Elkington's of Birmingham patented their process in about 1840, and then licensed other manufacturers to produce it. Initially copper was the base metal upon which the silver was applied; later Britannia metal and nickel-silver were used (one couldn't see so quickly that the plate was wearing thin). The marks E.P.B.M. and E.P.N.S. indicate the formula used; many spurious silver marks and cowboy legends (such as 'Nevada silver') were added to mislead the unwary. Good quality plate is often stamped with 'A1' or the names of high-class retailers, such as Mappin and Webb.

   Since electroplating is a chemical process, the replating of pieces which have worn thin is straightforward enough. The replating of Sheffield plate (a mechanical process) by electrolysis is not advisable.

elm   Handsome though it looks when growing in the ground, the timber of the common elm (*Ulmus procera*) is not the most glamorous of woods for making furniture. Its light colour and coarse grain make it suitable for table tops and chair seats — it is ideal for the seats of Windsor chairs — and also for coffins. If such gloomy talk depresses you, elm was also traditionally used for shuffle-boards, tables upon which shove-halfpenny was played.

engraving The earliest of the *intaglio* processes for making prints out of pictures, in use since the early fifteenth century. A design is incised in a copper or zinc plate with a burin, a sharp tool not unlike a gouge. The plate is then inked but the high-standing areas are wiped clean before damp paper is pressed against the plate. The printed image emerges from the incised areas of the plate, and a plate-mark is left on the paper itself. In the bottom margin of an engraving one might expect to see 'pinx.' followed by the name of the painter and 'f.' or 'fec.' or 'sc.' or 'sculp.' followed by the name of the engraver.

envelope table A table over which four hinged triangular leaves fold (like envelope flaps) to cover the working surface of the table. Often such tables were — indeed are — used for card playing, and, since the surface has usually been protected for most of its life, its condition is often very fine.

epergne One sympathises with those doomed to spend night after night at banquets: rising to one's feet endlessly for loyal toasts, the awful struggle to keep one's cigar alight, and that cataclysmic problem of which *petit-four* to choose. The Victorians did what they could to help them. The epergne was specially designed to make things easier (*épargner*) for the diners. It was a decorative centrepiece with dishes for fruit, breath sweeteners and *bonbons*; one didn't have to pass things, just help oneself. Some epergnes were merely flower-holders, others had mirror glass bases. Curious shapes, colours, and materials were frequently used for these epergnes, which could be of huge and horrifying aspect.

Curiously the French don't call an epergne an epergne. They call it a *surtout de table*.

ephemera Since ephemera, by definition, means things which are short-lived (literally mayflies which live only for a day) it is a paradox to talk of collecting them. However the Ephemera Society and its members do just that, collecting and studying 'the transient minor documents of everyday life'. So next time you turn out your desk contact the Society at 12 Fitzroy Grove, London W.1.

escapement Without being too technical, the escapement in a clock or watch is that part of the mechanism which locks and unlocks the train, thereby controlling the driving power of the pendulum or balance.

The oldest form of escapement is the verge, used from the thirteenth century until the late eighteenth century in bracket clocks and until the mid-nineteenth century in watches. The anchor or recoil system was used only for pendulum clocks and was more accurate than the verge. The cylinder (invented 1695) depended on a slotted hollow ruby cylinder and was used only for watches, as was the lever escapement, invented in the mid-1760s by Thomas Mudge, and so well invented that it is still in use in an age of quartz and silicon chips. The grasshopper had a jumping action, as you might expect, while the deadbeat (invented by George Graham) was a modification of the anchor escapement.

Escapements

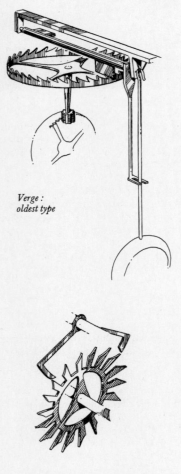

Verge :
oldest type

Anchor : credited to
William Clement, c. 1657

Dead beat : modified anchor
invented by George Graham, 1715

Lever : attributed to
Thomas Mudge, 1770

escritoire   Call it an *escritoire*, *secrétaire*, secretary, *scriptoire*, or *scrutoire*, what you are referring to is a fall-front bureau, or writing cabinet. To try to draw a distinction, as the admirable John Gloag does in *A Short Dictionary of Furniture*, between the first three, which he claims have 'a hinged front that lies flat when a drawer is pulled out', and the last two ('fall-down front writing cabinets') is perhaps sliding in the direction of pedantry. All are quite simply writing cabinets.

escutcheon or **scutcheon**   (a) A metal plate of ornamental design covering a keyhole, as may be seen on a knife-box, bureau, and so on; (b) a small plate bearing the maker's name on, say, a gun or a clock; (c) a carved armorial shield decorating the pediment of a large piece of cased furniture; (d) a shield bearing a coat of arms, or (e) the coat of arms itself, or (f) the field upon which the coat of arms appears.

étagère   A tier of shelves for displaying trinkets and *objets de vertu*, usually designed in a square Louis XVI style with ormolu decorations and a brass gallery. As you might expect, cabriole legs were *de rigueur*, and *étagères* were usually made from tulipwood, kingwood, or inlaid satinwood.

etching   One of the *intaglio* processes of printing pictures. An acid-resistant substance (wax or varnish) is laid on a metal plate (usually copper or zinc), and the artist scratches his design through this ground with an etching needle. The plate is then dipped in an acid bath, so that the acid 'bites' the exposed metal. The depth of the line can be varied by exposing the metal to the acid for longer or shorter periods. The plate is then inked and printed as an engraved plate would be.

Fabergé

> *Yea, faileth now even dream*
> *The dreamer, and the lute the lutanist;*
> *Even the linked fantasies, in whose blossomy twist*
> *I swung the earth a trinket at my wrist.*
> Francis Thompson, *The Hound of Heaven*

So must Fabergé have felt when his beautiful trinkets, so dreadfully fashionable, so fashionably expensive, were confiscated by the Bolsheviks in 1918.

Peter Carl Fabergé (1846–1920) was the first son of Gustav (1814–93), who in 1842 had founded the firm of goldsmiths and jewellers in St Petersburg which bore the family name. But it was only when Peter Carl took over the running of the business in 1870 that international success was assured. He became the Russian Imperial Court's official jeweller. Every year from 1884 he made an Easter egg for presentation to the Empress

Maria Fedorovna, and other fantasy objects produced at Fabergé's included trees, animals, flowers and fruit in jade, and precious and semi-precious stones. Useful gifts included scent-bottles, pencils, cigarette-cases, and bell-pushes. Materials used included gold, diamonds, emeralds, rubies, enamel, indigenous Russian stones like chalcedonies, tourmalines, amethysts and moonstones. Besides Peter Carl's brother, Agathon, Zaion-tchovsky, the silversmith, and of course Peter Carl himself, the most notable talents were August and Albert Holmström and August Hollming.

Books: *Peter Carl Fabergé* by H. C. Bainbridge (Hamlyn, 1966); *Easter Eggs: A Collector's Guide* by Victor Houart (Souvenir Press, 1978); *Fabergé* by Geza von Habsbourg and Alexander Solodkoff (Studio Vista, 1979); *Carl Fabergé* by A. K. Snowman (Debrett's Peerage Ltd, 1979)

faience There is a Faenza, near Bologna, and a Fayence, in France, and tin-glazed earthenware was made at both, which is confusing. The term faience has come to stand however for any tin-glazed earthenware from France or Germany (Bayreuth, for instance), to distinguish it from Italian maiolica, Dutch Delft, or English delftware. For further help, see *Delft*.

fairings Originally fairings were small china ornaments which the fortunate and the skilful could win at fairground stalls. They were known as bed pieces, since beds figured prominently in most of them; a little sententiously as cottage mantelshelf china; and, in Lancashire, as fairings. Towards the end of the last century their popularity was such that they did not always go to fairgrounds at all, but were simply sold across the shop counter. Their manufacture lasted for fifty years from 1860, and the most surprising thing about them is that, although they appear as British as marmalade tart and grumbling about the weather, they were made in Germany and (a very few) Austria.

There are two sorts of china ornament which, by general consent, qualify as fairings: groups of figures up to mischief, and boxes with small decorations on their lids. The groups have captions, the boxes rarely so. The subjects treated range from the indelicate to the sentimental. Indeed the early fairings, with such titles as 'Two Different Views' (one gentleman with a telescope admiring the natural habitat, the other, unobserved, glancing down the front of a demure lady's frock) tend towards rudery, and the later ones (girls with puppies, young match-sellers) towards the whimsical.

They can be characterised under six broad headings: the relationship between the sexes; household matters; soldiers (usually from the Franco-Russian War of 1870 in which Britain remained neutral, but occasionally from the Crimea); cynical legal and political scenes; children; and animals. The first category is by far the biggest, the humans depicted behaving in a rather beastly manner, unlike the animals who behave like humans. Quite the most common and hence the cheapest is the ubiquitous 'The last in bed to put out the light'. Other familiar subjects include a lovesick landlord with a fondness for peeping through keyholes, 'An Awkward Interruption', which needs no explanation, and 'Three O'clock in the Morning', in which a baby has to be rocked to sleep. The attitudes are those of comic postcards, with henpecked husbands drowning their sorrows, and puppies misbehaving in the hall.

The East German factory responsible for producing the majority of fairings was Springer and Oppenheimer (now in Czechoslovakia and still in business as Karlovarsky Porcelain). There were other German factories, plus a factory in Japan in the early twentieth century which seems improbably to have favoured Welsh scenes.

Book: *Victorian China Fairings* by W. S. Bristowe (A. & C. Black, 1964)

One of the 'Vienna Series' of fairings made in 1860 at the Royal Vienna Factory

fakes Strictly speaking, to forge is to copy something that already exists, while to fake (originally thieves' slang for beating someone up) is to produce an item, hitherto unknown, in the style of somebody else, or to make an existing article (for instance a piece of white china) look like something else by adding ornamentation (for instance, fruit and flowers in the Worcester manner). Neither forgery nor fakery is illegal, unless it can be proved that there exists an intention to deceive. Forgers who only wish to show up experts as not worth the paper their authentications are written on, may be acting within the law. Reproductions are honest forgeries.

A rough estimate by John FitzMaurice Mills, who has made a detailed study of this subject, puts the percentage of fakes and forgeries passing through the antiques trade at $12\frac{1}{2}$ per cent. He also suggests that the annual turnover in the trade is a formidable £1500 million. Add to the $12\frac{1}{2}$ per cent the number of pieces which are not wholly original and one realises that the business is very big indeed.

It is in the picture galleries that the most expensive fakes can be found. The criminals have become quite expert, and the sophisticated equipment needed to trap them is both costly and hard to get hold of in a hurry. The most difficult fakes to spot are contemporary pastiches — Dürer and Cranach were much copied in their lifetime. Artisan fakers should not be too difficult to identify: their work may be accurate as to pigment, brushwork, and so on, but it cannot come close to the spirit of the originals. Artists like van Meegeren came very close to their models, and some of their fakes are now fetching considerable prices themselves.

So far as furniture is concerned, the age of the wood is the element that can never be satisfactorily reproduced. Young wood produces 'white edges' when chipped or cut. Antique wood would certainly have been left to mature for ten years before being worked. Large cased pieces are less likely to be ungenuine than small elegant pieces (commodes and bureaux), and the more intricate the craftsmanship the surer you can be of its authenticity. Machine screws ought to indicate a date later than 1852. Brass mountings are frequently anachronistic and give the game away. Warping is usually a sign of age, but not inevitably. When a piece of furniture has been artificially aged it is said to have been 'distressed', and when it has been made up from components of two or more pieces, it is said to have been 'married'.

So far as ceramics go, a great deal of pirating of patterns went on in the early days of porcelain manufacture, which makes it difficult now to separate supposed sheep from suspected goats. A mark may easily be removed by using an acid solution or a quartz stick; a more desirable mark may then be painted on and lacquered over.

Silver is little faked, though hallmarks have been fiddled from time to time. Horse brasses, on the other hand, are rarely genuine. Fairings — and especially the rarer items — are also best treated with caution. Coins were forged in the Lebanon on a vast scale. Scientific instruments, copper, cast iron doorstops, ships' decanters, warming pans, cased glass, pistols and long guns (especially those with percussion actions), pewter, Rockingham pastille-burners, lustreware, Toby jugs, Mary Gregory glass, Fabergé eggs, oil lamps, sporting prints, money banks from Taiwan, there is almost no area which has not now been worked over by the fakers.

Jewellery is currently one of the thickest jungles. The latest artificial diamonds (djevalites) appear authentic down to the sooty impurities, and *real* diamonds, by scientific definition, have been created, albeit expensively, in Schenectady.

It's tough, but there are precautions which the innocent can take to protect himself in a wicked world. He can demand an invoice from a dealer, which invoice should contain details of all purchases. If the purchases then turn out to be inferior models, he can get the dealer under the Trades Descriptions Act. He can concentrate at auctions on sales of 'effects'. He should avoid buying a 'name', or at least avoid paying extra for one. Signatures and marks of all kinds are very tempting, but may well be unauthentic. He should get an expert to help if possible; *never* buy when he has suspicions; beware of improbably generous 'bargains'; and, finally, trust the evidence of his own eyes and buy what he likes. Unless you intend to resell, it matters little who made your chair, or painted your picture; what matters is that you're happy with it.

Books: *How to Detect Fake Antiques* by John FitzMaurice Mills (Arlington Books, 1972); *The Genuine Article* by John FitzMaurice Mills and John Mansfield (BBC Publications, 1979)

fall-front A rather grand phrase calculated, like so many in the antiques business, to frighten off the ingenuous. It simply refers to the writing part of a desk or cabinet which has to be lowered to be written on.

famille jaune A variety of decorative Chinese porcelain produced during the early years of the K'ang-Hsi period (1661–1722) of the Ch'ing Dynasty. The ground is pale yellow, the prevailing colours are shades of yellow, while the contrasting decorations are coloured in enamels.

The following note is applicable also to the next three entries. Chinese ceramics are so bound up with the history, the mythology, the literature and the religions of the Chinese people that it is not easy to study them in isolation. Dragons, for instance, are not just dragons, but symbols, and the number of their claws has its own significance. Similarly with colours: each dynasty has its colour, each colour its symbolic reference. Only in the West is it safe to assume that a rose is a rose is a rose.

famille noire Fine Chinese decorative porcelain of the K'ang-Hsi period in which a black ground, sometimes unglazed, and tinged with green, is used to display white sprigs of prunus or cherry blossom.

famille rose An exceptionally fine variety of Chinese decorative porcelain celebrated and honoured for its rose-pink tinge. The first blushes crept into Chinese porcelain *c.*1720, or at the very end of the K'ang Hsi period (1661–1722), and continued through the Yung-Cheng period (1723–35) and the Ch'ien Lung period (1736–95). Typical ornaments featured include the peony, the chrysanthemum, the lily, the mushroom, plus elaborate processions of elders. The enamel painting on *famille rose* pieces is slightly raised over the whole or a part of the pattern. Towards the end of the Ch'ien Lung period, which was the last great period for Chinese porcelain, Western culture began to cast its baleful influence over *famille rose*, although in Europe the Chinese influence on Western porcelain was almost entirely healthy.

famille verte A major class of Chinese decorative porcelain produced initially towards the end of the Ming Dynasty (1368–1644). The characteristic colour is, of course, green in many different shades, with the addition of pale yellow panels. The subjects treated, dragons, baskets of flowers, and Buddhist symbols, are painted over the glaze, and stand out in slight relief. Besides green, yellow, and blue, the principal colours include iron-red and purple. The effect sounds daunting, but is mysterious and brilliant.

fans   Stick fans originated in the East thousands of years ago and were brought west by Portuguese traders who knew a good line when they saw one. It was Queen Elizabeth I who created a vogue for folding fans. Early European fans were Chinese in style, ornately carved, with scenes painted across the leaves of chicken-skin parchment. (Chicken-skin is not what you think but worse, being a vellum, exceptionally thin and supple, made from the skins of newly born lambs.) *Brisés* were folding fans composed entirely of overlapping sticks, and bound by ribbon threaded through slots in the tops of the sticks.

The French tradition of fan-making outlasted the English. There was not a single British-made fan at the Great Exhibition of 1851. Regency silk fans gave way to lace, sticks and mounts were of mother-of-pearl, ivory or tortoiseshell. There were monogrammed fans, jewelled fans, and fans with matching parasols. One could have a Dubarry fan with a peep-hole in it, a mirror fan to enable one to see what was going on behind one, a telescopic fan to fit into a purse.

After 1876, when there was a grand fan exhibition in South Kensington, one could hardly move for the things. Huge ostrich-feather fans, tambour fans which opened when one pulled a cord in the handle, black mourning fans, all with satin lined boxes to keep them in. By the end of the century, fans had become thoroughly vulgar, being used to advertise tradespeople and hotels.

Books: *Collectors' History of Fans* by Nancy Armstrong (Studio Vista, 1974); *The Fan* by Mary Gostelow (Gill & Macmillan, 1976); *A Collecting Guide to Fans over the Ages* by Bertha de Vere Green (Frederick Muller, 1975)
Collections: Waddesdon Manor, Aylesbury; Grosvenor Museum, Chester; Tudor House, Southampton (Franks Collection); Castle Museum, York

felspar, feldspar or **feltspar**   A group of silicates of alumina found in rock formations. Felspathic glaze has the property of fusing only at a very high temperature. Josiah Spode II and John Rose of Coalport both made use of deposits of felspar found on the Welsh-Shropshire border to produce a hard and durable white ware similar to bone china. Felspar porcelain is also the trade name used by Spode for a type of china made in the 1820s.

fiddle-back   Musical instrument shapes are so satisfactory that they are frequently included in furniture designs. Thus a lyre-back chair; thus too the fiddle-back, in which the shape of a violin appears in the splat design at the back of the chair. Fiddlebacks are eighteenth-century chairs.

finial Originally an architectural term, a finial is a terminal ornament of an apex or a corner. The 'pepperpots' on the old Ministry of Defence building in Whitehall, London, are finials. In antique jargon the term finial applied to anything spike-shaped decorating the top of a piece of furniture, silver, plate, etc. Finials were themselves subject to the changes in classic styles. A unicorn is a horse with a finial.

fireback As soon as the open fire, so necessary to heat the huge Elizabethan banqueting halls, had been moved from the centre of the room — not a good place to put a fire since there was no way of dispersing the smoke — to the wall, a new problem presented itself. How could one preserve brickwork from the heat? The answer was the fireback, which, in its most primitive form, was simply a square or rectangle of cast iron.

Obviously the iron founders (the most talented were those of the Sussex Weald) regarded such an artifact as something of a challenge, and after a while — we are talking now of the end of the sixteenth century — decorations were added. Rope borders would do, prints of hands and feet, whether human or animal, patterns created by any domestic tools close at hand. Coats of arms, Biblical and historical scenes, mythical figures burgeoned forth behind the friendly glow of the log fire. Such pieces were primitive in their design but exceptional in their craftsmanship.

There are many fakes on the market but these may be spotted by an observant collector. If a fireback has been exposed to smoke for centuries, expect it to have substantial deposits of lead. A thin layer, which is easily removed, indicates a recent reproduction. Genuine antique rust is nice and dark but the ersatz variety is an unhealthy orange.

Collections: Hampton Court, Greater London; Art Gallery and Museum, Brighton; Anne of Cleves House, Lewes; Petworth House, Petworth (Mitford Collection)

firedog, otherwise known as **andiron** Firedog is the most appropriate name (they're also called 'cob irons' and 'brand irons') because these pieces look a great deal like dogs. Their essentials are four legs (two at either end), heavy round heads, and some sort of horizontal bar, the billet bar, doing duty as the body on which the logs could be laid. For the purpose of these homely animals was to support the logs and prevent them from rolling onto the floor, while permitting an under-draught of air to keep the flames merrily blazing.

Early firedogs were made of cast iron by the iron founders of the Sussex Weald (other, though less skilful, practitioners came from the Forest of Dean, Yorkshire and Derbyshire), and these sixteenth-century examples are heavy, honest and straightforward. By the mid-seventeenth century firedogs were becoming more ornamental, being made of brass, either plain or enamelled in the colourful style known as Surrey enamel. Small central dogs would support the fire, large dogs would stand guard at either end. A writer in 1662 commented: 'The little creepers, not the great Brass shining Andirons bear up all the heat of the fire.'

By the mid-seventeenth century the dog grate had taken over the role of the firedogs; it was a simple matter to convert the litter of pups into one large freestanding structure. Coal was rapidly replacing wood as the basic fuel to be burned in the home; by the reign of Queen Anne the firedog no longer had any significant job to do, and became a decorative feature.

French firedogs — or *chenets* — of the eighteenth century were made of ormolu in the elaborate prevailing styles, while in the Metropolitan Museum, New York, a fine example of a pair of firedogs by the noted silversmith, Paul Revere (1735–1818) may be seen. By then houses were no longer being built on the massive Elizabethan scale, and the huge old firedogs would have had nowhere to put their paws.

Collections: The Museum, Battle; The Museum, Horsham; Anne of Cleves House, Lewes

firemarks In 1774 an Act of Parliament made London churchwardens responsible for maintaining a fire appliance within their parish. Insurance companies formed irregular fire-brigades through their clerks and executives. In 1833 these companies combined to form the London Fire Brigade, under the command of one James Braidwood, himself to die in a fire twenty-eight years later. In 1866 the Metropolitan Board took over the whole operation of fighting fires in London.

Firemarks were issued by insurance companies and were fixed to an exterior wall of buildings which had been insured. Thus you could depend on the fire-fighters, especially if they were your own employees, to do their best to extinguish the fire, and to protect your property.

Since not all the firemen were literate it was necessary that firemarks be figurative. A seven-pointed star, for instance, stood for the 'Suffolk and General County Amicable Insurance Office' (one of these was recently sold at auction for £540). Early firemarks were of lead, and had different devices for the building and for the chattels. Later versions were made of copper and cast metal and tin, one device doing double duty for building and chattels.

Firemarks

A word of warning. As with other collectable items, there are many modern reproductions of firemarks. But it should be possible to tell the real antiques, when you consider how they must have been exposed to the elements throughout all the seasons of many, many years.

Collections: Chartered Insurance Institute, London (and the head offices of many insurance companies); Belvoir Castle, Grantham; City Museum, Winchester; Castle Museum, York

firescreen That there were firescreens in the fifteenth century we know from a Campin picture in the National Gallery, London, and occasional metalwork firescreens from the sixteenth century have survived. But it was not until the reign of William and Mary that firescreens came into general use. These were cheval screens, free-standing wooden frames with sliding panels of fabric, usually displaying French influence in the carving.

Pole screens, standing on tripods and with movable panels, became fashionable during the eighteenth century, as did small folding firescreens, sometimes of fretwork and in the Chippendale style. Thereafter the styles of firescreens followed those of other furniture, slimming during the eighteenth century to elegantly slender proportions, then becoming more grandiose with the Victorian desire for portentousness. Banner screens with rosewood stands and silk banners bearing coats of arms were consistently popular.

Firescreens were made from metals, various woods including bamboo, *papier mâché*, glass, needlework, and beading. Many have not survived, or have been adapted to create other pieces of furniture. The most frequently found nowadays are tapestry firescreens in mahogany frames.

flashed glass Flashing means dipping a piece of clear lead glass (incorrectly known as flint glass) into molten coloured glass. A thin coat of colour then adheres, and several layers are thus built up, into which engravings may be cut in the manner of cameo glass (see *cased glass*).

flatbacks These earthenware groups made in Staffordshire have few pretensions. Their press-moulding is unsubtle, their colours are not what you might call sophisticated, and the best that can be said of them is that they are cheerful. Highwaymen, Wesley, political figures, highlanders, a prince and princess (based on Victoria and Albert), the Prodigal's Return: these are the sort of subjects you will find. Their backs were flat because they were made to be viewed from one side only, thus the price could be kept down. The price is down no longer, although there are so many modern reproductions around that trying to buy an old flatback is a hazardous undertaking.

Books: *Staffordshire Portrait Figures* by P. D. G. Pugh (Barrie & Jenkins, 1970); *Staffordshire Chimney Ornaments* by R. G. Haggar (Phoenix, 1955)

flatware   A term used by people in the know to describe anything, well, *flat*, such as cutlery, dishes, plates, and trays, used on the table. The converse, therefore, of hollow-ware.

flintlock   A simplification of the snaplock, this mechanism, invented by the French gunsmith Marin Le Bourgeoys, was to become the standard for two hundred years from the mid-seventeenth century.

The firing mechanism was held fast by the 'tumbler', upon which two notches were cut, thus the firearm could be kept at half-cock (safety lock) or at full-cock (ready for firing). The flintlock was much easier to load and to fire than earlier weapons, and was extremely reliable. It could be fitted (and was) to every conceivable type of weapon: single-, double-, and multi-barrelled, travelling, belt, holster, and duelling pistols, sporting guns, muskets, and carbines. It could even be fitted with spring bayonets. The blunderbuss was usually flintlock-fired.

Book: *Flintlock Guns and Rifles* by F. Wilkinson (Arms and Armour Press, 1971)
Collection: City Art Gallery and Museum, Kelvingrove, Glasgow

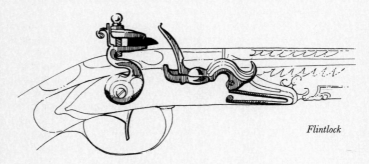

Flintlock

footstools   In the Middle Ages, kings on their high thrones needed footstools or at least cushions for their feet. Footstools usually accompanied chairs in Elizabethan and Jacobean furniture. Gouty or gout stools were, said Hepplewhite, 'particularly useful to the afflicted', and when Boswell visited Pitt in Bond Street, he found his friend dressed in black 'with white nightcap and foot all wrapped up in flannel on a gout-stool'. These gout stools were usually made in mahogany, and were sometimes adjustable.

The golden age of footstools was the Victorian age. They were usually produced in pairs, and were round (occasionally oval or rectangular) with low cabriole, bun, or pad feet. Needlework, woolwork, and beadwork provided the decoration; long fender stools were almost always upholstered with Berlin woolwork and a design of lilies. The footstool was sometimes hinged to expose a spittoon (or *salivarium*).

forks   The use of forks at table as the regular means of conveying meat to the mouth is comparatively recent, only about three hundred years old in fact. Previously one simply used one's fingers, except in Italy where table manners were most refined. It was acceptable for a number of people to eat from the same dish with their fingers, because in Britain precedence at the dinner-table was strictly observed. Things were not so in Germany. Richard Smith, travelling there in 1563, wrote: 'In every inne where we came all the gests must sit to gether be they never suche slaves, as we were in many places at syt with suche slaves that a man would abhor to se suche fylthye hands in his dishe.'

Obviously the refinement of table-forks would have to be introduced into England, but it took time, and foreigners visiting in the early years of Charles II's reign were miffed to find that they were expected to eat with their fingers. Some travelled with their own forks, matched with spoons — sometimes also with knives — fitted in a leather or shagreen case. In the Victoria and Albert Museum you may see a silver table-fork with the hallmark for 1623, which is one of the very earliest. (Forks were used at table as early as the fourteenth century, but only for delicacies.

If the hallmark on a silver fork has been rubbed away, the best means of dating it is to hunt around for a spoon with a similar handle. But if you are concerned with a fork with steel prongs, look for a knife with a matching handle. Very early forks had sharply pointed prongs to hold the joint of meat while it was being carved and for serving. Later forks were blunted, as they are today, to save injury.

It is not possible to date a fork by the number of prongs it bears, but generally the three-pronged fork was the most popular during the eighteenth century, and the four-pronged during the nineteenth. Two-pronged forks are also common enough.

Collection: City Museum, Sheffield

four hundred day clock   This was also known as the anniversary clock for the very good reason that it would run for a year — indeed for four hundred days — on a single winding. Invented by Anton Harden, a German clockmaker, in 1880, and run by an anchor escapement, the four hundred day clock has not been an unqualified success, since, once it goes wrong, it is extremely difficult to regulate. These clocks are often displayed under glass domes, and are still made today.

friggers   At the end of the day the glass blower frigged, that is to say he used up any oddments still lying on his bench to make whimsical presents for the children, or utensils for the wife. Apparently the practice was most energetically indulged in at Nailsea, near Bristol. Friggers included such items as walking sticks, bugles, pipes, rolling pins, whips, pens, top-hats, 'dumps' (doorstops), pistols filled with liquorice, and tadpoles which stayed intact however hard you hit them on the head, but shattered as soon as you tapped them on the tail. Friggers were usually of coloured glass, threaded, flecked, or latticed. Towards the end of the last century their commercial possibilities were appreciated and they were mass-produced in Stourbridge and Alloa, as well as in Nailsea.

frog-mug   The frog-mug was a mid-nineteenth century practical joke. The idea was to provide one's drinking companion with a vessel at the bottom of which there was a modelled frog (or sometimes lizard) attempting to climb up the side. Frog-mugs were usually made of a white stone china, known as granite ware, and had a hard and durable glaze. They were produced chiefly at Leeds, Sunderland, and Nottingham, but plenty of other centres must share the blame.

fruitwood   A generic term covering trees bearing apples, cherries, pears, and plums. Applewood (*Malus pumila*) is a heavy reddish-brown hardwood with a healthy, straight grain, used as a veneer, and also for the turned legs, spindles, and stretchers of country furniture. Cherrywood (*Prunus avium*) is a handsome, red, close-grained hardwood used for much the same purposes as applewood. The Morris men of the arts and crafts movement used it attractively for decorative inlay.

Pearwood (*Pyrus communis*) is a fine light-coloured hardwood recommended by John Evelyn for 'Stools, Tables, Chairs, Pistol-Stocks, Instrument-Maker (*sic*), Cabinets, and very many works of the Joyner . . . and Sculptor, either for flat, or emboss'd-works, and to Engrave upon, because the Grain intercepts not the Tool.' It was used for country furniture, for inlay (stained black to imitate ebony), for picture and mirror frames, for clock brackets, and various smaller items. Plumwood (*Prunus domestica*) is a heavy hardwood, coloured from yellowish to reddish brown, and used for turned work and inlay.

Fulham pottery   It is not true to claim, as many have done, that John Dwight, who obtained a patent in 1671 to manufacture 'transparent porcellane' at his Fulham works, was the first to make porcelain in England. He wasn't, because his 'porcellane' is really only a translucent earthenware. However, he was a remarkable modeller, and takes the credit for fine stoneware busts of, among others, Prince Rupert and Mrs Pepys, both of which are now in the British Museum. In the Victoria and Albert Museum is a particularly poignant halflength figure of a dead child, inscribed: 'Lydia Dwight, dyd March 3 1673'.

Other examples of Fulham ware are reddish brown and saltglazed, while tankards and jugs are decorated in relief with hunting scenes, beefeaters, celebrities, and humorous and satirical vignettes. Fulham also produced domestic, sanitary and chemical items.

After the death of John Dwight, the pottery was carried on for a while by his daughter, until it went bankrupt. After many vicissitudes and little success, it was improved and enlarged by C. J. C. Bailey in 1864. Jugs, mugs, and vases were then produced in the newly fashionable Japanese manner. In 1888 the pottery was taken over by the tile-maker William de Morgan (1839–1917), whose designs in art nouveau styles were executed by Italian artists. In 1905 de Morgan bravely left the works to write novels (in which field he had some success) and the pottery closed again in 1907. However, the last time I drove down the New Kings Road, it was still there, and still in business.

furniture See under types of furniture (e.g., *Windsor chair*), styles of furniture, (e.g., *Hepplewhite*), types of ornamentation (e.g., *cabriole legs*), and varieties of wood (e.g., *oak*).

fusée Dating from the fifteenth century, a fusée is a spirally grooved tapering cone found in the movement of a spring-driven watch or clock. When the key is turned a gut, chain or wire is drawn on to the spiral, thus ensuring that the tension remains even as the spring uncoils. Good time-keeping results.

gadrooning An eighteenth-century stylised decoration used on the edges of tables, silver trays, glass bowls, and so on. Gadrooning usually takes the form of convex curves, or sequences of convex and concave ones.

Gallé, Émile Émile Gallé (1846–1904) came from Meisenthal, where his father made china, glass, and furniture. He made his name at the various Paris expositions with his re-interpretations of the art forms of medieval Europe and Japan. His knowledge of horticulture was also turned to good advantage. In 1874 he established a workshop in Nancy for the production of earthenware, stoneware, and porcelain. His pots were decorated with heraldic designs and developed ideas initiated by the Dutch designers at Delft. Believing, as he did, that for every desired effect a particular technique would have to be developed, he moved into glassware, designing a vertical disc for engraving deep into tinted glass. But this was only one of a number of innovations Gallé introduced at Nancy, where he became the influential prophet of the École de Nancy.

Gallé made cameo glass, an ornamental glass of two or more coloured layers in which the decorations stand out in high relief. He used the contrasts between transparent and opaque glass, and clear and coloured glass to get his effects. The technique had been popular with the Romans and had resulted in the Portland Vase, which Wedgwood copied in jasperware and with which he marked much of his finest china. Examples of cameo glass were also produced by the Chinese in the eighteenth century with their snuff-boxes; by John Northwood, the glass engraver from Stourbridge in the nineteenth century, who also copied from the Portland Vase with notable success (winning a prize of £1000); and by the nineteenth-century German and Bohemian glassmakers.

Gallé went on to make *clair-de-lune* glass, an opalescent glass which apparently becomes blue under certain light; *marqueterie sur verre*, coloured glass sections inset into a larger glass object and then wheel-carved; and *verreries parlantes*, decorative glassware upon which have been incised symbolic fragments of verse, the design and coloration of the whole being intended to illustrate the quotation. He worked on *verreries tristesses*, sombre vases with sombre verses reflecting upon the nature of mortality and the hopelessness of the human condition; and *verre triplé*, in which three layers of glass are superimposed to give depth and contrast to the designs.

From 1900 onwards Gallé turned his talents to the decoration of electric lamps, his most famous (and most frequently imitated) design being an illuminated flower, poking its head shyly from between half-opened petals. The glassworks at Nancy continued — with an interruption for the Great War — until 1935. The earliest pieces from the works (1880–89) are the finest; from 1889 onwards all were signed.

Gallé also designed characteristic furniture, in which the ideas explored in pottery and glass were further tested in wood. The shapes were based on natural models (trees and flowers, etc.) with marquetry decoration in fruitwood and inlaid inscriptions. He also undertook major commissions for private clients. A notable collector of Gallé vases was King Farouk who had a collection of over a hundred pieces at the time of his death, as well as numerous lamps. These were all sold for the derisory sum (with hindsight) of between £15 and £20 each.

Book: *Émile Gallé* by Philippe Garner (Academy Editions, 1976)

garnets The name for garnet comes from the Latin *granatum*, a pomegranate, and it is well chosen since the pulp of the pomegranate seed is red. Garnets are very much more ancient than their reputation as one of the mainstays of Victorian jewellery suggests. It is highly probable that the Biblical carbuncle was, in fact, the garnet. If so, it was a garnet that was set in Aaron's breastplate.

In the early eighteenth century when garnets came into fashion they were elaborately set, but towards the end of the century garnet jewellery became a great deal plainer. Garnets in closed settings frequently had a bit of foil inserted underneath to make them sparkle more brilliantly. Cabochon garnets were often hollow-cut for much the same reason. During the nineteenth century there was a revival of interest in garnets for secondary jewellery. Small pieces of garnet set in clusters came from Austria, Germany, and Czechoslovakia. These stones were inferior ones. Garnets are not all red: yellow, violet and green are also found (the colour varying with the minerals present in the rocks). The green demantoid garnet is probably the most valuable.

garniture de cheminée   The full set of five pieces — clock, two urns and two mirrors — which comprises a *garniture de cheminée*, is rarely found together; in most cases the mirrors have been dispersed. These sets, often extremely ornate with ormolu decorations sometimes in the rococo style, were designed — as the name suggests — to be displayed on a mantelpiece. They date from the late seventeenth century.

gate-leg table   Gate-leg tables first came into popular use in the post-Restoration period when it was fashionable to dine at small, separate tables. The earliest ones, which date from the seventeenth century, were triangular or semicircular, and stood against the wall when not in use. These were commonly made from oak, fruitwoods, and yew. Gate-leg tables may have one or two hinged flaps, supported by 'gates' which swing out from the central section. They are also known as drop-leaf tables, but the drop-leaf table need not have 'gates'.

gesso   A composition of plaster of Paris or whiting and size used in the construction of bas reliefs and other architectural features. A dollop of gesso would be added to a base of softwood (usually deal), and shaped to follow the line of a traced pattern. The surface would then be sanded and gilded. The vogue for gesso lasted from about 1700 until the mid 1730s. It was generally applied to such pieces as side-tables, candlestands, and mirror frames (for which it was particularly suitable). It looks fine in good condition, and particularly unattractive when disintegrating.

girandole   See *sconce*.

glass   There are some liquids which may be cooled below their freezing point without crystallising. What happens to them then is that they become increasingly viscous and stiff until they appear to be solids. Then, technically, they can be called glass, as — to extend the parallel — can toffee which is a supercooled sugar solution. Almost all commercial glass is made from sand, limestone, or sodium carbonate (soda ash). Rock-crystal is natural quartz, and is almost colourless and translucent.

Glass can not only be treated like jewellery, and turned, cut and engraved, but, when warm, it becomes plastic and can be inflated with a blow-pipe or poured into a mould, decorated with trailing threads, coloured with metallic oxides, gilded, cameo-carved through layers of opaque glass, or 'overlaid'. When the artist-craftsman responds to the peculiarities of this most unusual substance, the result will be artifacts of great beauty.

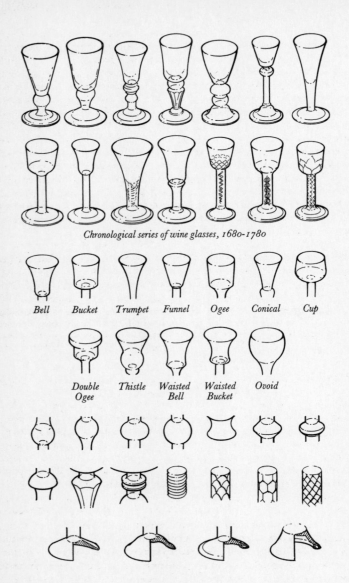

Chronological series of wine glasses, 1680–1780

Bell   Bucket   Trumpet   Funnel   Ogee   Conical   Cup

Double   Thistle   Waisted   Waisted   Ovoid
Ogee   Bell   Bucket

In the sixteenth and seventeenth centuries Venetian glass was supreme. George Ravenscroft (1632–83), a shipowner and chemist, established a glasshouse in the Savoy in London in 1673, where he developed flint glass, containing oxide of lead, which reflected the light brilliantly and in which were produced monumental glasses of great simplicity.

Cut-glass, that is to say lead-glass cut into facets, grooves, and depressions by the use of a rotating wheel, was very fashionable during the Regency period, at which time the Waterford Glasshouse in Ireland was enjoying its golden age, to be followed by the vogue for bohemian coloured glass in all its gaudy magnificence. During the Victorian era transfer-printing and acid-etching, 'satin' finishes and electrolytic processes, and all kinds of twistings and ribbings, and shadings and threadings, and bubblings and printings, and silverings and gildings were developed. Press-moulding was developed in America to bring cheap glass within reach of the poorer classes, while the art nouveau movement, embraced by such innovators as Eugène Rousseau and Émile Gallé in France, Louis Comfort Tiffany in America, and various glassmakers in Scandinavia and else-where, catered for aesthetes and collectors.

For greater detail see the entries for the major glass centres (e.g., *Stourbridge*), the types of glassware (e.g., *decanters*) and styles of decoration (e.g., *latticinio*).

Books: *An Illustrated Dictionary of Glass* by Harold Newman (Thames & Hudson, 1977); *Glass, A Guide for Collectors* by Gabriela Gros-Galliner (Muller, 1970)
Collections: There are many fine collections of glass throughout the country, of which the finest are in the British Museum, London; Victoria and Albert Museum, London; Royal Scottish Museum, Edinburgh; National Museum of Antiquities, Dublin; Fitzwilliam Museum, Cambridge; Pilkington's Glass Museum, St Helens, Lancashire (Glass Gallery)

glaze   Broadly speaking, a glaze is a hard, glassy, water repellent coating which gives to pottery or porcelain a smooth shiny finish. For pottery, an opaque glaze made from lead or tin and silex is used. For saltglaze stoneware, as you might expect, salt is thrown into the kiln where it fuses with the clay, forming a hard, clear glaze, sometimes rather pitted. Tin glazes are used for maiolica, and many other formulae have been tried by potters seeking to give their pots durability and distinctiveness.

gold   See *silver*.

Goss china   In 1857 at the age of twenty-four, William Henry Goss was chief designer at Copeland's London factory. In 1858 he set up his own works in Stoke-on-Trent, to produce Parian ware and terracotta of good quality. His jewelled porcelain was especially fine. A sideline of the Goss factory was the production of souvenir pieces of porcelain decorated with the arms of Eton and Harrow and the Oxford and Cambridge colleges.

*Goss model of
John Knox's house*

Adolphus, William's son, a keen student of heraldry, had the idea that holidaymakers might care to take home as souvenirs archaeological china models bearing the civic coats of arms of the resorts of their choice. These miniature models were instantly successful and very soon there was scarcely a mantelpiece which was not cluttered with ivory-glazed knick-knacks of no special distinction: tygs, ewers and urns, vases, lamps, shoes, lighthouses, and milk churns.

In fact the Goss craftsmen were capable of much more sophisticated designs, and it was when they turned their fingers to busts and cottages that they surpassed themselves. The first cottages to be produced were intended as nightlights and appeared in 1893. Shakespeare's house was followed by Burn's cottage, Ann Hathaway's cottage, Manx Cottage, and 'The First and Last House in England'.

Half-size models, three inches in length, followed, though these were merely for display. Great attention was paid to detail, so that when the ivy was cut back from Charles Dickens' house at Gad's Hill and two windows were revealed either side of the porch Goss immediately set about producing a house with windows to replace the existing house with ivy. Fifty-one cottages were produced over a period of thirty years, and production was only halted by the Great War. Goss also produced rare and very attractive wall pockets in the form of cherubs.

In 1928 the firm faced bankruptcy and was sold to George Jones and Sons who had already bought up other firms making crested china, including Arcadian and Crescent. Today all the designs, patterns, and moulds are held by the Ridgway potteries, which acquired them together with the right to use the Goss name and trademark in 1954. Ridgway could well cash in on the craze for collecting Goss china which was reactivated in the 1960s.

If models bear impressed marks 'W.H.G.' or 'W.H. Goss' they may be dated c.1862. The Falcon or Goshawk mark was printed from 1862, 'England' being added from 1891. However, the age of Goss china is less important than the detail. Any model with a military, naval, commemorative, or pictorial crest is especially in demand, as is a 'matching' crest (a Worcester crest on a Worcester jug for example). So far as the cottages are concerned, it is important to study them carefully for damage, ideally in natural light, concentrating particularly on the chimneys. Restoration is not easy to spot.

Books: *The Price Guide to the Models of W. H. Goss* by Roland Ward (Antique Collectors Club, 1975); *The Models of the W. H. Goss Factory — a Priced Guide* (Milestone Publications, 1975)

Great Exhibition, 1851 It was proposed by Sir Henry Cole, Prince Albert helped to organise it, and Queen Victoria headed the list of subscribers. Sir Joseph Paxton designed the Crystal Palace in Hyde Park for it, and it was indeed a palace. Over 600 yards long, a quarter of a mile wide and 66 feet high, this glittering rectangle of prefabricated iron and glass played host to 13,000 exhibitors who set up their wares over eight miles of display tables.

British exhibits, castigated by the jury for lack of artistic integrity and over-ornamentation, came under the headings of Minerals and Raw Materials, Machinery, Manufacturers, and Fine Arts. Nonetheless, there must have been fascinating entries from Minton (majolica by Arnoux), Pratt (coloured transfer-printing), Copeland, and Wedgwood. Thomas Webb & Sons showed cut glass, M. Thonet bentwood furniture, Jennens and Bettridge *papier mâché*. Many new fashions were started at the Exhibition including a significant one for Indian and Kashmir carpets. From America came false teeth, artificial legs, a Colt pistol and a reaping machine.

More than six million visitors helped the Exhibition towards a huge profit, which was subsequently used to endow the Victoria and Albert Museum. However, it is doubtful whether the Exhibition did anything to raise the standards of public taste, and, sadly, the Crystal Palace burned down in 1936.

Books: *The Great Exhibition: 1851* by Y. Ffrench (Harvill Press, 1950); *The Great Exhibition of 1851: A Commemorative Album* by C. H. Gibbs, a Victoria and Albert Museum publication (HMSO, 1964); *High Victorian Design: a Study of the Exhibits of 1851* by Nikolaus Pevsner (Architectural Press, 1951)

Greenaway, Kate Kate Greenaway (1846–1901) was a hard working, shy woman, and a close friend of John Ruskin. She first exhibited at the Dudley Gallery in 1868, and rose to become a much admired Academician. Her most enduring popularity came from her book illustrations: her vision of childhood was idyllic and quaint. For a while all nannies dressed their little girls in high-waisted muslin gowns with sashes and beaver bonnets; little boys were squeezed reluctantly into frilly shirts and pantaloons. Very soon Kate Greenaway became an industry. Wallpapers, prints, ceramics, clothes, trade cards, and tablecloths all bore her

..._'The Greeting' by Kate Greenaway_

whimsical illustrations. In recent years Charlie Brown and Snoopy, Roger Hargreave's 'Mr Men', and the Muppets have enjoyed similar exploitation, but in the nineteenth century such crazes were more unusual.

Book: *Kate Greenaway* by Rodney K. Ehgen (Academy Editions, 1976)

grisaille   The name given to monochrome painting usually on porcelain, but also on murals, in which different shades of grey are used to give weight and perspective to a design. On a pale background, such as creamware, the effect can be stunning.

Enamel painting *en grisaille* was developed and popularised in sixteenth-century Limoges. Later, the use of *grisaille* enamelling for the reproduction of earlier works of art became the fashion in Paris and Vienna.

hair jewellery   Although wearing a lock of one's beloved's hair was a very English custom, it is recorded that the fashion was exported to France in the years immediately preceding the Revolution when Anglomania was the thing. The hair would be plaited with horsehair to make it more workable, gold thread and pearls (sometimes) to make it more distinguished, and set in lockets, brooches, rings, and even earrings. Stiffened with glue, the hair would be mounted on enamel or opal glass and set in gold, pinchbeck, gilt, silver, or tortoiseshell. The hair might be shaped into the initials of the dear departed or worked to read 'In memory of'. It might be used as a weeping willow in a suitably funereal scene, or concealed in the back of a brooch or locket. Sometimes it would be plaited into a cord for a pocket-watch or bracelet.

Many amateurs indulged in this morbid, though hirsute, pastime; and so did plenty of talented people, Limmonier in France, B. Lee and Alfred Shuff in London amongst them. At the Paris Exposition of 1855 a full-length, lifesize portrait of Queen Victoria, made entirely from human hair, was exhibited; there is no record of whether or not the Queen was amused.

hallmark   A device stamped on pieces of British (and some foreign) silver and gold which denotes the assay office at which its purity was tested.

When one speaks of hallmarks, however, one means all the marks on pieces of silver. The principal devices are the heraldic lion and its head, the leopard's head, the three wheatsheaves (Chester), the crown (Sheffield), the anchor (Birmingham), the castle (Newcastle), the thistle (Edinburgh), an oak tree with a handbell hanging from its branches on one side, a bird on the top branch, and across the trunk a salmon with a ring in its mouth (Glasgow), and the harp (Dublin). Other Scottish marks include a pot of lilies (Dundee), a double-headed eagle (Perth), a dromedary (Inverness), a rose (Montrose), a portcullis (Arbroath), a green oak (Greenock), a fort (Forres), a cross (St Andrews), and a portcullis with an 'S' (Stirling). Ireland can offer a castle with or without a ship (Cork), another castle (Limerick), a yawl (Youghal), and an anchor (Galway).

Hallmarking dates from 1300 when the leopard's-head mark was adopted to indicate that the silver was 92.5 per cent pure — the same standard as coinage. In order to identify miscreants a maker's mark, which had to be registered, was added in 1363. This could be a symbol or a rebus; later initials were regularly used.

Silver marks

| London | Birmingham | Chester | Dublin | Edinburgh |

| Exeter | Glasgow | Newcastle | Norwich | Sheffield |

York

Sterling marks

Lion gardant   Lion passant   Britannia standard

Date letters started in London in 1478, twenty-year cycles of letters continuing until 1696, when a new series commenced with the new Britannia standard of 95.8 per cent pure. Each new cycle, which is distinguished by slightly differing graphics, has since then continued without a break.

The leopard's head, crowned until 1821, was the standard mark, but the lion passant was added to hallmarks (and remains as the London town mark) from 1544. In 1720 the lion was required to be stamped at all provincial English assay offices, and at Sheffield and Birmingham when they opened in 1773. Duty marks, bearing the sovereign's head, feature throughout the eighteenth and nineteenth centuries. Scottish marks run from 1457, with a date letter system from 1681, and a rather haphazard one in Ireland from 1638.

The hallmarking system gives only partial protection. There are pieces with old marks (often 'soft' and 'rubbed') which have been added later, and there are genuine pieces without hallmarks at all or with only bits of hallmarks. The placing of a hallmark may give a clue as to its authenticity. Pewter and electroplate sometimes carry marks intended to deceive the unwary, and Sheffield plate was stamped with imitation marks until 1784 when it became obligatory for the maker's full name to be included.

A new international system of hallmarking was introduced on 1 June 1976, and an additional mark, Queen Elizabeth II's head with necklace and tiara looking left, was struck during the Jubilee year of 1977 on all silver articles weighing 15 grams and over. The silver marks apply similarly (for the most part) to gold, which also bears carat marks. Initially you may find hallmarks confusing to interpret. But, like riding a bicycle, once you get the idea, it will become easy.

Books: *English Silver Hallmarks*, edited by Judith Bannister (Foulsham, 1970); *A dictionary of Marks* edited by Margaret McDonald Taylor (Book Club Association, rev. 1976)

hard-paste   A term applied to porcelain to distinguish it from so-called soft-paste. The distinction can be positively misleading since the 'hardness' and 'softness' refer to the degree of firing needed by the body, not to its inherent hardness or softness.

Hard-paste, sometimes known as 'true' porcelain, contains only china clay and felspar. It is impervious to acids from fruits and dyes, and when broken, exhibits a shell-like edge. Many myths are attached to the secret of its manufacture in China, some of which were invented by the Chinese themselves to discourage Western manufacturers from discovering the recipe. This they did in the eighteenth century, or at least William Cookworthy (1705–80), an apothecary, man of letters and Quaker preacher, did, at his New Invented Porcelain Manufactory in Plymouth (Meissen also made the discovery but only after investing vast capital and resources into experiments).

Hepplewhite (style) George Hepplewhite is a shadowy figure. We know that he was born in Yorkshire and apprenticed to Gillow's, cabinet-makers in Lancaster, and that he came to London to make his fortune. In 1760 he set up his own modest business in Cripplegate. He died in something like obscurity in 1786.

He owes his posthumous reputation to his wife Alice, who not only continued to run the business but published in 1788 *The Cabinet-Maker and Upholsterer's Guide*. This volume, which was reissued the following year, and in a revised edition in 1794, contained some three hundred different designs for almost every imaginable article of furniture engraved on 128 plates. Its intention was 'to combine elegance and utility and blend the useful with the agreeable'. It was very much a summary of existing middle-class taste rather than an expression of daring originality.

Hepplewhite's style was basically neo-classical, influenced by Chippendale, less formal than Adam, safer and more sturdy than Sheraton. (It is an intriguing fact that no piece of furniture made either by Hepplewhite or by Sheraton has ever been satisfactorily identified.) His particular emphasis was on chairs, with shield-back designs enclosing the Prince of Wales plumes, or swags, urns, or festoons of drapery, and on settees. He also favoured serpentine fronts. He removed the stretchers, pierced the backs, narrowed the legs and lightened the splats of the Chippendale chair. He used mahogany for the library and the dining-room, the more elegant satinwood for the bedroom, boudoir and drawing-room. Sometimes he used satinwood inlay on mahogany.

Said Sheraton of Hepplewhite's designs: 'We shall find that this work has already caught the decline and perhaps in a little time, will suddenly die in the disorder.' But he was not the first to underestimate the powerful instincts of the British middle-classes for the things that they know and love best, and Hepplewhite style remains as popular as ever.

Book: *Hepplewhite Furniture Design* by Ralf Edwards (Tiranti, 1955)
Collections: Holburne of Menstrie Museum, Bath; Audley End House, Saffron Walden

hollow-ware A phrase used by people in the know to describe anything, well, *hollow*, such as mugs, bowls and beakers, used on the table. The converse, therefore, of flatware.

horn An advertisement in the *Bristol Journal* for 28 March 1767 gives some idea of the variety of goods produced by the horner: 'Lantern leaves, Powder flasks, Drinking Cups, Ink horns, Horn Combs, Combs and Cases, Shoe Horns, Pepper boxes, Stay-sail horns, Gunners horns, Hunting horns, Marling spikes, Bell handles, Buttons, Button moulds, Shot pouches, and many other sorts of Horn goods too tedious to mention.'

Certain types of horn, when immersed in boiling water, become plastic and may then be split into sheets or plates, or made to adhere by the application of pressure, or pressed in a die or a mould. Though a very useful trade, the job of the horner was not a polite one, for the stench of the boiling horn was extremely malodorous. Supposed to keep away 'Lowness of Spirits', it probably only succeeded in keeping away one's friends. This may be why few objects of artistic distinction have been produced in horn.

Snuff-mulls made from rams' horns are an exception, as are knife handles and snuff-boxes chased with silver. John Osborn, an Englishman working in Amsterdam in the early seventeenth century, produced some fine horn portraits, and a century later John O'Brisset (or Obrisset: it is not known whether he was Irish or French) became celebrated for his portraits of, among others, Drake and Charles I. Interesting novelties were the grog-spoons and horn tankards made in Elizabethan Britain and containing whistles in their handles, to be blown when a refill was required. From these comes the expression 'wetting your whistle'.

horse brasses It was once superstitiously thought that bright and dazzling amulets seduced the eye of the evil one away from the wearer of the amulet. Four thousand years ago, in the Near East, important figures wore amulets and also had them made for their horses. Thus arose horse brasses, which were traditionally hammered out of heavy sheets of latten brass by gipsies and tinkers, and sold at fairs and in markets. When the early cast brasses replaced hammered ones during the 1830s it became possible to produce more complex and elaborate patterns. But by the end of the nineteenth century stamped brasses from the Midland foundries supplied an increased demand.

Notable designs include the Greek pattee cross, numerous other heraldic crosses and heart-motifs, the sunflash, moon and wheel, the potent crescent symbol, Tarots from the Romany Chal, agricultural and sporting brasses,

Horse brasses

private and county crests, clocks (from Wales), barrels (for dockyard horses), and trains (for goods yards) as well as a wide variety of commemorative brasses.

Old brasses have a great deal more weight, colour and style than the effete modern tat, of which there is a vast quantity about, and particularly desirable are those still attached to the harness leathers, especially if the harness maker's name is impressed in the bottom brass.

For more details than I can supply here contact the National Horse Brasses Society in Kidderminster.

Book: *Horse Brasses* by G. Hartfield (Abelard-Schuman, 1965)

icons As you will remember, had it not been for the miracle-working icon known as the Mother of God of Kazan, Ivan the Terrible would not have broken the yoke of the Golden Horde and taken Kazan in the late sixteenth century. Icons held a place of honour in every Russian home, but they were venerated rather than worshipped, and the Orthodox Christians from the East are no more superstitious about their icons than some Western Christians are about the effigies of their saints.

Icons first appeared in Byzantium and spread, as Christianity spread, to the Balkans and to Russia; their style developed from the tomb portraits of the Egyptians. The iconographers enjoyed little of the freedom of the Italian primitive painters: single figures of Christ and the Virgin Mary, who was incidentally not confirmed as Mother of God (*Theotokos*) until AD 431, were traditionally popular. But it was increasingly realised that icons had considerable educational value, and artists were encouraged to depict a wide range of Biblical scenes. Most were designed to occupy a particular niche (*iconostasis*) in the church, but large icons, painted on both sides, were intended to be carried in processions.

The traditional symbolism of icon painting was subjected to a crisis in the sixteenth century. Some Moscow painters, frustrated by the obligation to paint according to canon, attempted a more realistic approach, but were disciplined and their panels destroyed. Since then Russian icons have adhered to the old traditions.

The icon was painted on a panel made from local wood: lime, pine, or alder in southern Russia, fir or cypress in the north. Early on, the panel was shaped with an axe, later a plane was also used. It would then be strengthened at the back with pieces attached against the grain to prevent warping — though this was not always successful.

The panel would be prepared and primed and, in Russia, given a bevelled edge. Gesso would be laid on, sometimes over a layer of canvas. The outlines of the subject to be depicted would then be drawn in (or 'pounced' in inferior examples), the background filled with gold or silver, and the details expertly painted with colours — white, yellow, black, ochre, crimson, azure, cinnabar, maroon, chrome, green, and umber —

diluted in egg-yolk, fish-glue, and a preservative, which was sometimes wine (*rvas*). The Byzantines preferred gold backgrounds, the Russians, besides gold and silver, adopted other colours as trademarks for various cities: Novgorod used white, Pskov green, for instance.

Perhaps the finest painter of icons was Andrey Rublev in the fifteenth century. Modern examples are still being made both by indigenous artists and by fakers.

Book: *Icons and their Dating* by D. and T. Talbot Rice (Thames & Hudson, 1974)
Collection: Icon Museum, Recklinghausen, West Germany

Imari   Japanese porcelain made in the province of Hizen and shipped via the port of Imari to the West. Imari is now taken to refer to the design itself, which is based on textile patterns and worked out in bold enamel colours. The design was much imitated in Britain, most successfully by the Derby factory; as a result the term 'Imari' is loosely used for variations, as well as for theme.

inlay   A most popular and ostentatious technique of enriching furniture and metalwork by filling grooves with other woods, ivory, tortoiseshell, nautilus shell, brass, mother-of-pearl, precious metals, and so on. See *boulle*, *damascene*, *marquetry*, *parquetry*.

inro   The word derives from the Japanese *in*, a seal, and *ro*, a container. Originally these boxes were used to carry the seal and ink of dignitaries accustomed to signing documents. Later on, they became repositories for such things as medicines and herbs. *Inros* were regarded as an expression of one's personality and there was much competition for the best and richest designs. The most famous designer was Hokusai and the most famous lacquerer Shibata Zeshin.

A cord passed through holes in the *inro* and when this was tightened with the *ojime* (bead) the compartments of the *inro* were secured. At the end of the cord a *netsuke* stopped the *inro* from slipping out of the obi (sash). *Inros* became necessary because the Japanese national dress was devoid of pockets. After Western dress was popularly adopted, the *inro* no longer had a useful function to perform and became something of an irrelevance, whose value was chiefly in the export markets. See also *netsuke*.

Jacobite glasses   The Jacobite period lasted a century, from 1688 when James II was deported to France until 1788 when Prince Charles Edward died. A Jacobite was a supporter of the Stuart dynasty in England after the expulsion of James II, the last Stuart king. Sadly the romantic nature of the Jacobite cause was not always reflected in the energetic determination of the Jacobites to do anything about it. One result of this was the proliferation of Jacobite glasses, used by drinking clubs whose members clinked glasses of wine over a bowl of water, to toast the King in exile across the English Channel.

Many early Jacobite glasses are either of the acorn-knopped baluster variety, or trumpet-bowled with air-twist stems. Air tears were often contained in the stems, the tear an appropriate symbol. Jacobites, being secretive, appreciated symbols, and later Jacobite glasses are engraved with many such, from the Rose with two buds (representing the Crown of the Three Kingdoms with James, the Old Pretender, and Charles Edward, the Young Pretender) to the Star (the guiding light of the Jacobite movement), the Oak Leaf (from the Boscobel Oak in which Charles II hid after the Battle of Worcester), the Stricken Oak (the unfortunate Stuart lineage), the Thistle (the Crown of Scotland), and the Daffodil (an emblem of mourning).

Inscriptions are frequently found on Jacobite glasses, such as *Fiat* (Let it be done), *Redeat* (May he return), and *Hic vir hic est* (This is the man). Amen glasses, the most desired of all Jacobite glasses, were made for the exclusive use of dignitaries. They express loyalty to the cause and are engraved with verses from the Jacobite anthem, concluding with 'Amen'. They also bear the cipher IR, surmounted by a crown, with the figure 8. Fewer than twenty authenticated amen glasses have survived, so it is not surprising that they have been extensively and sometimes successfully forged.

jade A vague word used to describe various substances. The real, classical nephrite is calcium magnesium silicate with a hardness of $6\frac{1}{2}$ degrees on the Mohs scale. It was found in river beds and was extracted from rocks, frequently in Turkestan, although it was not a native product of China. Our name for it comes from the Portuguese *pedra-de-mijada*, which suggests that it was supposed to prevent kidney and urinary diseases.

Jade was carved in China as long ago as the neolithic age, and found its way into the country as a tribute to the emperor from his terrified subjects. To give some idea of the reverence felt by the Chinese towards what to Westerners is simply a stone, consider that the Chinese character for 'jade' is the same as for 'nobility'. It is also worth quoting from a seventh-century ritual:

> *If Jade is highly valued, it is because, since very olden times, the wise have likened it to virtue. For them the polish and brilliancy of jade represent the whole of purity; its perfect compactness, and its extreme hardness represent the sureness of the intelligence; its angles — they do not cut although they seem sharp — represent justice; the pure and prolonged sound which it gives forth when one strikes it represents music. Its colour represents loyalty; its interior flaws, always showing themselves through the transparency, call to mind sincerity; its iridescent brightness represents Heaven; its admirable substance, born of mountain and of water, represents the Earth. The price which all the world attaches to it represents the truth.*

Jade comes in a variety of colours, from white (when it is almost without silicate or oxides) to the darkest of dark greens. Green, especially the greeny-grey known as cabbage green, is the most common; creamy-white, or mutton-fat jade, is one of the most desirable colours. Yellows and greys, pinks and purples are also found.

Many objects have been fashioned from jade, including jewellery, human and divine figures, ritual vessels, panels, seals, and sceptres. Six ritual objects mentioned in the *Book of Rites* feature prominently, and four mythical creatures, a dragon, a phoenix, a kylin (or bushy-tailed stag), and a lion (to our eyes more like a pekinese). All these have mythical and symbolic significance. During the Ming Dynasty (1368–1644) one also finds figures of the Eight Immortals.

The finest jade objects were probably carved during the reign of the great Emperor Ch'ien Lung (1736–95), who commissioned a number of pieces made from huge blocks, depicting landscapes (including jade mountains) and embellished with poems by the Emperor himself. The best examples of jade in Britain are probably those in the Fitzwilliam Museum, Cambridge, where the fine triumvirate of Reclining Buffalo, Black Horse, and Dragon-Headed Horse (c.1670) may be seen. There is a fine Yuan Tortoise in the British Museum, and a bright green horse of the ancient Han period (fourth to second century BC) in the Victoria and Albert Museum.

Collectors must be careful that what is called jade is not in fact soapstone, marble, or alabaster. The comparative hardness of jade means that it will not scratch. Stains due to oxygenation and carbonisation are very often a sign of age, and make the piece more desirable. However, stains are now being artificially created and, since jade is still being produced in the Far East, one needs to be extremely cautious before paying large sums for jade objects. Other stones also known as jade, include jadeite (sodium aluminium silicate), which has been worked since the eighteenth century, and Chinese serpentine.

Books: *Chinese Jade Throughout the Ages* by S. C. Nott (Tuttle, 1969); *Chinese Jade Throughout the Ages: Catalogue* edited by Gray, Basil *et al.* (Oriental Ceramics Society, 1976)
Collections: Fitzwilliam Museum, Cambridge; St Osyth's Priory, Clacton; Gulbenkian Museum, Durham (Sir Charles Hardinge Collection)

japanning See *lacquer* and *Pontypool*.

Collection: Museum and Art Gallery, Newport

jardinière In town what was one to do for birds and flowers, how was one to manage without nature? One didn't have to. One got oneself a jardinière.

A jardinière might be no more than a carved wood stand on which to display flowers, or an ornamental pot in which to grow them, or between

1820 and 1840, it might be a substantial structure containing a birdcage and an indoor garden with room for lady authors, vicars, and Percy Grainger.

Earthenware jardinières became popular with the *fin de siècle* art pottery designers, such as Charles Brannam, William Ault, and Henry Tooth, and also with Doulton, Minton and so on.

Collection: Quintiques, New King's Road, London

jasperware   One of the longest-running hits in the pottery playland. The small souvenir pieces you find in the High Street stores are little changed from the first pieces Josiah Wedgwood produced in about 1774. This jasperware was hard, unglazed stoneware stained throughout or dipped in dye. The popular colours were predominantly blue — followed by green, mauve, and yellow. The body was decorated with a white moulded band of classical figures, playing flutes, hunting and generally putting on an Attic disposition. Jugs and vases were among the larger items made in jasperware. Medallions of the famous were another profitable line.

Book: *Wedgwood Jasper* by Robin Reilly (Letts Collectors Guides, 1972)
Collection: Etruria Museum, Burslem

*Jasperware vase decorated
with The Apotheosis of Homer, 1785*

jet   A fossilised wood found in bituminous shale, a sort of anthracite in other words, dug up in huge quantities in Whitby, Yorkshire. Its mining began in 1826 but its popularity as a form of inexpensive jewellery dates from the death of the Prince Consort in 1861. Thereafter the court went frequently, obsessively, and, it must sometimes have seemed, almost permanently, into mourning, and the gloomy nature of carved jet, in the form of rings and pendants, earrings and bracelets, necklaces, beads and crucifixes, was just what the widowed Queen Victoria wanted.

Beware of French jet, a cheap substitute for the real thing which is no more than faceted black glass given a high polish.

Collection: Castle Museum, York

Kakiemon   Kakiemon decoration is named after a family of potters who lived at Arita, near the port of Imari in the province of Hizen, Japan. This seventeenth-century design, incorporating sprigs of foliage and small quails spaciously set out with a colour scheme of rust, turquoise, blue, and yellow, was enormously influential in the West, inspiring designers at Meissen, Chelsea, Bow, Worcester, Derby, Chantilly, Vincennes and other factories, to imitate it, and therefore to flatter it. Thirteen generations on, the descendants of Sakaida Kakiemon I (1596–1666) are still working the Nangawara Kiln.

kaolin   A refractory clay which, allied with felspar, produces hard-paste, or 'true' porcelain as it is sometimes known. The best china clay comes from near St Austell, but the clay considered most suitable for pottery comes from Devon and Dorset. Kaolin is purified in a series of 'catch-pots', whence it is conveyed, dried and cut into squares, to the potteries.

Kauffmann (style)   Angelica Kauffmann was born in Switzerland and settled in England in 1765. She became a much sought after portrait painter, received commissions from the royal family, and became an R.A., a rare distinction for a woman in those days. Her most notable work was achieved as Robert Adam's assistant. Here she worked alongside Pergolesi and Antonio Zucchi, a Venetian painter. For Adam she painted furniture and ceilings, favouring pastoral and classical scenes well suited to Adam's taste. In 1780 she married Zucchi, and left England for Italy, where she died in 1807.

A great deal of decorated furniture attributed to Angelica Kauffmann could not possibly be by her when you consider the brief time she lived in England. However, many coloured engravings were made of her pictures, and these were imitated by other furniture painters, so that one can expect facile copies of her work also to appear on furniture. Many of her designs are to be found on furniture *en grisaille* (that is to say, in monochrome) surrounded by swags and wreaths of flowers in full colour; the central panels are usually either oval or octagonal.

Characteristically most of Angelica Kauffmann's work appears with a satinwood veneer, to great effect.

Book: *Angelica Kauffmann: Her Life and Works* by V. Manners and George C. Williamson (Hacker Art Books, 1977)

king's pattern A cutlery design which developed from the fiddle pattern. Handles remained fiddle-shaped but were enriched with scrolls, shells, honeysuckle flowers, and similar motifs. The king's pattern dates from the early nineteenth century and is still popular with those who believe that the sun has yet to set on the Empire. It may be found in silver, Sheffield plate, electroplate, and so on. (The king's pattern, that is, not the Empire.)

King's pattern

kitchenware 'The great laboratory of every household' is the vivid way Mrs Isabella Beeton described the Victorian kitchen in her *Book of Household Management* (1861). One has to date Mrs Beeton's books because she was as liberal with words as she was with pastries, blancmanges, and stews. In the 1895 edition of her book she listed the requirements for the kitchen of 'a small house'. They included: three copper stew-pans, a copper sugar boiler, sauté and preserving pans, iron pots (various), tin fish kettles, sets of meat-skewers and hooks, round and fluted pastry-cutters, a spice box, a marble mortar, a hardwood pestle, a weighing machine, a colander, a coffee mill, a coal scuttle, and fire irons.

Naturally one might also expect to see jelly, chocolate and cake moulds, ladles, skimmers, spoon-racks, and chopping boards. Coffee mills of tin or wood, butchers' steels and choppers, butter-churns, butter-pats and 'The Servant's Friend', a large, circular knife-cleaning machine on a cast iron frame, such as may still be found quite frequently at country auctions.

In addition the Victorians were obsessed with mechanical devices. Since science was going to save the world, why should it not also make the housewife's and the cook's chores a little less onerous? Thus we find self-pouring teapots, apple-peelers and cherry-stoners, marmalade-cutters, vegetable-choppers, and vacuum cleaners of fearsome appearance. More curious perhaps is Warren's Patent Fish Kettle and Invalid Cooking Pot; Captain Warren was also responsible for a Patent Corrugated Bachelor's Broiler.

The pressure-cooker we owe to Denis Pepin (1647–1712), who presented the Royal Society with his steam 'Digester' as early as 1681; but the application of the principle of the safety valve to cooking failed to make any money for its inventor. Larding needles, potato pastry pans, podgers, bottle jacks (for spit-roasting meat), porridge-stirrers, cabbage-pressers, and bean-slicers are just a few more of the odd devices without which a well stocked Victorian kitchen was incomplete. A laboratory indeed.

Book: *Kitchen Antiques* by Mary Norwak (Ward Lock, 1975)
Collections: Christchurch Mansion, Ipswich; Ordsall Hall Museum, Salford; Brighton Pavilion, Brighton; Art Gallery and Museum, Cheltenham (Victorian kitchen); Sulgrave Manor, Banbury (Tudor kitchen); Huntly House, Edinburgh (Scottish eighteenth-century kitchen); Honiton and All Hallows Public Museum, Honiton (old Devon kitchen); Talton Park, Knutsford; Rapallo House Museum, Llandudno (old Welsh kitchen)

knives   In the fifteenth century etiquette required that, instead of seizing one's meat with both hands, one should convey it to one's mouth with three fingers only and in small quantities. But knives had been in use since pre-history. One hunted, cooked and ate with the same utensil. With the introduction of the fork in the sixteenth century it was no longer good manners to spear one's meat on the end of one's knife (as the Anglo-Saxons had done with their scramasaxes). Accordingly knives acquired parallel blade edges, rounded points, and long, solid handles of wood, bone or ivory, many of which were elaborately inlaid or damascened. During the seventeenth century knife blades were frequently rectangular and handsome variations were produced in which the blades curved one way, and the handles the other.

Collection: City Museum and Art Gallery, Sheffield

knife boxes or **knife cases**   Towards the end of the seventeenth century dinner parties became increasingly elegant affairs. No longer were guests expected to bring their own cutlery, attractive as some of these individual sets of knives, prongs and spoons had become. Now, the host had his own cutlery with fine handles of silver, ivory, agate, or onyx; and he had cases or boxes in which to display it.

Although (or perhaps because) the shape of early knife boxes was governed by their function, very handsome examples of cabinet-making were produced, in which the craftsman could use all his skills. The cutlery was to be displayed when not in use, so the boxes had to be attractive both closed and hinged open. The knives were graduated in size from front to back, and were stored blades down.

The shape that was most convenient turned out to be serpentine-fronted boxes with sloping lids. The earliest of these were covered in shagreen; not sharkskin shagreen, but specially prepared leather. (Interesting to note that shagreen was also used in the East as a covering for the sheaths of daggers.) Intricate brass or silver mounts included locks in the shapes of hooves and tiny claw-feet. These early examples would have been lined in red or green silk velvet, interspaced with metallic galloon.

With the introduction of mahogany sideboards, designed by Robert Adam in the 1760s, and Adam's insistence that all accessories should blend into an overall design, mahogany knife boxes came into fashion. These were inlaid with satinwood, ebony, and boxwood, and with holly when a black and white check was called for. A typical example would have a star or a Sheraton-type shell inlaid centrally both on the exterior and interior of the lid, and mounts rather less ornate than earlier examples.

The neo-classical revival also introduced knife urns (usually of satinwood) of severe classical design and in sets of three. Two urns would hold the knives, while the third would be lined with metal to hold hot water, so that the knives could be washed between the courses. In the early nineteenth century 'sarcophagus' knife boxes were made, in much the same style as similar tea caddies of the period.

I know of no more pleasant way of collecting, reasonably economically, perfectly characteristic examples of the work of the great cabinet-makers of the past, than through these charming and practical knife boxes.

knife rests Traditionally these were dumb-bell shaped objects for resting the carving knife and fork on during the meal to prevent the cloth being stained. They were made from clear or coloured crystal, Bristol glass, silver, pewter, ivory, carved wood, and porcelain. From Stourbridge came *millefiori* and filigree glass examples with coloured twists mainly in red, white, and blue. Animals, birds, human figures, and sporting and military symbols are also found. More imaginative designs include two elephants joined together at the trunk.

lace It is important to make a distinction between needlepoint lace and bobbin lace.

The art of needlepoint (*point à l'aiguille, punto in aco*) is similar to bridge-building or soufflé-baking. You have to contrive a self-supporting embroidery. *Reticella* and spiderwork mean that a few supporting threads from the parchment base remain; *punta in aria* is entirely free of any umbilicus. The art, which was hard on the eyes and on the patience, was developed in the convents of Italy. The resulting needlepoint, very much in vogue in seventeenth-century Europe, was considered suitable for church vestments and all important occasions, unlike . . .

Bobbin lace which is light and delicate. Also known as pillow lace and bone lace, it is either made on a pillow held on the lacemaker's knee, or on an elevated frame. The design is drawn on parchment; this is picked out with pins. A thread is looped round each pin, then around a bobbin, and the bobbins — there may be two hundred of them — are intertwined to form the groundwork of the fabric. Bobbin lace is thought to have originated in Flanders, and was used to embellish personal linen; also as an accessory around the collars, cuffs and flounces of costumes. Very pretty.

The Huguenots brought this art (as so many others) to Britain in the early seventeenth century. Honiton, in Devon, became a centre, as later did Carrickmacross in Ireland. Other fine lace is produced in Holland, Belgium, Spain, and Malta. During the nineteenth century hand-embroidery on machined net was substituted for the real thing and now, of course, the process is almost entirely automated.

Book: *Lace and Bobbins: A History and Collector's Guide* by T. L. Huetson (David & Charles, 1973)
Collections: Honiton and All Hallows Museum, Honiton; Blair Castle and Atholl Museum, Blair Atholl; City Museum and Art Gallery, Nottingham

lacquer The Chinese and Japanese used this sap of the tree known as *Rhus vernicifera* in the last few centuries before the Common Era, as a protective glaze around small personal objects of wood and earthenware. The Japanese were more skilled than the Chinese, although the tree grew naturally in China. The Emperor K'ang-Hsi generously acknowledged that his countrymen's products were inferior, but blamed it on the climate. Among its many other properties lacquer is airtight, so it was used to line Japanese coffins.

In the sixteenth and seventeenth centuries lacquer objects began to find their way to Europe, to Holland and thence to Britain where their appeal was immediately recognised. Craftsmen imitated oriental models and in 1688 John Stalker and George Parker published *A Treatise of Japanning and Varnishing*. This detailed volume spoke highly of the technique: 'No damp air, no moulding worm or corroding time can possibly deface it, and which is more wonderful, though its ingredients, the gums, are in their own nature inflammable; yet this most vigorously resists the fire, and is itself found to be incombustible.' The following year we find Edmund Verney agreeing to pay a guinea for his daughter to learn japanning at school, with another forty shillings for materials to work upon.

But European imitation never quite matched the real thing. We did not understand about the slow simmering of the *urushi* (the resinous sap) or the peculiar blacking properties of *huguro* (women's tooth dye). Oriental lacquer had a perfect almost metallic gloss; the English version has a satin quality. Oriental lacquer had more sharply etched designs and the distribution of the detail was more 'connected'. Unmounted oriental panels were imported into Britain to be made up into furniture but finished oriental cabinets are obviously more desirable. In other ways too Western craftsmen compromised the philosophical sophistication of the oriental pieces. Western faces with wide round eyes stare out from oriental costumes, and furniture is constructed in styles which would have been offensive to Chinese and Japanese craftsmen.

Most lacquer furniture is black with gold designs; occasionally the ground is red, green, blue, orange or cream. Particular details are picked out in a kind of gesso. The oriental taste was most popular in about 1710, and continued for many years. Later pieces can usually be dated by the foundation woodwork and tend to be inferior.

When the fashion was at its height few escaped its influence. One can only sympathise with an anonymous correspondent to the *Spectator* in February 1712 who complained about his wife. It seems she 'set herself to reform every Room of my House, having glazed all my chimney-pieces with Looking glass and planted every corner with such Heaps of China, that I am obliged to move about my own house with the greatest Caution and Circumspection for fear of hurting brittle Furniture.'

There is much reproduction lacquer, some dating from the 1880s, the 'aesthetic' period, some more recent. Though superficially attractive, it has none of the quality of the older pieces.

Book: *Lacquer of the West: History of a Craft and an Industry* by Hans Huth (University of Chicago Press, 1971)
Collections: Victoria and Albert Museum, London (Chinese); Chiddingstone Castle, Edenbridge (Japanese)

ladder-back The ladder-back chair is also known as the slat-back chair and has retained its popularity for three centuries. It is usually a high-backed chair, sometimes rush-seated, with four or five horizontal slats between the uprights. In the seventeenth and eighteenth centuries the ladder-back was a popular 'country' chair, but the design was elaborated by Chippendale and others. In the late nineteenth century the tradition received new life with the pioneering work of Ernest Gimson (1864–1919), the leader of the Cotswold school, and Sir Gordon Russell (b. 1892) of Broadway, Worcestershire.

Lalique, René René Lalique (1860–1945) was a French jeweller, silversmith, glassmaker, and decorative artist, who was influenced as a young man — he would have to have been blind not to be — by Émile Gallé. Like Gallé, Lalique was fascinated by the colours and textures of precious stones, by the shapes and patterns of the natural world in general, and insects in particular. After his studies at the École des Arts Decoratifs he became the most sought after jeweller in Paris, hanging his creations around the fashionable neck of Sarah Bernhardt, among many others. His most profitable assignment was probably the collection of 145 pieces of frivolous fantasy he designed for Calouste Gulbenkian (these may be seen at the Paombel Palace near Lisbon).

He had incorporated glass panels into his jewellery, but after being exposed to Gallé's work — notably at Samuel Bing's shop, L'Art Nouveau, in Paris — he turned his attention chiefly to glass, designing perfume bottles for Coty and buying his own glassworks in 1910. His characteristic innovations included a milky white opalescent glass in which his nude figures float, elegantly ethereal; he also had a predilection for fish and ferns, dragonflies and hair. Among the artifacts he produced were lamps, plaques, dishes, fountains, screens, chandeliers, door panels, dishes, clock-cases, statuettes, and car mascots, which are now *très snob*. In 1930 he designed one of his most triumphant pieces, an altar-rail made of long glass strips, decorated with lilies. The 1920s and 1930s were his best decades.

The possibilities of glass in architecture intrigued him, for he realised that it was strong enough to be used monumentally in conjunction with steel, and he anticipated that its luminosity would enhance the appearance of many modern buildings. This discovery may well have been his most influential contribution to twentieth-century aesthetics.

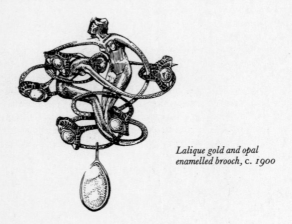

Lalique gold and opal enamelled brooch, c. 1900

Lambeth delftware   A generic term to cover the ware from a number of London factories from the sixteenth century onwards. Since Flemish painters and potters were employed in these early factories, the products were tin-glazed and blue and white in the prevailing Dutch fashion. A dish dated 1600 has survived with the inscription:

> *The Rose is Red*
> *The Leaves are Green*
> *God Save Elizabeth*
> *Our Queen.*

Other seventeenth-century pieces — whether from Lambeth, Southwark or elsewhere is difficult to establish — include chargers commemorating the coronation of Charles II, wine bottles inscribed with the names of wines, 'Merryman' plates (sets of six or eight plates, each with one line of a humorous poem), pill slabs, drug jars, and bleeding bowls. For Doulton's Lambeth pottery, see *Doulton*.

Book: *English Delftware* by F. H. Garner and Michael Archer (Faber & Faber, 1972)
Collections: City Art Gallery, Bristol; Guildhall Museum, London; Museum and Art Gallery, Brighton (Willett Collection); Museum and Art Gallery, Reading (Blatch Collection)

lantern clock   Also known as a 'birdcage', this clock, the successor to the German Gothic clock, was the first domestic chamber clock in Britain and appeared *c*.1620. Made almost entirely of brass, the lantern clock had a wholly unprotected movement (pendulums from 1656), and, only rarely, a minute hand. Key-wound copies in the Gothic style were produced towards the end of the nineteenth century, and recently forgeries (some say from Hungary) have been shouldering their way on to the market. Examples signed by Thomas Moore of Ipswich, a very prolific clockmaker, are especially suspect.

Provincial balance-wheel lantern clock, 1663

latticino or **latticinio**   Terms applied to clear glass embedded with strips of (usually white) glass. It should not be, but often is, confused with lattimo glass, which is opaque white glass, similar in appearance to porcelain. Since the words are all derived from the Italian *latte*, meaning milk, coloured strips of glass cannot be *latticinio*.

Leeds Pottery   The situation of the Leeds Pottery, established halfway through the eighteenth century, meant that by using the waterways it could easily obtain white clay from the West Country and flint from Sussex. As a result characteristic creamware was developed, which was of sufficient quality to rival the best from Staffordshire in general and Wedgwood in particular. From 1775 when William Hartley established a dominant position in the firm, it began to enjoy much success and a considerable export trade. However, the numerous imitators caused problems and the Leeds Pottery went bankrupt in 1820, although for some years attempts were made to keep the old place going. From 1888 Slee's Modern Pottery used many of the original moulds to produce pieces in the Leeds manner, but today nothing remains of the Leeds works.

Besides creamware and pearlware the Leeds Pottery, trading as Hartley, Greens and Company (1781–1820), introduced blackware designs, printed over the glaze until the nineteenth century, and transfer-printing to replace hand enamelling.

Early Leeds ware is rarely marked and is not easy to distinguish from Staffordshire products. It has a less regular glaze than Wedgwood's Queen's ware. To identify a piece as Leeds look out for handles twined or plaited like straps or ropes; flower knobs on the lids, and flower or leaf-moulding where the handles join the bodies; plates with pierced rims and basketwork bowls (look carefully for damage); and, where there is an impressed mark 'Leeds Pottery', with or without the addition of 'Hartley, Greens & Co.', the less evenly the letters are spaced, the older the piece is likely to be.

Book: *The Leeds Pottery* by Donald Towner (Corey, Adams and Mackay, 1963)
Collections: Royal Pump Room Museum, Harrogate; Art Gallery and Museum, Cheltenham (Riskworth Collection); Astley Hall, Chorley; City Art Gallery, Leeds

Limoges   In the sixteenth century, Limoges, in the Haute Vienne region of France, was the centre for fine enamelling. Its factory claims to have made the first French hard-paste porcelain *c.*1771. In 1784 the Government purchased the factory from the Comte D'Artois, as a branch of its Sèvres operation; thereafter it was known as the Royal Limoges factory. Kaolin was brought from Marcognac, and felspar from Chantelope. The chief output from Limoges was table services with a slight ivory tint, decorated with sprays of flowers. By the beginning of the nineteenth century over a thousand men were employed at the works, and within fifty years there were almost as many factories producing useful china, which had a ready market in England and America. Haviland was one of the better factories.

linen press or **napkin press**   Victorian ladies stored their linen in a press, which was shelved in a cupboard or large chest (usually of oak). The name also applies to two flat boards, tightened together with a spiral screw, either free-standing or mounted on a table, and dating from *c.*1500.

lion mask   The lion mask is a feature found on furniture between 1720 and 1740, and later revived during the Regency. Lavishly carved and gilded, lion masks were usually accompanied by claw-and-ball or pad feet. Lions' heads are also found with rings through their brass mouths as door knockers, as handles to vases, and as ormolu mounts.

lithophane   There was a time when one could not go down a street in the East Riding of Yorkshire without seeing twenty or thirty lithophanes in the windows of houses. Now few dealers have even heard of them, and fewer still would recognise one if they saw one. A lithophane (also known as a Berlin transparency) is a nineteenth-century transparent sheet of porcelain, stamped on one side with a picture (usually of an emblematic, literary, or Biblical character) which counts for little until held up to the light. Most lithophanes came from Berlin where they were invented *c.*1830; a few came from Meissen and other centres. They were made from three to fifteen inches long to serve as window-panes, as ornaments to be hung in windows (see *witch balls*), as side pieces to lanterns, or as bases to teacups or beer mugs.

Liverpool   Porcelain and pottery have both been made since the early eighteenth century at Liverpool, the city where transfer-printing from copper plates on to pottery and porcelain was first practised by John Sadler of Harrington Street. (It is said that John got the idea from watching children playing with primitive transfers.)

The principal makers of porcelain were Richard Chaffers, Philip Christian, Zachariah Barnes, Samuel Gilbody, Seth Pennington, Reid and Company, and the Herculaneum Factory. (Such names these gentlemen had: they even sound like craftsmen!) Chaffers is the most notable. His porcelain was green, red, yellow, and maroon with a powerful green translucency; colour was applied over the glaze, and transfer prints were added to later examples. Christian's product is similar to Chaffers', but a little coarser and heavier and without the transfers. Barnes worked in underglaze blue and white, as did Pennington. Later Barnes concentrated on delftware, which was of fine quality. Herculaneum porcelain featured transfer- and bat-printing on tea and coffee services, and portrait busts.

Most Liverpool porcelain is unmarked and attribution and dating can be little more than intelligent guesswork. But the general characteristics are a soft white paste decorated in cobalt blue, slightly embossed, and decorated with charming if unauthentic 'Chinese' designs. Repeating border patterns aid identification (look at the examples in the Liverpool City Museum), and a design of fleur-de-lys with groups of dots occurs quite frequently.

With pottery, as with porcelain, attribution is a problem, but any of the following signatures will securely place the pot in Liverpool: John Sadler,

Joseph Johnson, Richard Abby, Guy Green on teapots, and Worthington and Green on jugs. Busts of local celebrities in biscuit, of naval and military heroes in basalt, were also popular. The basalt ware busts, from the Herculaneum factory, are $8\frac{1}{2}$ inches high and decorated with appropriate trophies. (A bust of Benjamin Franklin is named as being George Washington, but anyone can make a mistake.) Local views and sporting scenes are found printed on table services, and there are rather crudely potted figures with fern-leaf patterns decorating their bases.

After Sadler's discovery of transfer-printing his factory moved into tile-production in a big way. These tiles were often decorated with stage celebrities in their most famous roles, with animals from Aesop's *Fables*, or with rural scenes.

Book: *Liverpool Herculaneum Pottery* by Alan Smith (Barrie & Jenkins, 1971)
Collections: City Museum and Art Gallery, Liverpool (extensive); City Museum and Art Gallery, Birmingham (tiles); Museum and Art Gallery, Bootle (Bishop Collection of Liverpool Pottery); Botanic Gardens Museum, Southport

lockets Lockets have been popular since the seventeenth century, particularly so when fashion required that necks be bared. Gold, silver, crystal, tortoiseshell, enamel, and jet were among the materials most frequently used. Locks of hair and miniature photographs were generally thought suitable for wearing in lockets.

loggerhead Literally a thick head, or one whose head is too big for his body, the word has an old and respectable provenance, and is still colloquially used in Cumbria. In the Christmas number of the *West Cumberland Times* for 1892 you may find: 'Keep off them rods yeh gert loggerheeds!' The word was then colourfully applied to long-handled iron instruments with a ball at one end which rested on the hearth in pairs, and when heated in the fire could be used to melt pitch or mull wine. They were also used in the heat of the moment for more violent purposes, giving rise to the phrase 'to be at loggerheads' meaning 'to come to blows'.

longcase clock In 1632 a charter was granted to London clockmakers to encourage local manufacture, for most of the clocks around in the early years of the seventeenth century were foreign-made. Twenty-five years later the pendulum principle was applied to clocks, a development for which Galileo, of course, was in part responsible. The earliest weight-driven clocks were bracketed to the wall with their working parts hanging below; it was soon considered neater and more convenient to encase the pendulum and create a clock which could stand freely on the floor.

Seventeenth-century clocks are both rare and highly priced, and most surviving longcase clocks date from the late eighteenth century, by which time business was booming and quality declining. In the nineteenth

Longcase clock

century cases became coarser, with heavy scroll designs and huge pediments.

The term grandfather clock dates from 1876 when the song 'My Grandfather's Clock' was written. Technically a grandfather clock is a longcase clock of 6½ feet or more, while a grandmother clock (seldom as old as her mate) measures between 5½ and 6½ feet. Grand-daughter clocks, measuring between 3½ and 4½ feet, always date from the twentieth century.

To date a clock, first identify the materials:

Tudor	iron or brass
Jacobean and Cromwellian	oak
Carolingian and Queen Anne	ebony, marquetry, walnut, kingwood, olive wood
Georgian	mahogany, satinwood
Victorian	rosewood

If a clock bears the maker's name (as most good clocks do) it may be dated through the Clockmakers' Registry.

Book: *Longcase Clocks* by Eric Bruton (Hart-Davis, 1977)

Longton Hall   William Littler was born in 1724 and as a young man produced salt-glazed earthenware with his brother-in-law, Aaron Wedgwood, at Brownhills near Burslem. The earthenware was good of its kind but at that period porcelain was in vogue. So, when Littler attained his majority and inherited some money from his father (also a potter), he moved to Longton Hall, and set up the first factory in Staffordshire to produce porcelain. By 1852 he was advertising 'A large Quantity and great variety of very good and fine ornamental Porcelain or China Ware in the most fashionable and genteel Taste, where all Persons may be fitted with same at reasonable Rates either Wholesale or Retale.'

Littler was ahead of most of his competitors: at this date only Bow and Chelsea were fully into porcelain production. Yet sadly within a very few years, probably in 1758, the factory gates were closed and production ceased. It is probable that William Duesbury, who started his Derby works at Longton in 1756, bought the plant and transferred everything that was movable to his own factory. Littler later became manager to Baddeley and Fletcher at Shelton, but they too failed, and Littler died in extreme poverty at an advanced age.

The peculiarity of Longton Hall china is a streaky blue with either a heavy, glassy paste like early Chelsea, or a harder paste like early Worcester. Some excellent figures (such as 'Britannia') were produced, usually with a scroll ornament on the base, and large encrusted flowers and overlapping leaves (often in 'Littler's blue') decorated many pieces.

The rare mark of Longton Hall is two crossed Ls for Longton and Littler.

Book: *Longton Hall Porcelain* by Bernard Watney (Faber & Faber, 1957)
Collection: Fenton House, London

loo table Two of the most misleading names in the antiques glossary are commode and loo table. Commodes I have dealt with elsewhere; a loo table is simply a table at which the game of loo was played. Loo is short for lanterloo, a forfeit card game played originally in France but imported into England in the early nineteenth century.

Loo tables originally had a circular top, supported by a central column in the shape of a truncated cone at the triangular base of which would be four lion paws in brass. Such tables could seat eight in comfort — none of the participants being troubled with a leg. Halfway through the century the table top became oval and was sometimes inlaid, while the central column was either broken down into a cluster of smaller columns, or partially absorbed in curving legs. The pedestal carving, the scrolling on the base, and other 'improvements' continued to compromise the pleasing simplicity of the earlier design.

lowboy A low chest of (usually four) drawers, set on cabriole legs with a horizontal top and an undulating apron, which could be used either as an occasional table or as a base for a second chest of drawers, in which case it became a tallboy, or highboy. Lowboys were usually American-made.

Lowestoft For many years there was a widespread belief that a great deal of Chinese export porcelain, especially armorial services of the late eighteenth century, apparently made to order in the Orient and shipped back to England by the East India Company, had in fact been manufactured in little Lowestoft. This was clearly impossible: Chinese porcelain is hard-paste and Lowestoft basically soft-paste for one thing, and, for another, Lowestoft is extremely diffident and unpretentious, its works being described during part of its history as 'China manufacturers and Herring Curers'.

The Lowestoft porcelain factory opened its kilns about 1756. There were stories current that the Lowestoft workforce had been bribed by jealous London competitors to ruin their pots, but shareholders Philip Walker, Robert Browne, Obed Aldred and John Rickman remained undaunted. By 1760 an advertisement was appearing in the *Norwich Mercury* offering for sale: 'before Lady day next . . . a great variety of neat Blue and White China or Porcelain, at the manufactory in the Town. 'Tis humbly hoped that most of the shopkeepers in the County . . . will give encouragement to this laudable undertaking by reserving their Spring orders for their humble servants.' For the next fifteen years or so the entire Lowestoft output was 'useful' china in underglaze blue. Many of the most charming pieces (and charm is the principal characteristic of Lowestoft china) were relief-moulded with sunflowers and leaves; one notorious butter dish has the sunflowers growing *downwards*.

Printed designs appear after Robert Browne junior succeeded his father as manager in 1771. Many of these were pirated from Worcester patterns, and have been well described by John Howell as being 'as if drawn by a failing ball-point pen'. Apparently much of the Lowestoft printing was done by women — fishermen's wives, most likely — though many of the pieces featuring local scenes appear to have been done by fulltime experts. Typical lines produced at Lowestoft are souvenirs of the town — mugs, ink-wells and so on with goodwill inscriptions within fancy cartouches, and birthday medallions about two inches in diameter with a name and date of birth on the obverse, and a flower on the reverse. Only about two dozen of these in blue and white, and one dozen in polychrome, survive.

The factory closed in about 1800. Robert Browne junior wrote: 'I have heard my father say that they discontinued the works principally because they could not produce the ware so cheaply as the Staffordshire potters, and that they were getting old and wished to retire from the business, not from want of capital, as they were all wealthy men for the period.'

Book: *Oriental Lowestoft* by J. A. L. Hyde (Ceramic Book Company, n.d.)
Collections: Godden Collection, Worthing; Christchurch Mansion, Ipswich; Castle Museum, Norwich

lustreware   Lustred pottery has been made for over two hundred years, and is difficult to ascribe to a particular factory, a particular area, or even a particular country. This century a great deal of almost convincing lustreware has been imported from Czechoslovakia, so one must proceed with caution.

The whole idea of lustre was to make simple pottery look to a casual observer like something a great deal grander. The main categories are gold, silver, copper, and 'resist' lustre. The technique is to dissolve gold or platinum and apply them to pottery. Gold results in copper colour (on a dark body) and pink, red or purple (on a light body). Platinum produces a most convincing silver lustre — so convincing that tea and coffee services were made to conform to the prevailing styles of silver and Sheffield plate. With resist lustre, wax or grease was applied to a portion of the body before the piece was dipped: where the wax lay, the lustre would not take.

Richard Frank of Brislington is credited with the invention *c.*1740, but his was primitive stuff and by the early nineteenth century the process was well known and a free-for-all developed. The Staffordshire and Sunderland potteries competed, and Bristol, Leeds, Liverpool, Swansea, and Newcastle threw their hats into the ring. Wedgwood, always fascinated by novelty, produced his silver lustre in 1791. His pearlware, whiter than creamware and ideal for transfer-printing, was developed at about the same time. But his Moonlight Lustre (*c.*1810–15) and the fantastic Fairyland Lustre which Daisy Makeig-Jones produced at the Wedgwood factory during the 1920s are what the collectors are really interested in.

Book: *Lustreware* by John Bedford (Cassell, 1964)
Collections: Museum and Art Gallery, Mansfield; Museum and Art Gallery, Sunderland

mahogany In 1720 the French refused to export any more of their dwindling supplies of walnut so the British removed the tax on imports of colonial timber. In fact San Domingo, where the earliest supplies of mahogany came from, was a Spanish colony but importers and exporters are seldom too scrupulous about such matters and San Domingan mahogany (or Spanish mahogany) often slipped in via Jamaica, and was Chippendale's regular timber. Cuban mahogany, which was easier to work, better 'figured' and consequently ideal for veneering, became the more popular from about 1750. Mahogany from Honduras, also known as baywood, imported from about 1730 is still available today, long after San Domingan and Cuban supplies have been exhausted. However, it is lighter and softer than the others. African mahogany is used for modern reproduction furniture.

Sir Robert Walpole, having shown a profit of 1000 per cent on his South Sea Company stock (one of the very few investors to do so) built — or had Ripley build — Houghton between 1722 and 1732. This remarkable house was filled with Cuban mahogany furniture and pictures to the value of £200,000. On the first floor were over sixty mahogany doors, each three inches thick and heavily carved and moulded with matching window-shutters. One door alone is known to have cost £1000.

There are dealers who claim to be able to tell the origin of a piece of mahogany by feeling its weight; they should be listened to respectfully and ignored. Mahogany has a beautiful patina, which gets better as it gets older. It has strength and durability and a great range of colours and graining; it welcomes the attentions of the skilful carver and rewards his skills. The extent to which it dominated furniture-making in the late eighteenth and early nineteenth centuries may be seen from an entry in Crosby's pocket dictionary for 1810, where cabinet-makers are defined as 'workers in mahogany and other fine woods'.

maiolica In the second half of the fifteenth century when Italy was a conglomerate of small dukedoms, many artists and potters set up their *botteghe* (studios) under the patronage of the local duke. The main centres from which this tin-glazed earthenware emanated were Gubbio, Faenza, Caffaggiolo, Siena, Urbino, Castel-Durante (where Guido Andriesz, who brought Italian techniques to Holland, came from) and Pesaro. Gubbio, whither pieces from elsewhere were sent for additional decoration, specialised in a gold and ruby lustre. Urbino boasted what is known as Raffaelesque decoration in orange and blue. Caffaggiolo's ware has a white glaze, with rich blue decoration; the letters S.P.Q.R. or S.P.Q.F. or the words *Semper* (the motto of Piero de' Medici) or *Glovis* (Giuliano) frequently occur. See also *Delft*.

Collections: Victoria and Albert Museum, London; Polesden Lacy, Dorking

majolica A general term for nineteenth-century earthenware painted in imitation of fifteenth- and sixteenth-century Italian maiolica. (For a more detailed explanation of this confusing terminology, see *Delft*.) Minton's specialised in majolica, making such things as garden ornaments and small dishes from *c.*1850. The word is also vaguely applied to earthenware with a buff-coloured body and a coloured glaze over relief decoration. Wedgwood successfully revived earlier green leaf dishes in the majolica style.

mantel clock Any clock intended to stand on a mantelpiece may be known as a mantel clock. The mantelpiece, of course, was made fashionable in Britain by Robert Adam during the second half of the eighteenth century. Mantel clocks tended towards the ornate, particularly in France, and were often part of decorative sets (see *garniture de cheminée*). Victorian and Edwardian examples in black slate weigh a lot but may still be bought at modest prices. Should the slate be damaged it may be touched up with boot black.

Collection: Wallace Collection, London

maple The wood of the maple (*Acer saccharum*) is fine-grained, light brown and highly decorative. Bird's-eye maple comes from the sugar maple tree (which also gives us Golden Syrup) and is perfect for panels, frames, and inlay. John Evelyn in *Sylva* (1679) calls the bird's-eye maple 'the Peacocks-tail Maple' and notes that 'the knurs and nodosities are rarely diapered, which does much to advance its price.' Other figurations in maplewood are known as fiddle-back, blister, and curly.

Maple picture-frames were in regular use for Victorian sporting prints and marine subjects. Several maple substitutes are on the market now, but none has the satin richness or the glow of the real thing.

maps They were a brave bunch, the early British surveyors and cartographers. Conspicuous in their surveying gear, they explored daunting and little known areas of the British Isles. For the most part they followed river banks and erratic man-made tracks — there were no real roads in the sixteenth century — and lived on charity and their own wits. Their maps were sold by subscription: notables in each county subscribed towards the cost of a map of their county and had their coat of arms within a cartouche added to the map (an empty cartouche means that one gentleman failed to cough up his subscription).

In Britain, the cartographers would start with the most populous home counties and hope that the success of these would subsidise the less familiar counties, until in time a complete set of maps could be bound together as an atlas. The name atlas comes from Mercator's collection of maps bound together and published in three volumes from 1585 to 1595. Mercator took as his frontispiece the figure of Atlas bearing the World on his shoulders, for his maps covered the whole world. The first atlas of all the counties of England and Wales was published by Christopher Saxton in 1579. With true Yorkshire grit he surveyed and drew them all himself, a task that took him nine years. For the next hundred years all maps of the counties were based principally on his results. John Speed used Saxton's surveys for all counties except Kent, Cheshire, Lancashire, the Isle of White and the Isle of Man. Speed, who worked as a tailor and court jester to help raise money for map-making, added town plans, the sites of famous battles and an informative text based on Camden's *Britannia Abridg'd* (1607). Speed's own atlas, *Theatre of the Empire of Great Britain*, was published in 1611.

The following year saw the publication of the first part of Michael Drayton's *Poly-Olbion*, an eccentric volume if ever there was one. It was primarily an epic book of verses on the rivers of England and Wales with extraordinary coloured maps by William Hole. So that rivers might be included with their tributaries, county boundaries were ignored — as for the most part were place names, scales, titles, or any of that information which one expects to find on maps. What you *do* find are a few choice cities and towns depicted by Junoesque ladies, and rivers by naked gesticulating naiads. The effect is that of a sylvan masque.

In 1675 John Ogilby, the Master of the King's Revels, produced a set of road maps ingeniously arranged in strip form with each mile, each house and each bridge charted, and each gradient drawn in such a way that you can see at a glance whether the road goes up or down.

George Bickham, author of *The British Monarchy* (1754), produced maps that are effectively a bird's-eye view of each county, with Arcadian scenes complete with romantic ruins. William Blaeu, a Dutchman, produced with his sons a great many atlases and maps, both terrestrial and celestial, of the highest quality. In 1645 he produced an atlas of England (after Saxton) and in 1654 one of Scotland (after Pont).

Naval maps having proved dangerously unreliable in 1588 — though more so to the Spaniards than the British — Captain Greenvile Collins was commissioned to chart the coast of the whole of the British Isles. His forty-eight charts took him seven years to complete, and the results were eventually first published in 1693. The most important French cartographer was William Delisle, and he produced an atlas with 24 maps in 1700 and became First Geographer to the King in 1718. His maps were scientifically based. Jan Jansson, a contemporary of Blaeu and also a Dutchman, published an atlas of England the year after Blaeu had produced his. Both men adopted a similar technique; fewer Janssons have survived, however.

Better known as Ortelius and yet another Dutchman, Abraham Ortel was the first man to undertake an atlas of the whole world. *Theatrum Orbis Terrarum* was published in 1570, went into four editions in the same year, and many more thereafter. Ortel surrounded his maps with strapwork decoration. On a map of the Old World (1590) he wrote: 'The other countries which as yet do lie obscured within the frozen zones and under both the Poles, are left for succeeding ages to find out.' Ortelius is the most significant, and, as a result, the most frequently forged, of all map-makers.

Matthew Simmons published in 1635 *A Direction for the English Traviller By which he Shal be inabled to Coast about all England and Wales*. A work derived from a set of playing cards, Simmons' book is the earliest English roadmap. Lucas Janszoon Waghenaer, a Dutchman, published the first sea atlas in 1584–5; it contained forty-five charts of the European coast line. Waghenaer included plenty of sea monsters to decorate the dull bits; despite the beauty of his maps, he died in poverty.

Old maps were printed by wood-cuts in the fifteenth and sixteenth centuries, by copper engraving and, in the nineteenth century, by the lithographic process. The paper on which maps were usually printed (vellum, silk, and cotton were also used) contains a grid of pale lines visible when the map is held up to the light; and, sometimes, the manufacturer's watermarks as well. Maps were frequently published uncoloured and have often been coloured since, by Victorian children in particular, and amateur colourists generally. Good condition is desirable, and maps should be enclosed in a transparent envelope. They can be washed with warm water, but advice should first be sought. They are extensively forged.

Books: *Collecting Antique Maps* by Ronald Vere Tooley (Stanley Gibbons, 1977); *Maps and Map Makers* by Ronald Vere Tooley (Batsford, 1970); *Antique Maps for the Collector* by J. A. L. Hyde (Bartholomew, 1972)
Collections: British Museum, London; Bodleian Library, Oxford; Library of the Royal Geographical Society, London; National Maritime Museum, Greenwich; National Library of Scotland, Edinburgh; Cambridge University Library

marcasite   The crystallised form of iron pyrites, which, when made into brooches and clips, gives the casual observer the vague impression that he is looking at diamonds. Marcasite jewellery (it was also used to decorate small ornaments) has a brassy, not-safe-in-taxis kind of charm.

marquetry   A picture built up with tiny pieces of veneer, and used to decorate furniture. The age of marquetry began in England in about 1675. At that time it was already quite a sophisticated business on the continent where fine saws for cutting veneers and marquetry had been in use for many years. Early English marquetry was cut from holly, boxwood, and light and dark pearwood, and set into light-coloured backgrounds. The natural woods were then stained to heighten the contrast. Marquetry was usually applied to walnut furniture and was often enclosed in panels. Flowers, leaves, and birds were featured, as were acanthus patterns and scrolls.

During the reign of George I mahogany superseded walnut, and marquetry was replaced by the carving and fret-cutting which Chippendale recommended. But fifty years later marquetry was revived. Since many more woods were by then available, the range of contrasts was correspondingly greater. The eighteenth-century French *ébénistes* excelled in the use of marquetry, none more so than André Charles Boulle (1642–1732) who used brass, copper, white metal, ebony, tortoiseshell, ivory, and practically anything he could get his hands on. Some of his furniture was almost completely covered in marquetry design. Under Louis XV and Louis XVI some of the marquetry was technically so superb that it could easily be mistaken for painting. Having reached its zenith, the fashion for marquetry declined towards the end of the eighteenth century.

marrow scoop   Marrow scoops or spoons (marrow as in bones, not vegetables) were first produced at the end of the seventeenth century. Early scoops were long and narrow with grooved channels at each end; they were made from silver or Sheffield plate. When the marrow scoop was revived in the late nineteenth century it was usually electroplated nickel silver (E.P.N.S.) and single-ended, the handle probably of bone.

Martinware   Here is a contemporary (1912) impression of the curious shop in Brownlow Street, Holborn, where the four Martin brothers sold their wares:

These potters do not approach you as shopmen, and I dare not think what would happen if you attempted immediately to open commercial relations. I have seen many pieces of stoneware bought of Wallace and Edwin Martin but I have never seen them sell a piece. The pots are there, they have their prices marked on them, you may examine them and admire and, if you wish, purchase them, but if you only admire you are just as — and, I sometimes think, more — welcome. For the Martin brothers are reluctant to part with the treasures they have made; they are jealous of other ownership even after they are convinced of its worthiness.

All that remains, then, is to explain who these brothers were and what strange treasures they had in the shop to inspire such fierce possessiveness. There were four of them, Robert Wallace (1843–1923), the eldest and the last to die, the modeller of grotesque birds, portrait plaques and human face jugs; Charles Douglas (1846–1910), who organised the shop; Edwin Bruce (1860–1915), who incised flowers and leaves, fish, lizards, and dragons in the unfired clay; and Walter Frazer (1859–1912), who was responsible for the preparation of the clay.

Together the brothers opened a studio in Fulham in 1873, and a workshop at Southall in 1877 (an old soap factory) in which, at great risk to all concerned, they fired their salt-glazed stoneware in their own kiln. Besides their famous — one might say notorious — leering and grinning birds with detachable heads and grotesque face jugs, they produced goblets, candlesticks, clock faces, and vases.

Considered among the earliest of true art potters, the Martin brothers brought a sort of gruesome humour into what is normally considered an

*Martinware bird,
dated 18 April 1905*

altogether solemn undertaking. But after Charles died in 1910 and Walter in 1912, the heart went out of the business and the shop closed in 1914.

Book: *Victorian Art Pottery* by E. Lloyd Thomas (Guildhart, 1974)
Collections: William Morris Gallery, Walthamstow; Public Library, Southall (Martinware Pottery Collection)

Mary Gregory glass Mary Gregory glass is the name given to those whimsical white-enamelled children who dance and play around the coloured glass jugs and vases and decanters of the mid-Victorian era. We know that Mary Gregory worked for the Boston and Sandwich Glass Company from 1826 to 1888, and we know that she specialised in these glass items. But we do not know whether it was Mary Gregory, or one of the glassworkers at the Hahn Factory in Jablonec, Czechoslovakia, or an Englishman from the Midlands or Tyneside, who first put brush to enamel to produce these enormously popular, sentimental pieces. All go under the generic name of Mary Gregory glass.

What we do know is that there are two distinct varieties on the market: those in which the children are painted entirely in white enamel on a coloured ground, and those in which white enamel is dabbed on to give relief and texture to an existing design. The first category usually displays superior craftsmanship. We know too that the glass was a big success at the Great Exhibition of 1851 and at the 1853 New York exhibition.

Cranberry glass — wrongly known as ruby glass — was the most popular background for the childish figures. Various shades of green and yellow and blue are also found. Quality is of the essence, and you can judge quality by studying the details of design. Much of the output was machine-made; you should be able to distinguish easily between these pieces and the rarer handmade ones.

Mason, Miles Miles Mason (1752–1822) came from an agricultural family in Westmorland. As a young man he opened a business in Fenchurch Street selling imported Chinese porcelain. He enjoyed the work because he loved what he sold, but when he reached the age of forty, he was obliged to close a shop which was no longer profitable. Bravely he determined to set up a manufactory of his own. He apprenticed himself to William Duesbury of Derby and then to the Worcester factory, learning all he could from those best qualified to teach. In 1794–5 he set up his own works at Lane Delph (now Fenton), Stoke-on-Trent, and produced a translucent, hard-paste porcelain, generally printed in a light underglaze blue, which he called British Nankin.

It was attractive and of good quality, but didn't pay the rent. To subsidise his income Miles Mason developed his Ironstone China which he claimed was unlikely to chip. This claim is supported by time, for many dinner services in Mason's Ironstone China survive today. They are very attractive with their reds and blues, and yellows and golds, cheerful and homely copies of superb Chinese originals. In 1804 he advertised that he could 'match' any parts of foreign services which were missing. This service was intended 'for the nobility and gentry, trusting that if these efforts are successful he may be favoured with further patronage.'

In 1805 he moved to a larger factory and was joined by his fourteen-year-old son, Charles James (1791–1856), another son, George Miles, following later. However, this is a sad saga for in 1851 Charles had to sell his patent, his moulds, his copper plates, all that makes a potter's life worth living.

Among less usual pottery items Mason produced were mantelpieces (a very few), posts for four-poster beds, cisterns for goldfish, and huge punch-bowls. Some of the Mason vases were enormous, fifty-two inches high and more. But probably the most characteristic Mason wares, and those which frequently come up for auction, are the jugs with elaborate Chinese ornamentation, and dragon handles — much imitated by Ridgway's, among others.

Books: *Mason's Patent Ironstone and Related Wares* by Geoffrey Godden (Barrie & Jenkins, 1971); *Mason Porcelain and Ironstone* by R. Maggar and E. Adams (Faber & Faber, 1977)

Matchboxes

| *Engine-turned* | *Decorated* en grisaille, *1889* | *Penknife* | *Whistle* |

matchboxes John Walker, a Stockton-on-Tees chemist, invented the friction (or lucifer) match in 1826 or 1827; and very unpleasant it was too, giving off a noxious gas when struck. However, matches were rapidly improved thereafter, becoming smaller as well as safer. Boxes were first provided for them around 1830; these held no more than half a dozen matches, which is not surprising when you remember that matches cost twopence each. (Matches are one of the few things that are cheaper now than they were 150 years ago.) Probably the idea for matchboxes came from the base metal boxes which the manufacturers supplied with their various brands. Thus we find Fusee, Vesta and Congreve boxes. The earliest non-trade matchboxes came in leather and wood; gold, silver, plate, gunmetal, and various alloys were also used.

Silver matchboxes (or match-cases, or strikers) may be collected by shape. Rectangular boxes with rounded corners, hinged along the short side, were the classics. Oval, round, and heart-shaped boxes are less common, and boxes in novelty-shapes (common in non-precious metals) are much to be treasured when in silver. The man-in-the-moon, elephants, clowns, pigs, and tortoises are just a few that have been recorded.

Decoration was by engine-turning, chasing, embossing, enamelling, *appliqué*, or by the encrustation of precious stones. Some early matchboxes had dual compartments for matches and for tinder. Many silver matchboxes had rings by which they could be attached to a watch-chain.

The phosphorus-head match was abolished by the White Matches Prohibition Act of 1908, and the heyday of the silver matchbox was over. For some, of course, they had never been necessary: the seat of the trousers was quite good enough, although as W. Macqueen-Pope remarked, that was for 'men of no social pretensions'.

matchlock Developed at the end of the fourteenth century, the matchlock had a curved, pivoting arm, known as a serpentine, attached to the stock. A match was applied at the top of the serpentine and lowered to the touch hole, at which point it fired very inaccurately towards, one hoped, the enemy. The addition of a longer barrel and sights turned the matchlock into a matchlock musket, and gave the musketeer a chance, however remote, of hitting his target.

In due course a ramrod was developed to drive the powder and ball into the breech. Though unreliable and slow-firing, the matchlock remained in use in Europe until the late seventeenth century. Japanese and Indian matchlock muskets of some quality are found more frequently nowadays than European models.

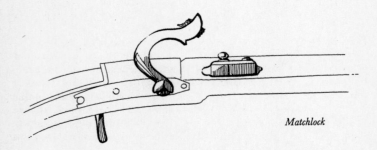

Matchlock

medals There are six categories of medals on which collectors chiefly concentrate. In the armed services, there are decorations for gallantry, campaign medals, and long service medals. Then there are the ancient orders of chivalry with their insignia, the Jubilee and Coronation medals, and miscellanea. I shall take them separately.

Decorations for gallantry. One has to start with the Victoria Cross. It remains pre-eminent despite the efforts of other countries to emulate this most celebrated medal, including Idi Amin's despicable 'Victorious Cross', given to many of his friends and himself and made (by Spink and Sons Ltd) to look as much like the real thing as possible. Instituted by Queen Victoria in 1856 at the instigation of the Prince Consort, the V.C. is made from the bronze of the Russian Cannon captured at the Battle of Balaclava, and bears the simple inscription 'For Valour'. There are still some 40lb of the gun metal left, so soldiers need not stop being brave. To date 1350 V.C.s have been awarded, 633 in the First World War. There have been three recipients of double V.C.s. The price of a Cross (if you can bring yourself to own one which you have not earned) depends upon which branch of the services the recipient was in, the total number awarded to his regiment — the Guards being the best — the theatre of war and how many were awarded in that particular battle, the details contained in the citation, whether the V.C. was awarded to an officer (best) or other rank, the condition and what other medals might accompany the V.C. You can check details, the careers of those who won V.C.s and most other gallantry and campaign medals by referring to the army and navy lists, the War Office, regimental records, the *London Gazette* and the Records Office. It is this that makes collecting medals so fascinating.

Next in rank to the V.C., the George Cross was initiated by George VI in 1940 and may be given to civilians as well as to the armed forces for actions which would not normally receive a military decoration. Like the V.C., the G.C. carries an annuity of £100 a year. Military versions are more highly regarded by collectors than civilian ones.

Other highly desirable decorations include the New Zealand Cross, awarded only on 23 occasions and always against the unfortunate Maoris, the D.S.O. (especially the gold ones issued in the first two or three years of its existence), the D.F.C. (especially if issued by Queen Elizabeth II), the Albert Medal for life-saving, and the Conspicuous Gallantry Medal.

Book: *British Gallantry Awards* by P. E. Abbott and J. M. A. Tamplin (Seaby, n.d.)

Campaign medals. The campaign medals which are generally collected today and even worn on certain poignant occasions originated in the commemorative medals struck by sovereigns from Henry VIII onwards to record splendid victories. Charles I and Cromwell both had medals struck to raise the morale of their supporters. But the first medal to be awarded to all those who took part in a battle — on the winning side of course — was the Waterloo Medal (1815) which was struck in silver for both officers and

Indian Mutiny medal
1857-58

Afghanistan medal
1878-80

other ranks and which was inscribed with the name, number and regiment of each recipient, as were all British military medals until the Second World War. The value of such medals is enhanced by the rank and regiment of the holder.

Currently the most valuable campaign medals include a gold Nile medal of 1798, the East India Company's gold medal for Egypt (1801), the Naval Gold Medal (1785–1815), the Relief of Lucknow Bar to an Indian Mutiny Medal (1857–58) and, as you might expect, medals issued to participants in the Charge of the Light Brigade. As a general rule medals to native troops are rather spurned by collectors, which is due partly to the problems of researching these medals and partly to snobbery.

Some collectors preserve the ribands of their medals in the worn condition in which they find them; others have new ribands made for them by dealers. Some collect groups of campaign medals which will give the entire history of a man's career. Together with uniforms, swords, war diaries and so on, these form collections which should never be dispersed. Catalogues of such medals and groups of medals make fascinating reading.

Long service medals. Since these were issued in great quantities and are seldom named, they command nothing like the glamorous prices of gallantry and campaign medals. They have been awarded for all kinds and conditions of long service and good conduct, from the St John's Ambulance Brigade to the Colonial Prisons, from the Royal Navy Wireless Auxiliary Reserve to the Ulster Special Constabulary.

Orders of chivalry. The insignia of the Great Orders (the Garter, the Thistle, and St Patrick) have always been returnable to the Crown by the heirs of the recipients. However, many knights of these orders had stars, badges, and insignia privately made, and still do. Vanity sometimes insisted that these be a *little* more magnificent than the official orders, so variations must be expected.

As a general rule the higher up the chivalric list the more valuable the items. Insignia made for foreign countries tend to be highly theatrical and magnificent, but are a recondite area for collectors. The insignia of these orders is usually a star or badge, a neck chain, a sash, or just a simple medal. *Jubilee and Coronation medals.* These date only from 1887, the year of Queen Victoria's Golden Jubilee. Subsequent medals were issued in 1897 (Diamond Jubilee), 1900 (her visit to Ireland), 1902 (Edward VII's Coronation), 1903 (various occasions), 1910 (George V's Coronation), 1935 (Silver Jubilee), 1937 (George VI's Coronation), 1953 (Elizabeth II's Coronation), and 1977 (Silver Jubilee). Except for the odd gold medal, none of these command very high prices, although the Queen's Coronation medals issued to the team that was the first to climb Mount Everest were officially impressed, and are highly desirable.

Miscellaneous. This small category includes a few rare and valuable items, such as Polar medals of 1904 in bronze and silver, military best shot medals, Defence of Ookiep (April-May 1902) medals, and so on.

For all the above categories, and for all medal collectors the essential *aide-mémoire* is . . .

Book: *The Standard Catalogue of British Orders, Decorations and Medals* by E.C. Joslin (Spink & Sons Ltd, continuously revised)
Collection: Imperial War Museum, London

medical instruments If you are less than happy with your local G.P., think yourself lucky that you never fell into the hands of the famous surgeon Robert Liston (1794–1847), reputedly 'the fastest man with a knife', a giant who could amputate a thigh single-handed and who cut notches on his knife after each operation. A contemporary of his reported his technique:

> One man was so terrified at the thought of his impending operation he went and hid in the lavatory. Liston strode after him, cut open the lock with his amputation knife, hauled him out, strapped him down and cut for stone in two minutes. He was once said to be so anxious to break his own record for speed (and bets were placed on his performance) that in amputating a leg he took off one of the patient's testicles and two of his assistant's fingers at the same time.

The first people in Europe to undertake surgery were the barbers who used to go into the monasteries to trim the monks' tonsures. The monks were learned in scientific matters, but not themselves permitted to consecrate the Host if they had touched blood. Instead, they instructed the barbers in such matters as leeching and bloodletting and the barbers took it from there. The stripes round the barber's pole represent bandages and remind us of those barber-surgeons of the past.

Most medical instruments collected today date from between the mid-seventeenth century and *c.*1870, when the introduction of antisepsis by

Joseph Lister meant that many of the prettier materials used to decorate medical instruments (wood, ivory, tortoiseshell, etc.) were no longer permitted in operating theatres.

Silver and pewter bleeding bowls and scarificators, or scarifiers, are not uncommon, since bleeding was the universal panacea (even for anaemia), while lancets, amputating saws, sets of trepanning instruments, forceps, catheters, tongue-depressors, aural specula, stethoscopes, ear-trumpets, pap-boats and nipple-shields are just a few of the more mentionable items collected by strong-stomached antique dealers.

Book: *Antique Medical Instruments* by Elisabeth Bennion (Sotheby's, 1978)
Collections: Simon Kaye Ltd, London; teaching hospitals generally

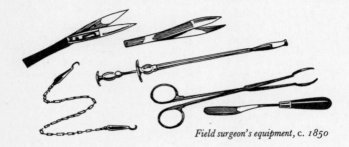

Field surgeon's equipment, c. *1850*

meerschaum   You are not required to believe the following story.

Rather over two hundred years ago a certain Count Andrassy brought a lump of meerschaum, which had been presented to him in Turkey, to Karl Kowates, shoemaker of Budapest. The Count asked Karl, who carved pipes in his spare time, if he would make him a pipe from the meerschaum, and Karl made not one but two, keeping one for himself. Later the shoemaker noticed that where his fingers touched the bowl of his new pipe, the meerschaum turned a beautiful golden brown. It was the cobbler's wax, which Karl had constantly on his fingers, that so affected the pipe. Karl waxed the whole of the pipe, and found to his delight that not only did the pipe 'colour' all over, it also gave a sweeter smoke than before.

Meerschaum, or *l'écume de mer*, so called from its likeness to petrified sea foam (in fact it is a silicate of aluminium), comes chiefly from Eskisehir in Turkey. The bowls of meerschaum pipes were always roughly shaped before being exported to Austria-Hungary (especially Vienna) for carving. They are large in diameter, thick at the base and sustain carving beautifully. The ideal mouthpiece for a meerschaum was amber, which was also worked in Vienna. It was the first pipe seriously to challenge the popularity of the clay pipe in England, and the porcelain pipe in Central Europe. See *pipes*.

Book: *The Pipe Book* by Alfred Dunhill (Arthur Barker, 1969)
Collections: Clive House Museum, Shrewsbury; British Museum, London (Bragge Collection); Guildhall Museum, London; Gorey Castle Museum, Jersey

Meissen See *Dresden.*

menu cards and **menu card holders**   Perhaps one of the most curious meals of this century, and one to rival the Mad Hatter's tea party, must have been the 'Upside Down' dinner given in 1914 at the R.A.C. Club in London. The occasion was held to honour Mr Hucks and Mr Hamel who had distinguished themselves by looping the loop and flying upside down. The guests of honour sat under large mirrors at a loop shaped table, the legs of which pointed upwards. The dinner was served backwards, beginning with coffee and ending with the *hors-d'oeuvre.*

Dining clubs have commissioned the most ingenious menu cards down the years. Walter Crane, Kate Greenaway, and Beatrix Potter all designed cards. Stanley Morrison, Graham Sutherland, Osbert Lancaster, and Vivian Ridler all worked for the Double Crown Club in the twenties and thirties. Noel Carrington designed a menu card in 1937 in the manner of a railway timetable with times of arrival and departure of courses. Cecil Beaton, Osbert Lancaster, and David Hockney are among more recent contributors. The menus at Simpsons-in-the-Strand with their celebrated Bateman cartoon of 'The Gentleman who asked the Carver whether the meat was English or Foreign!' are also intriguing.

Victorian menu cards, printed on fine cardboard or silk and satin with fringed edges, were often hand-painted and engraved. Doyleys (invented by Thomas Doyley, the warehouseman who made his fortune out of 'cheap and genteel' plate coverings) and place cards would often match the menu cards. But such menu cards and place cards were only elegant if standing in little holders. These were designed at Doulton's in the 1880s and 1890s by George Tinworth among others, and featured musical mice, organ grinders, and so on. Though made from moulds, they were finished by hand, and no two examples are quite the same. Royal Worcester, too, used the opportunity to design some frivolous cards, which now fetch nonsensical prices, especially when sold in sets.

Menu card holders

millefiori Literally 'a thousand flowers', the technique of fusing together bundles of coloured glass rods, drawing them out, and then slicing them across, was known to the Egyptians some three and a half thousand years ago, and revived in sixteenth-century Venice.

miniature furniture There are three possibilities: either these miniature, scaled down examples of bookcases, tables, wardrobes, etc., were made as travellers' samples; or they were made to stand in shop windows to advertise what the cabinet-maker could provide; or they were 'Prentices' Pieces', made by apprentices to display their skills. Many arguments have raged during those long bleak afternoons when business is slow as to which explanation is the most feasible. I should suppose that the most sophisticated examples were used by travellers and window-dressers, the more naïve pieces made by apprentices.

Book: *Book of Miniatures: Furniture and Accessories* by Helen Ruthberg (Chilton, 1977)

Minton Founded at Stoke-on-Trent in 1796 by Thomas Minton, pupil of Thomas Turner of Caughley and one-time employee of Josiah Spode, Minton's very swiftly became established and affluent. From 1821 a fine, white, soft-paste porcelain mimicking Sèvres ware was produced. From 1828 Thomas' son, Herbert, set about potting encaustic tiles, based on medieval designs found in ancient monasteries. Another speciality of the firm was the Parian ware figures, modelled by John Bell (sculptor of the Guards Memorial in Waterloo Place) and by the imposingly named Frenchman, Albert-Ernest Carrier-Belleuze, among others.

Majolica in the Spanish and Italian styles was designed by Léon Arnoux, the artistic director of the firm from 1848, and from 1870 or 1871 Marc-Louis Solon, transferred from Sèvres, supervised the *pâte-sur-pâte* ware which was so enthusiastically admired by those who understood about such things. In the 1870s William Coleman, the director of Minton's Art Studio Pottery, was among the most energetic disciples of all things Japanese.

As you will have gathered, Minton's was a sort of artistic Vicar of Bray, cutting its cloth with every wind that blew (if I may mix a metaphor). But it was also admirably empirical in its policy of employing the best artists, wherever they could be found.

For a hundred years from 1842 Minton's employed a year-code, enabling its better pieces to be easily dated. From 1943 this code was replaced by using just the last two digits of the year of production.

Book: *Minton Pottery and Porcelain of the First Period* by Geoffrey Godden (Barrie & Jenkins, 1968)

mirrors Until the seventeenth century mirrors, though backed with metallic substances, gave poor, dark, and distorted reflections. Then Sir

Robert Mansell (1573–1656) brought over from Venice a number of craftsmen: he had just been granted a monopoly of plate-glass making and wanted to get the most out of it. He was extremely successful and in 1664 the Worshipful Company of Glass-sellers and Looking-glass Makers was incorporated in London. The previous year the Second Duke of Buckingham had established a manufactory at Vauxhall, which was to become celebrated for the quality of its plate glass.

The French and English competed during the eighteenth century to supply plate glass for mirror-frames. High import duties were imposed but even so most of the large plates of glass were imported from France. In 1773 the British Cast Plate Glass Company was established at Ravenhead, St Helens, a site now occupied by the Pilkington Glass Works, among the largest suppliers in the world. Early mirrors were very small, and carried in the hand, dangled from a belt, or placed on a dressing-table. The word 'looking-glass', dubbed non-U by Alan Ross in 1956, became current during the seventeenth and eighteenth centuries, and this was the very period in which looking-glasses were covered in reflected glory.

Early English frames were almost square with wide convex moulding around the glass, and were made of oak, veneered with walnut, or lacquered. Many English mirrors were tall and narrow and were intended to fill the 'piers' between windows, while over-mantel mirrors with bevelled glass were framed in carved giltwood. It was the custom for several plates to be contained within the same frame. Dressing-tables with toilet-glass and elaborate free-standing cheval mirrors were also fashionable in bedrooms and dressing-rooms.

The materials and design of mirror-frames followed the prevailing furniture fashions throughout the eighteenth century. The rococo style led to some impressively ornate examples from Chippendale, until the influence of Adam, with his neo-classical imagery, made itself apparent. Sheraton was keen on circular convex mirrors, and copied some which had been manufactured in Nuremberg from the fourteenth century. William Ince and John Mayhew also advocated them. The familiar convex giltwood mirror decorated with balls and suspended from a chain held in an eagle's beak was a feature of the early nineteenth century. Art nouveau and art deco designers seized on the mirror as a wonderful excuse to explore different mounting and framing materials. Pewter, copper, chrome, and aluminium are just a few materials used; since glass can now be supplied to more or less any specifications, the designers may be given free rein.

Book: *English Looking-Glasses* by G. Wills (Country Life, 1965)

model ships   Evelyn Waugh's fascination with cruise liners, and his descriptions of life on board in *Brideshead Revisited* and *The Ordeal of Gilbert Pinfold* border on the obsessive. They are closely related to his fascination with the decline of the West, for some of the more extravagantly fitted

Cunarders — the SS *Normandy* in particular — made a religion of luxury and a spiritual pilgrimage out of a visit to the cocktail bar. Now the big ships are gone, and there was irony in the manner of their going; for they were so solidly built that it became uneconomic to scrap their saleable parts.

The aristocrats of model ships are the ten- to twenty-foot models which once dignified the showrooms and boardrooms of the shipping lines. Bassett-Lowke was the firm responsible for many of these beauties. Steam-yachts are much in demand, their luxury fittings being difficult to reproduce in miniature. Warships are rarer than merchant-vessels. Block models which are half boats, sometimes only hulks, were made to guide the builders in the shipyards and tend therefore to be in poor condition. Plating models are block models with scale details of the necessary plating; sectional models give cutaway views of public rooms, cabins, and so on.

> *The stately ship is seen no more,*
> *The fragile skiff attains the shore;*
> *And while the great and wise decay,*
> *And all their trophies pass away*
> *Some sudden thought, some careless rhyme,*
> *Still floats above the wrecks of Time.*
> William Edward Hartpole Lecky

Collections: Rotunda Museum, Woolwich; Arlington Court, Barnstaple; Transport Museum, Belfast; Museum and Art Gallery, Sunderland; Library and Museum, South Shields; Public Museum, Rochester; City Art Gallery and Museum, Kelvingrove, Glasgow; City Museum, Liverpool; Dorman Memorial Museum, Middlesbrough; Buckland Abbey and City Museum and Art Gallery, Plymouth; Doughty Museum, Grimsby

model soldiers   Toy soldiers have been popular since the Egyptian civilisation. Paper cut-out soldiers existed in France during the childhood of Louis XIV; they were obviously fragile and as a consequence have become very rare. Carved wood soldiers from Bavaria, between two and twenty inches high, were sometimes mounted on springs and wheels. Plastic soldiers in Britain since the war have enabled manufacturers to keep prices down, though there is little pleasure in handling plastic. When collectors speak of model soldiers, they are usually referring to metal.

The very earliest metal soldiers were developed in southern Germany. They were quite sizeable, the horses and knights being cast in solid bronze, gilded and enamelled, while the soldiers were made of slate. The first commercial tin soldiers were about six and a half inches high and were produced by Johann and Andreas Hillpert, from Nuremberg (*c*.1760). During the next hundred years the soldiers shrank in size until the big producers, such as Allgeyer and Heinrichsen, agreed on standard sizes conforming to the Nuremberg scale. By then Hillpert and his successors had made models of just about every contemporary regiment, as well as representative Roman, Saracen and medieval troops, and impedimenta.

These models were all 'flats', which is to say they were two-dimensional figures on small stands. There also developed *c.*1850 'semi-flats' or 'semi-solids' in low relief, while 'solid' figures which had been produced in small quantities since the sixteenth century were developed commercially by the French, especially Mignot, in the 1870s. The French called these models *rond bosse*. Towards the end of the century William Brittain, an English-man, produced the first hollow-cast, three-dimensional figures. These were more realistic than the continental models and cheaper, since they contained less metal. Brittain completely dominated the world market and by the outbreak of the Second World War claimed to be able to supply every regiment in the British Army.

Books: *Model Soldiers* by W. Y. Carman (Letts Collectors Guides, 1973); *Model Soldiers* by Henry Harris (Octopus Books, 1972); *Model Soldiers* by Massimo Alberini (Orbis Books, 1972) — finely illustrated; *Collecting Old Toy Soldiers* by Ian McKenzie (Batsford, 1976); *Collecting Model Soldiers* by John Garratt (David & Charles, 1975)

Mohs scale   Devised by Friedrich Mohs, the Austrian mineralogist, in the late nineteenth century, the Mohs scale is a test of hardness in stones, climbing from 1, the softest (talc) to 10, the hardest (diamond).

1 Talc	6 Felspar
2 Gypsum	7 Quartz
3 Calcite	8 Topaz
4 Fluorite	9 Corundum
5 Apatite	10 Diamond.

To give an indication of how hard is hard, a fingernail would rate $2\frac{1}{2}$, a copper coin 3, window glass $5\frac{1}{2}$, a knife blade 6, and a steel file $6\frac{1}{2}$.

money-boxes and **money banks**   The piggy bank originated in the eighteenth century. Pigs were thought to be lucky, and a smiling pig with a slot in its back was meant to encourage children to part with their pocket money. Mechanical money-boxes of cast-iron were extremely ingenious and popular during the last century. Teddy Roosevelt shoots a coin into a tree in which a bear is hiding (see *teddy bear*). Two monkeys shoot a coin into the mouth of a lion about to consume a baby monkey. A coin put into the hand of a black man or woman is raised to the mouth and swallowed, gratitude being expressed by the flashing of the whites of the eyes. American banks encouraged designers to ever more inventive mechanical devices. An Honest Labourer hits an anvil labelled Monopoly, and a coin is deposited in a slot marked Bread Winner's Bank. William Tweed, the Tammany Hall boss, receives a coin and nods in appreciation.

A word of warning. Many cast-iron money banks are being reproduced quite convincingly. Underneath some of them there should be the legend 'Made in Taiwan', but this has frequently been erased on importation.

monteith   Rather disappointingly, the monteith appears *not* to have been named after a Scottish earl who slaughtered five hundred carousing Cromwellians by poisoning their punch, but after a certain Frenchman, a Monsieur Monteigh. Dating from the seventeenth century, a monteith is a large bowl, originally silver or pewter, but later china or glass as well, with a scalloped brim from which wine glasses hung down into iced water. Sometimes the rim was detachable so that the bowl could be used as a straightforward punch bowl, and very often the monteith was dignified with lion-mask drop-handles.

Moorcroft, William   One of the few potters whose work is sufficiently individual to be collected during his lifetime or within a generation of his death. Others who spring to mind include Bernard Moore, Clarice Cliff, Susie Cooper, and Dorothy Doughty. Moorcroft (1872–1945), whose bold signature appears in green or blue underneath most of his wares, was trained as an art teacher, and became a leading designer with the Burslem firm of James Macintyre and Company. Here his bold floral designs made an immediate impact: Aurelian ware and Florian ware (1898–1904) featured stylised flowers, and later trees were introduced (1902) with toadstools (1903) and pomegranates (1911).

In 1913 Moorcroft established his own pottery at Cobridge, where he specialised in monochrome lustreware and flambé effects. As he grew older, his colours became darker, his flowers and plants more exotic. But the designs themselves were constantly simplified, much as Miró in his late years produced four huge canvasses, each covered with a rich sheet of a simple colour. Writers find it far harder to attain such dignified simplicity.

William was succeeded at his factory by his son, Walter, in 1945.

Book: *William Moorcroft and Walter Moorcroft* by Richard Dennis (Catalogue of Fine Art Society Exhibition, 1973)

Morris, William   When William Morris died in 1896 at the age of sixty-two, his doctor remarked that he died simply 'of being William Morris and doing more work than any ten men'. Consider:

He was a poet, a propagandist, an architect, a painter, a furnisher, a jeweller, a textile designer, a dyer and carpet-weaver, a lecturer, a conservationist in the days when such creatures were scarcely known about, a social democrat, a Marxist, a museum adviser and college examiner, a typographer and printer, a glazier, a tile-maker; in short, an artist-craftsman and a one-man revolution.

He was brought up in Walthamstow, educated at Marlborough and Exeter College, Oxford, studied architecture for a year under George Street, painting with Edward Burne-Jones (1833–98) and Dante Gabriel Rossetti (1828–82), and built Red House with Philip Webb (1831–1915). In 1861, with £100 from his mother and £1 from each participant, he

William Morris chair

founded a cooperative of seven artists known as 'The Firm', which introduced innovations in every area of design. In 1874 The Firm (Morris, Marshall, Faulkner and Company) was bought out by Morris (Morris and Company), after which woven and printed fabrics became an increasingly important part of its output.

He was now an active campaigner for socialist reforms, particularly through the Art Workers Guild and the Arts and Crafts Exhibition Society. The dignity of labour and physical, spiritual and social liberty were basic tenets of his work. In the 1890s his interest extended to typography (he designed three types, Golden, Troy, and Chaucer) and he founded the Kelmscott Press which produced sixty-five volumes and was most influential in the private press movement.

It seems sad and rather ironic that a man so diverse and so dedicated should be chiefly remembered by fashionable, modern, and not always honourable, reproductions of his wallpaper and fabric designs. We would do well to remember his philosophy: 'It is the allowing machines to be our masters and not our servants that so injures the beauty of life nowadays', and his last words: 'I want to get mumbo-jumbo out of the world', which seem as pertinent today as when this remarkable man set out to change the quality of our lives, and did so.

Book: *William Morris: from Romantic to Revolutionary* by E. P. Thompson (Merlin Press, 1977)
Collections: William Morris Gallery, Walthamstow; Wightwick Manor, Wolverhampton

motor-vehicles   Since the first horseless carriage there have been well over five thousand different makes of car, some (the Model T) whose success has been legendary, others (the Edsel) so disastrous as to support

*1935 Bentley 3½-litre
saloon by Park Ward*

one of Pascal's *Pensées*: 'Men are mad so unavoidably that not to be mad would constitute one a madman of another order of madness.'

Technically speaking one needs to know that veterans are cars produced in or before 1904. Edwardians date (a little unhistorically) from 1905 to 1919, while vintage cars are sports cars of the 1920s and 1930s. Pedants also refer to post vintage thoroughbreds (P.V.T.s) — cars of a later date, whose quality of design makes them worth collecting.

Although Britain has always had the most sentimental attitude to old cars — the Veteran Car Club, founded in 1930, is the oldest in the world — the collecting of fine cars, and the investment in them of fine sums of money, is now an international sport. Sotheby's held two sales of old cars as long ago as 1969. This is not the place for a lengthy survey of the most desirable vintage and veteran cars — there are several specialist magazines which do that quite adequately — but the Blue Chips, as listed by James A. Mackay, are as follows:

Alfa Romeo The 2.9 litre, 8 cylinder version of 1934
Aston Martin The 1.5 litre 'side-valve' model of the 1920s
Ballot The 2 litre, 4 cylinder model of 1923–28 or the RH3 'straight 8' of 1929–30. The Ballot company was taken over by Hispano-Suiza in 1929
Bentley The 8 litre Bentley of 1931
Bugatti The Royale 15 litre (probably only six of these Bugattis still exist — only seven were built — but any Bugatti is a treasure)
Duesenberg The J and SJ Models of the 1930s
Delage The 'Straight-Eight' D8.5S 100
Frazer-Nash Any of the post-1930 models
Hispano-Suiza The 5 litre, 6 cylinder Type 68 bis of 1932 (with an engine capacity of 11,310cc!)
Isotta-Fraschini The 8-B of 1931
Lagonda The V12 of 1937
Mercedes-Benz Since only two examples of the 38/250 Model exist, it can hardly be called a Blue Chip. Any S-type Mercedes would do nicely, however

Packard   The 8 cylinder Speedster
Rolls Royce   The Silver Ghost, between 1907 and 1925

Other cars now being much collected include the Alvis, Lanchester, Rover, Talbot, Austin 7, Morris Minor Traveller, Sunbeam Talbot, Riley, MG TC and TD, Morgan, Jaguar XK 120 and XK 140 and E-type, Rover P4 range, Austin Healey, Triumph Mayflower, and Lea Francis. Also the Volvo P1800 S 'Cow Horn' model, which I loved like a baby.

Book: *Book of the Veteran Car* by Phil Drackett (Pelham Books, 1973)
Collections: National Motor Museum, Beaulieu; Cheddar Motor Museum, Cheddar; Myreton Motor Museum, East Lothian; Pembrokeshire Motor Museum, Pembroke; and many others (refer to *The World's Motor Museums* by T. R. Nicholson — Dent, 1970)

musical instruments   Casals described his cello as 'a beautiful woman that has not grown older . . . but younger with time, more slender, more supple, and more graceful.' And here is Menuhin on his Prince Khevenhuller violin made by the ninety-year-old Stradivarius: 'ample and round, varnished a deep, glowing red, its grand proportions were matched by a sound at once powerful, mellow and sweet.'

Perhaps the most satisfying aspect of collecting musical instruments is that their quality is evident not just in their appearance but in the sound they make. The market for them is an artificial one, since prices for antique instruments in good working order are inflated by solo instrumentalists, whose fees are fat and whose pockets are deep. The young cello player, for instance, will have the greatest difficulty in buying an instrument of quality at a price less than the price of a large car, if not a small house. The inflation has spread to bows too. A fine bow by François Tourte, 'the Stradivarius of the bow', will sell for many thousands of pounds.

Collections: Horniman Museum, Dulwich; Fenton House, Hampstead (for keyboard instruments, which for a small fee you may even play); British Piano and Musical Museum, Brentford (especially automatically played instruments); Michelham Priory, Hailsham (Alice Mummery Collection); City Museum, Liverpool; Carisbrooke Castle Museum, Newport, Isle of Wight

Two-keyed boxwood oboe, c. 1800

Seventeenth-century Dutch ebony tenor recorder

musket A smooth-bore firearm fired from the shoulder, the musket was used by the infantry from the late sixteenth century until the early nineteenth. Its length was gradually reduced from five to three feet, and it was fitted with whatever firing mechanism was currently in vogue.

mustard pots Before the eighteenth century mustard was served dry in a caster and sprinkled as we sprinkle salt and pepper. It was sold in 'Tewkesbury balls', otherwise known as 'fire balls', small agglomerations of dried mustards mixed with damp pea-flour. In the eighteenth century the Durham process of milling mustard seed to produce mustard flour became generally accepted.

Mustard pots date back three centuries. They were sometimes made of glass and china, but it is the Georgian silver ones which are so charming. Small pots with hinged lids, blue glass liners and spoons were and are quite rare and expensive. Commemorative mustard pots are not unknown. A fine collection of pots is maintained by Messrs Colman of Norwich.

Nailsea glass Glassworks were founded in this Somerset village in 1788 and 1790 by John Lucas and William Chance respectively: the two then amalgamated in 1810.

Originally crown-glass window panes, eulogised eloquently by Sir John Betjeman in *The Village Inn*, were produced at Nailsea. These are panes made with concentric wavy lines of glass around a 'bull's eye' in the centre. Various domestic glassware was thereafter produced in the works, but a great deal of what the trade refers to as 'Nailsea glass' probably came from Bristol, Stourbridge, and elsewhere. Such items as gemel and bellow flasks, witch balls, walking sticks, bugles, rolling pins, etc., made from flecked, festooned, and filigreed multi-coloured glass are optimistically supposed to originate in Nailsea. The table-bells certainly didn't.

Book: *Nailsea Glass* by Keith Vincent (David & Charles, 1975)
Collections: Municipal Museum, Warrington: Gilchrist Collection, Cowes, Isle of Wight

Nankin In the early years of this century any evidently antique pieces of blue and white Chinese porcelain would be catalogued as 'Old Nankin', or 'Old Canton'. There never was a porcelain factory at Nankin, a river port in Kiangsu Province, although porcelain from nearby centres may have been decorated there; Nankin was simply the port from which much Chinese porcelain was exported. But it had been established as capital of the Ming Dynasty in 1368.

'British Nankin' is the name which Miles Mason gave to the hard-paste porcelain in the Chinese manner which he manufactured at Lane Delph. See also *Canton*.

Book: *Oriental Blue and White* by Sir H. M. Garner (Faber & Faber, 1970)
Collection: Percival David Foundation of Chinese Art, London

Nantgarw William Billingsley painted flowers on porcelain as though the paintbrush were the tip of an angel's wing. By using a dry brush to wipe away wet pigment he was able to create flowers that looked as though they had been picked with the dew still on them. Unfortunately he was not an angel in other matters and you cannot wipe away creditors with a dry brush.

He learnt his trade from Zachariah Boreman at Derby, but left and went into partnership with John Coke at Pinxton. This partnership was dissolved in 1799 after three years, and he then set up a decorating establishment at Mansfield. By 1803 he was at Brampton-in-Torksey, but after five lean Lincolnshire years, certain pressing financial matters necessitated his changing his name to Beeley (sometimes Bailey). Now he took his two daughters and Samuel Walker, his future son-in-law, to Swansea, and eventually to Worcester, always on foot and living rough. At Worcester the two men were contracted to Messrs Barr, Flight and Barr to whom they sold the secret of their soft-paste porcelain for £200, entering into a thousand-pound bond to reveal it to no one else. The following year Billingsley and Walker decamped from Worcester, breaking their contract in doing so, and taking their secret and the two girls with them.

At Nantgarw in Glamorgan they set up their own factory, requesting a grant from the government since, as usual, they had what is now called tactfully 'a cash-flow problem'. The man from the ministry, Mr Dillwyn, was most impressed and built the partners a larger works in Swansea before discovering that they had left Worcester under rather a dark cloud. They returned once again to poverty and Nantgarw. Now they organised things better. In 1818 they found ten country gentlemen to subscribe £100 each, but within two years the cupboard was once more bare, and they sold up and offered their services to John Rose at Coalport, whose emotions at seeing two such notorious gentlemen must have been mixed. William Weston Young, a local land surveyor, naturalist, and dealer who had been a loyal friend in the past, bought up the remaining Nantgarw House stock and decorated some of it himself, but again the business failed.

It should at once be emphasised that the quality of the work produced at Nantgarw approached the quality of Sèvres, which it much resembled. And it should be added that many other notable porcelain works also failed about this time, namely Chelsea, Bow, Bristol, Longton Hall, Liverpool, Lowestoft, Caughley and Plymouth, to mention but a few. It was a liquidator's market.

With two such peripatetic gentlemen, there are bound to be confusions as to what came from Nantgarw, what from Swansea, what from elsewhere, who painted what, and whether it matters. Flatwares are invariably marked with the name Nantgarw and 'C.W.' (for China Work), and sometimes letters and numbers. So is the work they did at Swansea. As to the china itself one should be clear that there were three distinct periods,

1813–14, 1817–20 and 1820–22, the period during which Young and Pardoe ran the works, probably only decorating existing stock and not firing any new. The second period is the finest: the porcelain is brilliantly white and translucent with a clear glaze. Billingsley's flower paintings, often featuring briar roses, are of course outstanding. Many of the pieces sent off to London to be painted are also very fine.

Besides the men mentioned above, Thomas Baxter, a friend of Nelson and Lady Hamilton, painted landscapes; John Latham, William Pegg, and Matthew Colclough (whose speciality was birds) are thought to have decorated Nantgarw plates, dishes, and vases. The most famous pieces to leave the factory were those which made up the Mackintosh service: these have a border of gilded shells, reserve panels of flowers, and, centrally, an exotic bird in a floral landscape.

Book: *Nantgarw Porcelain* by W. D. John (Ceramic Book Company, 1948, with 1956 supplement)

Collections: National Museum of Wales, Cardiff; Royal Institute of South Wales, Swansea; Glynn Vivian Art Gallery and Museum, Swansea; Royal Museum, Canterbury; Art Gallery and Museum, Cheltenham

napkin rings   The napkin carelessly cast aside over the debris of the dinner table is the sign of the true aristocrat. The careless indifference, the casual selfishness, how little of such things television directors know!

Napkin rings appeared at the start of the eighteenth century. Since only the privileged classes could afford napkins, the only napkin rings which survive from that period are extravagant examples, gold, silver-gilt and silver predominating. As I have suggested, those who used the napkins did not themselves ring them; the sequence would have been as follows: (a) napkins are folded into elaborate shapes in preparation for the dinner party; (b) after the meal they are casually cast aside; (c) the following morning they are re-damped, ironed and slipped through their rings to be used by the family at breakfast and lunch.

Sometimes the rings would be engraved with the owner's name, initials or family crest. Very often a silver ring, boxed with a matching mug and porringer, would be given as a christening present. Many silver rings are characteristic examples of the work of the great silversmiths, reflecting styles from regency to art deco.

Cheaper but still attractive rings come in mother-of-pearl, ivory, carved wood, and beadwork, or are embroidered on Berlin wool, inlaid with Tunbridgeware, and printed with tartans.

necklaces   In Czechoslovakia a grave estimated to be 20,000 years old was excavated and found to contain a male human skeleton wearing a necklace of fishbones, deer's teeth, birds' legs and shells. Men wore necklaces long before women (some, such as mayors and Masons, still do).

Modern collectors concern themselves only with necklaces from the Renaissance onwards. Pearls and diamonds have always been the most desired stones for necklaces, although amber, jet, coral, amethyst, seashell, citrine, and other more dubious materials have often been used. To study necklaces as they are designed to be viewed, that is to say round necks, visit the National Portrait Gallery, London. See also *lockets*.

netsuke   The *netsuke* (pronounced *netski* by those who wish to be treated seriously by dealers and auctioneers) is a toggle, used at the end of two threads which are attached to an *inro*, which is closed by tightening the threads with an *ojime* — a bead. And, in the days before pockets, the *netsuke* was tucked through the *obi*, the sash worn with the kimono by Japanese men and, sometimes, women. The golden age for *netsuke* was the late eighteenth and early nineteenth centuries; after the Meiji restoration in 1868 European costume came into fashion and, as a consequence, *netsuke* were made for the export market, becoming decadent and trashy.

Early *netsuke* (they originated in the fourteenth century) were made of wood. Other materials include lacquer, mother-of-pearl, tortoiseshell, enamel, horn, bone, amber, metal, and even dried mushroom. But most *netsuke* are carved, often minutely, from ivory. The types are as follows: *ichiraku*, with a basketwork design; *kagamibuta*, a shallow bowl, 1½ inches in diameter, fitted with an ornamental metal disc; *katabori*, miniature sculpted figures, the most popular form of *netsuke*; *kurawa*, which did double duty as an ashtray and was used with a tobacco pouch; *manju*, which was circular, flattened in the shape of a miniature Japanese rice-cake, and was either solid or hollow; and *sashi*, which were rod-shaped, often in the form of an insect on a twig, and were up to five inches long.

Netsuke may be homely and jocular, grotesque, erotic or inscrutable. They may imitate natural objects or symbolise spiritual values. The best examples are finely carved with rounded corners, good coloration and patina, and are signed. Prices received a dramatic boost with the sale of the Hindson collection at Sotheby's (1967–69), since when the market has been hectic. In 1978 the first international *netsuke* convention was held, and in 1979 a new record for a *netsuke* of £19,000 plus premium was established.

Books: *Netsuke* by N. Davey (Faber & Faber, 1974); *Netsuke Familiar and Unfamiliar* by Raymond Bushell (Weatherhill, 1976)

Ivory netsuke

New Hall   Richard Champion (1743–91), a Bristol shipowner, took over a porcelain factory in Bristol from his cousin, William Cookworthy (1705–80), who had discovered the secret of making 'true' or hard-paste porcelain. But the factory proved something of a white elephant. Cookworthy's patent came up for renewal by Parliament in 1775, but the renewal was opposed by a powerful consortium of Staffordshire potters. As a result Champion won the right to produce 'translucent' but not 'opaque' porcelain in Bristol. However the case cost him a great deal of money and, with competition from Derby and Worcester (cheaper) and Meissen and Sèvres (more fashionable), he was unable to stay in business. With a wife and eight children to support, Champion had to sell his patent, which he did to the Staffordshire consortium. He left England and settled with his family in South Carolina where he flourished as a farmer.

Meanwhile the consortium opened their factory at New Hall, Shelton, in Staffordshire, in 1782. They produced domestic china of considerable charm. The influence of Chinese *famille rose* is apparent, and the typical decoration is sprays of flowers and sprigs of leaves applied with some restraint. Painting, gilding, and transfer-printing were employed, and in about 1810 the New Hall mark (the name of the factory in a double circle) appeared. The regular New Hall paste is very hard, glossily glazed, and milk white. Some lustreware was produced. Like so many other porcelain works, New Hall closed its kilns in 1825, but its influence among numerous imitators remained powerful for some years.

Book: *New Hall and its Imitators* by David Holgate (Faber & Faber, 1971)
Collections: Christchurch Mansion, Ipswich; Luton Museum, Luton

newspapers   The earliest newspapers were published as 'newsbooks' in the 1620s and it was forty-five years before the single sheet made its appearance. Those early newspapers were fiendishly expensive to produce, and became more so in 1712 when the Tax On Knowledge, as it was romantically dubbed, was introduced. The result was that syndicates of people clubbed together to buy such papers as Cobbett's *Weekly Register*. At the end of the year the leaves would be bound together into volumes, a practice which has created problems for collectors of single sheets. From 1695 the press was technically 'free', that is to say no editor needed a licence to run his newspaper, although he naturally remained subject to the laws of the land.

Collectors of old newspapers tend to specialise according to subject, geographical location, or historical event. The highest prices are reached for newspapers recording important events like the Battle of Trafalgar, but there is a growing interest in more recent issues, such as *Picture Post*. Bound copies of *Punch* are always popular, especially in complete runs.

Collection: British Museum Newspaper Library, Colindale

Nymphenburg Nymphenburg, which is near Munich, had a porcelain factory from 1747; in 1761, the factory was transferred to the Nymphenburg Palace, where it still is. In 1766 two hundred men were employed there, but in 1771 the work force had dropped to thirty.

Early Nymphenburg porcelain is whiter than white. Miniature figures, groups, vases, and table services formed the major part of the factory's output, and examples are extremely graceful. Melchior, from the Frankenthal factory, Bustelli, famous for his Commedia dell' Arte figures, and Auliczek were three of the finest modellers. Since 1862 the factory has been privately owned, but it is not a notable advertisement for private enterprise. The current owner is the grandson of Ludwig III of Bavaria.

oak The earliest English furniture of the Middle Ages was ecclesiastical in origin. Since the monastic architect was the one who set the styles, the designs were austere and uncompromising. Oak was the principal material: it was the representative English wood, and it was very durable. Oak furniture of the Gothic period was brightly coloured, decorated with tapestries and softened with valances and cushions. The paint has long since flaked off, the tapestries, valances, and cushions have rotted, but the wood itself has survived, and early Gothic furniture has a stark beauty reminiscent of Edinburgh on a lowering day.

Rooms were panelled and furniture consisted of tables, chests, benches, buffets, cupboards, beds, stools, and *prie-dieux*. Floors would have been strewn with rushes, clothes kept in a *garderobe* (a small room by itself, not a piece of furniture in a room), and baths taken in wooden tubs in front of the fire. Chests and coffers were popular, both for storage and sitting on.

At the end of the fifteenth and beginning of the sixteenth centuries the linen-fold pattern, having originated on church screens, became a popular decoration for furniture panels. Some Gothic designs became highly elaborate and intricate; the choir stall canopies in Westminster Abbey are a good example. During the sixteenth century Gothic taste was gradually replaced by the Renaissance style, and oak by walnut.

Collections: Aston Hall, Birmingham (fine furnished Jacobean house); Elizabethan House, Totnes; Museum and Art Gallery, Maidstone

ogee The 'line of beauty', or *cyma recta*: a slender S-shaped curve, the upper concave, the lower convex. Frequently applied to drinking glasses, namely the ogee bowl. The shape is also seen in bottles and, ornamented, in cabriole legs. My own legs are a bit ogee.

ojime See *netsuke* and *inro*.

ormolu The word comes from the French *or moulu* which means 'ground gold'. In fact it is only gilded brass or bronze. An object would be cast in bronze, using the *cire perdu* method, in which a model is made of wax over an armature, with clay around the wax. When the wax melts, molten metal is poured into the mould. Then the hollow object receives an application of mercury and gold, and, after the mercury has vaporised, verdigris is added as a fixative. After *c.*1840 electrogilding was used. Ormolu brackets, mounts, and decorations were applied to most of the best pieces of eighteenth-century French furniture and clocks. Much Chinese porcelain was disfigured by the addition of ormolu mounts.

There are a number of substitute materials, usually involving spelter, which you should guard against, for the real thing is luxuriously expensive these days.

Collection: Wallace Collection, London

ottoman The Turks were responsible for the low, broad bench known as the ottoman, which dates in its British version from the late eighteenth century. The ottoman could be circular or octagonal, and was frequently button-backed. It might be divided into four seats by upholstered arms, or have a cone-shaped back rest, with or without carving, upon which an aspidistra might stand and glower. And you will remember that Winnie the Pooh 'gets what exercise he can By falling off the ottoman'.

paperweights The attractions, both for the aesthete and for the investor, of old French paperweights became apparent in June 1953 when Mrs Applewhaite Abbott sold her large collection at Sotheby's. Among those impressed by the attractions of these artifacts was King Farouk, not a man to draw a bow at a venture. During the 1950s he bought up most of the best examples to come on to the market. Maybe he liked them because the techniques of some of the *millefiori* (thousand flowers) pattern paperweights had their origins in the mosaic glass beads of the ancient Egyptians.

The paperweights for which Mrs Abbott and King Farouk shared such enthusiasm are not all that old. Pietro Bigaglia, one of a Venetian family of glassworkers, is credited (by Frank Manheim) with the production of the first paperweight. This he exhibited at an industrial fair in Vienna in 1845 where it found an enthusiastic disciple in the French Professor Peligot. The eulogies of the professor to his friends in Paris were so infectious that an industry to produce similar paperweights in France (and notably at the Baccarat, Clichy, and St Louis factories) got under way forthwith. Of course they were not the main business of these factories, but they were profitable sidelines.

A *millefiori* weight is made up of bunches of coloured glass canes arranged in patterns. The technique is fascinating and complex, every part of the paperweight being made by hand. But these are not the most desired of the nineteenth-century French paperweights. It is the butterflies and dragon-flies, the birds and reptiles, the mushrooms and vegetables, above all the fruit and flowers in beautifully accurate representations that attract the most enthusiastic attention of the collectors.

Books: *Glass Paperweights* by Patricia McCawley (Letts Collectors Guides, 1975); *Antique Glass Paperweights from France* by Patricia McCawley (Spink & Son Ltd, 1968);
Collections: Littlecote House, Hungerford; Farnham Museum, Farnham

Mid nineteenth-century Baccarat paperweight

papier mâché   Originally patented in 1772 as 'paper-ware' by Henry Clay of Birmingham, the name *papier mâché* was not used until Richard Brindley from the same city produced a much cheaper version of a similar material. Clay had decorated his furniture, trays, and smaller items with paintings (usually landscapes) in oils; Brindley preferred the fashionable lacquer. Clay commissioned original works; Brindley copied old masters.

The intention of Henry Clay was to produce an English equivalent of Japanese lacquer — the Pontypool ironware and tinware took painted decoration nicely but was not suitable for furniture. Paper-ware proved ideal: it was light; it was stronger than it looked; and, properly japanned, it was oriental in a pleasantly British sort of way. It was made by stiffening paper pulp with glue, chalk, plaster, sand, sizing, and gum mastic. Layers would be added *ad libidum*, then paint and varnish. It was heat- and damp-resistant, and Adam found it just the job for cornices and other architectural decorations. The firm of Jennens and Bettridge adopted Clay's invention and dominated the world market during the first half of the nineteenth century.

Papier mâché proved to have limitless uses: boxes, trays, ink-stands, screens, coasters, blotters, fans, vases, teapots, writing cases, cabinets, letter-racks, pen-trays, canterburys, tables, chairs, and beds (though these thankfully had an iron framework). By 1900 there was little *papier mâché* being made, except in kindergartens. The tin age was upon us, the plastic age just around the corner.

Papier mâché may be repaired with plastic wood, touched up with India ink or stove black, heightened with gold paint. It may be cleaned with furniture cream. The best examples are signed Jennens and Bettridge, but

Victorian papier mâché
*jewellery cabinet, inlaid
with mother-of-pearl*

even unmarked pieces are sometimes charmingly embellished with
mother-of-pearl, tortoiseshell, nautilus shell, and ivory designs or oil-
painted panels.

Book: *English Papier-Mâché of the Georgian and Victorian Periods* by Shirley Spaulding De Voe
(Barrie & Jenkins, 1971)

parasol   The parasol, like the poodle, was as much a matching accessory
as an object of utility. Ladies in the mid-nineteenth century who did not
wear broad-brimmed hats, carried parasols to match their dresses, and fans
to match their parasols. Often the parasol had a fringed lace covering on an
ivory stick, although there are many variations on the theme.

Parian   Parian, a statuary porcelain imitating marble and receptive to
fine modelling, was invented at the Copeland factory by a certain Mr
Battam. Neither he nor the factory patented the new invention with the
result that it was exploited by many other firms, notably Minton and
Derby. Parian is very similar to biscuit, but it uses a felspar that fuses at a
lower temperature. It shrinks by up to one quarter of its mass during firing,
which can pose interesting problems for the modellers. It has been chiefly
employed for classical subjects, and it has to be said that nude limbs look
particularly smooth and enticing in Parian ware.

Book: *Victorian Parian China* by C. and D. Shin (Barrie & Jenkins, 1971)

parquetry   A decorative technique of inlaid wood similar to marquetry,
except that the pieces of wood used in the designs are straight-edged. The
effects are achieved by contrasting the grains in the wood, as they should
also be contrasted in good quality parquet flooring. An obvious example of
parquetry design is the chessboard.

pastille burners These small containers in silver, in bone china, or in Staffordshire earthenware had perforations at the top through which the scent of charcoal-burning could cleanse the air of a room in which a meal had recently been eaten, or in which an invalid was lying. The ceramic versions, from Swansea, Rockingham, and the Staffordshire potteries, were often in the shape of castles, cottages or animals.

Collection: Art Gallery and Museum, Cheltenham (Kingsworth Nye Collection)

patch boxes Both men and women of the seventeenth and eighteenth centuries wore patches, which were small pieces of taffeta attached to the skin. The theory was that by drawing attention to a large artificial blemish, smaller natural ones might pass unnoticed. And the most offensive pock-marks could be covered by a patch. Boxes made to contain patches were usually of porcelain, and sometimes had a mirror set into the lid.

pâte-sur-pâte Marc-Louis Solon (1835–1913) invented the process known as *pâte-sur-pâte* while employed at the Sèvres factory. It involved the application of low relief decoration in white slip on to celadon grounds in grey, green, or chocolate. 'A cloud of cream in a cup of tea' is a vivid description of the effect achieved, and the designs in this paste-on-paste technique were usually classical figures rich in poetic allegory and semi-draped. From Sèvres, Solon moved to Minton in 1870 or 1871, and produced more *pâte-sur-pâte* pieces there until his retirement in 1904, after which he worked on just a few pieces of special significance. The technique was adopted also at Meissen, Moore Brothers, Worcester, and other factories, but it was time-consuming and expensive and was rarely produced after the turn of the century.

patina Originally 'patina' referred to the oxidisation which occurs on bronze after long exposure to the earth's atmosphere or long burial underground. Examples of this may be seen on ancient Chinese bronzes, now green with age. Artificial patina was applied by treating with acids, and dignifies old Japanese sword-mounts. By extension the term has come to be applied to any material which acquires a skin after weathering. Patina cannot be bought in a tube or applied with a piece of leather.

pediment Properly a pediment (something like a gable) is a technical term from classical architecture, meaning the triangular part of a building enclosed by raked cornices above an *entablature* and under the roof. In case-furniture of the seventeenth century the word was applied to the equivalent part of the furniture. Later on it was used to describe the moulding on the pediment, as well as the pediment itself. In the eighteenth century and thereafter it could also be applied to tallboys, cabinets, and the hoods of longcase clocks.

Pembroke table Why is the Pembroke table so named? It has nothing to do with the county of Pembroke in west Wales; according to Sheraton, it was named after the Countess of Pembroke (1737–1831) who 'first gave orders for one of them and who first gave the idea for such a table to the workmen.' Others make a claim for Henry Herbert, ninth Earl of Pembroke (1693–1751), known as the Architect Earl and admired by Horace Walpole for his good taste.

The Pembroke is a smallish drop-leaf table with shallow leaves that are supported on brackets when the table is open. In a true Pembroke, the hinges are placed along the long sides of the table; when they are on the short sides it is a sofa table. Pembroke tables were very popular in both the eighteenth and nineteenth centuries; you will remember that Mr Wodehouse in *Emma* had a small Pembroke 'on which two of his daily meals had for forty years been crowded.' The majority of eighteenth-century Pembroke tables stand on four legs, which were square until 1770, afterwards becoming square and tapering, and sometimes turned. The last quarter of the century was the finest for these tables, with satinwood veneer a fashionable choice. Marquetry and painted decoration (which Sheraton recommended as an attractive and economical alternative) were also used to embellish the elegant Pembroke table.

Two warnings. It is not unheard of for a Pembroke table which appears honourable at first sight to turn out to be an illicit union between top and frame. And you would not have to travel far to find a simple and unfussy old table which has been 'improved' by Victorian or Edwardian painting.

pewter There are peculiar problems associated with the collecting of pewter. First of all nobody has yet agreed about what it is. Secondly, the forging of pewter with modern touchmarks is perfectly legal; since many genuinely antique pieces were never marked in the first place, this leads to a good deal of confusion. Furthermore until this century and the notable scholarship of H. Massé, it had received scant attention from academics and collectors. But antique pewter has such a moonlit glow, such unassuming candour, that I find it hard to resist.

The Romans made pewter from Spanish or Cornish tin, mixed with lead. After they left Britain pewter continued to be made, both grand pieces, chalices and candlesticks fit for altars, and secular items, such as bleeding bowls and slop-pails — and you can't get much more secular than that! For churches, pewter medallions were struck with the images of saints, and those who could not afford silver for their ecclesiastical plate used pewter instead and were none the worse for it.

In the fourteenth century the first controls for pewterers were introduced in London, and in 1350 the unfortunate John de Hiltone, 'peautrer', was arrested and his stock forfeited for making vessels 'the greater part of the metal of which was lead'. As to what the constituents of pewter should properly be, opinions vary. Eighty parts tin to ten lead and ten copper was standard, but Massé sorted pewter into thirteen grades of alloy. Some silver is usually present, but it is there 'not because anyone put it in, but because nobody could get it out.'

The Worshipful Company of Pewterers received its charter from Edward IV in 1473, and members were required to register an individual 'touch', which would identify them should any of their pieces fail to conform to the requisite standards of composition and workmanship. These touchmarks are both attractive and extremely useful, but they should never be taken on their own as evidence of authenticity. The 'table' upon which the records, delineating which mark belonged to whom, were set, was sadly destroyed in the Great Fire of London. But in 1929 Howard Herschel Cotterell, the Tolstoy of British pewter, listed no fewer than 6000 pewterers whom he had identified. Platters, dishes, saucers, cups, bowls, goblets, salts, spoons, porringers, and almost everything which you would have expected to see on a middle-class English table between the fourteenth and seventeenth centuries could have been made of pewter. It had a life expectancy of no more than thirty years, and if it did not succumb to natural wear it would frequently be melted down for re-use. The most desirable surviving pieces are probably the broad-rimmed chargers of from 15 to 20 inches in diameter, made between c. 1650 and c. 1680. The multi-reeded plate replaced these chargers, to be followed, in its turn, by single-reeded plates, and then, between the early eighteenth and early nineteenth centuries, by plates with entirely plain rims.

Besides ecclesiastical and domestic pewter, tavern pieces are well worth latching on to. These include baluster wine measures from half a gill to a gallon ('hammerheads' from 1600 to 1670, 'buds' from 1670 to 1730 and 'double volutes' with Prince of Wales feathers on the thumb pieces, from 1730 to 1800). These measures became pot-bellied in the early Victorian period and straight-sided later in the nineteenth century.

The challenge to pewter by the cheaper and inferior Britannia metal was hard to meet (partly because it is so difficult to tell that it *is* cheaper and inferior), and pottery was able to do all that pewter could do at a price which it couldn't, so that only in pubs, where Britannia metal and earthenware were simply not strong enough, did pewter survive into this century. In fact the arts and crafts movement produced a minor revival of interest in pewter with the Tudric range, sold by Liberty's from 1875 and vaguely influenced by medieval Celtic art.

Traditionally pewter was cast in moulds with five types of decoration, namely relief casting, engraving, chasing, punching, and overlaying with such materials as brass, plate, lacquer, and paint. It tended to copy the styles employed by the silversmiths (and their hallmarks too on occasion) with very elaborate rococo examples being produced on the continent where pewter already had a long and distinguished history.

Corrosion to pewter may be removed by soaking it in paraffin, and dents by hammering it with a horn-head hammer, resting the article on a sandbag. Valuable pieces and those that appear old should be taken to a specialist. Abrasives should never be used, nor acids. Indeed the grime on an old piece of pewter, induced by wood smoke and tavern fug, is a vital part of its charm, and I should leave it alone. See also *Billies and Charlies*.

Books: *A History of English Pewter* by John Hatcher and T. C. Barker (Longman, 1975);
       English Pewter Touchmarks by Radway Jackson (Foulsham, 1970); *British Pewter* by
       R. F. Michaelis (Ward Lock, 1969); *Pewter* by Gabriele Sterner (Studio Vista,
       1979)
Collections: Victoria and Albert Museum, London; Guildhall Museum, London; Kelvin
       Museum, Glasgow; Pewterer's Hall, London (by appointment)

phonograph Thomas Alva Edison (1847–1931) was not a man to let the grass grow under his feet. In America alone he took out a total of some twelve hundred patents, and when he discovered (by mistake, for he was working on a morse code machine at the time) the means of reproducing the human voice, it was no more than three months before he had produced the first phonograph. This operated on the same principle as almost all succeeding phonographs, gramophones, record players, 'music centres', what you will. But Edison's phonograph was not commercially successful and nine years later in 1886 Alexander Graham Bell, his cousin Chichester Bell, and an instrument-maker called Charles Tainter were granted a patent for their graphophone, an electric machine where

An Edison 'Amberola'
concealed-horn phonograph of 1909

Edison's had been hand-driven. An improved phonograph by Edison competed with Bell's graphophone during the last years of the century for use as a dictaphone. But bosses preferred secretaries, and the machines were more successful reproducing music than business letters.

Unfortunately, until master cylinders were invented, artistes and musicians could only produce one disc from each recording session; this tried their patience, and their musicianship, more than a little. Early cylinder machines had spring-drive with a governor rather than direct electric drive until 1907 when AC mains drive was introduced. Edison machines include among others the Gem, Standard, Triumph, Balmoral, Home, Idelia, and Fireside. Edison Bell Machines (*not* Edison's company) introduced a Gem and a Standard too, as well as an Elf, Imp, and Eva. Columbia had over forty different models in America, but fewer in Britain. These include the Q, Eagle, Standard, Grand, AZ, Sovereign, Jewel, and Trump. The Crown (1907) and the Coronet (1908) featured a tone arm, which disc machines already had.

Cylinder machines continued to compete fiercely with disc machines until the outbreak of the Great War. Four-minute cylinders were the answer to twelve-inch records, and both machines displayed the exterior horns which are so much part of the early music reproduction instruments in the imagination of the public. Cylinders were produced until 1929.

photographs   'From today painting is dead!' cried Paul Delaroche, the painter, when he saw his first daguerrotype. One can appreciate his enthusiasm and alarm. But it was not painting that died: it was privacy.

The first photograph was a heliograph, taken from Delaroche's attic window by the ageing French scientist, Joseph Nicéphore Niepcé in 1826. This led to collaboration with Louis Jacques Mandé Daguerre which resulted in the publishing of a daguerrotype in the late 1830s. In England William Henry Fox Talbot had been leaving what his wife called 'little mousetraps' around the house to photograph such things as chair legs and breakfast tables. Talbot's process, the first to use a negative from which any number of paper prints could be produced, was championed by Sir John Herschel, of the Royal Academy, who invented both the word 'photography' and the 'hypo' (hyposulphite of soda) which contemporary photographers still use.

Early photographers frequently worked in pairs, partly because the equipment was so cumbersome. In the 1840s David Octavius Hill and Robert Adamson collaborated on a composite portrait of 470 delegate ministers of the Scottish Free Church. The photograph measured over 11 feet long by 5 feet high and took twenty-three years to complete.

In 1851 Frederick Scott Archer invented the wet collodion process involving glass plate negatives. Not only did the process produce wonderfully clear images, but it was published without patent restrictions, and it was this more than anything else that encouraged the hordes of amateur photographers who established societies, held exhibitions, and earnestly debated whether this new activity was an art or a science.

For Roger Fenton it was art, science, and propaganda: his coverage of the Crimean War with a team of photographers showed the conflict more realistically and therefore more poignantly than the traditional war artists. (An album of Fenton's Crimean studies was sold at Sotheby's Belgravia in 1975 for £8500.) He also produced some superb studies of Britain's finest country houses and gardens. In 1862, however, Fenton abandoned photography and resumed his legal career. In the same year Queen Victoria instructed Francis Bedford, an associate of Fenton's, to accompany the Prince of Wales as official photographer on a tour of the Near East. It had not taken long for the new art form to become respectable. When the dry-plate process replaced the wet-plate in the 1880s, photography became accessible to those without much chemical expertise, but not until this century did cameras become easily portable.

Other Victorian photographers whose work is significant must include the formidable Julia Margaret Cameron, who specialised in portraits of all the most eminent *literati* of her time. The wife of an ex-Indian Army civil servant, she did all her developing in a converted chicken shed in the garden, but she was totally dedicated and serious in her work. Posing for her required patience: one had to hold a pose for up to ten minutes without moving or smiling. She lit only from above and produced only contact prints (which she neither retouched nor enlarged) from her huge wet-plates, and continued her sittings until she was satisfied; in Browning's case, for instance, she took three hours.

David Wilkie Wynfield and Frederick Evans also photographed eminent artists, their counterpart on the continent being 'Nadar', whose portrait of Sarah Bernhardt enables us partially to understand why so many discerning critics thought her divine. Lewis Carroll preferred little girls, while John Thomson, Adolphe Smith, and Paul Martin took magnificent, candid photographs of the working classes.

Foreign travellers who brought home albums of their travels included the Bisson Brothers (the Swiss Alps) and Francis Frith (Egypt and the Nile). More parochial travellers, who snapped nature landscapes at home, included George Washington Wilson, George Shaw, the Reverend John Wheeley Gough Gutch (really!), and Joseph Cundall, who was expert at Yorkshire abbeys. Eadweard Muybridge, Eakins, and Marley all conducted experiments into animal and human locomotion with strips of photographs, not at all dissimilar to film-strips.

By the 1920s a less formal approach to photography had become fashionable. It was not blasphemous to proclaim that accident could be involved in design. Surrealists, such as Man Ray, used startling juxtapositions of animate and inanimate objects to great effect. Signed photographs by modern photographic artists fetch substantial prices, although, if the artist is still alive, there is no guarantee that he has destroyed the negative from which your print has been taken.

Books: *Early Photographs and Early Photographers* by Oliver Matthews (Reedminster, 1973); *Collecting and Valuing Old Photographs* by Peter Castle (Garnstone Press, 1973)
Collections: Kingston Public Library (for Eadweard Muybridge); National Portrait Gallery, London; Victoria and Albert Museum, London

photograph albums and **scrap albums**   The early family albums of 1840–50 were no more than albums for souvenirs, somewhat haphazardly arranged, with no special provision for photographs; indeed at that time photographs were something of a rarity. Later on albums were made especially for photographs. A characteristic one would be heavily bound in leather-covered, bevelled boards. The pages would be white or cream card, the edges gilded, with metal clasps. The front would be embossed or tooled with coats of arms or crests. Some might even display patterns in lacquer with inlaid ivory and mother-of-pearl decoration. The pages, enhanced with floral sprays or country views, would have frames for one, two or four photographs, from the small *carte-de-visite* size ($4 \times 2\frac{1}{2}$ inches) to the cabinet size ($6\frac{1}{2} \times 4\frac{1}{2}$ inches). Below the photographs you can usually find the name and address of the photographer, while on the back of the mounts are trade advertisements elaborately engraved.

For the portrait photographs themselves the effect is usually a little grim, but this is because the sitters were formally posed and had to remain immobile for several seconds. Sunday best is worn. The man often holds a walking stick, or rests his elbow on a pedestal, while the woman carries a book, a letter, or a small spray of flowers. Children may hold tennis racquets or hoops. The studio props, besides those mentioned above, include drapes, baskets of flowers, button-back chairs, urns, and trellis-work.

By the turn of the century there were some 17,000 registered professional photographers. Albums of specialised subjects by famous photographers, such as landscapes by Hill and Adamson, fetch substantial sums at auction. The record of £52,000 given in 1975 for an album of portraits by Julia Margaret Cameron (1815–79) is unlikely to be surpassed for many years.

More modest scrap albums are full of charm. They flourished from the middle of the last century and give vivid insights into the lives of those who kept them. You may find menu cards, dance cards, programmes, pressed flowers, postcards, verses, and quotations. Watercolours, caricatures, and sketches are often as engaging for their amateur enthusiasm as for any aesthetic qualities. Arrangements of 'scraps', which were bought individually and feature rosy-cheeked children, holly, robins, comic cats, and all the sentimental paraphernalia of Victorian taste, are often highly imaginative.

piecrust border On eighteenth-century furniture and silver you will often see a scrolled border, with alternate concave and convex curves separated by straight sections. This 'piecrust' border is usually found on a circular table.

pinchbeck An alloy of rose copper and zinc which closely resembled gold, and which was invented by Christopher Pinchbeck (d. 1732), clockmaker extraordinary. Just as pinchbeck is an inferior imitation of gold, so there are now plenty of inferior imitations of pinchbeck. So secret was the formula of this alloy that in 1733, the year after Christopher's son, Edward, succeeded to the business, the following advertisement appeared in the *Daily Post*: 'Notice is hereby given, that the ingenious Mr. Edward Pinchbeck, at the Musical Clock, in Fleet Street, does not dispose of one grain of his curious metal, which so nearly resembles gold in colour, smell and ductility, to any person whatsoever; nor are the toys made of the said metal sold by any one person in England except himself.'

pin cushions Pin sticking was a pretty pastime to give Victorian schoolgirls training in the finger dexterity so necessary if they were to play the piano. Regency pin cushions were flat and thin so that they could easily be carried in a reticule. As chairs became fat and overstuffed so did pin cushions, growing huge, encrusted with beads and pearls, ruched and flounced and threaded with ribbon, or patchworked. These monsters came in strange shapes too, of shells, stars, or animals.

Some had ceramic or metal bases with plush on top to take the pins; these could be wittily made to look like improbable household articles. Silver slippers or boots, Tunbridgeware, tortoiseshell, pearl-shell, ivory, *papier mâché* may all be found with a little patience. And if you think the whole business *petit bourgeois*, then I would remind you that Victoria made a white and gold pin cushion for her governess, 'dear Lehzen'.

Collection: Luton Museum and Art Gallery, Luton (Doris Homan Collection)

pine Any soft wood from a coniferous tree is generally known as pine. The timber from the Scots fir (*Pinus sylvestris*) is known as deal and was used for drawer-linings and other parts of furniture that would not be immediately visible. Yellow pine (*Pinus strobus*), also known as Weymouth pine or New England pine, was introduced in the mid-eighteenth century to replace deal, to which it was superior.

pipes Pipes do have splendid names: large bents and churchwardens, round pokers and dublins, wafered chubby apples and cadgers.

Until the end of the eighteenth century pipes were usually of clay. Only a very few of these early clays were stamped with the makers' marks, and attribution and dating is therefore something of a puzzle. In any case few

*Meerschaum pipe
with silver mounts*

*Erotic pipe-cum-cheroot
holder, c. 1885*

survived, for they were very fragile, especially the long-stemmed varieties, such as London straws. Cherrywood pipes were subject to carbonisation and cracking, porcelain pipes overheated, glass pipes from Bristol and Nailsea were fun to look at but impossible to smoke, and pottery pipes were not much stronger than clay.

The sensible solution was the meerschaum, which was made from tiny fossilised sea creatures. The meerschaum itself came chiefly from Turkey, but the pipes were carved (often in weird and wonderful shapes) in Vienna. Claws clutching at eggs, ladies in picture hats, Arabs, skulls, Bismarck, Napoleon, Cleopatra's Needle, George and the Dragon, Leda and the Swan, there was very little that the skilled meerschaum carver was not prepared to tackle. Erotic subjects in particular were discreetly displayed on pipes, perhaps because they were usually smoked in all-male company. The advantage of the meerschaum is that it remains cool and dry to smoke, and is light and pleasant to handle. The ideal mouthpiece was amber, which could be carved in any number of adventurous, provocative ways.

The modern briar, usually with a vulcanite mouthpiece, comes from the root of the tree heath, or *Bruyère arborescente*, found in Corsica, Calabria and Algeria. It is pleasant to smoke, absorbent and robust, but it will not submit to carving as the meerschaum will. According to Alfred Dunhill,

> *Give a man a pipe he can smoke,*
> *Give a man a book he can read,*
> *And his home is filled with a calm delight,*
> *Though the room be poor indeed.*

Book: *The Pipe Book* by Alfred Dunhill (Arthur Barker, 1969)
Collections: Guildhall Museum, London; London Museum; House of Pipes, Bramber,
    Steyning, Sussex (25,000 items)

piqué An inlay of gold and silver set into ivory or tortoiseshell, and very nice too. There are three main types: *piqué point*, comprising tiny nail heads set into a pattern; *piqué clouté*, using slightly larger nails; and *piqué posé*, flakes of gold and silver inlaid in cut-out sections which can be swiftly inserted into tortoiseshell made more amenable by heating. *Piqué* was chiefly used for boxes, fans, buttons, buckles, earrings, and brooches. After 1872 it was stamped out instead of handmade.

playing cards   The oldest playing cards are thought to date from Chinese paper notes of the T'ang Dynasty AD 618–908. These were both what you played *with* and what you played *for*. In the West too the first paper money seems to have been playing cards with IOUs scrawled on them. Edward Gibbon used cards for just such a purpose, as well as for indexing *The Decline and Fall of the Roman Empire*.

The design of the standard English pack of playing cards (that is to say, four suits of thirteen cards each) is French, from Rouen in fact, and it has changed very little in five hundred years. The French suits, *piques*, *coeurs*, *carreaux*, and *trèfles*, represent the class structure in medieval France of knights, churchmen, vassals, and husbandmen. The diamonds represent the arrowheads of the vassal archers; the clubs are the clubs of the husbandmen; and the spades are the points of the knights' lances. The hearts represent the churchmen. Thus the old chess-based war games became courtly games of chivalry. In 1440 came the first *named* court cards, and thereafter it was a witty satirical game to depict respectable personages, even popes, in a disreputable light on playing cards. The French revolutionaries deposed the court cards when they deposed the court and until 1813 French citizens played with philosophers, emblematic personages, and *sans-culottes*.

The printing press was invented in Germany, and the earliest cards were printed in Stuttgart from wood blocks. These cards featured hunting scenes with dogs, stags, ducks, and falcons as their suit signs and all the court cards depicted as seductive ladies. Hearts, leaves, bells, and acorns are the German national suits (cups, batons, money, and swords in hot-blooded Spain). Perhaps the most famous German cards are those made by Virgil Solis, the goldsmith of Nuremberg.

Churchill playing cards

Holland is famous for the Holbein 'Dance of Death' cards and the notorious pope sets proscribed by the Vatican, burned when found, and hence extremely valuable today.

The earliest English cards were not made until the end of the fifteenth century (before then sets were brought back from France by the English soldiery) and all our early cards bear costumes of the period of Henry VII. In 1628 the card makers of Britain received their royal charter and thereafter cards bore on them registered marks, such as the Great Mogul, Henry VIII, the Valiant Highlander, and the Merry Andrew. A tax first imposed in 1710 varied from threepence to half a crown, the duty stamp being printed within the fanciful design of the ace of spades, sometimes known as Old Frizzle, and almost always considered unlucky.

In 1832, De La Rue was granted letters patent to produce both backs and fronts of cards by letterpress and lithography, and from 1862 every imaginable variation was played on the basic theme. The joker was an American invention of the mid-nineteenth century. Twentieth-century cards are already being collected, particularly curiosities like the Belgian pack featuring Churchill, Stalin, Roosevelt, and de Gaulle as the four kings with Hitler as the joker; the notorious confiscated sets ridiculing Giscard d'Estaing and his administration; and the Kennedy Kards produced in 1963 as a tribute to the new president.

Books: *A History of Playing Cards* by Roger Tilley (Studio Vista, 1973); *Collecting Playing Cards* by Sylvia Mann (H. Baker, 1973); *Discovering Playing Cards and Tarots* by George Beal (Shire Publications, 1972)
Collection: Bowes Museum, Barnard Castle

Plymouth and **Bristol**   William Cookworthy, once a chemist's apprentice and a dedicated Quaker preacher, spent some twenty-eight years (*c.*1740–68) experimenting to find the secret of hard-paste or 'true' porcelain, as manufactured in China. His persistence was rewarded and he took out a patent and began production in Plymouth in 1768. Two years later in association with his cousin Richard Champion, a shipowner (see *New Hall*), and a delftware potter, Thomas Frank, he moved the business from Plymouth to Bristol, a suitable port from which to ship goods to the New World.

The Bristol manufactory only survived until 1781. Competition from cheaper British and smarter continental firms, combined with the disruptive effects of the American war, made the situation hopeless. Champion eventually managed to sell the patent for the new process to a consortium of Staffordshire potters who set up the works at New Hall — which in turn only survived for three years (1822–25).

Book: *Cookworthy's Plymouth and Bristol Porcelain* by F. Sevene Mackenna (F. Lewis, 1946)
Collections: City Museum and Art Gallery, Bristol; City Museum and Art Gallery, Plymouth

pontil   When a piece of glass has been 'marvered' it is transferred from its blow-pipe to its pontil (or punty, or puntee). In other words, when it has been roughly shaped it is attached to an iron rod for the final stages of styling and the addition of handles, etc. When finished, the object is snapped from its pontil, leaving a pontil mark underneath. On some early glass objects the pontil mark is pushed up inside the base. This is known as a 'kick'. Later on pontil marks were considered unsightly and were ground away. After the mid-nineteenth century they were eliminated entirely.

Pontypool   This town in Monmouthshire was the first centre for decorated tinware. Having been an iron manufacturing town, Pontypool was ideally placed to cash in on the late seventeenth-century craze for japanning, which aimed to imitate oriental lacquer work, but as often as not ended up looking like the cat's dinner. Besides *chinoiserie*, designs included rustic and sporting scenes, and among objects thus decorated are trays, caddies, boxes, and scuttles.

Collection: Newport Museum and Art Gallery, Newport

porcelain   See *hard-paste* and *soft-paste*, and factories (e.g. Worcester).

porringer   The derivation of this attractive word, which takes account of the intrusive 'n' and the change of 't' to 'r', gives the game away. A porringer is the same as a potager or, for that matter, a porridger. It is, in short, a bowl for liquid food.

Usually made from silver, pewter, or Sheffield plate, this small shallow basin, with or without a lid and with one or two handles, was also, I fear, used as a bleeding bowl. Indeed in America the bleeding bowl was called a porringer. Though the names may be confused, let us hope the contents never were.

Portland Vase   See *cased glass*.

Portobello   To clear up any confusion, Portobello ware refers to the pottery thrown at Portobello, Midlothian, Scotland. It does not, or should not, refer to the Staffordshire pieces made to commemorate the taking of Portobello in Spain by Admiral Vernon in 1739, nor to the ware for sale on stalls in Notting Hill on Saturdays.

There were several potteries in Midlothian between 1800 and 1850, and among other things they produced tiles decorated with allegorical subjects. William Baird in his *Annals of Duddingston and Portobello* mentions a Florentine lion, a watch-case shaped like a miniature clock with Britannia rampant, and a cow with a calf, as Rathbone's ware from Portobello. However, much of the output from Portobello is similar to run-of-the-mill Staffordshire ware.

postcards It was Emmanuel Herman who suggested to the Post Office that one might be permitted to send a piece of light card with limited space for words through the post at less than the price of a letter. In 1869 Austria issued the first postcards and Britain followed suit a year later. So successful was the idea (publicly commended by Gladstone) that 500 million cards were sent in 1900 and in 1917 the British Forces Postal Service dealt with almost two million cards and letters every day.

Rafael Tuck had encouraged the business with a hugely publicised competition for Christmas cards in 1880, and things got properly under way in 1894 when the Post Office allowed commercially printed pictorial postcards to be sent through the post. These early postcards were required to have the whole of one side kept free for the address so that any message had to be written on the illustrated side, but in 1902 printers were permitted to split the reverse of the card into two halves, one for correspondence and one for the address.

During the Edwardian era all kinds of novelties were introduced such as aluminium cards, pull-out cards, tinselled, embroidered, and illuminated cards that changed with the light. The three main producers were then Valentine, Bamforth, and Tuck.

The Great War saw the emergence of three main categories of cards: patriotic, sentimental, and comic. Silks with regimental crests and flags became very popular, as did the cartoons of Bruce Bairnsfather, also a great name in the sheet-music business. Recently cards have been widely collected, and they can be very expensive. Art nouveau cards by Kirchner or Mucha or Annie French can fetch over £50 each. Louis Wain cats, actresses, suffragettes, Donald McGill cards, royalty, topographical, glamour, there is almost no category that does not have its adherents.

Books: *Picture Postcards* by Marian Klamkin (David & Charles, 1974); *Picture Postcards of the Golden Age* by Tonie and Valmai Holt (MacGibbon & Kee, 1971); *The Picture Postcard and Travel* by Frank Staff (Lutterworth, 1979)

potlids After the sight of bewigged French aristocrats on the guillotine, wigs went out and were replaced by pomade (or pomatum). Gentlemen dressed their hair with bear's grease mixed with macassar oil: in the 1830s a Bond Street shop advertised that gentlemen's servants would be given an opportunity of seeing a freshly killed bear hanging over a hot grid, and the grease being prepared. It is no wonder the antimacassar became so essential a part of the soft furnishings in a Victorian household.

It was soon realised that the attractive pots in which the bear's grease was sold — and particularly their lids — provided valuable advertising space. A series of sixteen potlids featuring bears at play and at bay were produced and are now eagerly hunted down, as eagerly as the bears once were. The idea caught on for other products: potlids advertised 'Ambrosial Shaving Cream, Perfumed with Amonds', 'Old Civet Cat Cold Cream',

'Gorgona Anchovy Paste', 'Sweet Honeysuckle Tooth Paste, laden with the Scent of Flowers and breath of odorous spring', and many other enticing concoctions.

The main potteries responsible for the production of early potlids were Cauldon Potteries, Mayer Brothers and Pratts of Fenton, and C. T. Maling and Sons of Newcastle-upon-Tyne. The great Jesse Austin was the resident designer at Pratts; he not only printed the designs, but invented a multicolour printing process to reproduce them on earthenware. Prices were high; monochrome lids were then as now less expensive than coloured ones, although prices today are as dependent on rarity as on aesthetics. A regular price guide to potlids is published by the Antique Collectors Club and should be referred to.

Paste potlid, 'Preparing for the Ride', by Jesse Austin

In the end potlids priced themselves out of the market. Jesse Austin died in 1879, and people decided that they had had enough of potted shrimps from Pegwell Bay — one of the most successful lines. Crosse & Blackwell struggled on for a while, but tins were cheaper and more versatile than pots.

Many of the better examples of Victorian potlids were framed in circular ebony frames and hung on walls. Framed potlids are desirable (but be warned that forgeries are more convincing when framed), as are the copper plates from which the lids were printed.

Books: *Staffordshire Potlids and their Potters* by Cyril Williams-Wood (Faber & Faber, 1972); *Collecting Potlids* by Edward Fletcher (Pitman, 1975); *Price Guide to Potlids* by A. Ball (Antique Collectors Club, 1970; revised annually)
Collection: see *Prattware*

pottery   Anything which is made of clay and is opaque rather than translucent, is pottery. It is a general term which may be subdivided into earthenware and stoneware.

Collections: Museum and Art Gallery, Stoke-on-Trent; Museum and Art Gallery, Kirkcaldy

powder flask   Not to be confused with a powder compact. A powder flask was a container for gunpowder. Early ones were made from animals' horns, in their original condition, but later they were mounted with brass or other metals. Gold, silver, leather, wood, bone, and ivory were also used. The stopper would have a measuring device built into it so that the right amount of powder was dispensed. Often powder flasks came in pairs, the big one for the main charge, the small one for the primer. Naturally when muzzle-loading guns were replaced by breech-loading guns with percussion cap cartridges (c.1850) powder flasks rapidly fell into disuse.

I once had a silver flask on my stall, so blackened with age that I failed to recognise its quality: I had priced it at £2.50 and a canny dealer sold it for £40. I sometimes think that powder compacts are all I deserve!

Prattware   Fenton was (and is) a fairly large district in the Staffordshire potteries which contained the factories of — among others — Thomas Whieldon, once a partner of Wedgwood, Robert Garren, John Barker, Thomas Green, and Thomas Heath. The last of these had a pottery at Fenton as early as 1710, and his son-in-law was Felix Pratt, the maker of Prattware, who built his works on the site of his father-in-law's pottery. He produced his wares from c.1775–80 to c.1810–20, and specialised in national heroes such as Admiral Nelson and the Duke of York, children, animals including cow-creamers, relief plaques, stirrup cups, jugs with fabulous scenes and caricatures upon them, money-boxes, pipes, and watch-stands.

Many of these pieces were unmarked and may have been produced by other potteries, but there are distinctive features of Prattware to help us. The characteristic colour is creamy with a bluish glaze, although yellows, oranges, browns, blues, and greens are also found. Frequently Prattware is decorated with acanthus leaves. The quality is variable.

Collection: Laing Art Gallery and Museum, Newcastle-upon-Tyne (including potlids)

prie-dieu   Also known as a kneeling chair, a praying chair, a devotional chair, or a vesper chair. In order to make their devotions effectively Christians require comfort but not luxury. Hence the *prie-dieu*, which is a small praying desk with one shelf for the prayer's knees and another higher up near the wider top for the prayer book. Originally designed in the fourteenth century, *prie-dieux* were revived from c.1835 to c.1875 and,

*Eighteenth-century
Italian* prie-dieu

under the potent influence of the Oxford Movement, they became quite fashionable. Victorian models were either severely carved in the Gothic manner with blind tracery, or upholstered, sometimes in Berlin woolwork.

quaich or **quaigh**   The word probably derives from the Gaelic 'cuach', meaning cup or bowl, and this Scottish utensil was very likely used for both liquid food and drinks. The quaich could be made of marble, silver, pewter (rarely), brass, ivory, or wood. What was distinctive about it was its 'lugs': these are flattened handles, and there were always at least two.

The earliest traced example is a marble quaich of the late sixteenth century. Some of the silver examples of *c.*1700 are of extreme elegance. Often they have been used for taking collections at the sacrament and for holding the tokens at the communion table. They are still made to be given as prizes. By the nineteenth century the quaich had lost most of its distinction, along with other Scottish antiques.

quaint style or **fanciful style**   This was the trade version of art nouveau, and was popular at the turn of the century. It consisted of a conglomerate of writhing plants, arabesques, floral motifs, and suchlike whirligigs made from copper, enamel, mother-of-pearl, rosewood, and fumed oak. Greens and purples were popular quaint colours, and one should approach the more elaborate examples of this restless style with a clear head, a strong stomach, a jar of paraffin, and a match.

rat tail   A vivid description of a typical late seventeenth- and eighteenth-century spoon, which displays underneath its bowl a raised spine of metal tapering to a point. The intention was to add strength to the spoon; the effect was one of distinction.

Ravenscroft, George   A merchant and a chemist, George Ravenscroft (1632–83) perfected in 1676 the process of making lead glass (after previously inventing a defective 'crystaline glass'). He may safely be regarded as the most important figure in the history of British glass-making. It is therefore rather a shame that until 1975 many facts about his life, including the dates of his birth and death, were quite incorrectly reported. From 1677 Ravenscroft was permitted to seal his glass with a raven's head as a guarantee that it would not 'crissell', or decompose, as the crystalline glass had. Less than thirty of these sealed Ravenscroft pieces have survived. Ravenscroft made drinking-glasses, bottles (or decanters) and bowls. They are very beautiful.

refectory table   Dealers' jargon for a long oak table with six or eight hefty turned legs joined by square stretchers attached low on the leg. These legs were often extravagantly carved and bulbous.

reform flask   Between 1820 and 1856 a number of potters produced brown, saltglazed stoneware flasks moulded in the shape of celebrated personages. Among these potters were Bourne and Sons and Messrs Old-field of Derbyshire, and John Doulton and Stephen Green of Lambeth.

Reform flask by Oldfield & Co.

What they were used for is a matter of conjecture. Gin perhaps, or brandy, or both. Or could they have been sold empty? Some were certainly used for political propaganda, given away by canvassers maybe, and these are known as reform flasks, since reform is what they were concerned with. They supported Catholic emancipation, especially for Daniel O'Connell, elected M.P. for County Clare in 1828 but forbidden to take his seat; and the repeal of the Corn Laws by Richard Cobden — a successful campaign to which Peel gave in after a bitter struggle.

Other politicians featured include Lord Grey (Prime Minister in the Reform Parliament), Lord Brougham (Chancellor), Lord John Russell (the proposer of the bill) and Lord Melbourne. Royalty included Queen Caroline, the Duke of York, William IV, Queen Victoria (who always got in on the act), and Prince Albert. Historical events commemorated were the opening of Brunel's Thames Tunnel and the ending of the Crimean War. Jenny Lind, the Swedish Nightingale, and Thomas Dartmouth Rice, who introduced his coon-dance 'Jump Jim Crow' to an amazed and enthusiastic London audience in 1836, also merited flasks in honour of themselves.

In this century Doulton has produced six contemporary politicians on flasks (1912), and reproductions by Bourne and Sons of their earlier successes may fool some of the people some of the time.

Most reform flasks are impressed with the maker's name and the subject illustrated. This helps.

Collection: Harvey's of Bristol, Bristol

regulator   A regulator was a longcase clock of notable accuracy by which the many other watches and clocks in a large house could be set. Astronomers, clockmakers, and clock sellers also used regulators which, being functional, tended to be severe in design.

repoussé   Ornamental metal work which has been hammered or punched into relief decoration from the back.

ribbon-back   Ribbon-back (or ribband-back) chairs and settees were made in the mid-eighteenth century by Thomas Chippendale, who considered them his finest contribution to cabinet-making. And indeed they are glorious, with intricately interlaced and convoluted splats. This was rococo style at its highest, refined and dignified. Sadly, the chairs are so fragile that few have survived.

Ridgway   Job Ridgway, founder of the firm of the same name at Shelton in Staffordshire, was apprenticed to Josiah Wedgwood, and the experience benefited him. He built Cauldon Place in 1802, and his family continued to run the business in Shelton (later at the Bedford works) for several generations. Potlids were one of the specialities of the house; also a sturdy and attractive earthenware very similar to Mason's ironstone. Indeed Ridgway's produced jugs with blue and red *chinoiserie* patterns and dragon handles which are identical to Mason's but quite a lot cheaper. John Ridgway was appointed potter to Queen Victoria, and I'm sure he was a popular and diplomatic choice.

Book: *Ridgway Porcelain* by Geoffrey Godden (Barrie & Jenkins, 1972)

rings Why the third finger of the left hand? Some say that it's accounted for by the classical superstition that a vein ran straight to the heart from this finger. Others insist that the finger was chosen because it is the only one which may not be straightened by itself; a security, this, against the ring falling off and getting lost. In any case the giving of a ring as a plighting of one's troth is a very old custom.

Fede or fides rings have two hands clasped together, sometimes around a heart or hearts, and sometimes surmounted by flames, lilies, or a crown. They are usually of simple design in gold or silver. Gimmel rings have two loops which can be either separated or joined. Very often the betrothed couple would each wear one hoop until the wedding, when the two hoops would be joined. Puzzle rings are what you might expect. True lovers' knots are rings entwined with a symbolic knot, reminding the couple of the 'tie that binds'. Mary Queen of Scots wore such a ring to celebrate her engagement to Darnley. It consisted of three rings, the middle one being set with a large solitaire diamond, thought to be unlucky at the time, and soon enough shown to be so. Posy rings are inscribed with loving messages, while regard rings are an acrostic, the first letter of each set stone giving the name of the adored recipient, thus: Sapphire, Amethyst, Ruby, Amethyst, Hayalite would suggest that Sarah was the girl for whom the ring was made.

Book: *The Ralph Harari Collection of Finger Rings* by John Boardman and Diana Scarisbrick (Thames & Hudson, 1978)

rocking chair The first rocking chairs were designed in the eighteenth century, and were merely modifications of ladder-backs and Windsors. The rocker came into its own in America. The Boston rocker was the standard American rocking chair, with its S-shaped arms and its curved seat dipping from the back and scrolling over in front. It had (has) a high spindle-back with an ornamental panel usually depicting fruit or flowers. The Lincoln rocker, with its high straight upholstered back continuing into the seat and padded elbow rests on open arms, is supposed to have been Abraham Lincoln's favourite. Other varieties include Sinclair's American Commonsense Chair, exported to Britain during the 1870s and 1880s, Dr Calvert's Digestive Chair 'for invalids and women', exported to America c.1850, and, of course, Thonet's bentwood rocking chair, elegant, caned, and black-framed. The real authority is Hoagy Carmichael.

Rockingham The factory which was opened in 1745 on the estate of the Marquis of Rockingham, near Rotherham, was remarkable in several respects. It was celebrated for its teapots which everybody (except rival manufacturers) said extracted the fullest possible flavour from the tea, and it was the first maker of the Cadogan teapot, which, in imitation of the Chinese 'peach' wine jug, had no lid but was filled from beneath by a tube, and was therefore unspillable. The factory produced a characteristic purple-brown glaze, notably on coffee and tea services. Some of its porcelain was of such quality that royal approval was obtained to add the prefix 'Royal' to 'Rockingham'. John Brameld, who took over the factory in 1807, was the principal painter and his name, sometimes in a blue cartouche, is an alternative mark to Rockingham.

Dark brown glazed earthenware, also known as Rockingham, was made throughout America from about 1840.

Books: *The Rockingham Pottery* by Arthur A. Eaglestone and Terence A. Lockett (David & Charles, 1973); *Rockingham Pottery and Porcelain* by D. G. Rice (Barrie & Jenkins, 1971)

Collections: Royal Pump Room Museum, Harrogate; Museum and Art Gallery, Rotherham; City Museum, Sheffield

rocking horse

> *Dobbin came to us from Cremer's. He had two single green rockers, and a brown hair coat. How we despised later on, the unreal varnished breed of rocking horse with horizontal action back-and-forth instead of the authentic up-and-down! Dobbin was* real, *you fondled the ears and wore his smooth neck smoother still with kisses. One day we discovered that his horsehair tail pulled out.*
>
> *Nursery in the Nineties* by Eleanor Farjeon

The bloodstock lines of the rocking horse lead us directly back to its ancestor the hobbyhorse, a favoured toy of Greek and Roman children, and probably a good deal older than that. In Britain during the Middle Ages a hobbyhorse was a rich child's toy — and not just a toy, for on the back of the hobbyhorse you could learn a bit about knightly chivalry; he was a fine beast with his flying mane and raised forelegs. As soon as the rocking horse was introduced, probably in the first half of the seventeenth century, the hobbyhorse slunk back to his stable. More precisely in his simplest form — a roughly carved head with a pole for a body and a crossbar (sometimes) to hold on to — he was retained for poorer children.

The earliest rocking horses had boat-shaped solid wooden rockers on either side of the torso with realistic legs painted on the outside of this framework. In due course the wood was cut away from between the horse's legs, leaving him to stand magnificently, his neck arched, his hooves attached to curved rockers. Now he began to be glorified. Stirrups, glass eyes, manes and tails of real horsehair were added, and his size increased until it no longer made sense to import or export him. A healthy wooden bloodstock industry grew up in America, where a double rocking horse known as a Shoo-fly was an interesting development. Flying horses were also made.

Victorian horses had sprung suspension, or were mounted on three wheels (the velocipede horse). They could be covered in red cowhide or

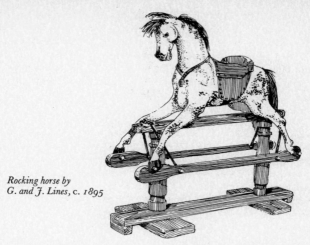

Rocking horse by
G. and J. Lines, c. 1895

paint (cowhide horses were more expensive than painted wood then). Safety rockers came in towards the end of the last century, and most surviving Dobbins date from this period, or later.

rosary The Virgin Mary has always been identified poetically with the rose. She was the Rose Without a Thorn, and roses tended to bloom around her in paintings. The chief prayer said upon the chaplet was the Hail Mary, and in time the beads came to be known as roses, the whole string of beads as a 'rose garland' or 'garden' of the Virgin. Hence the rosary, a word which means just that, a rose garden.

The first rosaries were little more than knotted string. But Lady Godiva, who so enlivened the eleventh century, possessed 'a circlet of gems that she had threaded on a string, in order that by fingering them one by one as she successively recited her prayers she might not fall short of the exact number'. Increasingly thereafter rosaries were worn for reasons other than purely devotional ones. They were attractive worn round the neck, the wrist, or the waist. They were made from everything and anything, including amber, coral, jet, gold, silver gilt, glass and wood, and especially cedar wood from the Holy Land.

A celebrated example is the Langdale Rosary, from the late fifteenth century, which consists of six large gold *Pater* beads and fifty smaller gold *Ave* beads, all engraved and enamelled with figures of the saints. The saints tend to figure prominently on rosaries, especially St Katherine, the virgin martyr, to whom single girls pray for husbands. Phials of holy water, medallions of all kinds, pomanders, votive hearts, reliquaries, and almost anything else of a superstitious significance may be found on rosaries.

Rosenthal   The porcelain factory established in Bavaria in 1879 by the German potter Philip Rosenthal has produced some of the best examples of art nouveau and art deco porcelain. Typically the dinner services, vases, bowls, and figurines are white or cream with a high gloss and simple elegant lines. The table services Darmstadt (1905), Donatello (1907) and Isolde (1910) were either undecorated or embellished with flowers and cherries. Cutlery is also produced at Amberg, and a Rosenthal glass factory makes items designed by Walter Gropius.

rosewood   There is no connection between rosewood and roses: the wood comes from a species of tree called *Dalbergia nigra*, which grows in Brazil. Another variety, known as Bombay rosewood, comes from India and Sri Lanka. It is a hard wood, dark red with blackish streaks, and in the eighteenth century it was used with satinwood for veneered borders. In the nineteenth century it became popular in its own right, and much Regency furniture was made out of solid rosewood; its use continued also in some characteristic art deco pieces. Laminated rosewood was used in rococo furniture in America during the mid-Victorian era.

rosso antico   A red stoneware invented by Josiah Wedgwood in imitation of classical Greek vases. The technique was later adopted by other factories.

rubies

> *That ruby which you wear*
> *Sunk from the tip of your soft ear*
> *Will last to be a precious stone*
> *When all your world of beauty's gone.*
> 'To Dianeme', Robert Herrick

Top quality rubies, known in the trade as 'exceptionally fine', are the most expensive gems in the world. The best come from Burma and are rich red, the second best, from Thailand, have an orange tinge. Others are found in Sri Lanka (lighter in colour), the USA and Australia. When a ruby is pale enough it is known as a 'pink sapphire'. Star rubies, that is to say rubies which exhibit six or twelve rays of light when cut *en cabochon*, are much to be desired, but not if they are brownish-red and come from India, in which case you may safely dismiss them with a snort.

rummers   Although the rummer has nothing to do with rum, it has not proved easy to find a likely derivation of the word. Probably it comes from the German *roemer*. Certainly these large drinking-glasses were very popular in Germany, especially in the Rhine Valley, from the sixteenth century. Originally rummers were short-stemmed, but they grew taller as the years passed. The stems were usually decorated with prunts, a prunt

Eighteenth-century ale rummers with hops and barley 'strong ale' motif

being a smooth or knobbly motif not unlike a boil or a raspberry. In the eighteenth century many English rummers were produced; these were rather more restrained than the German versions.

saltcellars If you say that a man is 'worth his salt', you are using an expression that dates back to a time when salt was a very valuable commodity. A covenant of salt is mentioned in the Bible, and no less an artist than Benvenuto Cellini turned his hand to the humble salt-dish. Saltcellars were made of many materials from gold and silver downwards. In late Victorian England examples made from pressed or cut glass were produced in huge quantities, some of which — and particularly those in bottle-green glass — were not used for salt at all but to protect the carpet from the legs of the piano. Salts in silver or Britannia metal had internal glass liners to prevent the salt from escaping through the pierced sides. Of course no cruet was ever placed on the table in properly genteel homes; it knew its place on the sideboard. It is interesting to note too that it was not until *c.*1875 that salt and pepper shakers were sold in pairs.

saltglaze A process which started in seventeenth-century Britain with delicate pieces of stoneware in the Chinese style, and is now used on a grand commercial scale for drainpipes, lavatories and so on. Saltglazing stoneware involved throwing salt into the kiln during the later stages of firing. The salt oxidises and forms a filmy surface, giving a glossy but colourless glaze. To the touch the feel of a saltglaze plate or figure is not unlike the feel of an eggshell, and very slightly pitted. John Dwight at Fulham and John Philip and David Elen at the Staffordshire potteries were among the earliest to test the possibilities of the technique. During the mid-eighteenth century it was discovered that saltglaze stoneware took very happily to the introduction of brilliant enamel colours, which look so good against a cream, buff, or light brown body.

Book: *Staffordshire Salt-glazed Stoneware* by A. Mountford (Barrie & Jenkins, 1971)
Collections: Fitzwilliam Museum, Cambridge; Victoria and Albert Museum, London (Room 137); Art Gallery and Museum, Brighton (Willett Collection); City Art Gallery, Manchester (Athenaeum Annexe); Castle Museum, Norwich

samplers Originally — and so far as Europe is concerned that means in the late fifteenth century — samplers consisted of patterns taken from printed pattern books. These were both decorative and instructive. That they were fashionable in the sixteenth century, we know from a number of literary references, the most celebrated of which is put into the mouth of Helena in *A Midsummer Night's Dream*. To Hermia she recalls how they had 'with our needles created both one flower, Both on one sampler, sitting on one cushion.' But there are only seven samplers surviving from that century.

The most common seventeenth-century samplers were long strips of linen with parallel bands of letters and numerals, and patterns taken from Turkish rugs. Others, of a squarer shape and usually anonymous and undated, featured 'spot' patterns, in which the bands of motifs were replaced by more random designs. Subjects included:

> *Flowers, Plants and Fishes*
> *Beasts, Birds, Flyes, and Bees*
> *Hills, Dales, Plains and Pastures*
> *Skies, Seas, Rivers, Trees.*

Stitches were many and various, including such outlandish-sounding ones as 'finney, new, chain, bread, fisher, rosemary, bow, whip and cross-stitches', while types of work included 'raised-needlework, pearl, Geneva, Virgin's device, cutwork, laid stitch and thorough stitch, lapwork, rock, frost, net, purle, tent and fingerwork'.

Eighteenth-century samplers continued to feature the popular honeysuckle and carnation motifs, but increasingly they were made as exhibition pieces for boastful parents to frame and hang on the wall and as school exercises for little girls and occasionally boys — at dame schools. Now a morbid streak of religiosity stains the unsullied linen of the sampler:

> *The soul by blackning defiled*
> *can never enter Heaven,*
> *Till God and it be reconciled*
> *and all its sins forgiven.*
> *Charlotte Robertson. Aged Six.*
> *Time Flies. Death Approaches.*

How scared these children must have been as they lay on their sickbeds (for infant mortality was common) working away at such alarming texts.

In the first half of the nineteenth century — the last period for British samplers — the stitching was almost always cross-stitch, which became known as sampler-stitch, with stereotyped patterns (the strawberry border, the pots of flowers, the letters, and the numbers) and commonplace colours. However the personality of the childish artist does still at times shine through and speak directly to us across the canyon of over a hundred years.

In America the sampler was extremely popular and highly pictorial, with a particular penchant for genealogical trees and tables.

Books: *Samplers* by A. Colby (Batsford, 1964); *Samplers* by D. King (Victoria and Albert Museum, 1960)
Collection: Museum and Art Gallery, Stoke-on-Trent

sandalwood   An Indian hardwood (*Santalum album*), brown and aromatic, sandalwood is chiefly used for inlaid boxes and chests. Its oil is pale yellow and viscous, and makes nice soap.

sapphires   Sapphires are from the same gem variety as rubies, the corundum (AI_2O_3). The best sapphires are violet-blue and come principally from Burma, the next best are pure blue and come from Kashmir. A star sapphire from Sri Lanka would be specially prized. Others come from Australia and the USA. 'Pink sapphires' are the same as pale rubies. Green sapphires should not be olive-tinged, grey-tinged, or mottled. Yellow sapphires are not much liked in common with other yellow gems: 'If you are going for yellow, go for gold', is a safe motto.

satinwood   East Indian satinwood (*Chloroxylon swietenia*) and West Indian satinwood (*Fagara flava*) were both used in the late eighteenth and early nineteenth centuries for decorative furniture, especially in the designs advocated by Thomas Sheraton. The Chippendale, Gillow, and Hepplewhite designs had called for it too. The beautiful colour of satinwood, a glowing golden yellow with magnificent figuration, made it ideal for panels, veneers, and inlays. Genuine old satinwood should have a mellow softness, a semi-transparent surface. Too much orange indicates too much polishing.   San Domingo satinwood, which becomes silver-grey with time, is also known as harewood. It is not unknown for the owners of modern pieces of satinwood to stain them with coffee to give them an 'antique' patina.

Satsuma   Some of the earliest Japanese porcelain and earthenware, known as Satsuma ware, was produced when Shimazu Yoshihiro captured some Korean potters and established them in the province of Satsuma. The characteristic Satsuma ware was a buff-coloured stoneware, brightly coloured and gilded; in the nineteenth century an ivory-white lustred ware with a crackled glaze was produced. Later Satsuma ware became gaudy to the point of absurdity with much blurring of detail, a long, long way from the delicacy of the early products. But most of this decadent ware was in fact made in Kyoto and decorated in Tokyo.

Books: *Japanese Porcelain* by R. S. Jenyns (Faber & Faber, 1965); *Japanese Pottery* by R. S. Jenyns (Faber & Faber, 1971)

scent bottles   There is a saying which runs: 'The smell of an onion from the mouth of the lovely is sweeter than that of a rose in the hand of the ugly.'

Down the years people have remained convinced that it is their duty to themselves and to society to smell sweet. The Elizabethans carried pomanders, the Stuarts and Tudors vinaigrettes. These served a dual purpose: they perfumed the owner and protected him or her from the stench of rottenness in the street.

Scent bottles were introduced during the seventeenth century, with a flattened pear shape proving the most popular. Scent was expensive, so the containers could be too, and gold and silver were employed as well as glass and porcelain. Porcelain scent bottles were produced at the Chelsea 'Girl-in-Swing' manufactory from the mid-eighteenth century, and in jasper-ware by Josiah Wedgwood some forty years later. Copper scent bottles covered with enamel were produced at Bilston, and in the Midlands.

Bulbous scent bottles made from crystal with *millefiori* stoppers came from Stourbridge, commemorative scent bottles with names and dates of giver and recipient were produced at Nailsea. Although Victorian glass scent bottles, often mounted with silver, were produced in great profusion, they were not ideal since scent deteriorates if exposed to too much light. Double-ended scent bottles (one end for scent, the other for smelling salts) were in vogue in the 1870s and 1880s. Generally the scent end unscrewed or uncorked, while the salts end was operated by a press stud.

Lalique, commissioned by Coty and Nina Ricci among other *parfumiers*, designed 'chunky' matt-finished bottles, and bottles shaped like doves, naked ladies, and so on.

Books: *Scent Bottles* by K. Foster (Connoisseur and Michael Joseph, 1966); *A History of Scent* by R. Genders (Hamish Hamilton, 1972)

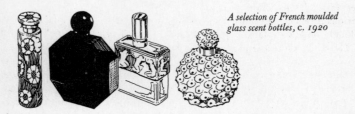

A selection of French moulded glass scent bottles, c. 1920

scientific instruments   The skilled business of making scientific instruments flourished in Islam from the seventh century AD. Scientific knowledge from Greece and mathematical scholarship from India were allied to an already rich tradition. In the ninth century scientific books were imported into Spain from Syria and Egypt and the first great Spanish scientist, Maslama ben Ahmad al-Majritê (died *c.*AD1007), wrote a treatise on the astrolabe. When the Christians took Toledo in 1085, they also captured an arsenal of scientific knowledge, and rapidly learned that most basic of lessons: Knowledge is Strength.

In England Thomas Gemini (who made two astrolabes for Queen Elizabeth) and Humfrey Cole were the two most celebrated instrument makers of the sixteenth century. By this time the making of instruments had become merely a popular industry producing sundials and other small items, rather than being a specialised part of an astronomer's scholarship. But Elias Allen (1606–54), Henry Sutton (d.1665) and John Rowley (d.1728) were all prepared to collaborate with scholars besides catering for amateurs. By the end of the seventeenth century most of the traditional instruments had gone out of fashion and the rapid growth of scientific knowledge led to a demand for telescopes, theodolites, and other specialised pieces of great complexity and accuracy.

Once the revolutionary (in both senses) Copernican theory that the earth went round the sun had been accepted by those whose opinions were thought to matter, the old-fashioned armillary sphere, a Ptolemaic instrument, was replaced by the orrery, which showed the movements of the planets around the sun. The great instrument makers of the eighteenth century, such as John Bird (1709–76), Jesse Ramsden (1730–1800), Benjamin Martin (1704–82) and George Adams (1704–73), were not just traditional artisans, but inventors and authors as well. Edmund Culpeper (1660–1738), noted for microscopes and sundials, was also an ecclesiastical brass engraver. Collaboration between various crafts was also necessary from time to time and bookbinders might be required to help with the protective leather and vellum surrounding microscopes and telescopes.

Should you be fortunate enough to possess any of these beautiful — which indeed they are — early instruments you should avoid cleaning or restoring them without expert advice. Fakes have recently become a serious problem, but most of the ones manufactured in this country — in Slough, no less — have, it seems, been exported to Japan.

Here follows a brief guide to some of the commoner instruments. The armillary sphere is a skeletal sphere, constructed according to the Ptolemaic, or geocentric, system showing a terrestrial globe centrally with fixed stars marked by pointers, and planets represented within the sphere. The astrolabe is an astronomical and astrological instrument of great antiquity, used for observing and charting the movement of stars. The mariner's astrolabe, made in Portugal towards the end of the fifteenth century, was used for measuring altitudes and was a simplification of previous astrolabes. The circumferentor is a surveying instrument made from the sixteenth to the eighteenth century, and containing sights and a joint for mounting on a tripod.

Sundials and dials fall into two main categories: altitude dials, which depend on the variation of the sun's altitude during the day, and

*Eighteenth-century
brass circumferentor*

directional dials, which depend on the variation of the sun's azimuth, measured along the equinoctial circle. There are very many varieties of dials, some including compasses which must be aligned along the meridian, others which are self-orientating. Those which are neither fixed nor suspended often have built-in plummets or spirit-levels.

Microscopes are either simple (with one lens) or compound with several). Simple microscopes were developed by Anton van Leeuwenhoek in the seventeenth century. Zacharias Janssen invented the first compound microscope in 1590; it had a convex objective and a concave eyepiece. The two-lens eyepiece, widely used today, was developed by Christiaan Huygens (c.1684). The orrery is a manual or clockwork-driven machine used to demonstrate the Copernican planetary system. The first orrery may have been constructed by clockmakers George Graham and Thomas Tompion c.1709. The orrery was named after Lord Orrery for whom John Rowley made such an instrument c.1712.

The quadrant is a flat wooden or metallic plane in the shape of a quarter-circle with 90 degrees marked along its curved edge and a plumb-line and bob suspended from its right-angle. With a pair of sights it could be used for computing the elevation of stars and planets; it was also used in surveying.

The first refracting telescope was made in 1608 by a Dutchman, Hans Lippershey (or Lippersheim), who discovered that spectacle lenses when held apart would magnify the object under observation. The first reflecting telescope in which the light was focused by a speculum mirror was conceived by James Gregory in 1663 and built by Sir Isaac Newton in 1671. A radio telescope in Puerto Rico covers an area of $18\frac{1}{2}$ acres.

Books: *Scientific Instruments* by H. Wynter and A. Turner (Studio Vista, 1975); *Collecting and Restoring Scientific Instruments* by Ronald Pearsall (David & Charles, 1974); *Scientific Instruments of the 17th and 18th Centuries and Their Makers* by Maurice Daumas (Batsford, 1972)

Collections: Royal Scottish Museum, Edinburgh; Whipple Museum of the History of Science, Cambridge; Museum of the History of Science, Oxford; National Maritime Museum, Greenwich; British Museum, London; Science Museum, London

sconce Although generally used to describe various antique light fittings, the word sconce is properly applied to a wall bracket with candleholders extending from its back plate. In the sixteenth century this light fitting was known as a candle plate. In the sixteenth and seventeenth centuries sconces were made of earthenware, silver, copper, brass (frequently), pewter, and latten, an alloy of copper and zinc. Later they combined embroidered panels with walnut frames, ormolu, japanning, and gesso. A rococo sconce would be known as a girandole, and often incorporated a panel of mirror glass to reflect the candlelight into the room. Some of Chippendale's designs in his *Director* for rococo girandoles are fanciful to a degree.

In a novel published in 1796 a young lady considers taking 'a naked peep into my heart to see if it is composed of true feminine matter; if it prefers girandoles and the heartache, to a simple candle and content'.

When the gas bracket was introduced the days of the sconce were numbered; however, sconces still graced pianos, and a few were converted to gas.

screens There were draughts and so there were screens. Making a virtue of necessity, craftsmen seized on the possibilities of the folds of a screen for either contrasting or continuous designs; artists of the arts and crafts movement and the Bloomsbury Group found screens almost irresistible. And screens were a godsend to dramatists too:

Sir Peter Teazle:	You can make even your screen a source of knowledge — hung, I perceive, with maps.
Joseph Surface:	Oh yes, I find great use in that screen.
Sir Peter Teazle:	I dare say you must, certainly, when you want to find anything in a hurry.
Joseph Surface:	(Aside) Ay, or to hide anything in a hurry, either.

This, of course, is from *A School For Scandal*, first produced in 1777, a period when screens (which originated in seventh-century China) were at their most popular in interior decoration and when the French influence was most potent. There were many combinations, tapestries or silks with mahogany, embossed leather panels on a carved oak frame, lacquer or *papier mâché* screens inlaid with mother-of-pearl or *piqué*. In the early nineteenth century the taste was for fabric rather than panelling. Berlin woolwork (from *c.*1830) was usually a mistake, but enabled the amateur artist to enjoy the public exhibition of his or her work. Painted screens became unrestrained with all the misplaced enthusiasm of the over-confident: they sparkled, they glittered and they shone with mother-of-pearl, nautilus shells, powdered gold, and bronze. 'A mass of barbarous splendour' was the verdict on some screens at the 1851 Great Exhibition.

About ten years later ostentation was replaced by charm as the vogue for scrapwork began. Collage screens featuring greeting cards, commercially

Vellum covered, tasselled screen by Carlo Bugatti, c. 1900-10

produced 'scraps', chromolithographs, and old master prints were cheerful and, yes, charming. The Japanese movement (*c.*1870–80) produced oriental designs in silk and watercolours, and tapestries of medieval subjects *à la* Burne Jones were also popular.

In the twentieth century Dunand revived lacquer screens in France while the Irish designer, Eileen Gray, produced screens of startling beauty, featuring nude figures against richly coloured backgrounds.

scrimshaw These are the words from an inscription carved by a sailor on a stay busk, an oblong strip of whalebone used as a corset stiffener:

> *Accept, dear girl, this busk from me*
> *Carved by my humble hand,*
> *I took it from a sperm whale's jaw*
> *One thousand miles from land.*
> *In many a gale had been the whale*
> *In which this bone did rest.*
> *His time is past, his bone at last*
> *Must now support thy breast.*

Scrimshaw is a strange word. So many versions of it exist (scrimshandy, scrimshoning, scrimshorn, scrimpshong, skrimshouting, skrimshontering, and squimshon are just a few) that there is little hope now of finding a satisfactory derivation for it. But the meaning is clear enough. Scrimshaw is any craftwork made on board a ship. The ship is usually a whaler, and the craft usually involves the teeth or jaw of the whale, but it need not. Besides busks, articles made from marine ivory include boxes, rolling pins, ladles, pastry crimps, riding whips, canes, umbrella handles, and stocks.

Such pieces were usually fashioned from whatever materials and with whatever tools the sailor happened to have to hand, sometimes only his jack-knife, sometimes more elaborate tools, such as files and chisels, used on sharkskin. For the engraving of a whale's tooth (the lower jaw of the sperm whale by tradition belonged to the crew) a tracing was made from a spontaneous design or, less interestingly, from an illustrated paper, and pricked out with pin-pricks in the tooth itself. These pricks would be joined up with tiny scratches which would then be blackened and the whole polished with china clay and whale oil. Obviously many of the designs relate to sailing in general and whaling in particular, but some are nationalist, patriotic, or romantic.

Other scrimshaw artifacts include carved coconuts, woolwork pictures, decorative knots, and so on. The earliest dated scrimshaw works which have been discovered are two tobacco boxes, dated 1665 and 1712. They are wood inlaid with walrus ivory and are both in the Museum of Fisheries in Hull.

Book: *Scrimshaw and Scrimshanders, Whales and Whalemen* by E. Norman Flayderman (N. Flayderman, 1974) — distributed in Britain by Patrick Stephens, Bar Hill, Cambridge
Collections: Museum of Fisheries, Hull; National Maritime Museum, Greenwich

Decorated sperm whale tooth, c. 1830

seal The seal (mineral not animal) has been with us a long time, just as long as human beings have wished to impress others with a respect for property. Usually the seal, whether in ancient Egypt, the Middle East, or Britain, was a stone set in metal (normally a ring) with a personal emblem, monogram, coat of arms, or whatever, carved in *intaglio* upon it. The *secretum*, the personal seal of a man of some importance, was used from the twelfth century to authenticate documents. Religious, symbolic, and allegorical subjects are often featured on seals, and early glass bottles have a raised sealmark on them with the name or emblem of either the owner or the maker (for example the raven's-head seal of George Ravenscroft). From the nineteenth century company seals for sealing letters with wax became very fashionable. These had heavy ornamental handles, lavishly decorated with gold, lacquer, pinchbeck, ivory, porcelain, and so on.

sedan chair or **glass chair**   Miss Bolo (in *Pickwick Papers*) 'rose from the table considerably agitated, and went straight home, in a flood of tears and a Sedan chair.' She was lucky to have one for, by the mid-nineteenth century, these covered chairs carried by two men with poles were going out of fashion.

According to Evelyn's Diary for 8 February 1645 the sedan chair was brought to England from Naples by Sir Sanders Duncomb, and Evelyn may be right, for such conveyances had been in use in Italy for some time. Dr Johnson speculated wildly that they came from Sedan in France; most improbable. Wherever they came from, they rapidly became a most refined compromise between a large chair and a small room, quite sumptuous sometimes (French examples particularly), with fitted curtains, clocks and cushions. Public sedans were far more utilitarian, as you might expect.

Book: *Gregorian Grace* by John Gloag (Hamlyn, 1967) — Chapter 9
Collection: Avenue House, Ampthill

settle   It must have been cold and draughty in those old medieval houses. The fires were placed centrally in the middle of the hall and smoked atrociously; still, at least there was some form of heating. Tapestries on the walls and rushes on the floor may have helped a little; imagine, though, what it must have been like in church. The settle, an Anglo-Saxon word, was a long bench with a high or low back and arms, and sometimes an attached foot-rest. A hinged locker below the seat was used for storage. Here, at least, crowded together — for the settle was a communal bench — one had a measure of protection from draughts. The settle might be built into the wall or set into the fireplace of a farmhouse kitchen or the ingle-nook of an inn. In any event it was a warmly comforting piece of traditional furniture, and one can quite understand why the arts and crafts movement chose to revive it in the nineteenth century. Eastlake described it in *Hints On Household Taste* (1868) as 'The common wooden settle which forms so comfortable and snug-looking a seat by rustic hearths'. The old-fashioned settle was usually contrived of oak, often carved with whatever decorations were currently in fashion.

A settle table is a settle with the high-back hinged to fold over on to the arms to form a table. This is also known as a chair-table, a table-chair, a table-chairwise, a monk's seat or a monk's bench, the last two terms being modern and spurious.

Sèvres The early history of the Sèvres factory involving industrial espionage, royal patronage, heavy drinking, corruption in high places, and other such merry matters, resulted in the Vincennes works moving to a larger site, in Sèvres, which Madame de Pompadour graciously made available — well, sold — in 1756. Four years later the factory was purchased by Louis XV, and continued as a royal operation until the proclamation of the Republic in 1793. The director, M. Boileau, hired the best men he could find with Duplessis, goldsmith to the King, in charge of the modelling, and Bachelier superintending the decorations. No expense was spared to make Sèvres the finest manufactory in the world.

Representative ground colours of great richness were produced, dark blue (1749), turquoise (1752), yellow (1753), apple-green (1756), rose Pompadour or pink (1757), and so on. The style followed the rococo tastes of Louis XV with beautifully painted birds, landscapes and figures after Boucher, until a tendency towards classicism and restraint set in during the pre-Empire period. These early pieces were in soft-paste (*pâte tendre*), but in 1768 kaolin deposits were discovered at Limoges, and by 1804 all Sèvres production was of the hard-paste variety (some say that the youngest son of the Frankenthal potter sold the secret formula to Sèvres). Under Louis XVI the style became sumptuous, with enamelled 'jewelling' entirely covering the body of the piece.

For some years prior to the Revolution the factory suffered a decline, inferior work was produced, and the state could not afford to pay the employees — or so it claimed. But during the First Empire, attempts were made to restore its reputation, with Napoleon and his court ordering presentation vases and table services for the Tuileries, Versailles, the Trianon, Fontainebleau, and palaces in Rome and Milan. Fortunately Napoleon had many victories, and vases commemorative of these were produced. China plaques became an integral part of furniture design and Sèvres produced wall mirrors, clock-cases, and other ceramic furnishings. During this period the famous Sèvres biscuit groups were produced by such artists as Chéret, Barriat, and Dubois. The *pâte-sur-pâte* style, invented by the head of the painting department, was developed by Marc-Louis Solon (in about 1762), who later took the secret with him across the channel to Minton's. To give some idea of the scale of operations at the Sèvres factory, one need only mention the service made in 1778 for the Empress Catherine II, which originally cost £13,500 for 744 pieces, and was typical of several such presentation services.

In 1876 the factory moved to a new site near St Cloud, where Rodin was one of the more celebrated modellers. During the late nineteenth century it was influenced by the fashion for things oriental, but continued to reproduce its earlier successes.

The dating of Sèvres china is facilitated by a code-mark for each year, the letter A representing 1753, double letters starting in 1778. The

Revolution intervened and the traditional Sèvres mark, interlaced double Ls, representing the king, was no longer acceptable, so a new code was begun in 1801 (Year IX).

Book: *Sèvres* by Carl Christian Dauterman (Studio Vista, 1970)
Collections: Wallace Collection, London (very fine); Harewood House, Leeds; Windsor Castle; Upton House, Edgehill; Firle Place, Lewes; Waddesdon Manor, Buckinghamshire

sgraffito A type of decorative earthenware, made originally in the north of Italy. The body of the piece was coated with a slip, in which the design was engraved. In this way the colour of the slip could be contrasted with the colour of the body, often white on red. The article was glazed after engraving.

shagreen I'm sorry to have to mention this, but the word shagreen (and the resonant English word chagrin) comes from the Turkish for the rump of the wild ass. There are effectively three types of shagreen. The first is the hide from the wild ass (*saghri*) which, when dyed — usually green, from lime water — was used as a protective covering for boxes. The second type is camel, horse or mule skin into which small seeds have been pressed. This was then dyed green, or, rarely, another colour, and polished. Scientific and medical instruments were often protected by coverings in this material. The third is sharkskin, naturally rough and pitted, which has been dried and dyed, usually green. Many insignificant twentieth-century artifacts have been covered with sharkskin and it was something of a favourite with art deco designers.

share certificates The collecting of busted bonds and blocked assets is a comparatively recent hobby, which has been dignified by the name of scripophily. Old share certificates are of some intricacy and beauty, perhaps the most beautiful being American railway shares and Chinese bonds. The skills of the engraver and printer were an insurance against forgeries. Others, such as the more recently issued though defunct Playboy share certificates which feature milk-fed ladies covered in little but assumed confusion, are less enticing. Some British bonds, notably the Vauxhall Bridge and Strand Bridge issues, were printed on vellum.

There is always a chance that blocked assets, such as those held by the Chinese and Americans, may one day be redeemed. Such hopes tend to be reflected in the price at which they are traded. However it is generally safe to assume that the rarer issues, those with the highest face values (sometimes as few as seventeen of these were issued), and the most attractive ones in the best condition, are the only ones with which collectors should seriously concern themselves. There is an irony in scripophily, which is that it is only failed and unredeemed stocks that are now collected.

shawls The home of the shawl was Kashmir, and the traditional Kashmir shawls were woven from the fleeces of the wild mountain goats, wonderfully warm and so fine, by repute, that they could be drawn through a thumb-ring. These shawls were brought West towards the end of the eighteenth century, and local manufacturers imitated them, corrupting the ancient traditions but making a lot of money. Cashmere-like shawls were first made in Britain in Norwich, in the 1780s, and later in Edinburgh. The paisley shawl business, given a boost by Queen Victoria's partiality, initially pirated the Norwich designs, but employed the revolutionary Jacquard loom.

These paisley designs adapted and formalised the pine-tree motif of the original Kashmir shawls. The pine tree was the symbol of fertility and regeneration (having prophylactic and evergreen qualities). Several expeditions, mounted by French and English manufacturers, set off for Tibet, intending to bring back and domesticate the Tibetan mountain goat which had started the whole business back in the fifteenth century. But the goats stayed put, as goats will, and, by the time the Queen passed on, the fashion had too: paisley shawls were out in the cold like the goats.

Book: *The History and Romance of the Paisley Shawl* by A. M. Stewart (Paisley, 1946)
Collections: Paisley Museum, Paisley; Willmer House Museum, Farnham

sheet music Lithography, which was introduced in 1793, and chromo-lithography (1841) made the mass-production of sheet music feasible. Piano pieces, selections from the classics, transcriptions, duets, and accompanied songs were decorated in the characteristic styles of the period, and in what was considered an appropriate manner for the music; many of these sheets would then be bound into more permanent volumes.

In the 1900s, the greatest days of home entertainment, over two hundred titles were being produced each week, and a very profitable field for freelance artists was opened up. John Brandard specialised in opera and ballet music, Alfred Concanen in music hall songs. But many of these artists are unknown today, having only initialled their work or left it unsigned. Most collectors specialise in one area of sheet music, such as sporting songs or railway music. In few other fields of collecting has popular taste been so rapidly reflected in commercial design, and the jazz age of the twenties and thirties inspired some startling and charmingly suggestive illustrations.

Books: *Victorian Music Covers* by Doreen and Sidney Spellman (Evelyn, Adams & MacKay, 1969); *Victorian Sheet Music Covers* by Ronald Pearsall (David & Charles, 1972)

Sheffield plate A form of silver-plating was developed in the early seventeenth century, but was not a great success since the silver melted when it became hot, and the base metal (iron or steel) rusted when it became wet, causing the silver to detach itself.

In 1742 Thomas Bolsover, a Sheffield cutler, discovered that by fusing silver on copper a remarkably happy marriage resulted. For, once fused, the two metals expanded in unison when put through a rolling mill, and it was possible to produce a workable sheet of metal which looked like silver, felt like silver, yet cost a great deal less. In the early days of Sheffield plate the proportion of silver to copper was one to ten, though only one side of the article was plated. By 1770 'double-plating' was common, though gradually the layer of silver grew thinner until the nineteenth century, when the proportion might be as low as one to sixty.

Thomas Bolsover was a man in a small way of business: buttons and snuff-boxes were his stock-in-trade, candlesticks when he had breakfasted well. Horace Walpole, that most grandiose of collectors, wrote to a friend in 1760:

> As I went to Lord Stafford's I passed through Sheffield, which is one of the foulest towns in England, in the most charming situation . . . One man there has discovered the art of plating copper with silver. I bought a pair of candlesticks for two guineas, they are quite pretty.

The late eighteenth century was a fine period for English silver, and so it is no surprise to find Sheffield plate being used to copy contemporary silver designs. Indeed early pieces (and especially tankards) were stamped with punched marks intended to be mistaken for silver marks, a practice which was outlawed in 1757 when Parliament decreed that stamping misleading hallmarks was a felony punishable by death — a rigorous penalty never in fact invoked. In 1773 Sheffield gained its own silver assay office, and any marking of Sheffield plate was forbidden, though after 1784 makers were allowed to distinguish their wares by name and emblem. (Beware of pieces marked 'Sheffield Plated', which are just as likely to be electroplated.)

Bolsover's breakthrough was further developed by such men as Joseph Hancock, a cutler related by marriage to Bolsover, Charles Dixon, a candlestick-maker, Thomas Law, Henry Tudor, Thomas Leader, Thomas Bradbury, Samuel Roberts, Thomas Nicholson, and the celebrated Matthew Boulton, whose Soho manufactory (in Birmingham) produced domestic articles of excellent quality.

Since so many of the makers took such pains to conceal its composition, you might expect it to be difficult to recognise Sheffield plate, but really it isn't. If the copper shows through the silver (this is called 'bleeding'), there are no problems. The places where bleeding was most likely to occur, the foot rings, the edges and so on, were usually covered with silver wire, roping, and gadrooning. Being strong and workable, old Sheffield plate often displays beautifully detailed fret-work. Solid silver mounts were often soldered on to plated coasters, salvers, and trays. This permitted engraving, because, of course, you couldn't engrave on Sheffield plate without running the risk of exposing the copper beneath.

Just as Sheffield plate was successful because it was cheaper than silver, so it gave way to electroplate in the latter half of the nineteenth century because it was too expensive. It is inadvisable to subject Sheffield plate to electroplating, which destroys its character. Bleeding is an attractive sign of age and distinction; let it bleed and you will get a nice old bit of copper.

Books: *Antique Sheffield Plate* by G. B. Hughes (Batsford, 1970); *History of Old Sheffield Plate* by R. Bradbury (Macmillan, 1912)
Collection: City Museum and Art Gallery, Sheffield

Sheraton (style)   Adam Black, founder of the publishing firm A. & C. Black, shared lodgings with Thomas Sheraton (1751–1806) in Broad Street (now Broadwick Street), Soho, and described him thus:

> *A man of talents and, I believe, of genuine piety. He understands the cabinet-business — I believe was bred to it; he has been, and perhaps at present is, a preacher; he is a scholar, writes well; draws, in my opinion, masterly; is an author, bookseller, stationer and teacher . . . I believe his abilities and resources are his ruin in this respect — by attempting to do everything he does nothing.*

If his contemporaries had doubts about Sheraton, he had doubts about them. This is his comment on Chippendale: 'His designs are now wholly antiquated and laid aside.' On Robert Manwaring's book, he said that it contained nothing 'but what an apprentice boy may be taught by seven hours proper instruction', and on Hepplewhite's *The Cabinet-Maker and Upholsterer's Guide*: 'This work has already caught the decline and perhaps, in a little while, will suddenly die in the disorder.' For a Baptist preacher Thomas was sometimes rather less than charitable!

We know little about him other than that he was born at Stockton-on-Tees in 1751, where he learned the craft of cabinet-making. By his middle years he had come to London, and lived and worked variously in Davies Street, Wardour Street, and Broad Street, Soho, dying there at the age of fifty-five.

In Wardour Street he taught 'Perspective, Architecture and Ornaments', made 'Designs for Cabinet-makers', and sold 'all kinds of Drawing Books &c.' Whether or not he actually made furniture in London is an open question, but his contribution to the art was vastly influential through the publication of two great works, *The Cabinet-Maker and Upholsterer's Drawing Book* (in three parts published between 1791 and 1794) and *The Cabinet Dictionary* (1803), as well as the first volume of a third — a general encyclopaedia of taste. The first of these works was devoted as much to theories of perspective and geometry as to furniture, but his detailed studies into *why* things should please the eye were necessary if one were to understand *how* things pleased the eye. Certainly he was able to impose a supremely elegant style on those who came after him.

His designs owed a lot to France, although he always attacked the snobbery which insisted that French craftsmen were necessarily superior to English. In chairs his preference was for mahogany and beechwood. His chair backs were generally square rather than oval, shield or heart-shaped, as Hepplewhite advocated. They were divided into three vertical sections, the central section featuring a classical motif, such as an urn, a swag, or an ear of wheat. Legs were either square or round and tapering, arms curved and sometimes reeded.

Settees were upholstered with bolsters at either end. Firescreens in satinwood and japanning (both favourites of Sheraton) were either placed on tripods or straight supports. Pembroke and sofa-tables 'to breakfast upon' were featured, one 'Harlequin Pembroke Table' being ingeniously convertible into a desk. Games tables, side tables, bureaux, 'Carlton House Tables', and other writing cabinets, commodes, summer beds 'so that two people might sleep separately in hot weather' (and an 'Eliptic Bed for a single Lady'), dressing chests, wash basins, wall mirrors and sideboards, are just a few of the other furniture designs described and illustrated by Sheraton.

Generally Sheraton's influence was to lighten and make more elegant Hepplewhite's style. He preferred veneers, inlays, and painted decorations to carving, and he favoured straight lines rather than curves. Inlaid shell ornaments are typical. In France they pay Sheraton the great compliment of referring to his style as *Louis XVI à l'Anglaise*. When you remember what he thought of the French, they are more than generous to him.

Books: *Sheraton Furniture* by R. Fastnedge (Faber & Faber, 1962); *Sheraton Furniture Designs* by R. Edwards (Tiranti, 1962)
Collection: Holburne of Menstrie Museum, Bath

shield-back A popular design for a single chair in the Hepplewhite taste. The shield on the back of the chair was often used as a frame for Prince of Wales feathers, swags, urns, or festoons of drapery. It has remained popular ever since, perhaps because it fits the shoulders so very comfortably.

ships' decanters If you have ever travelled through the Minches in a MacBrayne's steamer when the wind is at its most Scottish you will appreciate that traditional table manners tend to go by the board. The problems of eating at sea are serious enough, but they are as nothing to the problems of drinking at sea. One practical solution was a spherical decanter which hung in a cord or wicker casing from a beam; such decanters lasted two centuries from c.1680, when English glassmaking got under way. Sadly, few have survived. An alternative solution was put forward towards the end of the eighteenth century, and this was the ship's decanter, much as we know it today, with a triangular base, somewhat squashed to encourage a low centre of gravity, and a long neck.

While this shape was retained the development of the ship's decanter followed the same course as that of the ordinary land-based decanter. When ships' decanters are good honest examples with little cutting or engraving, dating is facilitated by an examination of the stoppers. 'Disc' stoppers, plain, flat, and circular, appeared *c.*1760 to be replaced some ten years later by lozenge-shaped stoppers. In the 1780s other variations were introduced, including banded mushroom, knopped mushroom, and bull's eye or target stoppers. In early ships' decanters the neck and the stopper would be ground, both as a decoration and in order to ensure a tight fit. Beware of decanters when *either* neck *or* stopper has been ground.

Concurrently in the Bristol glassworks and in Liverpool decanters were produced in brilliant blues, greens, and purples, the stopper being cork-shaped and decorated in silver. Engraved motifs are frequently found on eighteenth-century ships' decanters. The name of the ship with or without a depiction of it is an obvious design. But trailing vines, patriotic slogans, family crests, commemorations of naval victories are also found. Quite frequently the engraving may be a later addition to a plain early decanter. The best way to identify these dubious pieces is to examine the quality of the engraving under a lens. Vintage engraving has a jaggedness and unevenness which is unlikely to be found on work done by a modern wheel. Cut glass and crystal examples are usually Victorian.

The Rodney decanter, named after Admiral Sir George Rodney, to whom went the credit for the victory at the Battle of the Saints, has five neck rings, instead of the traditional three, to give greater grip to the shaky hand of a thirsty admiral, and a cut design of elegantly classical simplicity.

Auction rooms have recently blossomed with examples of ships' decanters, which look respectable at first sight. It is as well to look twice.

sideboards Console tables, introduced from France, were the precursors of the modern sideboard. A sideboard, as invented by Robert Adam in the 1760s, would have been intended primarily as a table from which food could be served. It had two lead-lined drawers for wine storage, joined by a shallow drawer in which linen would be kept and above which the side dishes would be placed. The function of the sideboard thus imposed an elegant and characteristic shape, with six tapering legs supporting the heavy wine stores and an arched apron beneath the napery drawer.

Mahogany was the commonest material used to make sideboards, which grew to vast proportions to cater for vast Victorian households. Mirror-backs were added *c.*1860–75, wooden backs thereafter. Being such large pieces sideboards were particularly vulnerable to ruthless wood-carvers and some very elaborate specimens were produced, frequently in neo-Gothic style. An example at Warwick Castle has to be seen to be believed.

signs The best thing in Malta is the bus service: all the buses run from Valetta and their destination is indicated by their colour. This was the principle behind early shop signs: in Rome a goat represented a dairy, Bacchus pressing a bunch of grapes a wine merchant, and so on. In medieval England gable stones carved with an appropriate device helped customers identify the shops, until houses were supplied with street numbers. Inns were always identified. The Two Gentlemen of Verona arranged to meet, you will recall, 'at the sign of the elephant', and signs that could be instantly recognised were obviously good for business. A hand and mallet meant a goldsmith, scissors a tailor, a pestle and mortar an apothecary, and a monk's staff swathed in bandages a barber-surgeon — from which our barber's pole derives.

Book: *British Inn Signs and Their Stories* by E. R. Delderfield (David & Charles, 1965)

silver Until the discovery of palladium and platinum in the nineteenth century, gold and silver were considered to be the only two precious metals. And they have been worked by artists and craftsmen for a very, very long time: James Henderson points out that 'there exist ornaments which were twice as old in Cleopatra's time as Cleopatra's diadem would be for us.' Gold has always been scarcer than silver, except in Eldorado and a few other isolated spots, but the increasing demands for silver by industry are narrowing the gap. Both are malleable and neither is subject to oxidisation. Silver, which is harder than gold but softer than copper, is superior to both as a conductor of heat and electricity. It can be worked only by being alloyed with copper, which lowers its melting point. It was known by the alchemists as *luna*, the moon, while gold was always associated with the sun.

Silver was used as coinage in Babylon from about 4500 BC. By 2000 BC most of the techniques practised today by silversmiths were in current use, though not, of course, silver-plating. When Christianity was officially recognised in AD 313, the main task of the goldsmith (a little confusion here: goldsmiths were responsible for gold, silver and combinations of the two such as silver-gilt) was to create artifacts for enriching and beautifying churches.

French goldsmiths were supreme in the thirteenth, fourteenth, and fifteenth centuries. As the Gothic style evolved it was reflected in French silver pieces, whose influence spread rapidly to the rest of Europe. Silver was used in an architectural style, with enamel and precious gems being set where stained glass windows would have been in a church. During the Renaissance, Spain and Italy were central to the history of European silver, the influence of classical taste becoming paramount. Satyrs and cherubs cavorted, swags of fruit and flowers, acanthus leaves and scrolls made their cavortings aesthetic, and sea monsters and grotesques of all kinds leered and grinned. During the sixteenth century the German goldsmiths of Nuremberg and Augsburg showed what astonishing vari-

George III silver
tea caddy, 1809

ations could be played on the simple theme of the drinking vessel. Many German goldsmiths emigrated to Antwerp, and thence their influence spread to all parts of Europe and Scandinavia.

Initially then English silver, like so many other aspects of English taste, was adapted from continental models. Holbein designed plate for Henry VIII, that great despoiler of monasteries and debaser of currencies, and England became the adoptive home of many protestants from Europe. Towards the end of the sixteenth and beginning of the seventeenth century, as continental silver became ever more ornate (the astonishing baroque fantasies of Paul and Adam van Vianen for instance), so British silver simplified and dignified the ideas which had been brought from overseas; a style was created which was both immediately recognisable as English and, within a hundred years, as fine as anything produced anywhere. By the seventeenth century most households of any pretensions could count their wealth (for silver, being negotiable, was the outward and visible sign of wealth) in terms of silver salts, ewers, basins, tazzas (standing cups), tankards, and flagons.

During the Commonwealth almost all plate was melted down by Cromwell to arm and pay his troops, and scarcely any new pieces were produced: hence any surviving English silver from before 1660 is highly desirable. From 1685 began the richest period in the history of English silver. Huge pieces of silver furniture were commissioned. Table tops, mirror-frames, chimney furniture, toilet sets, flagons, pilgrim bottles, and wine coolers grew larger and larger. Wine coolers of over 3500 ounces have survived from this period known vaguely as 'Queen Anne'.

In 1697 the standard of silver for plate was raised to 95.8 per cent pure to distinguish it from sterling (92.5 per cent) and to save the Exchequer's embarrassment when bullion intended for the mint was diverted to the goldsmiths. The beauty of line and fine engraving of English silver was exemplified in the work of Paul de Lamerie (1688–1751) who came from Holland with his Huguenot parents *c.*1691. De Lamerie worked both in the plainer Queen Anne style and in the more ornate rococo manner, but rococo in Britain (unlike France) remained a controlled and distinguished exercise in elaboration.

In the 1750s the Grand Tour became a fashionable adventure for young men whose pockets were wide but whose outlook was narrow, and also for men like Robert Adam, the son of a celebrated Scottish architect, and Horace Walpole, son of the Prime Minister. They brought back with them tales of exciting finds at Pompeii and Herculaneum, and the neo-classical age began. Classical columns on square gadrooned bases, combinations of straight lines and symmetrical curves, formal borders, fluting and beading, and the familiar jumble of classical imagery, all contributed to coffee, tea and chocolate pots, candlesticks and candelabra, flatware and hollow-ware, and presentation items of great quality.

Paul Storr (1771–1844), who made his reputation with portentous pieces like the 'Battle of the Nile Cup', presented to Lord Nelson, opened a workshop which produced vast quantities of fine cutlery, as well as more ambitious pieces. But like de Lamerie he was more entrepreneur than artist-craftsman. Other excellent work of the period was produced by the Bateman family and Rundell, Bridge and Rundell.

The invention of Sheffield plate in the 1740s was now threatening to cream much of the profit off the silver business. Anything that silver could do, plate could apparently do as well — a great deal cheaper. Post-Regency and Victorian silver (itself to be challenged by electroplate) became increasingly eclectic, adopting the worst excesses of the French post-revolutionary style, as well as Gothic and oriental influences. Individual pieces of Victorian silver have quality, but much is heavily embossed, often dye-struck, and has little to recommend it except a boastful technical virtuosity, and a confidence that size and weight compensate for other shortcomings.

There is a great deal to be said for the collector taking a look at Scottish and Irish silver, since English silver has enjoyed so much of the limelight recently. Edinburgh silver of the early nineteenth century is probably of finer quality than most English silver of the same period, while Dublin silver between c.1720 and c.1820 is very fine indeed, though scarce.

Hints on hallmarking will be found under the entry for hallmarks, but it is always a good idea to look at the silver carefully *before* looking at the mark. Marks can be confusing, misleading, or, indeed, forged, while fine pieces of silver sing tunefully their own orisons. Damaged and blackened pieces should be taken to experts (inexpert repairers may just dip them in an electroplating bath), while silver should be cleaned in warm, soapy water and dried with a soft cloth — *never* put in a washing-up machine. Once clean, silver may be polished in the traditional way.

Books: *Silver* by Richard Came (Weidenfeld & Nicolson, 1961); *Book of Hallmarks* by F. Bradbury (Northend, 1975); *English Silver Hallmarks* by Judith Banister (Foulsham, 1970); *Collecting Antique Silver* by Judith Banister (Ward Lock, 1972)

skeleton clock   Originating in France in the late eighteenth century, these 'skellies' (as they are known in the trade) had their cases reduced to skeletal structures of bars, with dials pierced to expose the mechanism. Highly decorative, they were ideal for displaying in clockmakers' windows, and were sometimes made up for that purpose. In the nineteenth-century Gothic revival they took on weird and wonderful shapes. They have been much copied and faked (for early skeleton clocks were of excellent quality), so you should always look out for the number of spokes on each wheel. Four is suspect; five or six is encouraging.

Collection: Wallace Collection, London

Mid nineteenth-century single fusee skeleton clock

slagware   Also known as 'poor man's porcelain', slagware is, in fact, nothing at all to do with porcelain. It is a type of pressed glass, made by mixing molten flint-glass with slag from the local iron and steel works. There are three common types of slagware. The first is open mix, in which the colours (pale blue, green, brown, and dark mauve) and white portions are not blended. The second is fuse mix, in which the colours have been well blended, and the third is over-mix, which contains no white, only different shades of colour. Objects made from slagware include candle-sticks, spill-holders, plates, bowls, small squat vases and tumblers, cream jugs, and flat flasks impressed with illustrations from nursery stories.

The main centre for slagware was the north-east of England in general and Gateshead in particular. Millions of pieces must have been made at the glassworks there during the second half of the nineteenth century. Slagware remains cheap and easily obtained, although collectors are beginning to show signs of interest.

slipware   A type of primitive decorated English pottery. I can do no better than to quote from a reference book by John and Edith Hodgkin published in 1894: 'The material of the body of this ware was usually a coarse reddish clay, on which slip, a thin, creamy mixture of clay and water, was allowed to trickle through a tube by the workman, who thus produced quaint figures, conventional designs, borders, medallions, inscriptions, names or dates.' (One is irresistibly reminded of icing a cake.) The glaze of lead and manganese would then be applied before firing and the piece would acquire a rich yellow tone. Products made in slipware included tygs, posset pots, cups, plates, jugs, dishes, and candlesticks.

Collections: Museum and Art Gallery, Brighton; Anne of Cleves House, Lewes; Somerset County Museum, Taunton

snaplock or **snaphaunce**   This mechanism, which could be fitted to either pistols or longarms, was a sophistication of the wheellock. It was invented c.1544, and worked by striking sparks from a pivoting steel plate with a piece of flint held in a spring-activated cock. The sparks fell into the priming pan and fired the charge through the touch-hole. Its development was concurrent with that of the flintlock, and it remained popular in Spain, Italy, and North Africa long after the flintlock had been adopted elsewhere. The snaplock is the scarcest of all antique firearms. It is very beautiful and may often bear a date inscribed on the inside of the lockplate.

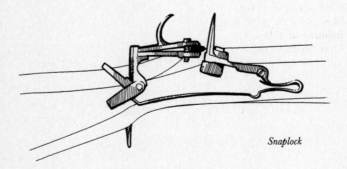

Snaplock

snuff-boxes   Sir Walter Raleigh may have discovered the potato but he certainly did not discover tobacco. In the year in which he colonised Virginia and is supposed to have discovered tobacco, Queen Elizabeth issued a decree condemning its use. Still, at that time even if you had no liking for smoking tobacco you sniffed it to keep the plague at bay, and you kept the powdered tobacco in a pouncet box. Presented thus it was called snuff. In Henry VIII's reign schoolboys were sometimes compelled to smoke or to sniff; it had the advantage of reducing healthy young appetites.

Until the end of the seventeenth century the craze for sniffing or snuffing (or snushing) was confined to the socially élite. Charles II is recorded on 24 September 1685 as having spent £85 on chocolate and snuff, while George IV took £7000 per annum from the Civil List to add to his collection of snuff-boxes. However, as snuff became cheaper (in 1605 an ounce would cost an average labourer's weekly wage), so the boxes tended to be made increasingly from everyday materials.

Generally one can say that gold Queen Anne boxes have rounded corners while under the first two Georges the boxes became oval. From 1760 to 1815 they were rectangular and from 1790 onwards they had concave or rounded sides. After 1798, 18-carat gold was introduced to bring Britain into line with continental practice, and after 1854 gold of 15, 12, and 9 carats was also permitted. A hallmark should enable you to date your box in any case. Where a gold snuff-box has a pull-on lid one can be fairly sure it was intended for *confits* (breath-sweeteners) not snuff.

More silver boxes have survived than boxes of any other material. Hallmarks may well have been rubbed off, and the interiors gilded to prevent discoloration. Octagonal silver boxes may be approximately dated between 1690 and 1740, triangular boxes are mid-nineteenth century, and boxes with sporting or topographical scenes let into the lid are very likely mid- or late-Victorian.

If you are lucky, you may come across a miniature painted on ivory by Richard Cosway (1742–1821), whose signature may be self-effacingly hidden under the mounts. Cosway and thirty other masters were engaged in painting snuff-box lids.

Most Sheffield plate snuff-boxes are rectangular, tin-lined, and very simple with perhaps some beading. Snuff-boxes in pinchbeck are notable for elaborate relief work. Battersea enamel boxes were produced only from 1753 to 1756, whereas enamel boxes from Bilston were produced for a hundred years from the 1740s. Genuine Battersea is therefore considerably rarer than Staffordshire, but both are charming and carry endearing messages on their lids.

Snuff-boxes were also produced from Britannia metal, moiré metal, gilt and Lancashire brass, mounted cowrie shells, tortoiseshell, mosaics of hard stones, amber, *papier mâché*, lacquer, mother-of-pearl, inlaid wood, and even potato skins, which offered excellent insulation against extremes of temperature.

Collections: The Stewartry Museum, Kirkcudbright; The Museum, Lancaster; Wellington
    Museum, London (gold)

soapstone   Otherwise known as steatite, soapstone is often mistaken for jade, particularly by dealers whose wish is father to the thought. No excuse for them really, because soapstone (1 degree on the Mohs scale) may be scratched with a fingernail and easily chipped, while jade (6½ degrees) may certainly not. Furthermore it has a waxy feel and warms quickly in the hand; jade is not so easily seduced.

Soapstone is hydrous magnesium silicate, or talc, in a massive form. As long ago as the Neolithic age small talismen were carved from it. The Egyptians made soapstone scarabs, the Assyrians, Babylonians, and Chinese used it for seals. Its natural colours range from black to grey and white, from brown to red and green. It was sometimes coloured artificially in the nineteenth century, but the dye in such cases failed to penetrate very deeply into the stone.

Although soapstone has been worked by Eskimos and Indians, most pieces which find their way here are Chinese, hailing from Fukien Province (the traditional home) or Chekiang Province. There are a few pieces surviving from the Ming Dynasty, and during the Ch'ien Lung period a number of large pieces were made in imitation of jade. Seals, which everyone had to carry, were regularly made from soapstone, as were flower vases. But perhaps the most interesting pieces are the eighteenth- and nineteenth-century carvings of the Eight Immortals, presented either singly or as a group. These are as follows (I quote from the excellent Michael Ridley):

1   *Chung-li Ch'uan, generally shown as a fat man with a bare belly holding a fan.*
2   *Chang-ko-Lao, usually shown with a mule, and holding a bamboo tube drum.*
3   *Lu Tung Pin, shown in the guise of a scholar with a fly-whisk.*
4   *T'sao Kuo-ch'iu wears court head dress and holds castanets.*
5   *Li T'ieh-kuai, represented as a beggar leaning on an iron crutch. He is shown thus because his spirit left his body, and on its return couldn't find him and so had to enter the body of a lame beggar.*
6   *Han Hsiang-tzu, whose emblem is the flute and who is credited with the power to make flowers grow and blossom instantly.*
7   *Lan Ts'ai Lo, who carries a flower basket.*
8   *Ho Hsien-Ku, a woman who became a fairy, having eaten a supernatural peach. Her emblem is the lotus in her hand.*

Kwan Yin, the Buddhist Goddess of Mercy, was also a popular subject.

sofa   From the Arabic *soffah*, a bench. Elegantly classical during the Regency period, this upholstered couch got pompous and neo-Gothic later on. The Sociable Sofa (with two seats) was introduced *c.*1850.

The sofa table had a rectangular top with flap-ends on a lyre-shaped pedestal support.

soft-paste   A term applied to porcelain to distinguish it from hard-paste. The distinction is positively misleading, as the hardness and softness refer to the degree of firing needed by the body in the kiln, not to the inherent hardness or softness of the porcelain. There are many varieties of soft-paste porcelain, resulting from attempts to imitate Chinese pieces. Mostly their components include clays, lime, sand, and animal and mineral ingredients (hard-paste has only two ingredients, china clay and felspar). Soft-paste may be stained by acids from fruits and by dyes. When broken its edges will exhibit a crumbly, granular surface, like a sugar cube. It was manufactured in Britain in the seventeenth and eighteenth centuries, after which it was generally superseded by hard-paste or 'true' porcelain.

spandrel   When a circle is drawn inside a square of the same diameter, there are little areas left in the corners of the square, and these are the spandrels. Now think of a clock face. Very often the spandrels of a longcase, bracket or other clock contain decorative devices in cast brass. These are often cupids or swags, and they are known as spandrel pieces.

spelter   When something looks almost like bronze and is light and a bit tinny to the touch it is probably spelter. Properly all spelter means is zinc, but the term is applied to cheap castings in zinc or zinc alloys, usually (though not always) taken from bronze originals. Statuettes, candlesticks, and clock cases offer the most common examples of work done with spelter.

spindle-back chair   Country chairs of the Windsor family. A spindle is a thin turned rod, shaped like the spindle used in spinning yarn. When the 'sticks' of a chair-back are spindle shaped the chair is known logically as a spindle-back. Sometimes rush seated, these charming chairs are what you automatically think of when you think of a kitchen chair. The design has survived unchanged for two hundred years, and we ought to appreciate it more than we do.

spinning wheels   Hand-operated wheels have been in use in Britain since the Middle Ages, but Germany was more advanced, since the treadle wheel was invented there in 1533. Obviously the advantages of having both hands free to manipulate the thread were enormous, and the foot-operated machine, with gears, was found throughout Britain during the seventeenth and eighteenth centuries. Hand-spinning is still practised in remoter parts of the British Isles, but not much. One wonders where all the spinning wheels went.

splat or **splad**   The splat is the central panel in a chair-back joining the seat to the top rail. It may be shaped (baluster-splat) or pierced, painted or inlaid, but it remains the focal point of the design.

Spode On 11 November 1749 Thomas Whieldon, at whose pottery so many able young apprentices were trained, hired 'Siah Spode, to give him from this time to Martelmas next 2/3d or 2/6d, if he deserves it.' Evidently young Josiah did deserve it, for within three years his wages had risen to 7s. He married, and in 1755 his son Josiah was born. He set up his own potteries, with William Tomlinson in the 1760s and with Thomas Mountford in the early 1770s, before going into business on his own some time in the 1780s.

His policy was to put quality before everything else, and it is for this reason that his business flourished when so many other potters in the eighteenth and nineteenth centuries failed. He was not an original, and copied patterns from Dresden, Chelsea, Nantgarw, and Swansea, signing his name to them from *c*.1800 (which was more than many did). He succeeded remarkably in imitating the Sèvres soft-paste porcelain (known as *pâte tendre*). His basalt, his dry-body ware, his caneware and creamware were equally successful — Whieldon had been a partner of Wedgwood, and Wedgwood's influence on Josiah Spode I was very powerful.

There were three generations of Josiah Spodes, and when Josiah Spode I died in 1797, Josiah Spode II took over the management of the Stoke factory. By then he was well qualified to do so, for he had been managing retail and wholesale outlets in London (Fore Street, Cripplegate, and Portugal Street, Lincolns Inn Fields) with conspicuous success and had learned that the British public, whether or not it knew anything about art, knew what it liked. He made two important innovations at Stoke. He perfected the technique, which had already been practised by a number of other manufacturers, of mixing bone ash with china clay, china stone, and a small proportion of alkalis to produce bone china. His recipe produces a beautifully white body, which is sometimes mistaken for Swansea ware, and is still used by most bone china manufacturers. He also created his felspar (or feltspar) porcelain with felspathic rock from the Welsh-Shropshire border; feltspar looks its best when painted the distinctive Spode green.

Spode's prolific and diverse output of earthenware, transfer-printed in underglaze blue, is of exceptional quality, although the stoneware (New Stone) services were more practical for domestic use, being harder to chip. Then there were the elegantly tasteful bat-printed wares, and, for the more bumptious, the heavily gilded and colourful patterns based on Japanese Imari porcelain.

When Josiah II returned to Stoke, his elder son, William, and his manager, William Copeland, took over the London end of the operation. In 1827 Josiah III succeeded to the Spode factory on the death of his father. The adroit William Copeland moved the Spode shop to Bond Street, and his son, afterwards Lord Mayor of London (1835–36), purchased the whole concern from Spode's executors in 1833. The firm traded as

Copeland and Garrett (1833–47), as W. T. Copeland, late Spode (1847–67), as W. T. Copeland & Sons (1867–1970), and since 1970 as Spode Ltd.

Other innovations included in 1846 the statuary porcelain in Parian ware — highly successful at the Great Exhibition — and the prettiest little dolls' tea and dinner services, some of them so tiny that there was no room for the Copeland and Garrett mark. Also produced were hand-painted tiles by R. J. Abraham (1850–1925), with titles like Health, Strength, Courage & Fortitude, and large allegorical vases by Samuel Alcock.

Book: *Spode* by Leonard White (Barrie & Jenkins, 1970)
Collection: Spode-Copeland Museum and Art Gallery, Stoke-on-Trent

spoons   Even today, I am assured, there are Scotsmen who drink whisky out of shells, an interesting link with the past for the earliest spoons were shells. Other materials used included stone (Upper Pleistocene Age), clay (Neolithic Age), bone (Roman) and metal (Egyptian). Some of these Roman and Egyptian spoons had spikes on the handles for extracting juicy bits from crustaceans, or, presumably, removing stones from horses' hooves.

The Anglo-Saxon word for spoon is *spon* which is derived from the word for wood-chip. Early English spoons were made of wood, bone, and horn. Copper, pewter, and brass were later employed for everyday use; the king used gold, the nobles silver.

Those who could afford to had their personal sets of cutlery which they carried with them, as we carry toothbrushes. Henry VI left his spoon with his boots and gloves at Bolton Hall after the battle of Hexham. (Hexham, incidentally, seems to have the highest incidence of antique shops per capita of anywhere in the country.) Elizabeth I had a gold folding spoon, and Bonnie Prince Charlie carried an engraved, two-piece lobed-end silver spoon in a black shagreen case. Although such spoons as these are unlikely to be picked up at your local antique market, there is still a pleasing variety of silver spoons for the collector to choose from.

The earliest recognised type of English spoon is the acorn-knop, dating from the fourteenth century. The acorns on these were tiny, but grew appreciably during the next century. Diamond-points were produced concurrently with acorn-knops. Maidenhead spoons feature the head and shoulders of the Virgin Mary at the top of the stem; they continued into the seventeenth century, and may be dated by the style in which the hair has been dressed. Strawberry-knops are topped with strawberries and other fruit. Wrythen-knops have spirally twisted cones on the stems. Other spoons are 'knopped' with falcons, doves, owls, balls, angels, spikes, mitres, and horses' hooves. Apostle spoons are very rare and valuable, the most remarkable set being 'The Tichborne Celebrities', which sold for £70,000 in 1975. Other early spoons include Lion Sejants (in which a lion sits proudly upright), Slipped-in-the-stalks, in which the stem appears to have been sliced transversely across, and Seal-tops, dual-purpose and decorated with acanthus leaves.

All these spoons have pear-shaped bowls, hexagonal stems tapering towards the top, and are hammered out of a single piece of silver. Rat-tails are an addition to the stem, strengthening the back of the bowl. Many of these early silver spoons were melted down at the time of the Commonwealth.

Later spoons, including caddy spoons, may be dated from their hallmarks. Fiddle pattern (the name precisely describes them), King's pattern, Queen's pattern and Princess pattern spoons each had their vogue — King's pattern remains popular today.

Book: *The Story of Cutlery* by J. B. Himsworth (Benn, 1953)
Collection: City Museum and Art Gallery, Sheffield

sporting trophies   In the jargon of the saleroom a sporting trophy is usually linked with big game. At a Christie's sale, the catalogue might contain such items as the skin of an abominable snowman, or Yeti, from the Himalayas, a reconstruction of a dodo, and the largest wild boar's tusk in captivity. Mounted gorillas and other game are almost a cliché. Obviously such items will become increasingly rare and expensive as restrictions on big-game hunting are tightened up. I would rather have a house filled with live birds (as Sir Thomas More did) than with dead gorillas.

Also collected, and only a little less bizarre, are late eighteenth-century racing trophies and testimonials, made in silver or silver gilt. Since the whole purpose of these objects was ostentation, the manufacturers (Hancock and Company, Elkington and Company, Garrard and Company, Hunt and Roskell) were given a free hand with their rose bowls, epergnes, candelabra, tazzas, and centrepieces. The results were frequently horrifying, some pieces containing as much as a thousand ounces of silver with the strangest conglomeration of classical, mythological, allegorical, topographical, and equine symbolism.

Staffordshire pottery   Unsophisticated earthenware figures of celebrated and notorious personages were produced throughout the eighteenth and nineteenth centuries in a number of Staffordshire potteries centred on Stoke-on-Trent. The seven towns are Burslem, Cobridge, Fenton, Hanley (with Shelton), Longton (with Lane End), Tunstall, and Stoke. The figures were what the people wanted at a price they could pay, and these, together with stoneware and earthenware table services, toby jugs, Staffordshire dogs (King Charles spaniels, dalmations, greyhounds, poodles), cats, zebras, and others, ensured the prosperity of the Staffordshire potters. Early figures and jugs — by 'early' I mean eighteenth-century — were more brightly coloured and more expertly modelled than

*Pair of cricketers, probably
Caesar and George Parr*

later examples, and some famous potters were involved in their production: men like Ralph Wood (father and son), Enoch Wood, Aaron Wood, Josiah Wedgwood, Thomas Whieldon, J. Voyez, John Turner, John Walton, James Caldwell, Ralph Salt, and many others.

Some of the most popular figures moulded in Staffordshire include Fred Archer (who was champion jockey from 1874 to 86 and rode 2748 winners out of 8004 rides), highwaymen Dick Turpin and Tom King, John Wesley, who looked upon all the world as his parish, the Duke of Wellington, Admiral Nelson, whose motto was 'Let him who merits bear the palm' and who lived by it, Queen Victoria and Prince Albert, the Four Evangelists, Britannia, and others too numerous to mention here.

Book: *Early Staffordshire Pottery* by Bernard Rackham (Faber & Faber, 1951)
Collections: Royal Museum, Canterbury (saltglaze); Corporation Museum, Dover (saltglaze); City Museum and Art Gallery, Stoke-on-Trent; Museum and Art Gallery, Brighton (Willet Collection); Stapleford Park, Melton Mowbray (Thomas Balston Collection)

stamps It is beyond the scope of this book to give any useful detailed information about philately. The only rule which remains valid in this as in every field is to specialise until you know more than those with whom you will be doing business. Such a degree of expertise can only be built up over some time. Increasingly now the stamp-collector needs to be a geographer, historian, and chemist if he is to succeed. Chemist, in order to spot the frequent forgeries, some of which, ironically, are now collected in their own right. Increasingly too, the philatelist collects stamps on their original envelopes, where the quality of the franking, the history of the mailing, and indeed the contents, all play an important part in the value of the item.

Here, for instance, is an entry with an estimated value of £1000 from a recent catalogue: 'Japan 1863 October 1, opened out envelope together with original letter headed HMS "Centaur", Yokohama, addressed to Wisconsin, USA, and sent via Hong Kong where the transit c.d.s. was applied on 14 October, London transit 2 December and Chicago arrival of 26 December, handstruck, 64/US Notes in blue. An extremely rare and very early piece of correspondence emanating from Japan.' It becomes difficult at times to define where philately ends and the collecting of banknotes, documents, and autographed letters begins.

Catalogues should not be regarded as bearing much relation to the price you would realise if you wanted to sell your stamps. It is fair to say that they represent what an *eager* buyer might pay a casual seller. With a reluctant buyer and a keen seller things could be very different. Then value also depends on *completeness*. In order to get a stamp which he needs to complete a set, a collector will probably have to buy a great many duplicates which he will then be eager to pass on. If, for instance, you could get every printing of a Penny Black marked with the code AA, that would be a triumph.

There are stamps which are valuable because of their rarity (Mauritius and Cape of Good Hope, for instance) but there are others equally rare, say, from some of the Latin American countries, which have never received such a good press. Condition is vital, of course. Ideally a stamp should be well 'centred', and have generous margins all the way round. Perforations should be complete and not 'short'. Crease marks, 'thinning', and 'toning' are defects; original gum is an asset. But condition relates also to the history of the stamp. One would not expect a much travelled stamp to be immaculate, or an unused block to be damaged.

A certain measure of security results from buying from or selling to a reputable auctioneer or dealer. Unfortunately, in the stamp business — and it is a very big business indeed — auctioneers and dealers are frequently one and the same, a disreputable state of affairs which is rapidly spreading to other areas of collecting.

Postal auctions are commonplace; you should watch out that these are not merely dealers selling their cast-offs. The best control is to see whether these auctions will accept some of *your* stamps. It is also a good sign if 'prices realised' lists are issued.

Books: *Collecting Stamps* by Alan James (Blackwell, 1973); *The Philatelist's Companion* by Bill Grunston (David & Charles, 1975); and of course the Stanley Gibbons catalogues
Collection: City Museum and Art Gallery, Birmingham (Evans Collection of 44,000 representative stamps)

Stevengraph   In 1854 Thomas Stevens (1828–88), a Coventry silk-weaver, started his own business, attempting to turn the newly imported Jacquard loom to profitable advantage. First he made silk ribbons, then bookmarks, which, with an improving text on them, were snapped up by schools as cheap but suitable prizes for pupils. Valentine and Christmas cards, lavender bags, hatbands, and calendars were all good selling lines, but none proved as successful as the coloured silk pictures on cardboard mounts, first produced in 1879. These Thomas called Textilegraphs, and over two hundred different designs have been recorded. The most popular themes included Lady Godiva, hunting and sporting scenes, royalty, politicians, transport, and historical tableaux. The quality of these Stevengraphs declined steadily after the turn of the century, and the Coventry factory was finally destroyed in an air-raid in 1940.

Stevengraphs were seriously introduced to collectors by Geoffrey Godden's exhaustive study (see below). They may be dated by reference to the backs of the mounts where a printed label gives details of previous Stevengraphs with a reminder that 'The following subjects can be had beautifully Illuminated in 10 or 12 colours.'

Although Thomas Stevens was not the only weaver of silk pictures in the nineteenth century, he is the only one around whom the majority of collectors have buzzed in their search for honey. It might now be better to look at such competitors as John Caldicott, John and Joseph Cash, Dalton, Barton & Co., William Henry Grant J.P., who specialised in Gladstone and Queen Victoria (as befits a J.P.), and J. Ratliff & Son.

Book: *Stevengraphs and other Victorian Silk Pictures* by Geoffrey Godden (Barrie & Jenkins, 1971)

stick-back The simplest form of Windsor chair, the stick-back has three or four thin turned spindles (known as sticks) flanked by two fatter spindles. It may have — and should have — turned legs. A bow-backed or double bow-backed Windsor chair in which all the sticks are thin may also be known as a stick-back.

stoneware Earthenware which has been fired at a temperature higher than 1200°C. It is then sufficiently solid to be non-porous and has no need of glazing. During the eighteenth century saltglazed stoneware, which developed alongside lead-glazed earthenware, was attractively similar to the more expensive porcelain it was designed to imitate.

stools The oldest kind of seat, used in myriad varieties for five thousand years. There are too many types to list here, but some of the more colourful of these backless seats are as follows:

creepie: a low stool used in Scottish churches, and dating from the late seventeenth or early eighteenth century.
faldstool: a medieval folding stool containing a cushion for kneeling on.
French stool: a stool with scrolled ends for placing in window recesses. The

term is used by Ince and Mayhew in their book *The Universal System of Household Furniture* (1759–62).

kneeler: a hassock.

necessary stool: a delicate seventeenth-century term for what became known in the eighteenth century as a convenience and in the nineteenth century as a night commode.

pouffe (also known as a *pouf, crapaud, comtesse,* or *senateur*): a large mid-Victorian stuffed footstool in which the framework is invisible. My local auctioneer, a man of some delicacy, refers to them as pouffés.

saddle stool: a three-legged stool with a seat shaped like a saddle, dating from the eighteenth century.

shop stool: four-legged and round-seated, these country-made stools may still be seen in traditionally fitted shops. They date from the eighteenth and nineteenth centuries.

tabouret or taboret: French stool from the court of Louis XIV. If you were a privileged lady you were permitted to sit in the royal presence, but only on a tabouret. The name, suggesting a drum, is incorrectly applied to oriental coffee-stools.

X-stool: any stool with an X-shaped frame, sometimes folding; an ancient design popular in most cultures. See also *footstool*.

Stourbridge   In 1567 Jean Carré, a glassmaker from Arras, emigrated to England and opened the Crutched Friars Glasshouse in London. Here he employed Flemish and Italian workmen, including the great Giacomo Verzelini (known as Mr Jacob). Only nine pieces have survived from the works, and all are goblets. Carré died in 1572 and Verzelini retired in 1592, leaving the works to his sons, Francis and Jacob. Many of the descendants of the Crutched Friars glassworkers made their way to the Stourbridge area of Worcestershire, where an existing manufactory was delighted to take them on. Glass is still made at Stourbridge today, and artist-craftsmen from that centre include the Webb family (at least four generations) and Arthur Nash, who travelled to New York in 1892 to help Tiffany.

The speciality of the Stourbridge works — or one of them, for they produced a wide variety of wares — was the cameo glass in which a white design was carved in relief on a dark body, a technique for which John Northwood (1836–1902) deserves the credit.

Book: *From Broad-Glass to Cut Crystal* by D. R. Guttery (Leonard Hill, 1956)

Sunderland   There were potteries in the Sunderland area from *c.*1740, but their output was nothing particularly fancy. They produced white domestic earthenware in competition with Staffordshire, and not until *c.*1800 did they produce a recognisable local style. The potteries then turned to transfer-printing in black or, more rarely, in red. Instead of pictures Sunderland preferred lines of verse: blank spaces were filled by hand with blotches of colour, or, alternatively, the whole piece would be lustred. Lustre became the Sunderland trademark, pink (from oxide or chloride of gold) leading the way *c.*1800, followed by copper and silver.

Evidently many of the customers of the dozen or so potteries were sailors, for mugs, jugs, and plaques were produced with lines from the 'Sailor's Farewell' and other such affecting classics. Commemorative pieces were also produced to celebrate victories at sea, events of national moment, the exploits of the local hero, Jack Crawford, in the Battle of Camperdown (1797), and the opening of the Wearmouth Bridge (1796), the longest single-span, cast-iron bridge in the world — at least 28 jugs with a view of its famous 236-foot span have been recorded.

Besides the above, Sunderland produced such items as chamber pots, bawdily inscribed, jugs and basins, punch-bowls, rolling pins, models of cottages, shepherdesses, portraits of celebrities, cats on cushions, cow creamers, lions, dogs, ink-stands, tobacco jars, watch-stands, and almost everything else that could be sold by the Staffordshire rivals. Frog-mugs and puzzle jugs, none of whose several spouts led directly to the ale inside, were for novelty-hunters.

It is surprising that such modest ware is so much reproduced, but it is, and, since the originals are unsophisticated, many of the reproductions are convincing. Few specimens are marked, so the best policy is to look underneath, for signs of wear and use. Dixon & Co, Phillips & Co, Sewell and Donkin, Dawson, and Fell are a few of the Sunderland potters whose marks may be found.

And, to cheer you up, an inscription from one of the above mentioned chamber pots, which could only offend those who enjoy being offended:

> *Dear lovely wife pray rise and piss,*
> *Take you that handle and I this.*
> *This present which to us is sent,*
> *To make some mirth it seems was meant.*
> *So let it be as they have said,*
> *We'll laugh and piss and then to bed.*

Collections: Laing Art Gallery and Museum, Newcastle-upon-Tyne; Museum and Art
    Gallery, Sunderland

Sutherland table Named after Harriet, the Duchess of Sutherland, Mistress of the Robes to Queen Victoria, this narrow-topped, gate-legged table with large folding leaves on both long sides occupies little space and was used for serving tea. It would be made of mahogany, satinwood, rosewood, or ebonised walnut.

swag An ornamental wreath or festoon of draped cloth, this classical device was employed to great effect by Adam and his followers in the late eighteenth century.

Swansea   See *Nantgarw*. Just as there were three periods of Nantgarw porcelain (with which the Swansea works was closely associated), so there were three at Swansea: before Billingsley and Walker joined, 1764–1814; when Billingsley and Walker worked at Swansea, 1814–17; after Billingsley and Walker left and the manufactory was run first by Dillwyn with the Bevingtons (1817–18) and then by the Bevingtons on their own (1818–24).

The first period is undistinguished, the porcelain being little better than earthenware. The second period produced china of the finest quality, very similar to Billingsley's products at Nantgarw. The artists, including Billingsley himself (flowers), Pollard and Morris, his pupils, Baxter (landscapes), Colclough (birds), Beddow (landscapes), and Weston Young (flowers), were much the same as those who worked for the Nantgarw factory. The third period was inferior to the second, the body of the china being less translucent. The usual Swansea mark is 'Swansea' in red with a trident.

Book: *Swansea Porcelain* by W. D. John (Ceramic Book Company, 1958)
Collections: as for *Nantgarw*

tallboy   Known in America as a highboy, the tallboy was originally and more helpfully referred to as a chest-on-chest. In the seventeenth and eighteenth centuries, this is what it was. Now it is a high chest of seven or nine drawers, divided horizontally by a cornice. As you might expect, a tallboy was sometimes made in association with a lowboy.

tantalus   You will recall Tantalus, the mythical King of Phrygia, who was condemned to stand in Tartarus up to his chin in water, and the water receded whenever he stooped to drink. Well, mythical or not, he gave two words to the English language, tantalise and tantalus.

The tantalus is well named. It is a container for decanters, usually made of oak, which has a retaining bar over the top with a keyhole in it. Thus the drinks can be displayed, but secured against the secret drinker.

tea caddies and **teapoys**   Tea came to Britain in the mid-seventeenth century, about ten years after coffee. There were then two kinds of tea, black or 'bohea' and green or 'hyson'. The black comes from the fermented leaves of the camellia bush, the green from the unfermented. The British East India Tea Company had the monopoly on the importation of tea, a profitable business. Initially tea, which was taken medicinally, was very expensive (£3 per pound) and in the early eighteenth century tea caddies were introduced so that the tea could be kept under lock and key. The word 'caddy' (originally catty) comes from the Malayan word for 1⅓ pounds avoirdupois, but these caddies, which often came in pairs, one for bohea and one for hyson, held no more than half a pound. Tea parties were elegant ceremonies, with the exception of a memorable one in Boston.

Tea was heavily taxed by the first three Georges. But gradually during the eighteenth and nineteenth centuries it grew cheaper and the practice of 'taking' it spread wide throughout all social classes. Caddies became larger as tea became cheaper, while silver gave way to baser metals. Tea urns appeared; wooden caddies, which had reflected the prevailing furniture styles, became less elegant with the end of the Regency, and Victorian sarcophagus-shaped caddies were not calculated to appeal to persons of discernment.

For them the teapoy, derived from the Hindi word for three and the Persian word for foot (though teapoys were more frequently quadrupeds), was the answer, for, manufactured from mahogany, satinwood, rosewood, or lacquer, teapoys would grace any room. They were easily mistaken for work-tables and often did double-duty. They should have two, or four, containers for tea and two mixing bowls, for in those days one blended one's own tea before making it. (Early caddies should feature a mixing bowl between two containers.) The characteristic decoration for the teapoy was brass inlay, but by the middle of the century all kinds of alternative woods and materials were used, including *papier mâché*, which was particularly suitable. See also *caddy spoon* and *teapots*.

teapots Originally there were no teapots. One sat cross-legged in front of a pot of boiling water in which camellia leaves were infusing their mysterious fragrance. Then one sipped the potion from a tiny eggshell porcelain bowl, and all the secrets of the universe would be revealed.

The teapot makes considerable demands upon the potter's skills. The body of the pot must be heat-resistant; its top opening must be big enough to facilitate cleaning, yet not so big that the contents spill out when the tea is poured; the handle must be conveniently positioned for pouring, and strong enough to take the weight of pot and tea; the spout must be correctly angled and must dispense the tea without dripping; the lid must fit tightly enough but not too tightly, and the knob on top of it must enable the lid to be easily removed or replaced. A teapot which fails to measure up to any of these requirements is going to be a disappointment to all concerned.

When the East India Company began importing tea from China in the mid-seventeenth century, it found that Chinese porcelain formed the ideal kentledge (heavy ballast) to make the ships seaworthy. The early Chinese teapots, packed among the china which performed this humble duty, were probably wine pots, though there is much debate on the subject. They had high handles extending over the lid of the pot, but did not pour too well and were soon superseded by more practical British teapots. However, teapot stands, imported with the original teapots, were obviously of practical use and remained a standard part of tea sets throughout the Regency.

Early English pots were very small — barely larger than a cup — and globular, and tea bowls were equally tiny. By the last quarter of the

Lowestoft globular,
c. *1770*

*Caughley porcelain
barrel shaped*, c. *1770*

Chinese famille verte,
c. *1710*

*Ridgway porcelain
'London shape'*, *1810-1820*

eighteenth century the barrel shape was preferred, and this was followed by the oval teapot, the canoe-shaped teapot, and the 'London' teapot with a large spout and handle and a bulbous tummy. Victorian pots, and especially those from the Rockingham and Staffordshire potteries, were on a raised base, or feet, and were extremely ornate. One produced for the Great Exhibition was much the same size as the Queen, who could have curled up inside like Lewis Carroll's dormouse.

The range of teapots is vast. It would take the rest of this book to detail those teapots which you are likely to find in shops or at sales. Wedgwood went for classical designs, Worcester — probably the finest teapot manufacturer — fancied shells and feathers, Nantgarw copied Sèvres patterns, Spode had cupids and coloured panels, Prattware was charming, Castleford extravagant, New Hall delicate, Coalport pretty, Lowestoft innocent, Lustreware lustrous, and Caughley desirably blue and white.

At the end of the last century cottage teapots were mass-produced to conform to the popular notion that happiness could only be found in rustic surroundings, while the art deco designers had a field-day with teapots, producing witty and ingenious variations on the basic shapes and patterns. Cube teapots, teapots like cats and dogs and racing cars, teapots with moral instructions upon them, it was as though the tea had slightly unhinged those who provided the pots for it to be made in. But certainly teapots are one of the cheapest and most amusing areas of collecting.

The fact that I have concentrated on ceramic pots should not be taken to mean that there were no others. Obviously teapots in silver, plate, brass, and so on, were also there to pour the tea. Not that it really matters where it comes from. Cowper puts it best:

> *Now stir the fire, and close the shutters fast,*
> *Let fall the curtains, wheel the sofa round,*
> *And, while the bubbling and loud-hissing urn*
> *Throws up a steamy column, and the cups*
> *That cheer but not inebriate, wait on each,*
> *So let us welcome peaceful ev'ning in.*

Book: *Teapots and Tea* by Frank Tilley (Ceramic Book Company, 1977)
Collections: Bulwer Collection at Castle Museum, Norwich (over six hundred teapots);
 Public Library and Museum, Castleford; Sharp Collection, Wonersh, Surrey

teddy bears The teddy made his appearance in 1907. Teddy Roosevelt was on a bear hunt in Mississippi when a more than usually appealing cub caused him to lower his gun. Whether or not he anticipated the incident being reported in the newspapers, it was, with a cartoon captioned: 'Drawing the Line in Mississippi'. A quick-thinking toy manufacturer asked Roosevelt's permission to name his soft toys 'Teddy Bears' and Roosevelt agreed — to their mutual benefit.

The popularity of these toys has never waned and early ones are now collected. Their cause has recently been enthusiastically espoused by a number of eminent men, notably the Poet Laureate Sir John Betjeman.

terracotta The classical terracotta was a small (four to eight inch) statuette, excavated from ancient tombs. Greek terracotta figures were better than Roman. The flower of all were the Tanagras, which depict youths and maidens with delicacy — Oscar Wilde's adjective for them was 'exquisite'. The word terracotta has since been applied to red earthenware similar to that developed for these antique figures. But modern terracotta is chiefly used for garden ornaments, fountains, vases, and some oven and table ware. Among other craftsmen George Tinworth (1843–1913) worked with terracotta at Doulton's Lambeth factory, and some fine ornamental pieces were produced at the Watcombe pottery in Devon, where the clay was exceptionally fine.

Book: *Classical Terracotta Figures* by James Chesterman (Ward Lock, 1974)
Collections: Twenty-one Tanagras, the gift of Lord de Samaurez, at Girton College,
 Cambridge; Greek Museum, The University, Newcastle-upon-Tyne

thimbles The Romans had thimbles, conical ones, bronze and smooth-tipped. The Saxons had bell-shaped thimbles of leather with a stitched-on metal cap. The Elizabethans had thimbles made from gold, silver, and silver-gilt, often with a motto engraved on the rim. (It is a mistake by the way to suppose that thimbles were only used for sewing; there was a children's game called 'thimbling', and there was the schoolmaster's game which had no name, of rapping recalcitrant children on the head with thimbles. There were even 'secret thimbles' containing a detachable shell concealing a glass phial for poison.) Up until 1800 thimbles were made in two sections, and until 1790 no hallmarks were required on gold and silver; this exemption was removed in 1790 for silver.

From the start of the nineteenth century china thimbles made their appearance; they bore indentations on both the sides and the top, and were glazed inside and out. Minton and Worcester marked theirs, although the majority of china thimbles were unmarked. During this inventive century many other materials were used for thimbles, including jade, ivory, bone, exquisite examples of the art of the miniaturist; enamel and gemstones were used. *Repoussé* scenes from nature or from literature were featured, as were emblems and coats of arms.

As for thimble cases, they could be yet more elaborate; even such men as Fabergé and Cartier troubled themselves with the humble thimble case. But of course for most of those who in past centuries actually did the sewing, thimbles were homely objects, thick and unwieldy, of bronze, brass or pewter, hand-punched and battered. They did the job pretty well.

Book: *Thimbles* by Edwin F. Holmes (Gill & Macmillan, 1976)

Tiffany Louis Comfort Tiffany (1848–1933) was born with a diamond encrusted spoon in his mouth, for his father Charles L. Tiffany had founded the New York jewellers, Tiffany's, and was a man who could have made a million shipwrecked on a desert island. By the late 1880s Tiffany's had the most valuable collection of diamonds in the world, and the company's interests extended to other precious stones, gold, silver, plate, and glass.

Young Louis studied painting in Paris and was much influenced by Émile Gallé. As an interior decorator he was responsible for some impressive designs, including the interior of the White House, Washington. His furniture reflected oriental, Indian and Moorish influences with much shallow relief carving.

He became excited by the possibilities of glassmaking, and patented an iridescent glass, known as favrile. He would have little to do with surface decoration, cutting or moulding, believing that the design should be integral to the material used and not imposed upon it. His fantastic peacock-feather and butterfly-wing vessels were produced entirely in the furnace without wheel or brush. Such pieces made their débuts at the Chicago fair in 1893 (just four years after Gallé's successes in Paris) and were a sensation. During the last years of the century, with the Tiffany name and resources behind him (in 1898 the stores consisted of 300 tons of glass in 5000 varieties), he was irrepressible. In 1892 he had been cunningly inspired to bring to New York the glassworker Arthur Nash, from Stourbridge: the complementary skills of these two men resulted in artifacts of great resource and beauty.

Among other items produced in the Tiffany studios were decorative tableware in coloured lustre, paperweight vases incorporating *millefiori* designs, Cypriote ware, with its rusty brown glaze, lava glass with abstract decoration of dark blue and gold lustre, bronze desk sets inset with glass, enamel, or mother-of-pearl, dragonfly lamps in ormolu and favrile glass, and art nouveau pottery with designs inspired by leaves and trees.

Tiffany continued to experiment until he withdrew from the studio in 1919; and he inspired many disciples, notably J. Lötz Witwe, of Klostermühle.

Book: *Louis C. Tiffany's Glass, Bronzes, Lamps; A Complete Collector's Guide* by Robert Koch (Crown Publishers, 1971); *Tiffany Silver* by C. H. and M. G. Carpenter (Peter Owen, 1979)
Collection: Haworth Art Gallery, Accrington

Bronze table lamp, 18 inches high with dragon-fly mosaic shade

Six-foot Tiffany standard lamp with Iceland poppy design

tiles   There have been tiles for at least six thousand years. The Egyptians, the Assyrians, the Babylonians, and the Persians (particularly) used them to please the eye, appease the gods, and keep out the rain, the wind and damp. An Italian tile showing a gorgon's head survives from the sixth century BC; another surviving example shows a double-bodied sphinx, and a third two birds being strangled by a nature goddess. These were roof tiles, placed low and vertically so that their designs could be clearly visible. In China, in Italy, in Turkey and the Arab countries tiles were an integral part of a house. Brick walls and earthenware tiles proved a successful combination to keep the home dry and cool.

In Europe it was not until the twelfth century that tiles came much into use, in the form of encaustic floor tiles for cathedrals and churches, made by monastic potters. However, the manufacturers ceased production (except in North Devon) in the mid-sixteenth century. The Dutch tile-makers of the seventeenth century turned out tiles of good quality in astonishing quantities. English delftware tiles, though of comparable and even superior quality, could not compete economically.

In 1756 John Sadler with the help of Guy Green 'did, within the space of six hours, to whit, betwixt the hours of nine in the morning and three in the afternoon of the same day, print upward of 1200 Earthenware tiles of different patterns at Liverpool . . . more in number and better and neater than one hundred skilful pot-painters could have painted in the like space of time.' Sadler's designs were entirely new; hunting and courting scenes contrasted with satire, and with actors and actresses. These mechanically printed tiles cost just half as much as traditionally painted tiles, although the clay for the tiles was still being cut and shaped by hand.

Minton's became a major manufactory of tiles, and Herbert Minton, son of Thomas, the founder of the firm, grew interested in the commercial possibilities of the medieval designs found on the ancient, monkish, encaustic tiles. After much sweat and some tears Minton's encaustic tiles became established. The tile was now an acceptable, indeed a fashionable adjunct to interior and exterior design. Minton's commissions during the mid-nineteenth century included a pavement for the Queen at Osborne House, the Sultan of Turkey's yacht, eleven cathedrals, the Capitol Building in Washington, and the Royal Albert Hall in London.

Transfer-printed tiles made at the Wedgwood factory from 1870 came in sets, with subjects like the months of the year, Little Red Riding Hood, American views, and A Midsummer Night's Dream. Still, the most prolific tile-maker was not Minton or Wedgwood, but William Maw of Brighton, a prosperous manufacturer of baby bottles who retired at the age of thirty-four to take up tile-making as a hobby. It was not long before he was making more tiles than anyone else in the world.

The apostles of the neo-Gothic movement, under A. Welby Pugin, and the pre-Raphaelites and the arty set, under Ruskin and Morris, believed that medievalism should be brought back into design and that indust-rialisation was betraying aesthetics. Their tile designs were significant, for they regarded tiles, being ancient, monastic, and utilitarian, as ideal materials for craftsmen to work upon. Another important tile designer was William de Morgan, a close friend of William Morris, and a designer of stained glass, furniture, and ceramics (including his delightful 'Moonlight' and 'Sunset' pottery designs). His tiles were handmade at every stage of their manufacture and featured birds, fish, flowers, ships, mythical beasts, and designs in the Persian Isnik manner. More recently charming farmyard tiles have been produced at the Poole Potteries.

Books: *Tiles, a General History* by Anne Berendsen *et al.* (Faber & Faber, 1967); *Victorian Ceramic Tiles* by Julian Bernard (Studio Vista, 1972)
Collection: Abbey Ruins Museum, Shaftesbury (medieval tiles)

William Morris tiles :
early Fulham period 1888-98

tin The invention of tin-making machines in 1872 was not as dramatic perhaps as the invention of gunpowder, or anaesthetics, or the lavatory cistern, but it changed our way of life. No longer did the big producers package their smaller goods in wood; tins were in.

Huntley and Palmers led the way. They had biscuit tins designed to look like inlaid mahogany, fishermen's creels, book bindings, or jewel caskets. Chocolate tins would be anvils or hearts or bells; lozenge tins would be shaped like lozenges. Tins were issued to commemorate national occasions involving royalty, and Queen Alexandra sent the troops little flat tins filled with chocolates and tobacco for Christmas. So many of these were supposed to have saved their owners' lives by deflecting bullets that one sometimes wonders whether the Germans fired directly at them. The tins were colour-printed in offset litho with the use of transfer prints.

Now tins are respectable. Warhol immortalised a tin of Campbell's soup and the Victoria and Albert Museum held an exhibition of them with full media coverage. Oxo cube tins, which may be dated by the change in their shape, are attractive, but my favourites are the little gramophone needle tins, of which close on two hundred varieties are thought to exist.

Lehmann clockwork toy, c. *1915*

tin toys Tin toys were first produced in the USA in the mid-nineteenth century, and the cheap new material soon spread to Europe, where automata had become expensive and sophisticated. These early tin toys were stencilled and hand-painted but the offset lithography process meant that full colour designs could be repeated easily on thousands of sheets of tin-plate, out of which the models could be cut. By the time of the Great War, Germany was a massive producer of tin toys, from huge battleships to the familiar and popular 'penny toys' — which were rarely if ever sold for a penny. Between the wars Japan moved into the market, copying European models zealously.

After 1945 the US Occupied Zone included Nuremberg, near where most of the toy factories were sited. With American money the industry was revived, all the new models, many of them made from pre-war designs, bearing the stamp 'U.S. Zone Germany'. They were beautifully made with excellent detail, though often rather grotesque. As the 1950s advanced these German toys became more positive, affluent, and optimistic.

It was a similar story in Japan where, with American money, models were churned out to meet the demands of the American market. The boys depicted are freckle-faced and chubby, not slant-eyed and sallow-skinned.

Other countries to produce tin toys in recent years include Britain, Spain, Portugal, France, and even Eastern Europe. As clockwork gave way to battery power, the mechanical possibilities of the toys grew greater, and they could perform for far longer. Names to watch out for include Wells Brimtoy, Chad Valley and Mettoy in England, Gunthermann, Arnold, Gama, Gescha, Technofix, Tipp, Kellerman, Distler, and Schuco in Germany.

Book: *Tin Toys (1945–1975)* by Michael Buhler (Bergstrom and Boyle Books Ltd, 1978)

toby jugs   It was not Sir Toby Belch who inspired the first toby jug. Sir Toby wore doublet and hose, Toby wore plain eighteenth-century dress. Nor do I believe that it was Uncle Toby in Laurence Sterne's eccentric novel *Tristram Shandy*, although the dates match perfectly: Uncle Toby was an old soldier and dressed like one; he was not an old soak. There are other claimants too, but the evidence seems overwhelming for Harry Elwes, nicknamed Toby Fill-pot (or Phillpot) who died 'as big as a Dorchester butt' from too much ale. Here then, according to an old ballad called 'The Brown Jug', is what happened to him after his fatal attack.

> *His body, when long in the ground it had lain,*
> *And time into clay had resolved it again,*
> *A potter found out, in its covert so snug,*
> *And with part of fat Toby he form'd this brown jug;*
> *Now sacred to friendship, and mirth, and mild ale;*
> *So here's to the lovely sweet Nan of the Vale.*

The earliest representations of Harry Elwes — and most of the later ones — came from the Staffordshire potteries, and particularly from the Wood family of Burslem. There were five Woods, Ralph and Aaron (brothers), Aaron's two sons, William and Enoch, and Ralph's son, Ralph. Ralph senior and Enoch were the toby specialists and their work is much sought after, particularly Enoch's 'Escutcheon' jugs. Tobies were instantly popular, and the 'ordinaries', or cheaper models, seem to have found ready customers for many years.

Early tobies are ten or eleven inches high and have a translucent coloured glaze. Later pieces, more suited to enamel paints, feature brightly striped waistcoats and so on. Constant variations on the Harry Elwes theme were thought up by Staffordshire potters, including miniature tobies, female tobies (Martha Bunn, the Brighton bathing machine attendant who used to dip Prinny), elderly tobies, and so on.

Besides the Woods, other desirable early tobies were made by Neal and Palmer, John Walton, Ralph Salt, and Felix Pratt of Fenton. Victorian and twentieth-century tobies are usually copies of earlier models (the colours of the reproductions are duller than the original and the base will show suspiciously little sign of wear), with the exception of Martinware and Doulton's face mugs, produced from the 1930s.

Book: *Collector's Guide to Staffordshire Pottery Figures* by Hugh Turner (MacGibbon & Kee, 1971)

torchères   *Torchères* were slender, decorative stands, produced in pairs, and made to hold candelabra elegantly either side of a blazing log fire. Like so many rather unnecessary pieces of furniture they were ideal items for master cabinet-makers to work on. Chippendale illustrates rococo *torchères* in his *Director*. Adam, as you might expect, based his on classical originals found at Pompeii and Herculaneum, with rams'-head carvings and fine ornamental detail. Hepplewhite decorated his with wheat-ears and acanthus leaves. Usually *torchères* stood on tripod legs.

tortoiseshell That which is usually passed off as tortoiseshell is not a shell and has nothing to do with tortoises. It is a compound of keratin, hydrogen, and hydroxyl, or it may be nothing more than mottled plastic — put a match to it and you will soon find out! Genuine tortoiseshell will fluoresce yellow-brown under an ultra-violet lamp; it will also smell powerfully when filed down. When it was genuine, that is, until *c.* 1900, it usually came from the hawk's-bill sea turtle (*Chelone imbricata*) which floats around the Florida coast. The colour varies from dark brown on the back to yellow on the belly. In the Far East the loggerhead turtle (*Thalassochelys caretta*) was used for combs, oikimono elephants, and *netsuke*; the green turtle (*Chelone midas*) yields a shell that is of little use except for veneering, and usually ends up in the soup.

On the continent tortoiseshell was very popular for boulle furniture, inlaid mirror-frames and so on; but it was little used in Britain until the early nineteenth century when Louis Craigneur opened a London workshop. He provided shell for tea caddies, fans, and musical boxes. But it was not long before *papier mâché*, used in association with mother-of-pearl and very cheap, put an end to all that.

trade tokens The bookshop owner does it at Hay-on-Wye, the Club Méditerranée does it in its camps, everyone does it on the Metro — uses tokens, that is. Historically wherever and whenever there was a lack of legal currency it became necessary to issue one's own. Generals in the American Civil War, local traders suffering from a lack of low-value coinage, regional governments, all did it. Most trade tokens were issued between the mid-seventeenth and early nineteenth centuries.

Tokens are interesting to collect, since their designs often reflect local preoccupations and personalities. T. S. Hobson and Sons, button manufacturers of Sheffield, issued tokens with angels and arrows on them, and Cornish money featured tin mines. The tokens redeemable at the Birmingham workhouse — eighty to the pound — are most portentous.

Trade tokens

John Wilkinson, the famous ironmaster, issued halfpenny tokens to his employees, and put his own profile on them. You find weavers on Norwich halfpennies, a woolsack on a Shrewsbury halfpenny, and Lady Godiva featured by John Reynolds of Coventry. 'Success to the Cider Trade' is proclaimed on a Hereford token, a rare example from the West Country. 'United For a Reform of Parliament' was the message from the London Corresponding Society. The advertising and propaganda power of trade tokens was not overlooked.

Much counterfeiting of tokens occurred, trade tokens being easier to forge than legal currency. Copper halfpennies fried in brimstone had a nice antique appearance, and it was worth remembering that counterfeiting copper money was only a 'temporal' offence, whereas for imitating gold or silver you could be sent to the gallows.

Books: *The Provincial Token Coinage of the 18th Century* by R. Dalton and S. Hamer (Seaby, 1967); *Nineteenth Century Token Coinage* by W. J. Davis (Seaby, 1968); *Trade Tokens: A Social and Economic History* by J. R. S. Whiting (David & Charles, 1971)
Collections: Museum and Art Gallery, Luton (seventeenth century); Salisbury and South Wiltshire Museum, Salisbury

treen   Quite simply treen is anything made from a tree. More precisely treen is any 'miscellanea of small wooden objects in daily domestic or family use and in trades and professions'. The definition is Edward Pinto's, who devoted his life to collecting these genteel mementoes of dignified labour. We are talking about back-scratchers and spurtles and dog-tongues, artificial legs, ox muzzles and muffin prickers, podgers (with which you fed the meat into a sausage machine) tennis-ball brushes and beekeepers' bellows, mole-traps, bird scarers and warbler discs, hecto-graphs, zograscopes and wimbles (for twisting straws), tatting shuttles, lacemakers' bats and niddy-noddies (or cross-reels), wig-powdering carrots, glovemakers' donkeys, and clickets (for calling children to order at school). All human life is there. Whatever your calling or profession, manual, semi-skilled, skilled or executive, something you use, some stock-in-trade, some tool, will be made of wood, and will be treen. Part of the interest in collecting treen is the detection of what precisely an object was *for*. Only occasionally are pieces of treen signed and dated. But such pieces are finely carved and turned, do deserve to be more appreciated, and doubtless will be.

Incidentally treen is a very old word. John Jewel, Bishop of Salisbury in the sixteenth century, is on record as remarking: 'In old times we had treen chalices and golden priests, but now we have treen priests and golden chalices.'

Books: *Treen and Other Bygones* by Edward H. Pinto (G. Bell & Sons, 1969); *Treen and Other Turned Woodware for Collectors* by Jane Toller (David & Charles, reprinted 1975)
Collection: City Museum and Art Gallery, Birmingham (Pinto Gallery)

truncheons Varying in length from fourteen to twenty-six inches, truncheons were turned from boxwood which had the useful property of withstanding hard wear without breaking. Some truncheons were merely polished, others decorated and varnished. The most frequently found were japanned (see *Pontypool*), black, much gilded, and painted with inscriptions and heraldic devices in gaudy colours. Now they call them batons.

Collections: Museum and Art Gallery, Birmingham; National Museum of Wales, Cardiff; Art Gallery and Museum, Cheltenham; The Museum, Greenock; Castle Museum, York; Bargate Guildhall Museum, Southampton

tulipwood A brownish yellow hardwood with pink stripes, tulipwood (*Dalbergia frutescens*) is used for cross-banding, veneers, and inlays.

Tunbridgeware Tunbridge Wells was a notable spa: Charles I brought Henrietta Maria there, Charles II his whole court. Queen Anne contributed to the cost of the paving from which the Pantiles took its name. Beau Nash made it his kingdom. Dr Johnson and 'all the good company came to stare at Mrs Elizabeth Carter, the woman who could talk Greek faster than any one in England.' And all this thanks to Dudley, Lord North, who in 1606 proclaimed the efficacy of the chalybeate waters. For so many rich visitors a souvenir trade was established, using the main local resource (besides the chalybeate waters), timber. For at Tunbridge three ancient forests met, Bishop's Down, Water Down, and South Frith.

Tunbridgeware box and bookrest

The Burrows family was among the first to develop the technique used to make what is now known as Tunbridgeware, in which bunches of chips of various woods were glued together to form blocks of some eighteen inches square, sliced across to show to good effect the end grain patterns of wood. These veneers would then be glued to the items to be decorated, ten veneers being cut from each inch of block.

Tunbridgeware was more generally appreciated after the Great Exhibition (1851) where such *tours de force* as Fenner and Nyle's graduated perspective block of Battle Abbey were exhibited. Another piece to attract attention was a table top with a bird design, for which 129,450 separate pieces of wood were employed. Larger pieces of Tunbridgeware include glove boxes, photograph frames, silk-skein holders, book stands, jewel cases, work-tables, desks, and chairs. But the smaller pieces, cribbage-boards, paper-knives, spinning-tops, pen-holders, brushes, darning eggs, trays, napkin rings, and so on, are more common.

Look out for the intricacy of Tunbridge patterns and makers' labels, often affixed underneath — but ideally *not* the stockists' — and beware of damage. Besides the names mentioned above, Thomas Barton and Robert Russell are good news.

Book: *Tunbridge and Scottish Souvenir Woodware* by Edward and Eva R. Pinto (Bell, 1970)
Collections: Royal Tunbridge Wells Museum; City Museum, Birmingham; Lancaster Museum

typewriters The first patent for a 'writing-machine' was taken out by a Mr Henry Mill in 1714, but the first machine that we know to have worked was the 'Typographer', invented by the American William Burt in 1829. A Remington machine of 1874, developed by Sholes and Glidden, and decorated charmingly with floral sprays, was the first to achieve popularity, and its success led to many others. In 1881 the YWCA of New York bought six typewriters and started a class for eight young ladies. Five years later it is estimated that some 60,000 typists were employed in the USA.

The early Remingtons and other contemporary typewriters printed only in upper case; Yost's 'Caligraph' was the first with a double keyboard. The Underwood no 1 (1896) was the first 'modern' typewriter with writing visible to the typist, shift keys, and some lightness of touch. Of course early models were large and heavy. The 'Blick' (invented by George Blickensderfer, 1893) was the first portable. Electric typewriters only became popular in the 1950s, although the first electric machine appeared in 1902.

urns The Greeks and the Romans devised urns to provide a practical but dignified receptacle for the ashes of the dear departed. The urns could be built into monuments in a distinguished sort of way.

The satisfying classically shaped urn was frequently worked by Adam and other neo-classicists. Sometimes their urns even had flames issuing from the lids to symbolise resurrection. As an architectural motif and in interior design the urn proved very useful — as a terminal on finials, as the centrepiece of a broken pediment, or free-standing in its own right, as a knife box.

Tea-urns, heated by a red-hot iron bar in the base, were produced from the mid-eighteenth century. Thus the mysteries of mortality were transformed into a nice cup of tea.

Valentine cards St Valentine was a bishop who refused to renounce his faith and was beaten with clubs and beheaded on the orders of the Prefect of Rome. He died on 14 February AD 270, the eve of Lupercalia, a fertility feast-day, thus immortalising himself in myriad bad verses.

Ever since, by one of those ironies of social history and aided by the commercial ambitions of stationers and printers, St Valentine's name has been associated with lovers and fertility. 14 February became, charmingly, the day upon which the birds were popularly supposed to choose their mates. By the seventeenth century it had become customary for lovers (or would-be lovers) to send hand-written *billets doux*, coloured and decorated with lovers' knots and other sentimental imagery, to the objects of their affection. Pepys wrote on 14 February 1667: 'This morning came to my bedside (I being up dressing myself) little Will Mercer to be her Valentine; and he brought her name writ upon blue paper in gold letters, very pretty; and we were both well pleased with it.'

The first *printed* Valentines came off the presses in 1761, flimsy things with ballads and hand-coloured engravings, some by Bartolozzi. By 1825 half a million were being sent through the post annually. H. Dobbs and Company, fancy paper manufacturers, were mass-producing Valentines at this time. Their inscriptions are a useful clue to the dating: 'Dobbs Patent' is pre-1816, 'Dobbs & Co.' 1816–38, 'H. Dobbs & Co' 1838–46, 'Dobbs & Bailey' 1846–51, 'Dobbs & Kidd' from 1851 onwards. Since postage was computed by the number of sheets enclosed, and an envelope doubled the cost of postage, Valentines were made complete with lacy envelopes.

As Valentines became more readily available, roses became redder and redder, violets unnaturally blue; and in due course no design was too ridiculous, no verse too mawkish to be sent to the object of one's love.

'Trade' Valentines came increasingly into use. These were sent by tradesmen to domestic servants, and were good for both business and pleasure. Other 'below-stairs' Valentines might include 'love-nests' (rustic cottages perched in the tops of trees), notes demanding payment of three hundred kisses, 'compensation for doctor's bills, palpitations of the heart, giddiness etc.' These notes, drawn on the Lovers Banking Company, were so realistic that they had to be withdrawn. There were also Cupid's Telegrams, which promised to pay the bearer £ove. 'Upstairs' Valentines might contain miniature portraits, flower-sprays painted on ivory, tiny mirrors, or photographs in locket-like frames. By the 1870s over one and a half million Valentines were posted annually and one large firm calculated an annual outlay of £2000 on scent and £1000 a week on artificial flowers. By the end of the century most Valentines had become crude, comical, vulgar, and even spiteful. The Valentine was not helped by the fashion, publicly approved by Gladstone, of sending picture postcards, and the custom died out with the first salvo fired in the Great War. There have been sporadic revivals, but the cards have never recaptured their winsome charm, nor their fey elegance.

Book: *Collecting Printed Ephemera* by John Lewis (Studio Vista, 1974)

veneer A thin slice of richly figured wood, cut by a saw till the end of the nineteenth century and by a knife thereafter. Ebony is almost always used as a veneer; mahogany, rosewood, tulipwood, and walnut are also much employed in this way. Combinations of wood may be used in a veneer, as may ivory, tortoiseshell, mother-of-pearl, and brass. See *boulle*, *marquetry*, *parquetry*, and *Tunbridgeware*.

Victorian jewellery The early Victorians were romantic, and Sir Walter Scott caught the mood by suggesting that all things ought to be mysterious, medieval and mouldering, and, if they weren't, they ought at least to be Celtic. Such ideas were represented in architecture and furniture by Augustus Welby Northmore Pugin (1812–52), while jewellery was decorated with knights and angels and heraldic animals, ivy-fronds and vines, serpents and berries and virgins tied to trees.

The jewellers of the 1860s and 1870s turned to purity of design, and purity of stone. Amber, agate, lapis lazuli, bog oak, and cairngorms were just a few of the materials employed. Tortoiseshell and mother-of-pearl provided interesting contrasts, and jet was employed extensively when the Court went into mourning after the death of the Prince Consort.

Diamonds were discovered in South Africa in 1876, and the opening of the first London theatre to be lit by electricity, D'Oyly Carte's Savoy Theatre in 1881, meant that masses of coloured gems began to look just a little garish beside the subtle sparkle of diamonds. Settings lost their significance. The stone was all.

The last great movement of the Victorian age was the aesthetic (1885 onwards) inspired by Ruskin and Morris, and C. R. Ashbee (1863–1942) was the pioneer aesthetic jeweller. He had no time for the secondhand or the machine-made. His shapes were sinuous, his silver dull; rose topaz, grey gold, and amethysts were his favourite materials. Arthur Gaskin (1862–1928), painter, illustrator, and metal-worker, used open-work silver in combination with pallid stones, such as opals and moonstones and blue and green enamelling. Liberty's was the chief patron for these new talents, giving respectability to what might otherwise have remained just quirkish. Cameos and lockets, hair-jewellery and *piqué*, corals and ivory are a few of the other ingredients in the mass of pretty, charming, and sentimental items that can still be found in an old jewelcase.

Books; *Victorian Jewellery* by Deirdre O'Day (Letts Collectors Guides, 1974); *Victorian Sentimental Jewellery* by D. Cooper and N. Butterskill (David & Charles, 1972)

Vienna With a name like Claude Innocent du Paquier one would expect to be able to inspire confidence, and so it was in the early eighteenth century that the Dutchman who bore that name wheedled out of the Emperor Charles VI a twenty-five-year monopoly to produce porcelain, and enticed the painter and gilder Hunger and his colleague Stölzel to leave Meissen. The confidence that du Paquier inspired was rather misplaced, for his Viennese works, which opened in 1718, was unsuccessful until the young Empress Maria Theresa took a personal interest in the factory, acquired by the Empire in 1744.

During the early period, vases, cups, saucers, and plates bore illustrations based on the highly fanciful work of such artists as Watteau and Boucher. Excellently executed groups and figures were modelled during the period of royal patronage. From 1749 the familiar beehive (*bindenschild*) was adopted as the official factory mark. The period of rich blue china overpainted with gold after the Sèvres style — known as the Sorgenthal period after the Baron who had been newly appointed — began in 1784. The celebrated *rothbrun* gilding was introduced, and brilliantly coloured painting 'after' Rubens and Angelica Kauffmann gave the china its distinction. Between 1784 and 1800 pieces were date-stamped with the last two numerals of the date; after 1800 the last three numerals were given.

The factory closed in 1864 when it was no longer profitable, although a number of artists who had been employed there set up *ateliers* of their own. Much Viennese porcelain is vulgar: tawdry and over-decorated. Only the best eighteenth-century pieces have real distinction.

vinaigrettes Whether one speaks of musk-apples, pomanders, pouncet-boxes or vinaigrettes, matters little, for they all performed the same very necessary function. They smelt good and they kept the plague away. The vinaigrette was the last to appear, arriving in the late eighteenth century. By then vinegar sticks (walking sticks containing vinegar) were rather out of fashion and the small box in silver or gold, worn on the watch-chain or châtelaine, was more discreet. A vinaigrette is much like a snuff-box, but has a pierced inner grille, allowing the aroma (95 per cent acetic acid, 5 per cent oils of flowers and spices, carried on a small piece of sponge) to escape when the hinged lid was lifted. The grille was always gilded to keep the rust away.

Silver vinaigrette by
J.L. Birmingham, 1817

The design of vinaigrettes followed the styles set by craftsmen in similar articles. Through the nineteenth century chasing, filigree, *repoussé*, *appliqué*, beading, engine-turning, moulding, enamelling, and gem-setting were introduced and discarded as fashions changed. Oblong vinaigrettes with rounded edges (*c.*1790–1820) were followed by straight-sided examples (*c.*1840). Dating vinaigrettes by hallmarks may be frustrating since many were too delicate to survive the attentions of the assay office. By the end of the century vinaigrettes had assumed all kinds of quaint disguises — articulated fish were popular, filled with smelling salts.

Names to watch out for are Samuel Pemberton, Matthew Linwood, Cocks and Betteridge, John Shaw, John Turner, Joseph Willmore, and Nathaniel Mills. These men all worked in Birmingham between the late eighteenth and mid-nineteenth centuries.

walking sticks   Until the fifteenth century walking sticks were plain staves about five feet long with a metal hand-grip at one end and an iron spike (known as a ferule) at the other. From the fifteenth century sticks were made of turned ebony or other heavy woods, and the spike was of silver. Silver and gold mounts were added, the head of the stick becoming finely carved and the wood being given a high polish. Sometimes the stick contained a pouncet box with perfume in it.

The cane was introduced in Elizabethan England. The wood was imported from the East Indies, and was light to carry and elegant. For the more traditional, staves were now chest high, with jewels set into their heads and tapering ferules of no more than six inches. These were reduced to three inches under James I, when ivory heads began to be fashionable.

In the eighteenth century one only carried a sword on ceremonial occasions, so that a stick (which might contain a sword, or a glass tube filled with spirits come to that) was necessary indoors. For gentlemen the exciting new mahogany wood looked virile. Ladies carried smaller sticks of ivory, whalebone or foreign woods, and decorated them with ribbons and engravings. By the nineteenth century sticks were reduced to no more than four feet, their shafts of such varied woods as ash, vine, teak, ebony, beech, and blackthorn, their heads of gold, silver, pinchbeck, bronze, tin, pewter, ivory, horn, mother-of-pearl, porcelain, glass, amber, and leather.

Collection: City Museum and Art Gallery, Nottingham (glass walking sticks)

Wall, Dr John   Dr John Wall was a highly respected Worcestershire gentleman, one of fourteen who signed the articles of association of a china factory at Warmstry House, Worcester, in 1751. Dr Wall gave his name to the first great period of Worcester porcelain, 1751–83, a period now regarded as the finest of all.

In 1772 the firm, which had been founded with the impressive capital of £4599, was sold to the Reverend Thomas Vernon for £5250. Vernon transferred it to John Wall junior who transferred it to a consortium of six including John Wall senior who died a year after selling his share for £1100 to William Davis junior, another of the shareholders.

No matter how dubious such transactions may sound to the ingenuous city gentlemen of today, there is no denying the beauty of Dr Wall china. The glazing is smooth and in shades of green; the patterns derive from English variations of oriental, Meissen and Sèvres originals; and some pieces were sent out to James Giles' workshop in Kentish Town for expert decorations.

Book: *Worcester Porcelain* by Henry Sandon (Jenkins, 1969)
Collections: Ashmolean, Oxford; Bantock House, Wolverhampton; Dyson Perrins Museum, Worcester

wallpaper   Oscar Wilde's last words are supposed to have been: 'My wallpaper is killing me — one of us must go.' Certainly wallpaper plays a crucial role in the interior decoration of one's house. With it the dullest of rooms can be turned into a sunny rose-garden, the most handsome degenerate into a liverish nightmare of clashing colours and warring patterns.

In the early sixteenth century when the first wallpapers were printed, a great variety of wall coverings were being used: wool, serge, silk and tapestry, wood panelling and embossed leather — this last being very popular and the forerunner of wallpaper as we know it. The earliest recorded wallpaper is a stylised pomegranate design, printed on the back of a proclamation of Henry VIII, discovered during restoration work at Christ's College, Cambridge. Thereafter the production of letterpress-printed papers continued sporadically throughout the sixteenth and seventeenth centuries. These black and white patterns have survived through having been used to line boxes and chests. Most were copied from contemporary embroideries.

Papers coloured with stencils became more common during the seventeenth century, and by 1699 John Houghton F.R.S. could say:

> . . . a great deal of paper is nowadays printed to be pasted upon Walls to serve instead of Hangings; and truly if all Parts of the Sheet be well and close pasted on, it is very pritty, clean and will last with tolerable Care a great while; but there are some other done by Rolls in long sheets of a thick Paper made for the purpose whose sheets are pasted together to be so long as the Height of a Room; and they are managed like Woollen Hangings, and there is a great Variety, with curious Cuts [wood cuts] which are Cheap, and if kept from wet very lasting.

Flock wallpapers from the early seventeenth century were regarded as the aristocrats of paperhanging, and treated as such, so that many fine examples of these have survived. 'Flock' was powdered wool scattered over painted, stencilled or printed cloth.

Simultaneously with these, Chinese painted papers (often known as 'India Papers', through being imported by the East India companies), marvellously coloured and detailed with trees, shrubs, flowers, birds, butterflies and small insects, were becoming fashionable. They were sold in sets of twenty-five rolls, twelve feet long and four feet wide, without any repeats. (Fine examples may be seen at Temple Newsam House, Leeds, and in the state bedroom at Nostell Priory, where Chippendale's Chinese furniture is so happily contemplated.) Of course the Chinese themselves would never have hung anything so gaudy on the walls of their houses, but they supplied the Western market to the advantage of both.

In due course and certainly by the middle of the eighteenth century, London had a thriving wallpaper industry of its own. Stationers, playing card makers, upholsterers, leather-workers, wood engravers, flockers and artists all gained employment, mostly in the City itself. The industry would have been yet more profitable had it not been for the duty of one penny per square yard of paper imposed in 1712 and increased to a penny halfpenny in 1714. Each sheet of paper had to be stamped by the excise officer, an unenviable task.

Working with new machinery the paper makers of the early nineteenth century evolved the 'endless sheet', and wallpaper, which had until then been an expensive luxury, was now available to almost everyone. However the quality of design suffered and, with the exception of the 'ivy patterns' (but not the tartan walls at Balmoral), standards were low. William Morris got to work and his designs are as popular today as when he originally devised them between 1862 and 1898 — indeed they are more so. The designs of Walter Crane, Lewis Day, Kate Greenaway, C. F. A. Voysey, and Bruce Talbert are equally deserving.

Book: *The Book of Wallpaper* by E. A. Entwistle (Arthur Barker, 1954) — a model of its kind
Collections: Victoria and Albert Museum, London; Museum, Library and Art Gallery, Worcester; German Wallpaper Museum, Kassel

walnut Walnut trees were imported from Persia into Italy some two thousand years ago. It seems probable that the Romans brought them to Britain along with elms, yews, and others. In the sixteenth and seventeenth centuries, walnut was the most popular furnishing wood on the continent; but in Elizabethan and Jacobean England its only use (such was its scarcity) was as a decoration in conjunction with the ubiquitous oak.

During Elizabeth's reign many walnut trees were planted, and the timber attained maturity about the middle of the seventeenth century. As a light and elegantly figured wood it was the answer to a cabinet-maker's prayer; it also carried silk and satin embroidery particularly well. Twists and curves, on the cross-grain, were less likely to chip in walnut than in oak; veneers and inlays and mouldings were also ideally served by walnut. What was not at once appreciated was that walnut was as popular with woodworms as with cabinet-makers; by the time this tragic truth had been fully understood mahogany had become available, a wood that was more than a match for the most enterprising worm. Towards the end of the seventeenth century the demand for plain walnut furniture increased, and a large amount of quietly elegant pieces were made.

English walnut is lighter in colour and more open in grain than most foreign varieties. The tree needs to be at least fifty years old before the trunk is large enough to be usable, for the portions next to the bark are worthless.

The golden age of walnut ran from c.1660 to c.1720, with the best marquetry decoration being worked between about 1680 and 1710. The wood's decline was rapid, but the advances made while it was popular had much influence on the mahogany design which followed.

warming pans Elizabeth I, Virgin Queen, had a beautiful warming pan, made of gold and garnished with small diamonds and rubies. It must have been one of the first warming pans to appear. Elizabethan examples were hinged metal pans, filled with glowing coals and placed between the sheets by means of a long handle.

In the seventeenth century warming pans were brass-faced, with solid cast iron and steel handles, whether flat or rounded like pokers. They must have been awkward and heavy to carry, but were very decorative, with holes in the lids of the pans (to ensure that the coals remained alight after the lid was closed) worked into the design. Some of these were of Flemish latten but the handles were always English. By the start of the eighteenth century there were plenty of utilitarian warming pans available, selling for around three shillings each.

In 1728 John Cook discovered how to machine-roll copper, and brass was replaced in many pans. Embers were used instead of coals, so holes were no longer punched in the lids. Since wooden handles had replaced cast iron ones, the whole package became a great deal lighter and more mobile. What decoration there was tended to get rubbed off, for warming pans had to be kept clear and bright to avoid soiling bed-linen. The lid no longer overhung the pan but fitted snugly into it.

By Victorian times the hinge had gone and the lid was sealed to the bottom of the pan. Kitchens were fitted with ranges now, so that hot water could be used to fill the pans by means of a small hole with a screw-on stopper. Sometimes the wooden handle unscrewed and the pan was filled through the hole left by the handle. But, when the water-filled pan was all that was left, it gave way to the familiar stoneware bottle.

Warming pans are prodigiously reproduced. Watch out for modern pieces. If the metal is not thick enough to carry embers, if there are no signs of regular wear and tear, if the handle is any old piece of broomstick instead of a nicely turned bit of fruitwood, if there are fractures around the hinge or shank, you have been sold a pup; and pups do nicely too to warm a bed.

watch paper Once upon a time it was customary to insert a circular piece of padding between the inner and outer cases of watches to prevent friction and to keep dust out. This padding was called a watch paper. It could be plain or elaborate and early examples are often of silk. Later cotton and muslin were also used, with floral designs and improving mottoes. Sometimes a map, sometimes a masonic emblem, sometimes a brain-teaser, the watch paper was versatile. Allegorical figures were often found and, since watches are suitable places for such things, *memento mori*. Towards the end of the nineteenth century advertising material began to appear on watch papers, which was the beginning of the end.

Collection: Library of the Clockmakers' Company, Guildhall, London

Watchpaper by Thompson's of Louth

Waterford glass Dating from the early eighteenth century, Waterford was the Irish centre for the production of flint-glass until the Great Exhibition of 1851, after which the Waterford glass company closed down, being unable to compete with English firms. The most substantial factory was founded by George and William Penrose in 1784 with the help of a subsidy from the Irish government. The Penrose brothers employed as works manager John Hill from Stourbridge, who took with him to Ireland 'the best set of workmen he could get in the county of Worcester'. Flint-glass was sold at Waterford for cash only, but, despite this, the company was bought in 1799 by a consortium including George Gatchell, who ran it as a family firm. In 1745 an excise duty was imposed on glass in England and until 1825, when a similar tax was levied in Ireland, the Irish glass-blowers had a considerable advantage over their English competitors. This was their golden age.

Waterford glass is notable for its bluish hue, though sometimes it is more dusky in appearance. Lavishly decorated and heavily cut, its weighty grandeur can be most impressive.

Other Irish glass-producing centres were located in Belfast, Dublin, and Cork.

Book: *Irish Glass* by Phelps Warren (Faber & Faber, 1970)
Collections: Ulster Museum, Belfast; National Museum of Ireland, Dublin

Wedgwood   Josiah Wedgwood (1730–95), despite losing a leg, was a complete English gentleman. He combined to a unique degree the arts and sciences, business and family, commercial pressures and aesthetic rewards. He was a radical, passionately opposed to the slave trade, a bibliophile, a member of the Royal Society, and a very wealthy man. A son, Thomas, became influential in the early development of photography; a daughter married the family doctor at Etruria Hall and fathered Charles Darwin.

The Staffordshire pottery, established in Burslem in 1759 by Josiah Wedgwood, is still administered by the Wedgwood family today. In fact there were two Wedgwood factories in Burslem, the Bell works where Josiah's cousin, Thomas, produced the 'useful' ware which was so profitable, and the Etruria works for ornamental ware.

Josiah's early experience was gained with Thomas Whieldon of Fenton. At this time he conducted an enormous number of wide-ranging experiments, meticulously recorded in his notebooks, into all branches of science, but particularly into chemistry as applied to ceramics and mineralogy. Such experiments led to the production of a fine glazed ware named Queen's ware after Queen Charlotte.

He had the ambition to export his ceramics to France, writing to his more worldly partner, Bentley: 'And do you really think we may make a *complete conquest* of France? Conquer France in Burslem? My blood moves quicker, I feel my strength increase for the contest.'

One of his developments at this time was Black Basalt, a highly vitrified stoneware, in which he was able to fashion realistic copies of the ancient antiquities that Sir William Hamilton brought back from Egypt. 'The black is sterling and will last for ever,' Josiah claimed, and so far it has. Jasperware was another successful invention. This had the peculiar property of being able to receive colours through its whole substance. Delicate and smooth-textured, it had imposed upon it friezes of classical figures, which went most happily with Sheraton furniture or Adam fireplaces. In jasperware Josiah produced some exact copies of the Portland Vase, which were, in his opinion, the supreme artistic expression of his potter's art. They were sold to a few privileged subscribers.

Other styles inaugurated at the Wedgwood works included *rosso antico*, a terracotta type earthenware; vases in the styles of marble granite, agate, and porphyry; vegetable and fruit ware (in which teapots mimicked pineapples, and coffee pots pretended to be cauliflowers); caneware (charming porcelain pieces of bamboo-like lattice work); shell patterns inspired by a visit to the seaside and a resulting passion for conchology; green-glazed wares, often shaped like leaves; and so on. One of the most important achievements was the production of a dinner service which Josiah made for Catherine the Great in 1773. The 952 pieces were individually painted with landscapes and priced at £2700; they may be seen today in the Hermitage Museum in Leningrad.

*Wedgwood copy of a
Barberini vase, c. 1790*

Later developments included Parian porcelain, usually portrait busts, elaborately and subtly coloured vases by Émile Lessore and lithographic designs closely copying contemporary oil-paintings. Majolica featured in a variety of designs (1860–1910), and biscuit-coloured porcelain (in flattering imitation of the output from the Worcester factory) was decorated with gilding and painted scenes from nature. The production of commemorative limited editions was popular with the American market, but was strictly controlled; no poor quality souvenirs were allowed to leave the factory. Imitations of Chinese porcelain were reproduced in the early years of this century, with the unique Fairyland lustreware designed by Daisy Makeig-Jones. A greater variety of colours was added to the jasperware range, and the New Zealand born architect and designer Keith Murray (b. 1893) was commissioned to produce matt white vases and mugs sparingly decorated with lathe-cut bands and grooves or fluting. In 1940 the factory moved to Barlaston and much of its output was thereafter sold in America.

'Elegant simplicity' was Josiah Wedgwood's motto, and one of his favourite phrases was: 'Everything yields to experiment.' His own life and the china which bears his name are a tribute to his vision.

China marked 'Wedgwood and Co.' and 'Vedgwood' is *not* genuine.

Books: *Wedgwood Ware* by Alison Kelly (Ward Lock, 1970); *Wedgwood* by Wolf Mankowitz (Batsford, 1953); *The Collector's Book of Wedgwood* by Marian Klamkin (David & Charles, 1971)

Collections: Museum and Art Gallery, Birmingham; Wedgwood Museum, Stoke-on-Trent

Welsh dresser Originally *French* rather than Welsh, the medieval dresser was very much a status symbol, the number of tiers one had being controlled by protocol. On special occasions it would be dressed with fine linens and the best of the family plate. In due course the *dressoir* became a 'court cupboard', literally a board for the display of cups, and in Wales the court cupboard became enclosed with doors into a *cwpwrdd deuddarn* with

two sections, or a *cwpwrdd tridarn* with three. These were made until the end
of the eighteenth century.

The Welsh dresser, as we know it, developed from these cupboards
during the eighteenth century; but there are so many regional variations
within Wales itself that 'Welsh dresser' is no more than a generic name.
The South Wales dresser, for example, is open-backed (though boards may
have been added to strengthen the structure at a later date). The further
north in Wales you travel the more solid and enclosed the dresser becomes.
Pembrokeshire dressers are utterly simple, but Glamorgan dressers boast a
varied arrangement of drawers with a decorated apron under the drawers
and a pot-board under the apron.

All one can say safely is that the best Welsh dressers were made of oak,
and looked sensational when dignified by some blue and white china.

Collection: Museum of Welsh Antiquities, Bangor

Welsh dresser

whatnot   A whatnot is not an *étagère*, though the distinction has been
blurred. A whatnot, which dates from the end of the Regency period, is a
three- or four-tiered stand, square, triangular or rectangular and made of
rosewood, burrwood, *papier mâché*, or bamboo. Its shelves are supported by
corner posts, which are very often turned with barley-sugar twists or other
decoration. The purpose of a whatnot was to display all the trinkets which
accumulated in a Victorian withdrawing room.

The lightweight elegance of the early whatnot became disfigured by
later additions. Fretwork was added to the upper tiers, vertical divisions to
the lower. Drawers were included. Mirror-backs, plush lining, bevelling,

Art nouveau whatnot

and ormolu were some of the features with which the designer burdened the whatnot when he could find no other repository for them.

wheel-back Either a Hepplewhite period chair with a back shaped like a wheel and spokes radiating to a curved rail, or a Windsor chair with a more primitive wheel motif carved in its splat.

wheellock The revolutionary idea (possibly invented by Leonardo da Vinci) was to replace the clumsy combustion system of the matchlock musket with a mechanical alternative. Hence the wheellock, in which a rapidly rotating metal wheel strikes sparks from iron pyrites, these sparks firing the charge. With powder and ball already in the breech, the wheellock was poised ready for action; all that was then necessary was to bring the pyrites into contact with the wheel by swinging the dogshead forward, and to pull the trigger. Since wheellocks were expensive to make

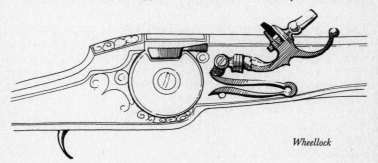

Wheellock

(most came from Germany) they were also highly ornamented. The stock would be inlaid with gold, silver, mother-of-pearl, ivory, bone, steel, or enamel. Wheellocks of the late sixteenth and early seventeenth centuries are the most elaborate.

However there were difficulties. The wheellock was liable to jam, and, when it was damaged, one needed to find a sophisticated armourer to repair it. Sophisticated armourers are not usually found on the battlefield, so this shortcoming proved serious.

Out of the wheellock rifle the wheellock pistol was developed. This first pistol was to change the nature of warfare.

Whieldon ware   Thomas Whieldon (1719–95 or 98) was making knife-handles at Little Fenton when he was twenty-one. At the age of sixty-seven he was acknowledged as a master-craftsman, had made himself a fortune, and was appointed High Sheriff of Staffordshire. An example to us all. The great John Astbury (1686–1743), was his master, and he himself employed such men as Aaron Wood, the famous modeller, Josiah Spode (later to be a partner), William Greatbatch, and other master potters. Quite early on in his career he became partner to Josiah Wedgwood, but they later went their separate ways.

Whieldon ware has a bright glaze which does not flake off the body, is light and well potted. Tableware was Whieldon's speciality, made in imitation tortoiseshell. Teapots in the shape of cauliflowers, melons, and pineapples are rather incongruously known as 'garden ware'. Besides excellent toby jugs, he made figures of musicians, horsemen, animals, and gods. He returned again and again to the agate ware he had used for his knife-handles. He also made toys and miniatures.

Collection: Museum and Art Gallery, Brighton (Willett Collection)

willow pattern   The interesting thing about this most successful pattern, the most popular ever printed on British china, is that it has no Chinese origins. The 'legend' was invented in order to explain the story, a marvellous gimmick. This perfect example of *chinoiserie* was supposedly invented by Thomas Minton, an apprentice engraver at the Caughley works. The pattern became standardised in about 1830: it featured a pagoda by a lake, two birds in the sky, a boat being punted across the water, a rickety-looking fence in the foreground, a three-arched bridge with three Chinese figures on it in the midground, and a willow tree overhanging the bridge. Most of the Staffordshire potteries — and some others — adapted the pattern to their own purposes, and it remains as popular as ever it was, way ahead of its nearest rival, the Indian tree pattern.

Collections: See *blue and white china*, and *Caughley*

*George III Windsor elbow chair
in yew and fruitwood*

Windsor chair Although Windsor chairs were made throughout the
Midlands and the South of England probably from about 1725, the
industry became centred around High Wycombe where paper-makers had
been at work for over a century. Local tradition insists that in 1805 Samuel
Treacher, a farmer, started making the chairs during the winter on
Marlow Hill. The nearby Quarry Woods would have supplied plenty of
beeches for the legs, and other local timber, such as ash, yew, and willow
(from the banks of the Thames), would be used for the bows. Elm for the
saddle seats would have been easily come by. Bodgers turned the legs,
benchmen made the seats, and framers put the parts of the chair together
and sanded it down. The result was the Windsor chair, which Thomas
Widgington manufactured successfully in High Wycombe in about 1810.
William Birch Ltd (established 1840) carried on the trade. Edwin Spull, a
High Wycombe manufacturer, *c.*1870, advertised over a hundred different
styles of chair, most of which could be classed as Windsors. Windsor chairs
may be with or without arms, high-backed or low-backed, with plain,
shaped, or pierced splats, and flat or shaped seats. Windsor chairs known to
be from High Wycombe are also known logically as 'Wycombe chairs'.

In America the Windsor chair has acquired an even greater reputation
than it has here; models were made in Philadelphia as early as 1730 and
Jefferson wrote his Declaration of Independence seated in a Windsor.

Book: *The Windsor Chair* by Ivan Sparks (Spur Books, 1975)
Collection: Art Gallery and Museum, High Wycombe

wine There is a paradox about collecting fine old wines, but a paradox
which seems not to concern many collectors, for classic wines have proved a

buoyant market in recent years. The paradox is this. Were you to buy a bottle, say, of Château Yquem, vintage 1858 (the opening vintage of the two decades of the 'golden' pre-phylloxera period), you would be paying in hundreds rather than tens (an 1832 Lafite would be thousands rather than hundreds) and you would have no guarantee that the wine was drinkable. It probably, almost certainly, would be, but the very act of discovering whether it was would destroy its investment value entirely. The choice is clear. Treat it like any other financial commodity, buying as a hedge against inflation and selling when market conditions are favourable, or open it on a special occasion, drink it, and hope to enjoy it.

For the investor the traditional gilt-edged wines are first growth château clarets. Until 1973 there were only three such châteaux (Lafite, Latour, and Margaux); but after years of campaigning by the Baron, Mouton Rothschild was admitted to this select company. You should further choose the classic vintages (1878, 1920, 1926, 1929, 1945 — possibly the greatest of all — 1947, 1949, 1953, 1955, 1959, 1961, 1966, 1970, 1975, and 1976); beware of the disaster years, 1956, 1963, 1965, 1968. Indeed you could drink a few cases and cover your costs on the rest.

Besides clarets, burgundies are an excellent buy, although the French prefer to drink them young. Port (vintages 1790, 1830, 1851, 1858, 1900, 1908 and 1912 are among the classics), madeira, sherry, sauternes, brandy (and especially the 'Napoleon' brandy of 1811), champagne, German wine and tokay, all appreciate with age.

Even if tasting the wine is not possible (all except the rarest wines are usually there for tasting at wine auctions), there are other indications as to quality. Richness of colour and clarity are important, as is the condition of the label and the amount of shrinkage. (The level of wine in a vintage bottle should reach up to the middle of the shoulder.) A great deal will depend on how the wine has been stored. Beware of cork-worm!

The record price for a bottle of wine is $18,000 for a Lafite 1864. This was drunk at a dinner in Memphis, where thirty guests paid $1,500 each to sample the wine, and the money raised went to a children's hospital.

Book: *Notes on a Cellar-Book* by George Saintsbury (Macmillan, first edition 1920 — reprinted 1979)

wine cooler See *cellaret*.

wine labels Early wine bottles had no paper labels to help identify their contents, and the bottles themselves were opaque. It was therefore vital to find a means of identifying at a glance which bottle contained which substance. Hence wine labels — or, to be quite accurate, bottle tickets, because your opaque bottle might have contained eau-de-cologne, vinegar, mustard, tooth-mixture, barley-water, or something called 'zoobditty-match', in place of wine.

Labels were produced from about 1725 and the earliest ones were either silver (made by such masters as the suitably named Sandylands Drinkwater and the Bateman family) or Battersea enamel. Sheffield plate, porcelain, pinchbeck, tortoiseshell, bone, ivory, mother-of-pearl, zinc, nickel, cork, and even tigers' claws are on record as having been used.

After about 1840 larger, more ostentatious and elaborate examples were preferred; these were engraved, chased, or pierced. From 1860 a licensing act permitted wine to be sold in single bottles with paper labels. Some of the names on wine labels are wild and wonderful. Bronte, Buda, Mountain, and Chusclan are all old varieties of wine, while it is not unknown to find a label with 'Nig' on it, for those too strait-laced to admit to drinking gin.

Collection: Royal Scottish Museum, Edinburgh

wine table In the late eighteenth century a wine table was a small, occasional table with a raised circular platform surrounded by a gallery and notches cut round the edge to take the stems of wine glasses, which would hang there until required. The sort of wine tables that come up often at auctions, on rather mean columns with half-hearted piecrust edges, are all modern reproductions, and have nothing much to do with wine.

wireless In November 1977 the Victoria and Albert Museum mounted an exhibition called the Wireless Show, which was just that. It dignified what had previously been little more than a hobby, the collecting of old wireless sets. The names of the early models are romantic enough: Alba, Cossor, Climax, Cromwell, Amplion, Portadyne, and Consolette, as well as the Golden Voice, the Twin Superbox, the New Arcadion, and the Little Maestro. What used to be rather nastily known as 'electrical brown goods' are now collectors' pieces.

The natural aristocrat of wireless sets is commonly accepted to be the 1934 AD65 model of Wells Coats, which was circular, in a moulded plastic case, and came with a custom-built wooden stand (29s 6d extra). In the 1930s EMI was producing over a quarter of a million sets every year, and by 1940 over nine million licences were being issued annually. So there must still be a great many early wireless sets about. Should you possess an Emor 'Globe', you are fortunate, for this chromium-plated sphere, which rotated on its axis, is now highly rated. Early Murphy sets, designed by R. D. Russell, had a sombre dignity. A substantial cabinet with a wooden veneer was considered appropriate for John Snagge, Alvar Lidell, and Professor Joad. Reproduction Chippendale with jazzy wood inlay over the loudspeaker grille was a bit more flash.

In the 1940s cheaper and more homely models in plastic and bakelite became popular, while the Government produced utility sets in simple oak cases, to which no one could take exception. Ever Ready produced their blue Saucepan Super 'to sell at less than £5', while Cossor put their set in a biscuit tin (just as today you can find sets in Snoopies and cans of Coke).

Collection: Helston Borough Museum, Helston, Cornwall

witch balls or **wish balls**   Witch balls were made of glass, sometimes silvered on the inside, or coloured green, blue, silver, and gold (at Nailsea), or merely plain glass filled with holy water. They varied from 3 to 36 inches in diameter, and were hung up in windows and doors to keep away evil spirits. What we don't know is whether they worked.

Worcester   Since there is so much about the origins of the great Worcester porcelain works which is still the subject of scholarly debate, it is best to concentrate on what we *do* know. On 4 June 1751, fourteen gentlemen formed a partnership to make porcelain in Worcester. They included Dr John Wall, who had a sketchy knowledge of how to make china, and William Davis. But they had equipment, materials, and the services of workmen from the 'Lunds' factory at Bristol. Men and equipment were removed to Warmstry House, Worcester (next to the cathedral) complete with Robert Podmore and John Lyes, who continued to produce the same reticent Chinese designs in underglaze blue, carefully potted and sweetly moulded — much as a canary will sing the same song, wherever its cage.

The ware of the first period (1751–83) under Dr Wall has a green translucency in the glaze, which is thin and clear. There is seldom any cracking or warping. Typical pieces include the globular teapot with a flower-knopped lid, the sparrow-beak jug with its loop handle, the cabbage-leaf jug, sauce-boats, tea services, tureens, cornucopias, open-work baskets, pickle-trays shaped like ivy leaves, and other small items. Although some of these may be marked with the Worcester crescent, the square mark or the letter 'W', others will bear in underglaze blue those tiny cryptic symbols known as workmen's marks.

After 1755 harbour scenes and landscapes in pastiche Meissen style were added to the repertoire, and some of these even had fake Meissen crossed-sword marks applied to them. After 1768 a number of superannuated painters from the Chelsea factory were added to the Worcester pay-roll. They contributed rich ground colours, allied with gilding and splendidly painted panels of flowers and birds, landscapes and figures. A number of first-period Worcester pieces were also sent to outside decorators, and particularly to the London studio of the celebrated James Giles. Giles and his staff had a fondness for exotic birds, 'sliced' fruit, large flowers, Aesop's Fables, and crests. I should add regretfully that early Worcester, like Chelsea porcelain, is very much faked these days, and rather expertly.

The death of Dr Wall in 1776 and William Davis in 1783 heralded the second period of Worcester (1784–1850), under Flight and Chamberlain.

Now times were hard. Thomas Flight bought the factory, but found strong competition in Staffordshire, where the discovery of bone-ash pastes had had an important impact. Through the ensuing years, during which the Worcester factory was managed by various Flights and Barrs in different combinations, the paste became harder and whiter, landscape painting, especially of local scenes, became popular, and lavish services for the élite brought prestige. Flowers and shells and birds in colourful profusion crowd out the more bashful blue and white, and unfortunate copies of Derby copies of Japanese Imari patterns hovered as close to vulgarity as was permitted in a county town like Worcester.

Robert Chamberlain, an apprentice at Worcester under Dr Wall, set up his own works in 1783 in opposition to Flight; his factory underwent many dubious boardroom shuffles until in 1840 it merged with its parent company, now known as Flight, Barr and Barr. Chamberlain had slightly more restrained taste than the Flights and the Barrs. After 1850 the rot set in. Occasional pieces, such as Kirk's Shakespeare dessert service for twenty-four people, featuring characters from *A Midsummer Night's Dream*, proved that the expertise was still there, but management quarrels meant a lack of direction and personality.

In 1862 the company became the Worcester Royal Porcelain Company Limited, and the portentousness of the title was reflected in much of the output. Rich colours, heavy gilding, meticulous painting were what the public wanted, and what it got. At the end of the last century George Owen produced marvellously fragile reticulated pieces, whose delicacy is ethereal. And in this century fine modelling by Dorothy Doughty (birds) and Doris Lindner (horses) produced presentation pieces many of which have since become fabulously expensive.

Other factories at Worcester worthy of attention are Graingers (1800–89), Hadley's (1875–1905), and Locke's (1895–1904), which was shut prematurely when the Worcester Company took exception to Locke putting 'Worcester' on his wares. All produced pieces of some quality.

Worcester is a fine city. Besides cricket and racing, succulent pears, gloves and a festival, it offers guided tours around the factory.

Books: *Worcester Porcelain* by Stanley W. Fisher (Ward Lock, 1968); *Worcester Porcelain* by Franklin A. Barrett (Faber & Faber, 1953); *Royal Worcester Porcelain* by Henry Sandon (Barrie & Jenkins, 1972)
Collections: Dyson Perrins Museum, Worcester; Ashmolean, Oxford (Rissick Marshall Collection of first-period Worcester); Art Gallery and Museum, Cheltenham; Art Gallery and Museum, Brighton (Stephens Collection); Victoria and Albert Museum, London (Rooms 139 and 140); Bantock House, Wolverhampton

yew   A hard, close-grained brown wood (*Taxus baccata*), well figured and native to the British Isles. Once used for the bows of archers, it found a new role during the eighteenth century, supplying the sticks, bows, and legs of Windsor chairs. It was also used for drawer-knobs, spindles, and veneers.

MONARCHS AND PERIODS	CHINESE DYNASTIES AND REIGNS	PORCELAIN	GLASS
	Ming Dynasty *1368–1644*	porcelain invented in China in the ninth century	
	Hung Wu 1368–1398		
	Chien Wen 1399–1402		
	Yung Lo 1403–1424		
	Hung Hsi 1425		
	Hsüan Tê 1426–1435		
	Chêng T'ung 1436–1449		
	Ching T'ai 1450–1457		
	T'ien Shun 1457–1464		
	Ch'eng Hua 1465–1487		
Tudor and Renaissance		Chinese porcelain increasingly exported to Europe from the sixteenth century	Venice sixteenth and seventeenth centuries
Henry VII 1485–1509	Hung Chih 1488–1506		
Henry VIII 1509–1547	Cheng Tê 1506–1522		
Edward VI 1547–1553	Chia Ching 1522–1567		
Mary 1553–1558			
Elizabethan		Medici soft-paste porcelain Florence *c.*1575	G. Verzelini at Crutched Friars *c.*1570–1592
Elizabeth I 1558–1603	Lung Ch'ing 1567–1573		
Jacobean or Early Stuart			Ravenscroft (1632–1687) at Henley-on-Thames
James I 1603–1625	Wan Li 1573–1620		
Charles I 1625–1649	T'ien Ch'i 1621–1627		
	Ch'ung Chên 1628–1644		
Cromwellian	*Ch'ing Dynasty* 1644–1912		
Commonwealth 1649–1660	Shun Chim 1644–1661		
Carolean or Late Stuart			baluster stems 1680–1730
Charles II 1660–1685			
James II 1685–1689			
William and Mary		*famille verte* from *c.*1700	Silesian stems 1700–1730
William and Mary 1689–1702	K'ang Hsi 1662–1722		
Queen Anne		J. J. Kaendler 1706–1775	knopped stems 1715–1735
Anne 1702–1714	Yung Chêng 1723–1735	Meissen from 1710	
George I 1714–1727		*famille rose* from *c.*1725	
(George II 1727–1735)			
Georgian		Chelsea *c.*1743–1784; Sèvres 1743 (Vincennes); from 1750 (Sèvres); Caughley 1751–1814; Worcester from 1751; Wedgwood from 1754; Lowestoft *c.*1756–1800; Derby from 1756; Spode from 1785; Coalport *c.*1796: Doulton 1815	Beilby family at Newcastle *c.*1760–1819 hollow stems 1760–1776 Penrose at Waterford 1784 Nailsea Glassworks founded 1788
George II 1727–1760	Ch'ien Lung 1736–1795		
George III 1760–1820	Chia Ch'ing 1796–1821		
Regency			John Northwood at Stourbridge 1836–1902
George IV 1820–1830	Tao Kuang 1821–1850		
William IV 1830–1837			
Victorian		Parian from *c.*1842; fairings from *c.*1850; Belleek from 1857; pâte-sur-pâte from *c.*1870. Use of lead abolished in potteries in 1900	hollow stems mid-nineteenth century art nouveau from *c.*1870
Victoria 1837–1901	Hsien Fêng 1851–1861		
	T'ung Chih 1862–1873		
	Kuang Hso 1874–1908		
Edwardian			
Edward VII 1901–1910	Hsuan T'ung 1909–1912		
Modern or House of Windsor	Republic from 1912		
George V 1910–1936			
Edward VIII 1936			
George VI 1936–1952			
Elizabeth II 1952–			

CLOCKS	FIREARMS	FURNITURE STYLES AND MAKERS	SILVER MARKS AND SMITHS
verge escapement c.1380	gunpowder c.1250 matchlock c.1390	Gothic thirteenth to fifteenth century	standard set 1238 leopard's head 1300 maker's mark 1363 assay offices in seven provincial towns 1423 annual date letter introduced 1478
table clock c.1580–1680	wheellock c.1515; snaplock c.1544; flintlock c.1550; matchlock musket and pike c.1550–1675	Renaissance fifteenth and sixteenth centuries	fine goldsmithing in Ausburg and Nuremberg early sixteenth century; lion passant standard mark 1544
	musket c.1570		
lantern clock c.1620–1700 Thomas Tompion 1639–1713		baroque c.1600–1760 rococo 17th, 18th centuries Boulle 1642–1732 Grinling Gibbons 1648–1721	Paulus Van Vianen d.1613
Daniel Quare 1648–1724 anchor escapement c.1656 longcase clock from c.1660 bracket clock from c.1660 pendulum from c.1660			
George Graham 1674–1751	blunderbuss c.1680	William Kent 1686–1748	Paul de Lamerie 1688–1751
cylinder escapement from c.1690			Britannia standard introduced 1696; lion's head erased
dead beat escapement from c.1715		Thomas Johnson d.1778 Hepplewhite d.1786 Chippendale ?1718–1798	Paul Revere 1735–1818
mantel clock from c.1760 lever escapement from c.1770	duelling pistol c.1750 percussion ignition c.1815	Robert Adam 1728–1792 A. Kauffmann 1741–1807 neo-classical 1750–1810 Thomas Sheraton 1751–1806 Augustus Pugin 1812–1852 Biedermeier c.1815–1848	Paul Storr 1771–1844 sovereign's head duty mark introduced 1784
skeleton clock from c.1820		William Morris 1834–1896	leopard loses crown 1821
American clocks from c.1840 Carriage clock from c.1850 four hundred day clock from c.1880	repeating rifle c.1880 mauser rifle c.1889 maxim gun c.1890	arts & crafts c.1875–1890 C. R. Mackintosh 1869–1928 Ernest Gimson 1864–1919 Ambrose Heal 1872–1959 art nouveau c.1890–1910	Omar Ramsden 1873–1939 sovereign's head discontinued 1890
	Lewis gun c.1910	art deco c.1910–1935	

Further Reading

The *Complete Encyclopaedia of Antiques* edited by L. G. G. Ramsey (Connoisseur, 1962) has stood for nearly twenty years as the definitive introduction to the subject. It contains articles on all the main areas of antiques, written by experts in their relevant fields. But, despite its 960 pages of text and 512 pages of plates, it is by no means comprehensive. More attractive is *The Penguin Dictionary of Decorative Arts* by John Fleming and Hugh Honour (Allen Lane, 1977). It has 4000 entries and over 1000 illustrations, and its scope is 'movable objects other than paintings and sculpture from the Middle Ages onwards'. *The Oxford Companion to the Decorative Arts* edited by Harold Osborne (Oxford University Press, 1975) has 76 contributors and a bibliography of 940 volumes. It is recommended for those with stamina.

World Antiques (Hamlyn, 1978) is extremely bitty, but is dignified with an introduction by the ubiquitous Roy Strong, who also introduces *The Collector's Encyclopaedia* (Collins, 1974). This deals with decorative objects, from the Great Exhibition (1851) to the outbreak of the Second World War, and is notable for its glorious photographs — over 300 are in colour. It has useful appendixes on marks and a quirky bibliography of books published in English. It is a sequel to *The Encyclopaedia of Antiques* (Collins, 1973) which details all antique artifacts from the post-Renaissance to 1875. George Savage's *Dictionary of Antiques* (Barrie & Jenkins, 1970) is considered rather controversial but should certainly be preferred to the *Antique Collector's Illustrated Dictionary* edited by David Mountfield (Hamlyn, 1975), which has 5000 entries, many of them obvious and some of them misleading, although the low price makes it a bargain if only for the excellent photographs (over 300 in colour). I can also recommend the dignified *Guardian Book of Antiques 1700–1830* by Donald Wintersgill (Collins, 1975), although its range is limited, and *The Antique Buyer's Dictionary of Names* by A. W. Coysh (David & Charles, 1970) which, despite serious omissions, is a valuable reference work.

Besides these, smaller chatty books by G. B. and Therle Hughes, Deborah Stratton, John Bedford, J. A. Mackay, George Savage, and Jane Toller may be recommended and can be found in most libraries. On such subjects as Victoriana, art nouveau, and art deco Bevis Hillier is exuberant, and Bea Howe's *Antiques from the Victorian Home* (Batsford, 1973) is whimsical and charming. *Junk* by David Benedictus (Macmillan, 1976) contains some good jokes and a valuable list of auction houses, but it should not be regarded as infallible.

The definitive work on furniture is that by P. MacQuoid (*A History of English Furniture*, 4 vols, Dover Publications, 1972). However, more accessible and extremely useful is *A Shorter History of English Furniture* by the estimable John Gloag (Allen & Unwin, 2nd ed. revised, 1969). In ceramics you should home in on John P. Cushion and W. B. Honey's majestic *Handbook of Pottery and Porcelain Marks* (Faber & Faber, 1965), Cushion's *Pottery and Porcelain* (Connoisseur, 1972), F. Litchfield's *Pottery and Porcelain, a Guide to Collectors*, revised by Frank Tilley (A. & C. Black, 1963), or any or all of Geoffrey Godden's volumes. When the astonishing Godden dies he will indeed return to clay! *The Observer's Book of Pottery and Porcelain* by Mary and Geoffrey Payton (Frederick Warne, 1973) is small enough to fit into a pocket, and excellent. Glass is less well served, but I can strongly recommend Harold Newman's *An Illustrated Dictionary of Glass* (Thames & Hudson, 1977) with 2442 definitions and 625 photographs, 17 in colour. If you are concerned with silver or plate, William Chaffer's *Handbook to Hall Marks on Gold and Silver Plate* (W. Reeves, 9th ed., 1966) should be your Bible, Koran, or Torah, while Norman Gask's *Old Silver Spoons of England* (1926, reprinted by Hamlyn, 1973) is an evident labour of love.

The Lyle series of price guides is produced annually and can help to prevent you making an ass of yourself, and Marcelle D'Argy Smith produces the *British Arts and Antiques Yearbook* (Phillips) which offers all sorts of useful tit-bits.

More specific recommendations will be found in the main body of the text.

Glossary of Names

This list is not intended to be exhaustive. With a few important exceptions, I have omitted those whose work was solely in ceramics, most of whom feature in the main body of the text. For further information consult the *Dictionary of National Biography*, an Encyclopaedia, or a specialist publication.

Adam, Robert (1728–92) See main text.

Aldin, Cecil Charles Windsor (1870–1935) Artist and author. Aldin illustrated Kipling's *Jungle Book* (1894–5). He specialised in country and sporting scenes, and in lovable dogs.

Alken, Henry (1784–1851) Engraver and book illustrator. Alken specialised in hunting and sporting scenes. One of his sons used his father's name or initials to sign his own prints, which were inferior to those of his father.

Amati, Andreas (1520–c.1577) Founded the celebrated school for makers of violins and other stringed instruments at Cremona, in Italy.

André, Major John (1751–80) A.D.C. to both General Grey and Sir Henry Clinton, Major André was a talented amateur silhouette cutter, who created likenesses of such as Benjamin Franklin and George Washington.

Archambo, Peter (working 1720–50) A Huguenot silversmith who worked in London, specialising in the rococo style. He produced a number of fine pierced baskets.

Arnold, John (1736–99) A watchmaker who also worked on marine chronometers. In 1782 he patented his improved detent escapement.

Ash, Gilbert (1717–85) An outstanding New York cabinet-maker who made fine chairs in the Chippendale style.

Ashbee, Charles Robert (1863–1942) Architect and designer. He founded the Guild of Handicrafts (1888), which practised the principles of the arts and crafts movement.

Audubon, John James (1785–1851) Ornithologist and water-colourist. His masterpiece *Birds of America* (published 1827–38) contained 435 hand-coloured aquatints in four volumes.

Baillie-Scott, Mackay Hugh (1865–1945) Architect and designer of metalwork, ceramics, and furniture, which was simple and linear but employed inlays of several materials.

Barlow, Hannah B. (1851–1916) Pottery decorator who worked at Doulton's Lambeth workshop. She incised saltglazed stoneware with horses, dogs, sheep, etc. Her sister Florence (d. 1909) produced similar designs.

Barnsley, Ernest (1863–1926) **and Sidney** (1865–1926) Furniture designer brothers associated with E. Gimson in the production of Cotswold School furniture. Sidney's son Edward (b. 1900) carried on the family tradition.

Bartolozzi, Francesco (1725–1815) See main text.

Barye, Antoine-Louis (1796–1875) The foremost animal sculptor who worked in bronze, and the founder of Les Animaliers in Paris. Noted especially for groups of fighting animals.

Baskerville, John (1706–75) The father of fine printing in England. His editions of the classics, Milton, and the Bible are works of genius.

Baxter, George (1804–67) See main text.

Beetham, Isabella (b. 1744) One of the best English silhouettists, especially on glass.

Beilby Family See main text.

Bewick, Thomas (1758–1828) Wood engraver, apprenticed to Ralph Beilby of Newcastle. His woodcuts are at their most masterly in his *History of Quadrupeds* (1790) and his *History of British Birds* (1797–1804).

Bigaglia, Pietro One of an old family of Venetian glassworkers, Bigaglia is credited with the production of the first glass paperweight.

Bologna, Giovanni da (1529–1608) French sculptor and architect, born at Douai. In 1558 he was attached to the court of the Medicis in Florence, and his famous bronzes were highly influential.

Bolsover, Thomas (1704–88) A Sheffield cutler who invented the process of fusing silver on copper, known as Sheffield plate. A distant relative, Joseph Hancock, exploited the process commercially.

Böttger, Johann Friedrich (d. 1719) An alchemist employed by the Elector of Saxony to discover the secret of 'true' hard-paste porcelain in the Chinese manner. He did.

Boulle, André Charles (1642–1732) See main text.

Boulton, Matthew (1728–1809) A Birmingham industrialist who was the only English manufacturer of ormolu and developed Sheffield plate. He also formed a partnership with James Watt to investigate the potential of the steam engine, and he issued copper coinage.

Boutet, Nicolas-Noël (1761–1833) A maker and decorator of guns and swords, working at Versailles, often for Napoleon I.

Brandard, John (1812–63) A lithographic artist best known for his music covers, which are distinguished by graceful, elegant lines and muted colours.

Brangwyn, Sir Frank (1867–1956) Painter, graphic artist and designer, assistant to William Morris from the age of 15. He designed pottery for Doulton's, panels and frescoes, books, tapestries, and furniture.

Breguet, Abraham Louis (1747–1823) Swiss watchmaker. With his son, Louis Antoine, he specialised in marvellously intricate watches.

Breuer, Marcel (b. 1902) A Hungarian furniture designer who applied the shape of bicycle handlebars to furniture, producing the first tubular steel chairs.

Briot, Francis (1580–1616) Pewterer at the court of Frederick, Duke of Württemberg, skilled in relief work.

Brittain, William The first model soldier manufacturer to produce hollow-cast three-dimensional figures.

Broadwood, John A pupil of Burkat Shudi, instrument maker in London, Broadwood developed the square piano from 1773 and grand pianos from 1781.

Burges, William (1827–81) Gothic revivalist, whose speciality was painted bookcases of castellated gloominess.

Caffieri Family (seventeenth and eighteenth centuries) Sculptors, bronze workers and decorators who worked in Paris under Louis XIV, XV, and XVI. They made magnificent gilt-bronze furniture mounts.

Cameron, Julia Margaret (1815–79) The most famous Victorian portrait photographer, who specialised in painstakingly posed likenesses of artists, scientists, and writers.

Caxton, William (c.1422–91) The first English printer, also a translator.

Cellini, Benvenuto (1500–71) Cellini made coins and medals in Rome, gold and enamel artifacts in Paris (including Francis I's saltcellar), and bronze and marble sculptures in Florence.

Chambers, Sir William (1723–96) The designer of the Chinese garden at Kew, and an important influence in the adoption of Chinese taste in eighteenth-century England.

Chiparus, Demetre A Rumanian sculptor, who specialised in bronze and ivory figures.

Chippendale, Thomas, the elder (c.1718–79) See main text.

Chippendale, Thomas, the younger (1749–1822) A partner in his father's firm, Chippendale and Haig, and a prominent designer and cabinet-maker.

Cipriani, Giovanni Battista (1727–85) Florentine decorator, painter, and engraver. He acquired a reputation in England as a painter of nymphs, etc., on satinwood furniture.

Clay, Henry The patenter of the first *papier mâché* in England (1772). Clay's ideas were turned to commercial advantage by Jennens and Betteridge of Birmingham.

Clement, William (1633–1704) Blacksmith, anchorsmith, and maker of longcase and turret clocks.

Cliff, Clarice (1899–1972) See main text.

Cobb, John (d. 1778) Upholsterer and cabinet-maker, and a partner of William Vile when trading in Long Acre.

Colt, Samuel (1814–62) American inventor of the first reliable revolving pistol, and other practical and decorative weapons.

Concanen, Alfred (1835–86) Victorian music-cover artist.

Cooper, Samuel (1609–72) The greatest

miniature painter of the Stuart period, and highly influential.

Crane, Walter (1845–1915) A designer of textiles, wallpapers, and ceramics, Crane is probably best remembered as an imaginative illustrator of children's books in the art nouveau style.

Cristofori, Bartolommeo (1665–1731) Italian harpsichord maker, who, by replacing the plucking jacks with hammers, produced the first pianoforte.

Daguerre, Louis Jacques Mandé (1789–1851) The developer of Niepcé's technique of recording an image on a silvered copper plate; he gave his name to the daguerrotype.

Daum, Auguste (1853–1909) **and Antonin** (1864–1930) Brothers who designed art nouveau glassware in Nancy.

Daumier, Honoré (1808–1879) Painter, modeller, wood-engraver, and, notably, lithographer, whose caricatures and cartoons made mordant comments on nineteenth-century France.

Doughty, Susan Dorothy (1892–1962) A modeller of flowers and birds at the Worcester porcelain factory. Her early pieces were taken from Audubon, her later ones from life.

Dresser, Christopher (1834–1904) Glass and metal designer. He visited Japan in 1876 on behalf of the British government, was much taken by what he saw, and was influential in the adoption of Japanese design in Britain.

Earnshaw, Thomas (1749–1829) A pioneer in the making of chronometers and watches, and a competitor of John Arnold.

East, Edward (1602–97) Watch- and clockmaker to Charles I. A craftsman of the highest quality, he often set his clocks in 'architectural' cases.

Edison, Thomas Alva (1847–1931) A professional inventor with some 1200 patents to his credit, he stumbled on the means of reproducing the human voice — hence the first phonograph.

Edouart, Augustin (1789–1861) Silhouettist in the freehand cut-out style. He kept duplicates of over 200,000 of his portraits, most of which were lost in a shipwreck.

Egermann, Friedrich (1777–1864) Bohemian glassmaker. He introduced a whole new range of colours with which to stain glass. Egermann applied enamel decorations to his coloured glass in the Mary Gregory style.

Fabergé, Peter Carl (1846–1920) See main text.

Fenton, Roger A Victorian photographer who took a team to the Crimean War, returning with a magnificent record of the lives of the soldiers. He also did a series of photographs of fine English houses and gardens.

Forsyth, Alexander A Scottish clergyman who invented the first percussion-lock gun; the mechanism was patented in 1807.

Gallé, Émile (1846–1904) See main text.

Gibbons, Grinling (1648–1721) An expert woodcarver who specialised in chimneypieces, mirrors, and picture frames. Wren employed him to work on St Paul's and Hampton Court.

Gilbert, Alfred (1854–1943) English metalworker, specialising in mayoral chains. Also a jeweller and sculptor, he is best remembered for his statue of Eros in Piccadilly Circus.

Gimson, Ernest (1864–1919) Architect and designer, much influenced by William Morris. Gimson practised as a cabinet-maker in Gloucestershire, making spindle-back chairs with rush seats.

Gosset, Isaac (1713–99) Wax cameo artist — probably the finest. He came to London from the Channel Islands and gained the patronage of George II.

Graham, George (1674–1751) Maker of clocks, watches, and instruments, who became a partner of the great Thomas Tompion. He is credited with the invention of the dead beat escapement for clocks and the cylinder escapement for watches.

Gray, Eileen (b. 1879) Irish architect and furniture designer. She also designed domestic earthenware and, notably, fantastic and mysterious screens.

Greenaway, Kate (1846–1901) See main text.

Gropius, Walter (1883–1969) The first director of the Bauhaus (1919–33), a revolutionary German design school. He believed in *Gesamtkunstwerk*, the dedication of all interior and exterior design to a single aesthetic.

Guarnerius Family (seventeenth and eighteenth centuries) Celebrated violin makers of Cremona. The first, Andreas, worked with Stradivarius under Nicolo Amati.

Hancock, Robert (c.1731–1817) An engraver who worked at the York House (Battersea) enamel works. When that closed down he did transfer-printing for the Bow, Worcester, and Caughley china factories.

Heal, Sir Ambrose (1872–1959) Furniture maker and designer. He became Chairman of Heal & Son Ltd and was influential in popularising well made, unpretentious furniture.

Hepplewhite, George (d. 1786) See main text.

Hill, David Octavius (1802–70) A Scottish landscape and portrait painter who turned later, in association with Robert Adamson, to landscape and portrait photography.

Hilliard, Nicholas (1547–1619) The finest of all miniature portrait painters, who counted among his models Mary Queen of Scots, Elizabeth I, and James I. Hilliard was also a goldsmith.

Hope, Thomas (1770–1831) Designer, architect, author, and collector of antiquities, Hope did much to make fashionable Greek and Egyptian taste.

Ince, William An eighteenth-century cabinet-maker and upholsterer. Ince went into business with John Mayhew in Soho and produced *The Universal System of Household Furniture* (c.1762).

Jacquemart, Henri-Alfred-Marie (1824–96) Leading French animal sculptor. The rhinoceros in front of the Trocadero in Paris is his.

Johnson, Thomas (d.1778) Woodcarver and gilder, possibly the most accomplished exponent of English rococo. He published a variety of designs between 1756 and 1758.

Jules, David (1808–92) Book illustrator and a leading designer of fashion plates.

Kaendler, Johann Joachim (1706–75) The finest European modeller of porcelain, based at the Meissen factory. Kaendler specialised in human and animal figures.

Kauffmann, Angelica (1741–1807). See main text.

Kent, William (c.1686–1748) An architect, master designer, painter, and landscape gardener, Kent's idiom was classical baroque. His finest monument is possibly Houghton Hall, built for Robert Walpole.

Knibb, Joseph (1640–1711) A notable craftsman of longcase and bracket clocks, which featured marquetry and parquetry elaborations, and silver mounts respectively.

Knox, Archibald (1864–1933) A designer committed to the Celtic revival. He designed 'Cymric' silverware and jewellery and 'Tudric' pewter for Liberty's.

Lalique, René (1860–1945) See main text.

Lamerie, Paul de (1688–1751) A silversmith who came to England with his Huguenot parents in 1691. His silver represented all that was finest in English rococo craftsmanship.

Langley, Batty (1696–1751) Langley established a school for architectural drawings, and published books on woodwork and building.

Le Blond, Abraham Inheritor of the Baxter print patent, Le Blond created small, oval pictures of rustic courtship and similar themes.

Le Corbusier, Charles Édouard (1887–1965) The Swiss-born, French naturalised designer of furniture manufactured by the Thonet brothers; a revolutionary and idealistic architect.

Lethaby, William Richard (1857–1931) Founder-member of the Art Workers' Guild, and influence on art nouveau furniture designers.

Liberty, Sir Arthur Lasenby (d. 1917) Founder of the Regent Street store and the arbiter of taste for most of middle-class England. A great patron of both the aesthetic and the arts and crafts movements.

Linwood, Mary (1755–1854) Famous for her wool embroidery which frequently copied the old masters, Mary Linwood should not be confused with . . .

Linwood, Matthew Early nineteenth-century maker of vinaigrettes in Birmingham.

Mackintosh, Charles Rennie (1869–1928) Scottish architect, designer, and leader of the Glasgow School. His work happily combined elements of Scottish baronial, arts and crafts, and art nouveau idioms. A notable originator, venerated abroad.

Mackmurdo, Arthur H. (1851–1942) Architect-designer. Mackmurdo founded the Century Guild (1882) to encourage craftsmen to work in guilds.

Manton, Joseph (1766–1835) A notable English gunsmith, famous for sporting guns.

Marinot, Maurice (1882–1960) A French art-glass designer whose trademark was deliberately created imperfections. He produced some 2500 original pieces.

Martin Brothers See main text under Martinware.

Meissonier, Juste Aurèle (1695–1750) A French designer, especially of silverware, who pioneered asymmetry in design, thus paving the way for the rococo movement.

Mercator, Gerhard (1512–94) Cartographer, whose heart-shaped projection was used by many subsequent map makers.

Miers, John (1756–1821) An expert 'profilist' or silhouette painter, who worked a great deal *en grisaille*. His son, William, picked up where he left off.

Minton, Herbert Son of Thomas, founder of the china manufactory. He produced encaustic tiles with patterns from the floors of medieval monasteries.

Montanari Family (nineteenth century) The seven members of this family produced plump, lifelike, expensive wax dolls.

Moorcroft, William (1872–1945) See main text.

Morgan, William de (1839–1917) A close friend of William Morris, Morgan was a designer of stained glass, furniture, ceremics, and tiles, which were entirely handmade. More remarkably he was also a successful novelist.

Morris, William (1834–96) See main text.

Mucha, Alphonse (1860–1939) A Czech painter and designer who achieved fame through the popularity of his Sarah Bernhardt posters. He also designed jewellery and murals, and illustrated books.

Murray, Keith (b. 1893) New Zealand born architect and designer in silver, pottery, and glass.

Nadar (Félix Tournachon) (1820–1910) A Parisian journalist and caricaturist who became a society photographer specialising in artists, writers, and musicians.

Niepcé, Joseph Nicéphore A French scientist who is credited with taking the first photograph — a 'heliograph' — from his attic window near Grasse, in 1826. It was Daguerre who exploited the invention.

Northwood, John (1837–1902) A glass engraver from Stourbridge. He achieved fame with his Elgin Vase (1873), and rediscovered the ancient technique of cameo glass.

Obrisset (or O'Brisset), John (early eighteenth century) An expert carver in horn and tortoiseshell; he even carved likenesses of royalty.

Oliver, Peter (c.1594–1647) Son of the miniaturist Isaac Oliver, Peter inherited his father's skills. With the exception of Hilliard, Oliver is as fine as any other English painter of miniatures.

Ortel, Abraham (1527–98) The Dutch cartographer, known as Ortelius, whose *Theatrum Orbis Terrarum* (1570) was the forerunner of the modern atlas.

Palissy, Bernard (c.1510–90) A French potter and designer of stained glass, whose glazed dishes and bowls featured reptiles, fish, and foliage in naturalistic abandon. Copied at Minton's and elsewhere.

Pellatt, Apsley (1791–1863) A London glassmaker who pioneered glass paperweights.

Pepin, Denis (1647–c.1712) A French physicist and co-inventor of the steam engine. In 1681 he presented the Royal Society with his version of a primitive pressure cooker.

Phillips, Robert (d. 1881) The one acknowledged master of coral carving in Britain.

Phyfe, Duncan (1768–1854) A Scot who moved to New York State at the age of 16, Phyfe used the best of English and French furniture designs to develop a style of his own that was both elegant and popular.

Pierotti Family (nineteenth century) The Pierottis produced wax dolls with puce colouring, blue eyes, and somewhat Italianate features.

Pinchbeck, Christopher (d. 1732) See main text.

Pistrucci, Benedetto (1784–1855) Italian engraver of gems and designer of coins and medals. Pistrucci settled in London in 1815 and became chief engraver to the Mint.

Preiss, Frederick A German sculptor of the 1930s who used bronze and ivory to suggest the athleticism and eroticism of young ladies.

Pugin, Augustus Welby Northmore (1812–52) This brilliant pioneer of the Gothic revival scored his most memorable success with his designs for the Houses of Parliament.

Quare, Daniel (c.1648–1724) Quare produced clocks and barometers of all shapes and sizes, some for palaces, some for domestic use. He was also responsible for the invention of the repeating mechanism for watches.

Ramsden, Omar (1873–1939) The English Fabergé, Ramsden was a silversmith, the son of a Sheffield engraver, who created jewelled and *repoussé* pieces of great magnificence, many in association with Alwyn Carr. Ecclesiastical work and commissions for the City livery companies were his forte.

Ravenet, Simon-François (1706–74) An engraver of enamel boxes, etc. at York House, Battersea. Later he worked at the Bow china factory, developing transfer-printing techniques.

Ravenscroft, George (1632–83) See main text.

Ravilious, Eric (1903–42) Engraver, designer, and painter of ceramics, glass, and furniture. Gardening, boat-racing, alphabet, and coronation motifs figure prominently on his pottery — chiefly commissioned by Wedgwood.

Revere, Paul (1735–1818) American silversmith, merchant, and patriot (remember his midnight ride?). He also engraved paper money.

Ricketts, Charles (1866–1931) Painter, sculptor, designer, and typographer, in the mainstream of the arts and crafts movement. He founded the Vale Press (1896) and was also a collector.

Riesener, Jean-Henri (1734–1806) The most celebrated *ébéniste* in the Louis XVI style, responsible for some magnificent marquetry bureaux.

Robbia, Della, Family (fifteenth and sixteenth centuries) Italian maiolica workers who specialised in free-standing figures.

Roentgen, Abraham (1711–93) A German furniture maker who also worked in England and Holland: an exceptional craftsman in marquetry. His son, David, was an exponent of neo-classical furniture.

Ruhlmann, Émile-Jacques (1879–1933) Possibly the finest art deco furniture designer. Ruhlmann worked in Paris and concentrated on bringing out the best qualities of the materials he used.

Ruskin, John (1819–1900) Writer, artist, critic, and educator. Ruskin's was the most influential voice in the late 1800s; he helped to found the Working Men's College, and also founded the Ruskin School of Drawing and the Guild of St George.

Saxton, Christopher A Yorkshire cartographer who produced in 1579 the first national atlas of all the counties of England and Wales, doing all the surveying and drawings himself.

Sheraton, Thomas (1751–1806) See main text.

Shibayama Family (eighteenth and nineteenth centuries) *Inro* artists in Japan, who developed a style of encrusted lacquer named after them.

Solon, Marc-Louis or Miles (1835–1913) Solon worked at the Sèvres factory, and developed the *pâte-sur-pâte* technique both there and later at Minton's.

Speed, John A seventeenth-century tailor and court jester, Speed published an atlas, *Theatre of the Empire of Great Britain* (1611), based in part on Saxton's surveys. His county maps are much reproduced.

Stevens, Thomas (1828–88) See main text under Stevengraph.

Storr, Paul (1771–1844) A London silversmith in the neo-classical tradition, who produced highly elaborate presentation pieces as well as utilitarian ware.

Stradivarius, Antonio (c.1644–1737) Pupil of Nicolo Amati in Cremona, Stradivarius made stringed instruments as fine as any ever produced. Beware of nineteenth-century copies.

Talbert, Bruce James (1838–81) Scottish architect and furniture designer who came to London in 1865. He worked in the early English and Gothic idioms.

Talbot, William Henry Fox (1800–77) Talbot developed the colotype process of photography, and was a renowned mathematician and scientist.

Tassie, James (1735–99) A Scot who specialised in the production of pink wax medallions on a backing of blue glass. He also invented a kind of lead-potash glass in which he carved small portraits. His nephew William (1777–1860) continued the work.

Templeton, James (b. 1802) A Scottish carpet manufacturer who set up his own business manufacturing and selling paisley shawls (1829).

Thonet, Michael (1796–1871) Viennese furniture designer. His experiments resulted in the internationally successful bentwood furniture, now made in Poland.

Tiffany, Louis-Comfort (1848–1933) See main text.

Tijou, Jean (c.1660–1720) French craftsman in wrought iron. He was responsible for much fine baroque ironwork at Hampton Court, Chatsworth, St Paul's, and elsewhere.

Tinworth, George (1843–1913) A Doulton artist who designed terracotta panels and animal figures at the Lambeth works.

Tompion, Thomas (1639–1713) An English watch- and clockmaker of genius. He went into partnership first with Edward Banger, then with George Graham. His longcase and bracket clocks are exceptional.

Tourte, François (1747–1835) A Parisian specialising in marvellously crafted violin bows.

Van de Velde, Henri Clemens (1863–1957) Belgian architect and designer. Influenced by William Morris, he established an avant-garde group of artists known as Les Vingt.

Vianen, Paulus Van (d. 1613), **Adam** (c.1565–1627) **and Christean** (d. c.1666) Dutch artist-craftsmen in silver whose work in the auricular style (i.e., shaped like the inner ear) was outstanding.

Vile, William (d. 1767) An upholsterer and cabinet-maker who went into partnership with John Cobb. Vile was cabinet-maker to George III and his work is of excellent quality.

Voysey, Charles (1857–1941) Architect and art nouveau furniture designer. He used oak, generally unadorned, and was very influential.

Wain, Louis William (1860–1931) The English illustrator and designer who specialised in comic anthropomorphic cats, especially on postcards and ceramics.

Webb, Philip (1831–1915) Designer of furniture, glass, metalwork, jewellery, and embroidery for William Morris, for whom he also designed the Red House in Bexley Heath (1860).

Wedgwood, Josiah (1730–95) See main text.

Whistler, Laurence (b. 1912) An English glass engraver who often engraves open old glasses. His style tends towards the baroque.

Zumpe, Johannes A piano maker who came to England from Germany in 1760. He modified Cristofori's piano into the English single, and later double, action.

Index

Many of the subjects listed in this index occur also under main headings in the text; page numbers given here are to important references elsewhere in the text.

Cross-reference is also made to main entries, shown here in bold type.